Second Chances

A national guide to adult education
and training opportunities

Fourteenth Edition

FOR
REFERENCE
ONLY

Lifetime Careers Publishing

374·941

Second Chances – fourteenth edition

Published by Lifetime Careers Publishing, 7 Ascot Court, White Horse Business Park, Trowbridge BA14 0XA.

© Lifetime Careers Wiltshire Ltd, 2005

ISBN: 1 902 876 91 1

No part of this publication may be copied or reproduced, stored in a retrieval system or transmitted in any form or by any means electronic or mechanical or by photocopying or recording without the prior permission of the publishers.

Printed and bound by Cromwell Press Ltd, Trowbridge

Cover and text design by Adrian Barclay

Contents

Section 1

Section 2

Section 3

Section 4

Foreword

This, the fourteenth edition of *Second Chances,* continues to provide a valuable one-stop reference guide for all advisers working with adults seeking information, advice or guidance in relation to learning opportunities.

Whether based:

- through next**step** information and advice (IA) networks

- in all-age careers services or Connexions services

- with education and training providers

- in Jobcentre Plus/Jobcentres

- with community or voluntary organisations that provide information

Second Chances can meet advisers' information needs, and signpost where to go for further information.

Second Chances is of benefit to:

- less experienced advisers, who may be learning their way around the range of learning opportunities, as it provides an overview of the range of available learning routes and provides up-to-date information about qualifications and student finance

- more experienced advisers, who may find, in particular, the more specialist information for particular groups a useful tool

- potential learners themselves, who may wish to use *Second Chance*s independently for their own reference.

Acknowledgements

The authors would like to thank all those individuals from organisations concerned with education and training who assisted with providing information for the compilation of this edition of *Second Chances*.

Lifetime Careers Publishing would like to thank the Department for Education and Skills for its contribution to the funding of this edition of *Second Chances*.

1:1

Introduction

Second Chances is a reference source for:

- staff working with agencies or organisations involved in providing information, advice and guidance to adults about education and training opportunities, such as Information, Advice and Guidance Partnerships

- adults wishing to research for themselves information about education and training opportunities.

Main features of *Second Chances*

- The information provided covers the whole range of learning opportunities, from basic skills through to postgraduate-level opportunities.

- It covers information relevant to adults aged from 19+, whatever their background or employment status, including those considering a return to learning or to employment, retired people, adults with special needs, or those who have recently arrived from overseas.

- It is designed as a useful reference both for less experienced front-line information staff as well as for more experienced adult guidance advisers.

- Sources of further information and advice are provided throughout.

Second Chances is divided into four sections:

- **General information** – provides the background information that most learners need to know about lifelong learning and the labour market. Sources of information, advice and guidance are listed.

- **How and where to learn** – information on the wide range of learning opportunities, a detailed look at finance for education and training, and at qualifications available across the UK.

- **Specialist information for particular groups** – unemployed people, people with disabilities, overseas students etc. Includes organisations set up to offer specialist support, information, advice etc.

- **The Gazetteer** – lists, by geographical area, organisations that may be involved in providing information, advice and learning opportunities for adults, including next**step** providers, careers/Connexions services, LSCs/LECs, LEAs, ELWa and DELNI, as well as further and higher education institutions.

Publishers' addresses – full contact details of those publishers most frequently listed are provided within the Gazetteer, after the organisations' listings (addresses of other publishers are given alongside the title of the publication).

The text of *Second Chances* can also be found on the website: www.second-chances.uk.com

Accuracy: the information provided in *Second Chances* was accurate at the time of publication. However, information changes quickly, so should always be checked with the contact sources provided.

Using *Second Chances* – Routefinder

As a supplement to the contents list and indexes, the brief guide below offers one approach to navigating Section 2.

While the routefinder provides some starting points, it may not be suitable for every query. Clients that fall into one of the groups listed in Section 3 should also consult the relevant part of that section.

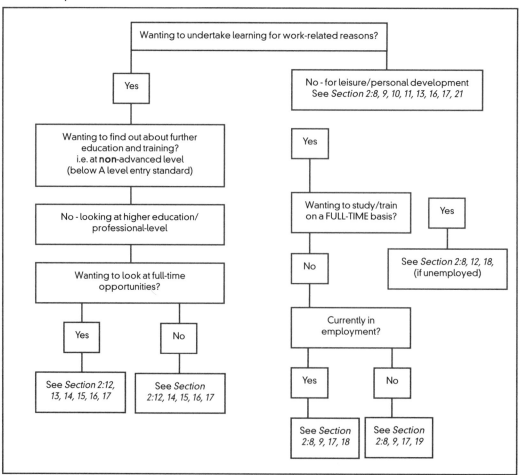

1:2

Lifelong learning

Topics covered:

- The importance of lifelong learning
- Initiatives to encourage participation in learning
- Checkpoints for advising potential learners

Why lifelong learning?

The Government is committed to the concept of 'lifelong learning', i.e. that it is important for everyone, no matter what their age or employment status, to continue with learning throughout their lives.

Some of the reasons that make lifelong learning important:

- **'Jobs for life'** are a thing of the past. People are likely to change jobs many times during their working lives. They will therefore continually need to learn new skills and new ways of working.

- **Skills and qualifications** are increasingly in demand. The proportion of unskilled and semi-skilled jobs is decreasing; a trend set to continue. Those who have not kept their skills up-to-date will be disadvantaged.

- The ever-increasing pace of change in **information and communications technology** is having a huge impact on the way organisations operate, and on the skills that individual employees need.

- Employees with **the right skills** will be valued by employers. Skilled employees help to improve productivity and profitability; crucial to the success of our economy.

- People who develop themselves are often able to achieve more varied and interesting work and/or may use their learning to **fulfil their ambitions**.

In 2002, the Government set the target of reducing, by 2010, the number of adults in the UK workforce who lack NVQ level 2 (or equivalent qualifications) by 40%. As a stepping stone to achieving this, the target has been set of one million adults in the workforce achieving level 2 between 2003 and 2006.

Initiatives to encourage participation in learning

A variety of initiatives has been introduced by the Government, by lifelong learning organisations, by the media and by employers, to help adults access appropriate learning opportunities. Initiatives are usually intended to do one or more of the following:

- improve information, advice and guidance about lifelong learning

- increase awareness of learning opportunities

- improve accessibility of learning

- help coordinate learning initiatives and improve collaboration between learning providers

- provide financial support for those participating in lifelong learning.

Examples of the main initiatives are described below.

learndirect

Since the Government introduced the learndirect initiative, learndirect centres have been set up all over the country, and can be found in places as varied as shopping centres, sports clubs, libraries and colleges. Some learndirect centres are based in companies, for the benefit of employees. Clients can follow a course at these centres through open learning, at a time and pace to suit themselves. Students learn using computer packages, and a tutor is on hand to give advice. A range of IT courses is available, from introductory to advanced level. Other courses available include basic skills, business and management skills, and languages. It is also possible to follow a learndirect course independently using a computer at home.

Apart from centres, learndirect provides a free national telephone helpline and website service for adults wanting to find out about learning opportunities and related matters e.g. about funding, childcare and local guidance provision.

> **learndirect advice** – Tel: 0800 100 900 for the national learning advice line, or 0800 101 901 to find out about learndirect courses and centres. Lines are open in England from 8am to 10pm seven days a week (9am-9pm seven days a week in Wales, and in Northern Ireland 9am-6pm Tues/Thurs/Fri and 9am-9pm Mon/Wed). The website offers a course search facility, and you can email learndirect from the site, or use the 'call me' telephone option on the website:
> www.learndirect.co.uk
> www.learndirect-advice.co.uk to search online for courses nationally.

learndirect scotland

learndirect scotland provides a similar role for Scotland. There are over 400 learndirect centres based all over Scotland. The learndirect scotland helpline provides information about the range of available learning opportunities and related matters.

> **learndirect scotland** – Freepost SCO5775, PO Box 25249, Glasgow, G3 8XN.
> Tel: 0808 100 9000 – lines are open from 7.30am to 11pm Monday to Friday, and 9am to
> 6pm at weekends.
> Email: info@learndirectscotland.com
> www.learndirectscotland.com offers a course search facility.

Local adult information, advice and guidance services

Various agencies within the UK offer information, advice and guidance for adults about learning opportunities. The following are the main agencies in the UK:

- England – next**step** local information and advice networks (formerly known as IAG networks)

- Wales – Careers Wales (an all-age service)

- Northern Ireland – the Educational Guidance Service for Adults network

- Scotland – Careers Scotland (an all-age service).

Further information on the above and other agencies can be found in *1:4 – Sources of information, advice and guidance.*

Learning Partnerships

There are 104 Learning Partnerships across England. Their main role is to promote provider collaboration in support of lifelong learning and to maximise the contribution of learning to local regeneration. Learning Partnerships are non-statutory, voluntary groups of local learning providers, with representation from providers ranging from voluntary organisations through to higher education institutions, together with others with an interest such as the LEA, local LSC, local guidance providers, employers and so on. Since April 2003, responsibility for Learning Partnerships has rested with the Learning and Skills Council, and each Partnership works closely with its local Learning and Skills Council. For more information, visit www.lifelonglearning.co.uk/llp which includes a directory of Learning Partnerships.

In Scotland, the Scottish Adult Learning Partnership (SALP) is a voluntary organisation created to encourage those who do not traditionally participate in learning to take up learning opportunities. SALP coordinates a number of campaigns each year, including Adult Learners' Week (see below), the *Sign Up Now* learning campaign each August/ September, and the *Signed Up Yet?* campaign each January, which encourage adults to enrol in learning, and Family Learning Week.

> **Scottish Adult Learning Partnership (HQ)** – 22 Hill Street, Edinburgh EH2 3JZ.
> Tel: 0131 220 5567.
> Email: salp@salp.org.uk
> www.salp.org.uk

Adult Learners' Week

Each year there is a special national focus on opportunities to learn, with local input, called Adult Learners' Week. It is usually in May and is coordinated in England and Wales by NIACE (the national organisation for adult learning in England and Wales) and in Scotland by the Scottish Adult Learning Partnership (see above). There are events all over the country to encourage UK adults to return to learning.

Learning at Work Day

Coinciding with Adult Learners' Week is Learning at Work Day, coordinated by the Campaign for Learning. The aim of the day is to encourage employers to give their workforce the chance to break from routine on that day, in order to learn some new skills – either work-related or other!

In addition, the Campaign for Learning runs a **Family Learning Week** in October.

The organisations below can provide further information:

➤ **NIACE (National Institute of Adult Continuing Education)** – Renaissance House, 20 Princess Road West, Leicester LE1 6TP.
Tel: 0116 204 4200.
Email: enquiries@niace.org.uk
www.niace.org.uk

➤ **Scottish Adult Learning Partnership** – www.salp.org.uk (see full contact details on previous page) or visit www.alws.org.uk

➤ **Campaign for Learning** – 19 Buckingham Street, London WC2N 6EF.
Tel: 020 7930 1111.
Email: mailto:campaign@campaign-for-learning.org.uk
www.campaign-for-learning.org.uk (includes contact details for the three regional offices)

National Grid for Learning (NGfL)

The NGfL acts as the gateway to educational resources on the internet by providing a network of carefully selected links to websites, including those aimed at adult learners. The NGfL portal is funded by the Department for Education and Skills and is managed by the British Educational Communications Technology Agency (Becta).

➤ www.ngfl.gov.uk

Media initiatives

The media sometimes develop initiatives to promote lifelong learning. For example, the BBC periodically runs programmes to encourage adults to consider opportunities, such as ICT. They may provide a helpline, website backup and other resources.

The BBC website www.bbc.co.uk/learning/adults has links to other web pages useful for adult learning, information about finding courses and details of BBC TV and radio programmes which might be of interest to adult learners.

Basic skills initiatives

In order to tackle poor standards of literacy and numeracy, various initiatives have been developed. For more details see *2:9 – Basic skills*.

The University of the Third Age (U3A)

The U3A aims to encourage lifelong learning for people who are no longer of working age. For more details refer to *3:25 – Third age*.

Employer initiatives

There are various private and public initiatives aimed at encouraging those in employment to continue with learning. These include projects funded through the Union Learning Fund, LSC Employer Training Pilots and the Investors in People (IiP) award (given to organisations which meet standards in relation to training and development) and schemes run by individual companies. Such initiatives are described in more detail in *2:19 – Learning in the workplace.*

Personal development plans

Individuals can find it helpful to draw up personal development plans in order to identify a general or specific progression pathway for their lives. Through the process of producing a plan, people will focus on their skills, abilities and achievements, and identify short- and longer-term goals, and the skills and knowledge they need to achieve their goals. *Progress File: Achievement Planner* is a set of interactive materials designed to help people manage their own learning and career development; the *Broadening Horizons* materials within *Progress File* are specifically designed to help adults make the most of themselves and their opportunities, helping with decision-making at different points of people's lives. Examples of how the materials can be used in employment and training, and for more information, visit: www.dfes.gov.uk/progfile

Career Development Loans (CDLs)

CDLs are available to help people pay for a vocational course. For details, refer to *2:7 – Money.*

Checkpoints for advisers

Advisers can encourage individual clients to enter learning, by helping them to realise the potential benefits and by enabling them to overcome any perceived barriers and difficulties. Here are a few of the ways advisers can help ensure a successful outcome.

Helping clients to overcome perceived barriers to learning

'It's so long since I've learnt anything... I don't think I could return to it now...'

Many clients have been away from a classroom for a long time, and are apprehensive about returning to learning. They do not always recognise that, in fact, they have never stopped learning, albeit in a different way from formal schooling. Clients can be encouraged to identify all that they have learnt to do, and the knowledge they have acquired, since leaving school. This could be through informal and formal training at work, evening classes, taking positions of responsibility in local clubs or organisations, participating in voluntary/community activities of all kinds, organising social events, managing a home and family budget, their own reading etc.

'I've always been hopeless at exams, so there's no point in doing a course.'

People who have not undertaken learning for some time may be unaware that a range of assessment methods is now used besides traditional exams, and that many qualifications can be gained via modes of assessment which do not involve exams at all.

Helping clients to be clear about their aims

If clients are clear about their own aims and objectives for learning, it will help to ensure that they select an appropriate learning opportunity, therefore reducing their chances of dropping out. Clients' learning objectives may include:

- updating skills in their existing field of employment

- gaining formal qualifications for the first time in their existing field of employment, or for a new field

- improving their chances of changing jobs

- improving their chances of gaining promotion

- proving something to themselves, or others

- learning for the personal challenge.

Raising issues about time

Successful learners are realistic about the time commitment necessary, and make good use of their available time. Clients need to research courses carefully, ensuring they have accurate information about how much time will be needed, both in formal taught sessions (where applicable) and time required for their own independent learning. Some clients find it useful to work out a personal time management plan.

Allaying fears about study skills and techniques

Fear of failing – lack of confidence in the ability to write essays/present assignments etc – may prevent some people from even considering returning to learning. New learners may be unaware of how much available help there is for study skills: some courses have study skills incorporated into the course; free-standing study skills courses/workshops may be available; there may be learning support services within the college that the student can take advantage of. The course tutor will be able to provide advice and guidance. Some of the publications listed at the end of this section also provide useful information.

Helping clients to get started successfully

Clients who have been away from study for some time, and are planning a lengthy period of learning, may be encouraged to consider doing some kind of short course beforehand. It could be a *return to learn* or *return to study* course (run on a part-time day or evening basis by an adult education service or a further education college), a weekend study course, or an Open University module (see *2:16 – The Open University*). This will help to increase the client's confidence as a learner, give them some learning skills, and demonstrate their capabilities to admissions staff for further courses.

Dealing with concerns about funding

Clients may be concerned about the cost of funding a programme of learning. Various initiatives and funds described in this section and in *2:7 – Money* may be available. It is also worth emphasising the long-term investment to clients. Many courses are now modular or can be taken on a part-time or distance learning basis. Flexibility means that a client's learning goal can be achieved without the need to give up work.

Further information

Further information on the topics, initiatives and agencies mentioned in this section may be obtained from local information, advice and guidance services, course providers and public libraries.

The Department for Education and Skills has a website dedicated to lifelong learning: www.lifelonglearning.co.uk while www.waytolearn.co.uk – developed by the DfES along with other organisations – brings together information for adults and potential learners.

NIACE produces a range of publications on topics related to lifelong learning, including the *Adult Learning Yearbook* – a directory of organisations and resources in adult continuing education and training. 2004-2005 edition, price £21.95.

International Dictionary of Adult and Continuing Education – published by Taylor and Francis, price £22.99 (paperback).

Opportunity – a directory of sources of lifelong learning and career development information, published annually by ADSET, price £45.00.

Coming Back to Learning – published by Lifetime Careers Publishing, price £11.99.

Returning to Education: A Practical Handbook for Adult Learners – published by How To Books, price £9.99.

Learning How to Study Again: A Practical Guide to Study Skills for Mature Students Returning to Education or Distance Learning – published by How To Books, price £9.99.

Keynotes – a series of photocopiable careers guidance leaflets for adults, covering general topics related to education and training, and career choice and change, published by Lifetime Careers Publishing. Price £140 for a single set (discounts for multiple sets). *Keynotes Plus!* is the computerised version.

1:3

The labour market

Topics covered:

- Factors that affect the labour market
- Industry trends
- Future work patterns

The labour market is the supply of and demand for labour – that is, how many jobs there are available compared with how many people there are qualified and able to do the work.

Forecasting where the jobs will be in future is almost as difficult as any other kind of fortune telling. Unexpected events, from terrorist attacks to foot and mouth disease, from the collapse of a major corporation to a sudden change in consumer confidence, can derail any attempts at predicting employment patterns.

Factors that affect the labour market

The match of jobs to workers depends upon a number of factors, such as how well the economy is doing globally and nationally, advances in technology and social trends.

The global economy and political factors

- A large proportion of world trade is carried out by multi-national companies. Because of their size they can establish or relocate factories, research and development facilities or head offices to wherever the economic climate is favourable and a skilled workforce exists. They can also contract work – such as printing or data processing – out to overseas companies to get it done more cheaply.

- Changes to the economies of other parts of the world, such as a downturn in the USA or a boom in China, can have an impact in the UK.

- Events which discourage people from travelling – whether terrorist attacks or higher air fares due to the price of oil – can disrupt particular parts of the economy, such as long-haul air travel and domestic tourism.

- The expansion of the EU and the strength of the single European currency can have an effect on the UK economy.

- Government and Bank of England policy can affect investment in UK industries.
- Increased affluence in the UK means more demand for non-essential consumer goods and services.

The strength of the pound will affect the competitiveness of UK exports.

The impact of new technology

Perhaps the largest cause of change at work in recent years has been the impact of the new information and communications technologies.

- In some sectors of industry and business, new technology has de-skilled jobs or changed them significantly – even replaced them completely. Increased productivity may save an industry but often means fewer jobs.

- The internet has had a significant impact on the way that many companies do business. Its effect is expected to continue, as more businesses use it to reach customers and carry out their business operations. It enables people to work at a distance from their employer – whether that means individual teleworking in the UK or firms moving their customer services to India.

ICT skills are among the key skills required by employers in all sectors.

Social trends

The make-up of the workforce, such as the number of people available to work, their age and gender, has an effect on the labour market.

- Women's activity in the labour market has increased, encouraged by flexible working hours, part-time employment and an increase in jobs within the service sector. The increasing provision of childcare and more employers adopting 'family friendly' working practices are having an effect.

- Existing legislation on the employment of people with disabilities and forthcoming legislation on age discrimination should mean a more diverse workforce.

- More young people are staying on in full-time education, so delaying their entry into the world of work as they gain higher levels of qualifications.

- The workforce is ageing. By 2020, 32% of the population will be aged between 50 and 64.

Industry trends

In the first half of 2004, 35,973 jobs were lost in British **manufacturing** – a trend likely to continue at least in the short term. However, there are still skills shortages in many management, engineering and technological areas of manufacturing. The manufacturing sector continues to employ nearly 15% of the UK workforce. High-tech industries, such as electronics and pharmaceuticals, may buck the trend.

Primary industries and utilities are in decline; North Sea oil and gas extraction is slowing down.

The **public sector** continues to expand; half a million new jobs were created between 1998 and 2003, particularly in the areas of education and health, due to increased public expenditure. However, the Government has announced cutbacks in the **Civil Service.**

Agriculture continues to shed jobs, although there is still work for people with the right qualifications and entrepreneurial leanings, as farmers learn to diversify and create niche markets.

The '**dot.com**' bubble was short-lived, but e-business and e-commerce are now an established part of our economy.

There continue to be serious skills shortages in the **construction industry**, for craftspeople, technicians and professionals, although demand may slow within the next decade.

Financial and customer services are expected to be on the rise, apart from some cutbacks in banking. While the rate of growth in the call centre/customer contact centre industry appears to be slowing, and some jobs have been lost overseas, it is anticipated that expansion will continue. Pay and conditions in this work are said to be improving, with the work itself becoming more complex and demanding.

IT and **telecommunications** are both recovering from recent slowdowns and some growth is expected.

There is a current high demand for skills in the **biotechnology industries, multimedia**, and **recycling and waste management**.

Leisure and recreation, retail and distribution, hospitality and catering, travel and transport and heritage jobs are all fairly buoyant, though some of these areas are low-paid for unskilled and unqualified work. There's a shortage of LGV **and PCV drivers**.

There are more jobs in **domestic help,** with better pay and status than of old, and also in **care for the elderly** – whether in people's own homes, hospitals or nursing homes – because of the growing ageing population. The Government has promised a huge increase in the number of childcare places available, so there is a shortage of **qualified childcare workers**.

All **healthcare workers** – including **nurses, midwives, radiographers, speech therapists, doctors, dentists and other professionals** – are in demand, as are **teachers** and **social workers**. **Police forces** and the **Armed Forces** are looking for recruits.

There is a trend towards contracting out services as businesses cut costs, improve efficiency and compete. This may lead to a reverse in the recent small decline in **self-employment** and the number of **small firms**.

Most of the extra jobs created over recent years across the economy have come in the traditionally **female dominated** employment sectors – losses in the male-dominated manufacturing industries are countered by gains in the female-dominated areas of public administration, education and health.

More available jobs are now **part-time**, and this trend is set to continue. Part-time employment is most common in the service industries, and therefore among women. However, more men are also working part-time.

Future work patterns

- There has been a shift away from manual and low-skilled occupations towards **higher-level occupations**, particularly to jobs at a managerial, professional and technical level. This trend looks set to continue.

- Employees of the future should expect to **change career** at least once during their working lives – which could include periods of temporary employment and/or self-employment.

- Traditional **career progression routes** will become rarer – people will need to take more responsibility for their own skills development and career planning.

- More jobs will be on **temporary or fixed-term contracts** – such as for a specific project.

- Employers will increasingly require **flexibility and adaptability** from their workforce.

- Employees will need not only job-specific skills, but also **key skills** for jobs at all levels: application of number, communication, problem solving, information technology, the ability to work with others, and the ability to improve one's own learning and performance.

- There is a gradual trend towards **flexible working** arrangements, away from the traditional full-time permanent contract. Flexible working arrangements can include **flexitime** (which allows employees to work an agreed number of hours over the week, month, or even year), **job sharing, term-time only working, working from home** and **career break schemes**. These arrangements can benefit both employers and employees.

- The total number of **teleworkers** in the UK increased by about 65% over the period 1999 to 2003 – that's well over two million people working from home at least one day a week, using a computer and phone to keep in touch.

Further information

The DfES *Skills Dialogues: Listening to Employers* series of booklets should be available in most careers libraries and information, advice and guidance offices. Between February 2001 and the end of 2002, reports on 16 industry groupings were published. A list of the *Skills Dialogue* titles can be seen, and individual titles viewed, on: ww.dfes.gov.uk/skillsdialoguereports

Alternatively, copies of the reports are available free from:

➤ **DfES Publications** – PO Box 5050, Sherwood Park, Annesley, Nottingham NG15 0DJ.
  Tel: 0845 60 222 60.
  Email: dfes@prolog.uk.com

Information on labour market information can also be accessed at the DfES's **Skillsbase** website. Whilst aimed primarily at analysts rather than the casual user, the site aims to make material as accessible as possible. The *Working Futures* section is particularly helpful. www.skillsbase.dfes.gov.uk

Labour Market Trends – published monthly by the Office for National Statistics. Available through subscription from The Stationery Office. Annual subscription price £95; single copies £9.50. Also available to view on the ONS website: www.statistics.gov.uk

Sector Skills Councils should have information on their industries. To find relevant Councils, see the Sector Skills Development Agency website: www.ssda.org.uk

The **Learning and Skills Council** national office sends out a free monthly email bulletin to education and training providers and other professionals, which includes some labour market information – the *Skills and Education Network Newsletter*. To receive the newsletter, register at: http://senet.lsc.gov.uk/join.cfm

The **Institute for Employment Research** at Warwick University publishes a free bulletin. Other information can be viewed online.

> **Warwick Institute for Employment Research** –University of Warwick, Social Studies Building, Coventry CV4 7AL.
> Tel: 02476 523284.
> Email: ier@warwick.ac.uk
> www.warwick.ac.uk/ier

Other useful websites

> www.nomisweb.co.uk

> www.scottish-enterprise.com

> www.invest-in-wales.com (click on Why Wales, then Key Sectors for industry information)

Local labour markets

Information on the labour market in a particular area can be gained from a variety of sources:

- Regional Development Agencies

- Learning and Skills Councils (LSCs) and Local Enterprise Companies (LECs)

- Chambers of Commerce

- adult information and guidance agencies

- local authorities

- local newspapers

- local television and radio.

These local organisations are likely to have information on attainment of qualifications, employment and unemployment figures, the skills shortages experienced by local employers and details of any employers or businesses who are investing in the area.

1:4

Sources of information, advice and guidance

Topics covered:

- The main providers of information, advice and guidance
- Computer-based information and guidance systems
- Using the internet
- Ensuring a successful outcome to learning

There are a variety of agencies across the UK involved in providing information, advice and guidance to adults about education and training opportunities.

These range from organisations providing factual information about learning opportunities through to those providing in-depth personal careers and educational guidance, where clients are helped to assess themselves, clarify their goals, and work out possible future options. Many agencies provide access to learning opportunity databases, which clients may use independently. Providers of information, advice and guidance include, of course, the providers of learning opportunities themselves. Fees may be charged for some in-depth guidance services.

The main providers

Information and advice networks (IAs) – next**step**

In England, information and advice is provided to adults through local **information and advice networks (IAs)** – previously known as information, advice and guidance (IAG) networks. These have been developed over recent years following the announcement in 1999 from the DfEE (now DfES) that it aimed to establish information, advice and guidance as a public service, in order to widen adults' participation in learning and enhance their employability. Responsibility for IA provision now rests with the Learning and Skills Council.

The establishment of local networks was achieved by the bringing together of local organisations/agencies which were, for the main part, already engaged in offering such services. Network members may come from a very wide range of backgrounds, such as voluntary groups and projects (e.g. those working with the homeless or families needing support), training providers, library services, local authorities, educational institutions and Jobcentre Plus, as well as careers/Connexions services.

In August 2004, the LSC contracted with IA contractors to provide IA services in each of the 47 local LSC areas. Although there is universal entitlement for adults to access the service, priority must be given to adults who have yet to achieve level 2 qualifications. How each local network achieves this balance, and exactly how the services are delivered, is locally determined by the contractor working with their local LSC and Strategic Board for Information and Advice. Therefore, the way each network operates varies from area to area, as services are designed to meet local needs. In addition, the way each network has developed reflects, and has built on, the services that were already operating in that locality.

Having stated the above, within an IA network, you may find:

● organisations (not in receipt of funding) providing information about the services provided by other organisations within the network, and directing clients to those agencies

● organisations (not in receipt of funding) delivering **information** to clients about learning and work – agencies may hold local and national databases and reference directories/ prospectuses of learning opportunities, and other publications relating to learning, job seeking and employment; learndirect will provide an entry point

● organisations offering **advice** (through a sub-contract from the main IA Contractor) to individual clients on learning opportunities and matters related to seeking and gaining employment

● in some networks, access to in-depth **guidance** services, and psychometric assessment. Such services will be funded by separate funding streams, such as the European Social Fund, and are free to the user, or charges to the user may be made for in-depth services.

Until now, IA networks have been locally branded, but a national branding has been introduced, and providers are known as next**step** – advice on learning and work.

➤ www.nextstep.org.uk

Quality assurance

The **matrix** quality standard for information, advice and guidance services provides a quality benchmark for organisations within the IAG networks. This standard is accredited by The Guidance Accreditation Board. Display of the **matrix** quality standard mark denotes the organisation works within the Guidance Council's Code of Principles which embraces impartiality, transparency, confidentiality, equality of opportunity, accessibility and individual ownership. Standards must be met in relation to five areas of service delivery and five areas of management of the service.

For more information about **matrix**:

➤ **The Guidance Council** – 2 Crown Walk, Jewry Street, Winchester SO23 8BB.
Tel: 01962 878 340.
Email: admin@guidancecouncil.com
www.guidancecouncil.com/matrix

For information about the accreditation process:

➤ **The Guidance Accreditation Board** – 3rd Floor, Edgbaston House, 3 Duchess Place, Hagley Road, Edgbaston, Birmingham B16 8NH.
Tel: 0121 456 6090.
Email: hq@gab.org.uk
www.gab.org.uk

Coordinators for each local IAG network are listed in the gazetteer, by geographical area.

learndirect

learndirect, launched in 1998, operates a telephone helpline which assists callers with learning and career enquiries. Callers may be anyone over 16 (whatever their employment status), employers and staff from institutions. Information about the range of learning opportunities across the UK can be provided, as well as information about costs and financial assistance. Enquirers can also be signposted to local childcare provision and to their local adult information, advice and guidance agency. The websites of both learndirect and its Scottish counterpart, learndirect Scotland, offer online course search facilities. (learndirect also offers open learning courses, see *2:17 – Open/distance and other independent learning* for information.*)*

> **learndirect – the national learning helpline**. Tel: 0800 100 900 for general careers and learning information (or 0800 101 901 to find out about learndirect's own centres and courses) from 8am to 10pm seven days a week in England, 9am to 9pm seven days a week in Wales, Tuesdays, Thursdays and Fridays 9am to 6pm, then Mondays and Wednesdays 9am to 9pm, with no weekend service in Northern Ireland. There is also a free 'call me' facility where you can type in your name and number on the website, and learndirect call you at a specified time. Callers with hearing difficulties may be transferred to a textphone service via the same number. Those with visual impairments should make their particular needs known, as information can be sent in a different format e.g. Braille.
> www.learndirect-advice.co.uk
> www.learndirect.co.uk

In Scotland, callers should telephone: 0808 100 9000 from 7.30am to 11pm Monday to Friday; 9am to 6pm weekends. (Minicom facility available through the same number.) www.learndirectscotland.com

Careers guidance services

England

Connexions services provide integrated support and advice for all young people aged 13-19 years, especially those who have been identified as being harder to help. Connexions services partnerships (each covering the same geographical area as the local Learning and Skills Council) are responsible for providing the service in their area, which is locally designed and delivered, but works to national standards. Careers services form part of the Connexions services, in partnership with a range of other agencies concerned with young people.

Connexions services may also offer assistance to adults – usually as part of the next**step** information and advice network (as previously described), or through European Social Fund funded projects or as Enhanced Services. Available services may include access to in-depth guidance, such as one-to-one interviews, psychometric testing, computer-aided guidance, and help with CVs and jobsearch skills, some of which may be priced (although charges may not apply to certain clients). Information and advice provided through next**step** is free. Connexions services also continue to assist young adults up to the age of 25 if they have severe learning difficulties or disabilities.

Some organisations also offer services to businesses, such as redundancy counselling, employee development, and help with recruitment and selection.

Connexions services are listed in the gazetteer.

Wales

Careers Wales is the national all-age careers information, advice and guidance service in Wales, which has combined the seven careers companies working across Wales. Careers Wales operates from over 70 centres, and provides free information and advice to all adults at its centres and through locally-based community outlets. Guidance is offered free of charge to unemployed adults, and those in community education considering moving on to training or vocational education. Free in-depth guidance and counselling is available to low-skilled employed adults wishing to access learning to enhance their job prospects. The seven companies that make up Careers Wales are listed in the gazetteer. www.careerswales.com

Northern Ireland

Guidance for adults is provided through the EGSA (Educational Guidance Service for Adults) network. Eight EGSA offices operate across Northern Ireland, providing independent information, advice and guidance to adults wishing to access or progress in learning. The EGSA service is grant aided by the Department for Employment and Learning. EGSA offices are listed in the gazetteer. www.egsa.org.uk

Advice about training, in particular opportunities for unemployed people, including the various schemes to help people back to work, is also available through the Department for Employment and Learning for Northern Ireland. The Department operates through a network of Jobs and Benefits offices/JobCentres, listed in the gazetteer. www.delni.gov.uk

Scotland

Careers Scotland offers information, advice and guidance services to anyone, of any age in relation to work or learning. It has brought together a range of existing agencies, including adult guidance networks, careers service companies, education–business partnerships and lifelong learning partnerships. Careers Scotland is part of Scottish Enterprise and Highlands and Islands Enterprise, and operates from a network of offices across Scotland, listed in the gazetteer. There's a national local-rate helpline: 0845 8 502 502. www.careers-scotland.org.uk

Further education colleges

All further education colleges offer information and advice to prospective students of all ages, and to students on college courses. Advice and guidance to prospective students may be offered through a central admissions service, or through the college student services or customer services departments. Prospective students may also find it useful to talk to teaching staff involved in the course they are considering. Most colleges offer open days and evenings when staff are available to provide information and advice.

Most FE colleges offer websites with a course search facility. FE colleges' contact details are listed in the gazetteer.

Higher education careers services

Higher education institutions usually have a careers advisory service offering help to their graduates and undergraduates. Some universities participate in the 'mutual aid' scheme, whereby recent graduates can receive help from a higher education careers service other than the one at which they studied, for example in their home town, for up to three years after graduation. However, not all institutions offer such a service, and priority is given to an institution's own students. Possibly, a limited service only may be offered, such as use of the information library, and a charge may be made for this.

AgCAS Graduate Careerline is a national telephone advisory service for people within three years of graduating. Enquirers pay for the telephone call but the advice is free. It is staffed by graduate careers advisers.

Tel: 0870 7702 477 on Tuesday, Wednesday and Thursdays from 3pm to 8pm.

Prospects – the UK's official graduate website is a guide to graduate jobs, careers and postgraduate study in the UK, containing occupational information as well as postgraduate course information: www.prospects.ac.uk

Graduate Prospects provides products and services to higher education institutions, including working with **AgCAS**, the Association of Graduate Careers Advisory Services, and other official bodies in the production of joint careers information publications.

Jobcentre Plus

The Jobcentre Plus network is currently taking over responsibility for many of the services previously provided by the Employment Service and Benefits Agency. It is thought that the introduction of Jobcentre Plus offices will be completed by 2006. As well as providing access to job vacancies nationwide through the touch-screen technology of Jobpoints, staff can advise on government-funded training opportunities, such as the New Deal and Work Based Learning for Adults/Training for Work in Scotland. Some offices provide access to careers information resources, including information about learning opportunities, which may be computer-based or through a personal adviser. Many Jobcentre Plus /Jobcentre services are members of the local IAG network, so can provide information and advice on the broad range of learning opportunities. www.jobcentreplus.gov.uk

Clients can also access vacancies, voluntary work opportunities, and details of 500,000 learning opportunities, through **Worktrain**, the national jobs and learning website. www.worktrain.gov.uk

Professional bodies

The professional bodies for particular occupations can offer advice about qualifications relevant to their particular occupational field. Some also provide careers information, and advice/information about finding employment in their field. Careers information reference books, leaflets and databases usually supply contact details of professional bodies.

Professional bodies which are concerned with guidance provision include:

> **The Institute of Career Guidance** – Third Floor, Copthall House, 1 New Road, Stourbridge DY8 1PH.
> Tel: 01384 376464.
> Email: hq@icg-uk.org
> www.icg-uk.org

> **The National Association for Educational Guidance for Adults (NAEGA)** – PO Box 459, Belfast BT2 8YA.
> Tel: 028 9027 1509.
> Email: admin@naega.org.uk
> www.naega.org.uk

Libraries

Local public libraries may provide some or all of the following:

- local further and adult education information – some may offer access to course databases

- general careers and educational reference books

- open learning materials

- access to the internet

- access to specialist journals and newspapers.

College/university libraries are obviously essential facilities to learners, and students who are attending courses at institutions will be introduced to the facilities available. These libraries are also likely to hold databases of learning opportunities and allow students access to the internet.

Citizens Advice Bureaux

Like the library, CABs can provide information, though not usually careers advice. They should be able to advise on aspects of finance and legal problems, or help students who are having difficulty obtaining information on benefit entitlements. Find your local branch on the website. www.citizensadvice.org.uk

Help for ex-Service personnel

Various agencies exist to provide ex-Servicemen and women with advice and assistance on retraining, employment opportunities and jobseeking. They include the following.

The Royal British Legion

The Royal British Legion runs a careers advice centre based in Birkenhead, to assist Forces leavers and the ex-Services community with information, advice and guidance. This includes anyone who has served in the regular and reserve Forces (however long ago) for a minimum of seven days, and their spouses and dependants (up to 18 years, unless they have special needs). The service operates through a national helpline. The service has access to training and education grants (subject to eligibility) and has links with a vocational assessment centre and supported employment schemes.

> **Legion Careers Advice Centre** – Unit 48, Woodside Business Park, Shore Road, Birkenhead CH41 1EL.
> Tel: 0800 169 4073.
> Email: careersadvice@britishlegion.org.uk
> www.britishlegion.org.uk

Career Transition Partnerships (CTPs)

CTPs work on behalf of the Ministry of Defence to provide a network of resettlement and jobfinding support. CTPs offer one-to-one counselling, courses and workshops to help eligible Service leavers of all ranks to have a successful career transition – whether into employment or starting their own business. Support can continue to be provided for up to two years after leaving the Services. Eligibility depends on length of service. CTPs work closely with other agencies that assist ex-Service personnel to find employment.

> **CTP HQ** – 7th Floor, New Zealand House, 80 Haymarket, London SW1Y 4TE.
> Tel: 020 7766 8020.
> Email: info@ctp.org.uk
> www.ctp.org.uk

Commercial providers

There are many organisations providing careers advice and counselling as profit-making companies. Many offer a range of psychometric tests and assessments. Fees vary enormously, so potential enquirers should check fees charged in relation to services offered before committing themselves. Companies are usually listed in local business telephone directories.

National education and training agencies

England – Learning and Skills Council

The Learning and Skills Council is responsible for the delivery of post-16 education and training in England (other than higher education). The LSC operates through a network of 47 local Learning and Skills Councils, and a national office in Coventry. The LSC's responsibilities include the funding of further education colleges, work-based learning, developing arrangements for adult and community learning, and information and advice for adults through next**step** providers.

> **Learning and Skills Council National Office** – Cheylesmore House, Quinton Road, Coventry CV1 2WT.
> Tel: 0845 019 4170.
> Email: info@lsc.gov.uk
> www.lsc.gov.uk

Wales – ELWa

ELWa – Education and Learning Wales – is the joint name for the National Council for Education and Training and the Higher Education Funding Council for Wales, which are both sponsored by the Welsh Assembly. The National Council for Education and Training is responsible for funding, planning and promoting all post-16 education and training in Wales (with the exception of higher education) – i.e. further education, private and voluntary sector training provision and adult continuing education. ELWa operates through a network of four regional offices, which are listed in the gazetteer, or can be accessed through its website. www.elwa.org.uk

Northern Ireland – Department for Employment and Learning

In Northern Ireland, responsibility for education, training and enterprise lies with the Department for Employment and Learning. Its responsibilities include helping people to find jobs and access careers advice, the development of training programmes and services to meet the needs of business and industry, and providing assistance to unemployed people. It operates a network of JobCentres/Jobs and Benefits offices across Northern Ireland (listed in the gazetteer).

> ➤ **Department for Employment and Learning** – Adelaide House, 39-49 Adelaide Street, Belfast BT2 8FD.
> Tel: 028 9025 7777.
> Email: del@nics.gov.uk
> www.delni.gov.uk

Scotland – Scottish Enterprise/Highlands and Islands Enterprise

Scottish Enterprise, funded by the Scottish Executive, is the economic development agency operating across southern Scotland. It has a network of 12 Local Enterprise Companies (LECs), each with its own board, made up of local people from the private, public and voluntary sectors. Areas of activity include running training initiatives such as Training for Work, which helps unemployed adults develop their skills, assistance with business start-ups and helping existing companies to grow.

Similar services are provided across northern Scotland by Highlands and Islands Enterprise, which operates through a network of ten LECs.

The websites of Scottish Enterprise and Highlands and Islands Enterprise offer links to the LECs, which are also listed in the gazetteer.

> ➤ **Scottish Enterprise** – 5 Atlantic Quay, 150 Broomielaw, Glasgow G2 8LU.
> Tel: 0141 248 2700.
> Network helpline: 0845 607 8787 (if calling from Scotland) or: 0141 228 2000 (if calling from anywhere in the UK)
> Email: network.helpline@scotent.co.uk
> www.scottish-enterprise.com

> ➤ **Highlands and Islands Enterprise (HIE)** – Cowan House, Inverness Retail and Business Park, Inverness IV2 7GF.
> Tel: 01463 234171.
> Email: hie.general@hient.co.uk
> www.hie.co.uk

Sector Skills Councils

Sector Skills Councils (SSCs) are replacing National Training Organisations as the industry bodies responsible for overseeing skill development and economic growth in their particular sectors. The Skills for Business network is made up of the Sector Skills Development Agency (SSDA) and the SSCs. SSCs are employer led, and involve trade unions, professional bodies and other interested parties. Their responsibilities include increasing opportunities for their sector's workforce to improve their skills. More information about SSCs is provided in *2:19 – Learning in the workplace*. www.ssda.org.uk

Computer-based information and guidance systems

There are many useful computer software programs related to education, training, careers, CVs and related topics.

They include:

- **information databases** – providing information about education and training courses, or about occupations
- **guidance systems** – self-evaluation programs, which suggest possible suitable career options on the basis of responses made by the client, often linked to an occupational information database.

Adults may access computer-based information and guidance systems through local providers of information and advice (next**step** in England) networks, Connexions/careers services and other advisory and guidance agencies. Educational institutions usually subscribe to various computer-based systems for the benefit of their students. Information databases may also be available through libraries, Jobcentre/Jobcentre Plus offices, community centres and other local public venues.

A few of the available systems most relevant to the adult user are described below.

Local databases of learning opportunities

In many areas, comprehensive databases of local learning opportunities have been developed, and may be available under a variety of different names (like the TAP network in the north-east, or information access points in Gloucestershire). Such databases usually cover the whole range of local learning providers, including the public, private and voluntary sectors. They include full-time, part-time and open/distance learning opportunities. They may be accessible through local libraries, information, advice and guidance services or on the internet.

It is also possible to research local courses online through the learndirect websites: www.learndirect-advice.co.uk and www.learndirectscotland.com

Course Discover

Course Discover is a recently redeveloped national database of further and higher education opportunities, produced by Trotman in association with ECCTIS Ltd. It is available by subscription, and is provided on CD-ROM and through internet access. It gives information on further and higher education courses throughout the UK, including postgraduate-level courses. It includes full-time, part-time and distance learning opportunities. Course Discover can be found in agencies providing information, advice and guidance on learning opportunities, educational institutions and libraries.

Teachers and advisers can obtain subscription details from:

➤ **Trotman and Company Ltd** – 2 The Green, Richmond, Surrey TW9 1PL.
  Tel: 020 8486 1200.
  Email: enquiries@trotman.co.uk
  www.trotman.co.uk

ECCTIS also maintains a database of postgraduate courses. www.postgraduk.com

Software from CASCAiD

Adult Directions multimedia

This is a career-matching program and occupational database designed for use by adults of all ages. It suggests careers based on the user's work and personal interests, and chosen occupational level. The job suggestions are described with direct reference to the responses made by the user in the matching program. General information is provided on issues such as age and employment.

Careerscape multimedia

Careerscape provides information on over 800 careers and other topics, and is suitable for young people and adult users. Occupational information includes details on adult opportunities. Subscription provides free access to CareerSphere – the internet-based version.

➤ **CASCAiD Ltd** – Holywell Building, Holywell Way, Loughborough LE11 3UZ.
   Tel: 01509 283390.
   Email: enquiry@cascaid.co.uk
   www.cascaid.co.uk

Software from VT Progressions

Odyssey

This is an occupational database with job information supplied by the DfES. It contains over 800 job titles with various searches to get the user to the job profile. It includes information on adult entry, and salary levels. Odyssey.2 is currently being developed to include more information for adults.

Pathfinder

Pathfinder (Standard Edition) takes the user through a series of questions, based on the VT JIIG-CAL Occupational Interest Profile and Job Suggestions program. (JIIG-CAL is a psychometric assessment tool.) The user is presented with an interest profile and job suggestions based on their responses. Users can see the pros and cons of each job suggestion, and detailed information about each job. Pathfinder has separate modes of operation for young people and for adults.

SkillCheck

SkillCheck is designed to help users identify their key skills and additional work-related skills. A profile is produced which indicates the strength of the user's skills. This is linked to job suggestions. Skillcheck is designed for young people and for adult users.

➤ **VT Progressions Ltd** – Sutton House, Weyside Park, Catteshall Lane, Godalming, Surrey GU7 1XJ.
   Tel: 01483 528871.
   Email: info@progressions.co.uk
   www.progressions.co.uk

Software from Lifetime Careers Publishing

Keynotes Plus!

Keynotes Plus! is a computerised version of Keynotes, a series of careers guidance leaflets for adults covering general topics in relation to career choice and change, education, training, jobhunting and employment. Keynotes Plus! allows clients to choose, view and print the information leaflets through selecting particular topic areas, or through a keyword search.

KeyCLIPS

KeyCLIPS is a computer package which allows users to explore the occupational information contained in the CLIPS careers information leaflet series. Users enter search factors such as qualification level, subjects and work skills, to generate a list of relevant CLIPS leaflets which users may view or print off.

ProMICAD

A self-assessment program which results in a computer profile describing the user's character and best qualities in positive terms only. Useful for advisers working with those who find it difficult to talk about themselves, or act positively, due to lack of confidence or low self-esteem.

> **Lifetime Careers Publishing** – 7 Ascot Court, White Horse Business Park, Trowbridge BA14 0XA.
> Tel: 01225 716023.
> Email: sales@lifetime-publishing.co.uk
> www.lifetime-publishing.co.uk

Using the internet

Access to the internet is now widespread; clients who are not online at home should be able to find internet access via their local library, or at an internet café. Educational institutions usually provide access to the internet for their students.

The internet is, of course, a useful source of information about education, training, careers and job opportunities, but users should check how up-to-date information is, and that it has been provided by an authoritative source. The following are just a few sites that may be of interest:

> www.dfes.gov.uk

The DfES website, which includes information on a wide range of government initiatives and policies, and links to related agencies and organisations.

> www.lifelonglearning.co.uk

The DfES-supported website for lifelong learning.

> www.waytolearn.co.uk

Another DfES site that brings together information about learning aimed at adults.

> www.lsc.gov.uk

The Learning and Skills Council for England website, which provides information about local Learning and Skills Councils.

➤ **www.scotland.gov.uk/topics/education/life-long-learning**

The website of the Enterprise, Transport and Lifelong Learning Department of the Scottish Executive.

➤ **www.elwa.org.uk**

The Education and Learning Wales website. Provides information relating to post-16 education and training in Wales.

➤ **www.delni.gov.uk**

The website of the Department for Employment and Learning in Northern Ireland.

➤ **www.worktrain.gov.uk**

The Government's national jobs and learning site, supplied by the DfES, Department of Work and Pensions and Jobcentre Plus. Provides access to job vacancies, learning opportunities (through learndirect), occupational information and childcare provision.

➤ **www.jobcentreplus.gov.uk**

Describes the service available; includes a job search facility and information about training.

➤ **www.newdeal.gov.uk**

For information about the New Deal.

➤ **www.learndirect.co.uk** (for learndirect's own course provision) or www.learndirect-advice.co.uk (for general information) and www.learndirectscotland.com

The websites of the national learning helplines, containing searchable course databases.

➤ **www.qca.org.uk**

The site of the Qualifications and Curriculum Authority, containing information about academic and vocational qualifications for England, Wales and Northern Ireland. For information about Scottish qualifications, look at the Scottish Qualifications Authority website: **www.sqa.org.uk**

➤ **www.ucas.com**

For information on higher education courses, including foundation degree listings and information and advice on all aspects of applying for higher education. A database of access courses can be found on www.ucas.com/access

➤ **www.foundationdegree.org.uk**

The DfES website listing foundation degrees.

➤ **www.prospects.ac.uk**

For information about graduate careers, jobs and postgraduate opportunities.

➤ **www.ukcoursefinder.com**

Higher education course database.

> www.british-learning.com

The website of the British Learning Association, formed as the result of a merger between the British Association of Open Learning and the Forum for Technology and Training; links to distance learning and e-learning providers.

> www.odlqc.org.uk/courses.htm

Lists accredited open and distance learning courses.

> www.ceg.org.uk

CEG, the Continuing Education Gateway provides information on lifelong learning and careers guidance. The PlanIT Plus website contains information about opportunities in Scotland, including links to community education and further and higher education providers. Also contains occupational information. www.planitplus.net

> www.skill.org.uk

The website of The National Bureau for Students with Disabilities.

> www.support4learning.org.uk

Information and resources for advisers, students and others involved in education and training.

> www.bbc.co.uk/learning/adults

Information for adult learners from the BBC, including online courses in a variety of subjects.

Ensuring a successful outcome to learning

Besides access to information about learning opportunities, there are other issues that new learners need to consider. Learners need to organise and plan their time, and to develop the necessary study skills.

Checklist for successful learning:

- well-managed time

- effective study skills

- the ability to organise self and resources

- finding the necessary space.

Time management skills

This is the key to successful study, especially if fitting learning around full-time work or family commitments. Potential learners should:

- find out how much time will be required for the course they are undertaking **in addition to** any scheduled classes, i.e. time for reading, researching, writing up notes, doing assignments etc

- review how they currently spend their time, and, if time is tight, try to re-organise their time more efficiently – re-prioritising daily activities etc, to create sufficient study time

- use their learning time effectively; it is helpful to devise a regular timetable of study periods, at a time of day when they can learn effectively, and then stick to it!

Effective study skills

Most course providers offer opportunities for students to develop their study skills. This could be as an integral part of the course itself, through short workshops or courses, via more informal 'drop-in' learning centres, or access to a learning support tutor on an individual basis.

Study skills include:

- note-taking – from oral presentations and from texts

- reading – how to read effectively when researching or reading set texts

- producing written work – essays, project reports and other assignments.

Organising resources

During most courses of learning, students will generate and accumulate a wealth of notes, handouts, leaflets and books, perhaps also tapes and videos etc, as well as computer-held documents. Learners will need to access this information for reference, revision and other reasons. Therefore, planning an efficient and secure storage and retrieval system is vital. Losing the final draft of an essay on the computer, or some essential handouts in messy ringbinders, can easily turn into a crisis!

Space to learn

Most learners need to spend some time studying at home, besides using libraries and other learning facilities. Space has to be found at home that is free from distractions and interruptions, and suitable for working – not always easy in a busy household. Ground rules may need to be negotiated with other family members.

Wordprocessing skills

Students undertaking courses requiring written essays/reports etc will find that having basic wordprocessing skills will be a huge asset, if not essential. If students do not have access to wordprocessing facilities at home, the institution offering the course is likely to have facilities that can be used by students.

Giving some consideration to the above issues will help ensure that the learner is well prepared, and has a positive outcome to their learning experience.

Further information

There are many reference publications on careers, education and training. Below are listed a few examples to provide a general starting point. Many of these will be available for reference in agencies offering information, advice and guidance, and some in local libraries. Most bookshops can order copies to purchase.

General

Keynotes – a series of photocopiable careers guidance leaflets for adults, covering career choice and change, education and training and job hunting. Published by Lifetime Careers Publishing. Price £135 (single copy); discounts for additional sets.

Learning opportunities

Coming Back to Learning – published by Lifetime Careers Publishing, £11.99.

The UCAS Mature Students' Guide to Higher Education – free booklet, published by UCAS.

Mature Students' Directory – published by Trotman, £19.99. Information on what each HE institution has to offer prospective mature students.

The Big Guide (2005 Entry) – published annually by UCAS, with an accompanying CD-ROM. Price £32.50. Provides information about all UK degree, foundation degree and HND courses at publicly-funded institutions.

Choosing Your Degree Course and University – published by Trotman, price £21.99.

Study Gap – published by ISCO, price £7.95 (plus £1 p&p). Aimed at gap year students, it includes a wide range of short courses in independent colleges.

Adult Learning Yearbook – published annually by NIACE; 2004/2005 edition price £21.95. A directory of organisations and resources in adult continuing education and training.

Career choice/life planning

The Which? Guide to Changing Careers – a Which? consumer guide. Price £10.99.

Planning a Career Change and *Returning to Work* – both published by How To Books, £9.99 each.

The Ultimate Career Success Workbook – published by Kogan Page, price £10.99.

The Career Change Handbook and *The Redundancy Survivor's Field Guide* – both published by How To Books, £12.99 each.

Surfing your Career – published by How To Books, £9.99. Details of 1500 careers websites.

Occupational information

Careers 2005 – published by Trotman, £39.99. A comprehensive careers directory.

A guide to careers, including information on the work, skills and interests, the pay and conditions, opportunities, prospects, entry requirements, training available and late entry to the work can be found on www.connexions.gov.uk/jobs4u

The Penguin Careers Guide – published by Penguin Books, £12.99. Occupational information; includes information on opportunities for part-time and flexible working, and advice for job changers and those returning to the workplace.

Jobseeking

What Color is Your Parachute? 2004: A Practical Manual for Job Hunters and Career Changers – from Airlift Book Company, price £14.99. Jobhunting advice; updated annually.

The Job-Hunter's Handbook: An A-Z of Tried and Tested Tips and *Your Job Search Made Easy* – both published by Kogan Page, £7.99 each.

2:5

A brief guide to education and training

Topics covered:

- Academic study
- Vocational education
- Vocational training

More detailed information on education and training opportunities is given in the rest of this section of *Second Chances*.

The education system in the UK covers a range of qualifications and subjects, from academic through to professional. The range of qualifications on offer is huge. Qualifications available are in line with the National Qualifications Framework, which places them into 9 levels. See *2:6 – Qualifications*.

Academic study generally leads to more traditional qualifications, based on theoretical study e.g. maths GCSE and history A level, as well as newer subjects in vocational and work-related areas such as GCSE engineering, or A levels in applied science and travel and tourism. Academic study can also lead to qualifications such as the International Baccalaureate (IB), foundation degrees, degrees, and Diplomas of Higher Education.

Vocationally-related learning is particularly important at the moment, and the Government is trying to encourage more people to participate. Many vocationally-related qualifications have only recently been developed, many more are being considered. These qualifications are relevant to the world of work and broad occupational areas, and now cover almost every industry sector.

Then, there are qualifications (usually gained in employment) that are about work and the ability to do a particular job. These **work-based qualifications** include NVQs, some BTEC Introductory, First, Higher and National qualifications. Other qualification bodies offering vocational awards are City & Guilds and OCR. Many professional bodies also offer their own qualifications.

Who offers education and training for adults?

Opportunities for adults are offered through the following channels:

- **public sector providers** of education – this includes adult/community education services, further education colleges, specialist colleges for areas such as art and design, agriculture, music etc, tertiary colleges or sixth form colleges, universities, colleges and institutes of higher education, and the adult residential colleges

- **independent training providers or colleges** – operating on a commercial basis

- **employers** – who offer training to their staff, and financial (and other) support for staff following courses at colleges, or through professional bodies

- **providers of government-funded training programmes** – these could include independent training organisations, further education colleges or voluntary organisations, which contract to provide training for unemployed people

- **voluntary organisations** – which often provide training, sometimes certificated, for their volunteers

- organisations offering **open or distance learning** courses – these could be public or private sector organisations

- **community-based training or education providers** – which may be supported by funding from public, private or voluntary agencies, but operate separately from mainstream educational establishments

- **internet-based** courses – such as the ones offered by the BBC. www.bbc.co.uk/learning/adults

Some definitions

Further education and tertiary colleges

These have traditionally offered work-related (vocational) courses. Most colleges offer a mixture of full- and part-time courses with qualifications at the equivalent of craft and technician levels, and many also offer courses up to professional or degree level. They cover general educational and recreational subjects as well as those relevant to employment.

The Government's plans for increased access to higher education are expected to involve further education colleges offering a wide range of foundation degrees.

Some colleges offer short courses geared specifically to the needs of people coming back into education after a number of years, often called Return to Learn, Fresh Start or something similar.

Adult education/community education services

These offer a range of courses for adults, mostly part-time, with some courses in the evening. Usually these courses are non-advanced. Subjects can be work-related, educational, leisure activities or hobbies.

Higher education

Higher education is advanced-level education (entry standard equivalent to A level or above), offered mainly through universities and colleges or institutes of higher education. Higher education includes degrees, foundation degrees, Higher National Certificates or Diplomas (HNC/HNDs) and Diplomas of Higher Education.

Most courses are full-time, but many courses are part-time.

Some universities run courses for adults through their Continuing Education, or Extra Mural departments or Short Course Units – the name varies. These courses do not have the breadth of the degree programmes.

Some institutions 'franchise' one, two or more years of a degree or HND course to another. So you may be able to take the first year of a course at your local further education college, and then go on to a university, or take a complete course at one college which is validated and awarded by a different college or university.

Independent providers

There are a number of independent providers of education and training, offering courses at all levels and in mostly specialist subjects – from management training to beauty therapy. One example is The University of Buckingham, an independent university offering intensive two-year degree courses.

Distance and open learning

Distance and open learning is the term used where the learner learns independently, using a variety of resources and ways of learning and keeping in touch with the tutor, other than attending scheduled classes. Open and distance learning includes correspondence learning, where students can use electronic means, as well as the post, to liaise with their tutors.

Contact with tutors on open learning courses may include occasional face-to-face meetings, to discuss progress. Open learning can involve the use of computer-based learning packages, which students may use at home, or through an open learning centre offering the necessary computer facilities, perhaps with tutor back-up.

There are often no entrance qualifications to distance and open learning courses, and a vast range of subjects is offered including degrees and postgraduate professional level courses (through the Open University). There is a lot of emphasis on self discipline as the courses are so flexible. Courses taken through the distance learning method may take many years to complete, especially if taken on a part-time basis.

The main providers

In England

The Learning and Skills Council is responsible for funding and planning further education and training for over 16-year-olds. Higher education courses are funded by the Higher Education Funding Council for England (HEFCE). www.lsc.gov.uk and www.hefce.ac.uk

In Scotland

The Scottish Executive Enterprise, Transport and Lifelong Learning Department is responsible for further and higher education, skills and lifelong learning. Funding for FE and HE is administered through the Student Awards Agency for Scotland (SAAS). Local Enterprise Companies (LECs) organise work-related training and other measures. www.saas.gov.uk

In Wales

ELWa (The National Council for Education and Training in Wales and the Higher Education Funding Council for Wales – HEFCW) is responsible for all post-16 education and training. www.elwa.ac.uk

In Northern Ireland

The Department for Employment and Learning in Northern Ireland (DELNI) is responsible for FE, HE and training and employment measures. Funding is administered by the local Education and Library Boards. www.delni.gov.uk

Local Education Authorities (LEAs), and Education and Library Boards

These fund most adult and community education services, community colleges and tertiary colleges, as well as schools in their area.

Business and industry

Many organisations carry out training. National Learning Targets have been set to help ensure improvement of the skills and qualifications of the workforce. Some larger employers have their own training and study centres, and employ their own trainers. Others buy in assistance from local colleges and consultants. NVQs allow people to be accredited on their competencies in the workplace.

The voluntary sector

This sector is a major provider of training and education which can often be transferred to professional paid work. Examples might be training for volunteers working with adult literacy groups, second language providers, counselling organisations, probation and social workers.

Further information

There are many reference directories of further and higher education; relevant publications are listed in the other chapters of this section. Here are a few examples to provide a general starting point. Databases of education and training opportunities, held at Connexions/careers services, can also provide useful information.

The Big Guide (2005 Entry) – published annually by UCAS, with an accompanying CD-ROM, price £32.50. Provides information about all UK degree, foundation degree and HND courses at publicly-funded institutions.

UCAS/Universities Scotland: Entrance Guide to Higher Education in Scotland 2005 Entry – published by UCAS, price £9.95.

Directory of University and College Entry 2005-2006 (DUCE) – published by Trotman, price £39.99. Includes foundation degrees.

The Mature Students' Directory price £19.99, lists all higher education establishments and covers what each has to offer the mature student, as well as admissions procedures.

For courses at all levels, see: www.learndirect.co.uk www.learndirectscotland.com

2:6

Qualifications

Topics covered:

- General information about qualifications
- The National Qualifications Frameworks for England, Wales and Northern Ireland and for Scotland
- Qualifications in England, Wales and Northern Ireland
- Qualifications in Scotland
- Accreditation of previous work and study
- Overseas qualifications

General points about qualifications

What are qualifications?

A qualification is formal recognition of skills and/or knowledge, awarded by a recognised body. They range from general, academic qualifications, through to those needed for specific occupations.

What are qualifications used for?

Recent qualifications are evidence of someone's commitment to learning and proof of their ability and achievement. Having qualifications is becoming increasingly important because:

- they may be required for admission to further and higher education courses
- they are usually asked for by employers when recruiting
- they allow access to membership of professional bodies.

How can qualifications be achieved?

- Through full- or part-time study on a formal taught course.

- Through open or distance learning – where students study independently using various resources, often with access to tutor support.

- Certain qualifications can be gained (in part or in full) through assessment in the workplace or accreditation of previous work or study.

- Some courses are structured so that learners can gradually build up to the full qualification by undertaking units or modules (which are each independently assessed) over a period of time, at a pace to suit themselves.

It is often possible for students to combine different types of qualifications and different levels to suit their needs.

Who needs qualifications?

Essential

There are some jobs for which specific qualifications are essential for entry – for example professional jobs such as nursing, law, architecture and teaching.

Desirable

To enter most professions and trades it is helpful either to have a general qualification at a certain level, or one relevant to a specific career. However, there are no hard and fast rules; some employers prefer applicants to have relevant, practical experience and others will require the right qualification.

Useful

Although experience is often enough for employment in smaller firms, or for self-employment, it is becoming increasingly important to have some formal recognition and proof of skills and knowledge, in particular for employment with larger employers.

Who awards qualifications?

There are many different awarding bodies. They include the various examination boards which award GCSEs and AS/A levels (e.g. AQA and WJEC), and bodies such as City & Guilds which are involved in awarding a wide range of vocational qualifications. Most universities award their own qualifications, although some smaller institutions offer degrees validated by larger universities.

The National Qualifications Frameworks

These have been developed to ensure that there is broad equivalence between the various qualifications at the same level.

There are now nine levels in the **National Qualifications Framework for England, Wales and Northern Ireland**:

NQF level	Qualifications			
8	NVQs level 5	Doctorates; Specialist awards		
7		Master's degrees; Postgraduate certificates/diplomas		
6	NVQs level 4	Bachelor's degrees; Graduate certificates/diplomas		
5		Foundation degrees	Diplomas of higher education	HNDs
4		Certificates of higher education		
3	NVQs level 3	AS/A levels	# Vocational A levels (AVCEs)	BTEC Nationals
2	NVQs level 2	GCSEs grades A*-C	Intermediate GNVQ	BTEC Firsts
1	NVQs level 1	GCSEs grades D-G	Foundation GNVQ	BTEC Introductory Certificates/Diplomas
Entry		Entry level certificates		

 # From September 2005, vocational A Levels (AVCEs) will be incorporated into the GCE AS/A level structure. They will simply be known as AS/A levels, but they are in applied subjects.

The table below shows the **National Qualifications Framework for Scotland**. There are twelve levels in the framework.

SCQF level	SQA National Units, Courses and Group Awards	Higher Education	Scottish Vocational Qualifications
12		Doctorates	
11		Masters	SVQ 5
10		Honours degrees Graduate diplomas	
9		Ordinary degrees Graduate certificates	
8		Higher National Diplomas Diplomas in Higher Education	SVQ 4
7	Advanced Highers	Higher National Certificates Certificates in Higher Education	
6	Highers		SVQ 3
5	Intermediate 2 Credit Standard Grades		SVQ 2
4	Intermediate 1 General Standard Grades		SVQ 1
3	Access 3 Foundation Standard Grades		
2	Access 2		
1	Access 1		

The Qualifications and Curriculum Authority (QCA) has overall responsibility for academic and vocational qualifications in England. ACCAC is the Qualifications, Curriculum and Assessment Authority for Wales, and the CCEA is the Northern Ireland Council for the Curriculum, Examinations and Assessment. Scotland has its own Authority, the Scottish Qualifications Authority (SQA).

Summary of qualifications in England, Wales and Northern Ireland

General qualifications

These are related to a specific academic subject and include:

- General Certificate of Secondary Education (GCSE)

- General Certificate of Education (GCE) at Advanced Subsidiary (AS) and Advanced (A) levels

- degrees – such as Bachelor of Arts (BA) and Bachelor of Science (BSc).

Vocationally-related qualifications

These provide a broad introduction to a particular vocational area, such as health and social care, business and manufacturing. They include:

- GCSEs in applied subjects

- vocational A levels (AVCEs)

- some BTEC Firsts, Nationals and HNC/Ds.

Occupational qualifications

These are related to a specific job and are based on the knowledge and skills needed in that job. They include:

- National Vocational Qualifications (NVQs), which are available in a wide range of occupations

- most BTEC Firsts, Nationals and HNC/Ds

- qualifications set by professional bodies for entry to that profession, for example in accountancy or surveying

- other occupational qualifications.

Summary of qualifications in Scotland

The educational system is different in Scotland from the rest of the UK. Scottish qualifications fall into three broad families:

- National Qualifications – Standard Grades, National Units, National Courses and Scottish Group Awards

- Higher National Qualifications – Higher National Certificates and Higher National Diplomas

- Scottish Vocational Qualifications – SVQs and Scottish Progression Awards.

The next part of this section describes the main qualifications more fully.

General academic qualifications in England, Wales and Northern Ireland

Entry level qualifications

Entry level qualifications are designed for learners who are not ready to take a foundation level (level 1) course in a particular subject or area of study. There are three sub-levels: entry 1, 2 and 3, with 3 being the highest. Entry level certificates can cover more than one of these sub-levels. Because of the diversity of people who can take entry qualifications, the range of entry level certificates is very wide. In total, there are more than 100 entry level certificates. They are in the subjects traditionally taught at schools and in vocational areas such as hairdressing and retail work, and in general subjects relating to life skills and basic skills, such as adult literacy and numeracy.

Entry level certificates are normally divided into units so that small steps of achievement can be recognised. The qualifications are designed to be flexible – the number of units and levels varies from one certificate to another. There are no particular time scales for completion.

At least 40% of the assessment of entry level certificates is external, but it can be based on practical, written or oral work. Internal assessment is often portfolio based and may include witness statements, audio, video and photographic evidence. In certificates based on the National Curriculum, 50% of assessment is external.

Around 18 awarding bodies currently offer entry level certificates. For more information about basic skills, refer to *2:9 – Basic skills*.

GCSEs (General Certificates of Secondary Education)

GCSEs are the standard way of recognising achievement at the age of 16 in England, Wales and Northern Ireland. GCSEs are also available to adults.

There is an extremely wide range of subjects: from English, maths and French, to Japanese, Russian and photography, amongst many others.

GCSEs are awarded by the following bodies: AQA, Edexcel, OCR, CCEA and the WJEC, and are overseen by the Qualifications and Curriculum Authority (QCA).

Each subject has a syllabus which describes what will be assessed and which methods (coursework and external examinations) will be used. Achievements are assessed by a combination of coursework (marked by teachers) and end-of-course examination (marked by external examiners for the examining board responsible for that particular GCSE).

GCSE certificates show achievements which must meet recognised national standards. Grades are awarded on a scale from A*-G.

Students who are aiming to use their GCSEs to help them enter work should note that many employers look for grade C or above in maths and English.

There are also GCSEs in applied subjects (e.g. applied science and health and social care), which are double awards. These are explained in more detail later in this section under vocationally-related qualifications.

Ways of preparing for GCSE

- **Rules, syllabuses and exam timetables** can be obtained from examination boards or downloaded from the internet.

- **Past examination papers** are useful for seeing the types of questions that are asked.

- **Examiners' reports** are published by exam boards, describing how past questions were answered and what the examiner was looking for.

Where to study

Students can study for GCSEs by attending a day or evening, full- or part-time course at a further education college or adult education centre, community college or through open or distance learning. Local secondary schools may allow adults to sit in on GCSE classes.

It is possible to take a GCSE without studying on a regular basis at a school or college, by registering as an external candidate. Candidates wishing to take a GCSE in this way will need to find out what the regulations are for the particular subject by contacting the relevant examining board and college.

AS (Advanced Subsidiary) and A (Advanced) levels

AS and A levels can be used to enter some careers; in particular they are the route for school leavers to get into higher education institutions. However, anybody, of any age, may study AS and A levels. They are widely offered in further education colleges and school sixth forms and can be taken through distance learning. In some subjects, for example chemistry or French, prior knowledge of the subject (such as that gained at GCSE level) is needed before proceeding to AS or A level.

An A level is divided into six units. Each unit is separately assessed. An AS qualification is achieved by successfully completing three AS units, which form the first half of an A level. An AS is also a qualification in its own right, and counts towards entry to higher education courses. To achieve the full A level, three A2 units are taken in the second half of the course. Passes at AS or A level are graded from A-E.

AS and A levels are currently offered by the following awarding bodies: AQA, Edexcel, OCR, WJEC and CCEA.

Vocational A levels (AVCEs) are described later in this section, under vocationally-related qualifications. N.B. From September 2005, vocational A levels are being restructured in line with A levels as described above.

AEAs (Advanced Extension Awards)

AEAs were introduced for the first time in summer 2002. They are designed to test students in greater depth than A levels and they aim to challenge the most able students. Universities can use AEAs to help them to differentiate between candidates with A grades at A level. AEAs are offered in various subjects. Students are graded merit or distinction. All assessment is external.

Access to higher education courses or return to study

There are many courses which cater for adults returning to formal education or study. Most of these are accredited through individual higher education institutions or authorised validating agencies, such as the National Open College Network. Many such courses are run at local further education colleges. Some Access courses are specific, such as Access to nursing, but others are more general. They can often be taken on a part-time basis.

Further information about Access courses can be found in *2:12 – Access and other adult routes* and also on: www.ucas.com/access which provides a course search facility.

Degrees

A higher education degree is a qualification which can provide an entry route to a wide range of professional jobs. Some degrees are more vocationally oriented than others; a Bachelor of Education is preparation for teaching, a law degree is a basis for further specialisation in the legal profession, engineering degrees for further training in engineering and so on.

A first degree (as opposed to a higher degree – described later) usually takes three or four years of full-time study (or longer part-time). At the end of the course students may be awarded an honours degree which is classified as a first, second or third class. If this standard is not reached, the student is awarded a pass degree. Examples are BA (Bachelor of Arts), BSc (Bachelor of Science), LLB (Bachelor of Law) and BEd (Bachelor of Education). An honorary degree is something quite different – see below.

A number of degrees are offered through a franchise arrangement between a further education college and a higher education institution. The first year of a degree offered in this way may be carried out at a local FE college with students moving to the HE institution for the rest. In some parts of the country, these arrangements enable students to do the whole degree in their local FE college.

Many institutions operate credit accumulation and transfer schemes (CATS). This means that it can be possible to accumulate credit through successful completion of modules of a degree course, and also to transfer that credit to a different learning programme. This is particularly useful for students who are not able to complete the whole course, as they can gain credits for the study they have successfully completed. CAT schemes are described in more detail later in this section.

Honorary degrees

Some universities award honorary degrees to famous or distinguished people who do not have to do anything by way of study but are simply distinguished!

Diplomas/Certificates of Higher Education (DipHE/CertHE)

These are offered by many higher education institutions as qualifications in their own right. A DipHE can be gained from a specific DipHE course which is normally two years full-time, equivalent in standard to the first two years of a degree. It can also actually be the first two years of a degree course, with the option of continuing into the third year. A CertHE is normally equivalent to one year of a degree course. Many higher education institutions offer CAT schemes (described above), so that students can gain credit points towards completing the degree at a later stage, as well as gaining the DipHE or CertHE.

More information on degrees, DipHEs etc can be found in *2:14 – Higher education – first degrees*.

Higher degrees

Master's degrees

Master's degrees are awarded after following a full-time programme, usually for a year, or a part-time programme for about two years. These are taught courses, which generally include some research. A Master of Philosophy (MPhil) is usually taken by doing research for one or two years.

Some people do a higher degree to enhance their professional knowledge and therefore fit it in around a job; others follow a first degree immediately with a master's degree, undertaken on a full-time basis.

Examples are MA (Master of Arts), MEd (Master of Education), MSc (Master of Science) and MBA (Master of Business Administration). Note that some universities (such as those in Scotland) call some of their first degrees MAs, and four-year engineering degrees etc may be called MEng (Master of Engineering).

Doctorate degrees

A PhD (Doctor of Philosophy) is awarded after doing several years' research in a subject. PhDs take at least three years full-time, more if the study is part-time.

More details on higher degrees can be found in *2:15 – Higher education – higher degrees*.

Vocationally-related and occupational qualifications in England, Wales and Northern Ireland

Entry level qualifications

Many entry level certificates are in vocationally-related and occupational subject areas. See under general academic qualifications earlier in this section for details.

GCSEs in work-related subjects and General National Vocational Qualifications (GNVQs)

GCSEs in work-related subjects were introduced in September 2002 and are offered by AQA, Edexcel, OCR, WJEC and CCEA. They are double awards (equivalent to two GCSEs). Eventually, the GCSEs will replace the existing Foundation and Intermediate GNVQs. Work-related GCSEs help to prepare people for entry to employment or to go on to further study. Although they are mainly aimed at young, full-time students, they can also be taken by adults.

GCSEs in work-related subjects are broad-based courses which cover different areas of employment. They are currently available in eight subjects – applied art and design, applied business, applied ICT, applied science, leisure and tourism, engineering, manufacturing, and health and social care. There are plans to introduce more subjects in the future

GCSEs in a work-related subject consist of three units. Usually, one unit is assessed by an external test, and the other two units by course work. They are graded from A*A*-GG.

Vocational A levels (AVCEs)

Vocational A levels (also known as AVCEs) prepare people for entry to employment or to go on to higher education. They are broad courses covering a particular area of employment e.g. applied business, leisure and recreation. Vocational A levels are awarded by three bodies – AQA, Edexcel and OCR.

Currently, a vocational A level may be available as a qualification of three, six or 12 units. Each unit of a vocational A level is separately assessed, either internally or externally. Vocational A levels are graded in the same way as GCE A levels, and can be used for entry to a higher education course.

At present, all the vocational A level units are of an equal standard, but, from September 2005, vocational A levels are being restructured to match GCE A levels. They will then have AS units that are assessed at the standard expected for a student halfway through an A level course, (as already happens with GCE AS levels) and A2 units. The qualifications will no longer be known as 'vocational A levels' or 'AVCEs', but will be called 'AS levels' and 'A levels'.

National Vocational Qualifications (NVQs)

NVQs are designed to reflect the skills, knowledge and understanding needed to do a specific job to the standards of competence set by industry, commerce or the professions. These National Occupational Standards are developed in collaboration with employers, employees' representatives and professional bodies.

The most important feature of NVQs is that it is not necessary to have attended a taught course in order to get the qualification, although further education colleges often provide courses leading to NVQs, if combined with work experience.

NVQs are split into units of competence. Candidates can achieve separate units and build up to the full NVQ over a period of time. NVQ candidates have to provide evidence, e.g. through being observed in the workplace, to demonstrate their competence in the various aspects of the work. Accreditation of Prior Learning and Accreditation of Prior Experiential Learning can be counted towards a qualification – see later in this section. Providing the evidence is authentic, relevant and current, it can come from previous work and life experience as well as from formal learning/experience.

NVQs are available in a huge range of work areas, and may be awarded at five levels, from level one covering routine jobs to level five for strategic management and other professional-level work.

BTEC First and National qualifications

BTEC qualifications are awarded by Edexcel. They may relate to particular fields of employment, such as agriculture, construction or design. Many others are in more specific job areas, such as hairdressing or blacksmithing and metalwork. BTEC qualifications may be taken on a full- or part-time basis and can be used for entry to higher education courses.

BTEC qualifications may be available as a:

- Introductory Certificate/Diploma (at level 1)

- First Diploma (at level 2)

- National Award – six units (equivalent to one A level)

- National Certificate – 12 units (equivalent to two A levels)

- National Diploma – 18 units (equivalent to three A levels).

BTEC Higher National Certificates/Diplomas (HNC/D)

HNC/Ds are awarded by Edexcel and are qualifications at a higher-education level. They relate to a particular vocational area or occupation. The courses combine theory and practice and prepare students for jobs at technician, supervisory or management level. Full-time courses lead to HNDs; part-time courses normally lead to HNCs. It can be possible to continue with a further year's study to 'top up' to a full degree.

Foundation degrees

These qualifications are offered in a wide range of vocational and occupational subject areas, aimed at meeting the skill requirements of industry and commerce. Part-time courses are particularly suitable for adults in employment who wish to further their careers. Foundation degrees take two years full-time, or can be studied part-time over a longer period. There are no set entry requirements; the university or college will decide whether a potential student is capable of study at this level. As with HNDs, it may be possible to continue studying to 'top up' the foundation degree to a full degree.

With the Government target of 50% of 18-30 year-olds experiencing some form of higher education, foundation degrees are likely to continue to increase in availability and popularity. They tend to be offered in FE colleges while accredited by higher-education institutions.

Other vocational qualifications

There is a range of other available vocational qualifications. Some of the main providers are described below.

City & Guilds

City & Guilds are involved in awarding 'own brand' qualifications in a wide range of industrial and commercial fields. It provides office-based qualifications through City and Guilds Pitman and management qualifications through the Institute of Leadership and Management.

OCR

OCR offers a wide range of flexible general, vocationally-related and occupational, qualifications, at more than 13,000 centres.

LCCI Examinations Board

The LCCIEB is a major examining and assessment body for business-related qualifications. Areas covered include secretarial work, finance, marketing, international languages, information technology and various basic skills courses.

Professional bodies

Almost every professional organisation, such as the Royal Institution of Chartered Surveyors, or the Chartered Institute of Marketing, has its own examination structures. Achieving their qualifications leads to full membership of that particular organisation. The relevant professional body can provide information – contact addresses can be found through public reference and careers libraries.

Scottish qualifications

The educational system is different in Scotland from the rest of the UK. Academic and vocational qualifications in Scotland, other than university degrees, are the responsibility of the Scottish Qualifications Authority. The Scottish Credit and Qualifications Framework (see earlier in this section) has brought together all the main Scottish qualifications from access (similar to entry level in the rest of the UK), right up to doctorate-level into a single structure of 12 levels which are described in terms of their credit value. The main qualifications specific to Scotland are described below.

National Qualifications

National Qualifications are available in a broad range of options and at the following levels:

- access (divided into three sub-levels, 1, 2 and 3)

- intermediate 1

- intermediate 2

- higher

- advanced higher.

Having five levels means there is more scope for candidates to demonstrate their abilities at whatever level suits them best. Each level is designed to encourage progression on to the next, helping candidates to achieve their true potential.

National Qualifications give candidates the flexibility to build up a recognised qualification while allowing them room to try something different, or build up new skills. There are National Units and National Courses in all the traditional 'school' subjects and there is also a choice of Units and Courses in subjects related to specific careers.

National Qualifications are usually studied at schools or colleges. They are assessed by a combination of exams and internal assessment.

National Units and National Courses

National Units and National Courses are usually taken by those aged over 16. National Units take about 40 hours to complete, and there are generally three Units plus an exam in a National Course. National Courses usually take around 160 hours (120 hours for three Units, plus 40 hours for review and consolidation) and include the Scottish qualifications described below.

Standard Grades (Scotland)

These are the Scottish counterparts to GCSEs. There are three levels of study and grades are given from 1 to 7 where 1 is the highest:

- Credit Standard Grade (grades 1 and 2 – equivalent to intermediate 2 level)

- General Standard Grade (grades 3 and 4 – equivalent to intermediate 1 level) – this is broadly the same as a grade C at GCSE

- Foundation Standard Grade (grades 5 and 6 are equivalent to access 3)

- course completed (grade 7).

Each Standard Grade has three or four separate elements. Assessment is usually through a mixture of formal examinations that are marked externally and internal, coursework assessment.

It may be possible for adults to take Standard Grades at community schools or further education colleges.

Scottish Group Awards (SGAs)

These are recognised packages of National Units and National Courses designed to give candidates coherent and relevant learning experiences. SGAs include core skills and represent the equivalent of a year's full-time study. The upper levels of SGAs have been designed with progression to higher education in mind.

There are 'named' SGAs in broad subject areas e.g. business or science. These are available at intermediate 2 and higher level. There are also 'general' SGAs in subject areas not covered by the 'named' SGAs. These are available from access level to advanced higher level.

Highers and Advanced Highers

Highers are normally taken after Standard Grades. However, they can be taken by adults, usually at further education colleges. Candidates in full-time education usually take five subjects. A wide range of academic and vocational subjects is available. Possession of an appropriate number of Highers and Standard Grades enables applicants to enter all the Scottish universities. Higher awards can also be used for exemption from the preliminary examinations of most professional bodies.

An Advanced Higher is broadly equivalent to an A level at grade A-C.

Scottish Vocational Qualifications (SVQs)

SVQs

SVQs are nationally-recognised awards, and are the Scottish counterparts to NVQs. SVQs demonstrate the candidate's competence to perform in a particular work area to the standards required by business and industry.

Scottish Progression Awards (SPAs)

SPAs are flexible qualifications, e.g. they could be a group of National Units to provide some of the knowledge and understanding required for an SVQ, or they could be a group of SVQ units. They are designed to prepare learners for work in a specific industry and are a way of showing that candidates have completed a programme of development to national standards. SPAs may be a stepping stone to a full SVQ, or another qualification. They are available in a growing number of occupational areas.

Higher National Qualifications

Higher National Certificates/Diplomas (HNC/D)

These are intended for students who have completed a relevant National programme, or who have an appropriate group of Higher and Standard Grades (or equivalent). Some students may qualify, at the discretion of a college, on grounds of maturity and experience. The length of the programme varies and whether a Certificate or Diploma is awarded depends on the level of study. Higher National qualifications are increasingly being offered on a part-time basis.

HNCs/Ds are available in a wide range of subjects including accountancy, travel and tourism, engineering and agriculture.

HNC/Ds are run at further education colleges and higher education institutions. They are recognised by many professional and technical bodies.

Degrees

Degrees in Scotland are generally of four years' duration; many first degrees in Scotland lead to the award of 'MA' rather than BA.

Awards offered by professional bodies

As for the rest of the UK, although there are some differences in professional qualifications, notably for the legal profession.

Professional Development Awards

Other qualifications available in Scotland include **Professional Development Awards** (PDAs), offered by colleges and some universities. PDAs include a range of qualifications in specific occupational subjects at postgraduate or post-experience level. PDAs are mainly aimed at people already in employment, to help with their career advancement. For instance, there is a PDA for classroom assistants, and others in computing, engineering and business subjects.

Key skills/core skills

Key skills (and core skills in Scotland) are considered to be the essential transferable skills which people need in order to function effectively as members of the workforce and in society as a whole. Skills may be studied and certificated in their own right, or are more usually achieved through work for other courses. Most post-16 courses include teaching and/or assessment of transferable skills.

In England, Wales and Northern Ireland, key skills units can be achieved at five levels. The key skill units at levels 1-4 are in:

- communication

- information technology

- application of number

- working with others

- improving own learning and performance

- problem solving.

The first three in the list above can be taken as a stand-alone key skills qualification. At level 5, the key skills are integrated into a personal skills development unit.

In Scotland, the core skills can be achieved at different levels up to Higher. There are core skills in:

- communication

- working with others

- numeracy

- problem solving

- information technology.

Credit accumulation and transfer schemes (CATS)

Many further and higher education institutions offer credit-based programmes, in which units or modules of study are assigned a number of credit points at a particular level. CATS allow learners to accumulate credit towards qualifications within an institution, and to transfer credit from one institution to another. Full-time, part-time, distance and open learning courses can all form part of a CATS. When assigning credit, account is normally taken of the total time that a typical learner would take to complete the study, and the level of the particular programme of learning.

Northern Ireland has a scheme (NICATS) which covers further and higher education and work-based training. Wales has a similar credit framework, called the Credit and Qualifications Framework for Wales (CQFW). In Scotland, SCOTCAT (which was mainly used for higher education) has been absorbed into the Scottish Credit and Qualifications Framework which covers all levels of qualification. 2006 is the target for all Scottish qualifications to be in the Framework. The Qualifications and Curriculum Authority is working towards establishing a credit framework for adult learners in England.

An increasing number of professional qualifications and in-company education and training programmes are credit rated by higher education institutions towards their certificates, diplomas and degrees.

Institutions may charge a fee for assessing previous study for credit.

More information on how CATS operate in higher education can be found in *2:14 – Higher education – first degrees.*

National Open College Network (NOCN)

NOCN is a recognised national qualification-awarding body and is the central organisation for Open College Networks – partnerships which collaborate to provide accreditation for adult learning in their local area. Accreditation helps learners plan their route through further and higher education. The Networks all adhere to a framework offering awards, from entry qualifications to level 3 (advanced level) equivalent.

More information about NOCN can be found in *2:12 – Access and other adult routes.*

APL and APEL

The process of gaining credit for existing qualifications or learning is known as the Accreditation of Prior Learning (APL). If prospective students want their experience taken into account and can demonstrate skills and knowledge, this is called the Accreditation of Prior Experiential Learning (APEL).

Sometimes qualifications are given an equivalence, but if not, applicants have to prepare evidence of relevant prior learning e.g. by compiling a portfolio of achievement. This has to be related to the learning outcomes of the units, or entry requirements for which they are seeking exemption. The portfolio can therefore give them credits for the formal entry requirements or for part of the course itself.

Applicants apply for APL or APEL to the individual institution which offers the service, and they will state whether it is worthwhile gaining credit in this way, and advise of any fees chargeable. Some institutions offer support to help applicants to compile their portfolio.

More information on how APL/APEL works at higher education-level can be found in *2:14 – Higher education – first degrees.*

Overseas qualifications

UK NARIC (the National Recognition Information Centre) provides information on the comparability of overseas qualifications to organisations through a subscription service, and individual students are able to use its general enquiry service. UK NARIC produces an advisers' database on the comparability of UK and international qualifications – *International Comparisons* – available, on subscription, through the internet or on CD-ROM. The database is updated throughout the year.

> ➤ **UK NARIC** – ECCTIS Ltd, Oriel House, Oriel Road, Cheltenham, Gloucestershire GL50 1XP.
> Tel: 0870 990 4088.
> www.naric.org.uk

Overseas teaching qualifications

Qualified Teacher Status (QTS) is normally granted automatically to teachers trained in the European Union, but such teachers still need to contact the relevant teaching body for verification.

Those with teaching qualifications from Switzerland and the EEA (which includes the EU), and who want to teach in England/Wales should contact the General Teaching Council for Wales or the General Teaching Council for England.

➤ **GTCE** – Victoria Square House, Victoria Square, Birmingham B2 4AJ.
Tel: 0870 001 0308.
Email: info@gtce.org.uk
www.gtce.org.uk

➤ **GTCW** – 4th Floor, Southgate House, Wood Street, Cardiff CF10 1EW.
Tel: 029 2055 0350.
Email: information@gtcw.org.uk
www.gtcw.org.uk

Those with teaching qualifications from outside the EEA or Switzerland, and who want to teach in England should contact the Teacher Training Agency:

➤ **TTA** – Overseas Trained Teacher Advice Line, Freepost ANG 2037, Chelmsford CM1 1ZY.
Tel: 01245 45 43 21.
Email: ott@ttainfo.co.uk
www.canteach.gov.uk

Those wanting to teach in Scotland should contact:

➤ **The General Teaching Council for Scotland** – Clerwood House, 96 Clermiston Road, Edinburgh EH12 6UT.
Tel: 0131 314 6000.
Email: gtcs@gtcs.org.uk
www.gtcs.org.uk

Further information

➤ **Qualifications and Curriculum Authority (QCA)** – 83 Piccadilly, London W1J 8QA.
Tel: 020 7509 5555.
Email: info@qca.org.uk
www.qca.org.uk

➤ **QCA Northern Ireland** – 2nd Floor, Glendinning House, 6 Murray Street, Belfast BT1 6DN.
Tel: 028 9033 0706.
Email: infoni@qca.org.uk

➤ **Scottish Qualifications Authority (SQA)** – based at two sites:

➤ **SQA** – Hanover House, 24 Douglas Street, Glasgow G2 7NQ.
Tel: 0845 279 1000.
Email: customers@sqa.org.uk
www.sqa.org.uk

➤ **SQA** – Ironmills Road, Dalkeith, Midlothian EH22 1LE.
Telephone, email and website as above.

➤ Information about Scottish qualifications can also be obtained from **learndirect Scotland**. www.learndirectscotland.com

➤ **ACCAC** – Castle Buildings, Womanby Street, Cardiff CF10 1SX.
Tel: 029 2037 5400.
Email: info@accac.org.uk
www.accac.org.uk

➤ **AQA** – Devas Street, Manchester M15 6EX.
Tel: 0161 953 1180.
Email: mailbox@aqa.org.uk
www.aqa.org.uk

➤ **City & Guilds** – Customer Relations Department, 1 Giltspur Street, London EC1A 9DD.
Tel: 020 7294 2800.
Email: enquiry@city-and-guilds.co.uk
www.city-and-guilds.co.uk

➤ **CCEA** – 29 Clarendon Road, Clarendon Dock, Belfast BT1 3BG.
Tel: 028 9026 1200.
Email: info@ccea.org.uk
www.ccea.org.uk

➤ **Edexcel** – Customer Services, One90 High Holbourne, London WC1V 8BH.
Tel: 0870 240 9800.
Email: enquiries@edexcel.org.uk
www.edexcel.org.uk

➤ **LCCI Examining Board** – EDI Plc, The Old School, Holly Walk, Leamington Spa, Warwickshire CV32 4GL.
Tel: 0870 720 2909.
Email: custservice@ediplc.com
www.lccieb.com

➤ **OCR** – Head Office, 1 Regent Street, Cambridge CB2 1GG.
Tel: 01223 552552.
Email: helpdesk@ocr.org.uk
www.ocr.org.uk

➤ **Welsh Joint Education Committee (WJEC)** – 245 Western Avenue, Cardiff CF5 2YX.
Tel: 029 2026 5000.
Email: info@wjec.co.uk
www.wjec.co.uk

Many of the resources listed below are available for reference in education, careers and public reference libraries.

British Qualifications – published by Kogan Page, price £45.00 (paperback). A complete guide to educational, technical, professional and academic qualifications in Britain.

British Vocational Qualifications – published by Kogan Page, price £37.50.

How to Choose Your GCSEs – published by Trotman, price £12.99.

Directory of Vocational and Further Education – published annually by Pearson Education, price £90.00.

Which A levels? The guide to choosing AS and A levels – published by Lifetime Careers Publishing, price £12.99.

NVQs and How to Get Them – published by Kogan Page, price £9.99.

The Big Guide 2005 Entry – published by UCAS, price £32.50. The definitive HE course guide. See also: www.ucas.com

2:7

Money

Topics covered:

- Planning ahead
- Sources of financial assistance for education and training
- Students with disabilities
- Career Development Loans
- Studying on benefits or through government-funded programmes
- Further education
- Higher education
- Postgraduate funding
- Dance and Drama Awards
- NHS bursaries
- Financial help for teacher training
- Adult education bursaries
- Individual Learning Accounts
- Sponsorships and scholarships
- Charities and trusts
- Employers
- Trade unions

N.B. Information on financial support is always subject to change. The details provided here is correct at the time of updating (September 2004). Make direct contact with the relevant sources to check that the information is still current.

Planning ahead

There will always be some financial outlay or pressure on existing finances when undertaking training, especially if embarking on a full-time course. This involves not just personal commitment, but often changes in the family lifestyle too.

Potential learners need to:

- **investigate** as many sources of funding as possible, and make sure that they are clear about all the costs involved besides the course fees: e.g. books, materials and equipment, registration and examination fees, travel costs etc

- **consider their liabilities** e.g. mortgage, rent, household bills, any outstanding loans etc and scale down their financial commitments as much as possible

- **check** whether things like national insurance contributions and any benefits received are going to be affected

- **review their assets and income** – e.g. house, car, savings, interest from savings and shares or partner's income.

Sources of financial assistance for education and training

This is a complex area. Most people who are studying or training are supported by more than one source. Any financial assistance available from public funds, which could be in the form of a loan, assistance with fees or a non-repayable grant or bursary, depends on:

- the course/training opportunity being taken

- the student's/trainee's personal circumstances.

As rules and regulations are often complicated, eligibility for the funding sources mentioned must not be assumed before consulting additional, more detailed, information from the relevant bodies, and an application is approved from the organisation concerned.

Students with disabilities

Some extra help is available. This may include:

- assistance for specialist equipment

- assistance with transport

- the Disabled Students' Allowance, for those on higher education courses (described in the higher education section)

- fee waivers, or reductions, in some cases.

Some state benefits, such as Income Support, that are not generally available for full-time students, may be accessible for students with disabilities on full-time courses. Disability Living Allowance should not be affected.

People with disabilities should always seek information and advice from course providers and Jobcentre Plus/Jobcentre staff about possible extra financial support.

For further information

> **Skill – National Bureau for Students with Disabilities** – Chapter House, 18-20 Crucifix Lane, London SE1 3JW.
> Tel: 020 7450 0620 (for general enquiries).
> Information Service: 020 7657 2337 or 0800 328 5050 (open Tuesdays, 11.30am-1.30pm and Thursdays, 1.30pm-3.30pm).
> Textphone for Information Service: 0800 068 2422 (open as above).
> Publications: 020 7450 0620.
> Email: info@skill.org.uk
> www.skill.org.uk

Skill publishes many useful information booklets, such as: *Funding for Disabled Students in Higher Education; Funding for Disabled Students in Further Education; Applying for the Disabled Students' Allowance; Funding for Disabled Learners from Scotland; Funding from Charitable Trusts* and *Income Support for Disabled Students*. These booklets can be downloaded from Skill's website or can be purchased at a £2.50 each (minimum order £5); disabled students, trainees and jobseekers can order up to five booklets free of charge from the Information Service.

The website provides links to **Skill Scotland** and **Skill Northern Ireland.**

Career Development Loans

Career Development Loans (CDLs) help people to pay for vocational education or training by offering a deferred repayment bank loan.

CDLs can be used for any course whether full-time, part-time or through distance learning, as long as it:

● is vocational

● lasts no longer than two years, plus, if relevant, up to one year's practical work experience, if part of the course. CDLs can also support 24 months of a longer course.

Eligibility criteria include that applicants:

● are 18 or over on the date of application

● live, or intend to learn, in England, Scotland or Wales (residents in Northern Ireland may apply for CDLs to learn in England, Wales or Scotland)

● intend subsequently to work in the UK or elsewhere in the EU, or within the European Economic Area

- are not employed by learning provider which offers the course

- do not have access to other funding for the course, such as through their LEA or employer – or from their own resources. However, in most cases, a CDL can be used to supplement a bursary or grant that does not cover the full learning costs.

CDLs are available through a partnership arrangement between the Department for Education and Skills and three major banks – Barclays, The Co-operative and The Royal Bank of Scotland. The banks have the right to refuse a loan – for credit worthiness or other reasons – so eligibility and acceptance on a course does not guarantee a loan.

Clients can apply to one of the participating banks to borrow between £300 and £8000 to pay for up to 80% of their course fees, plus the full cost of books, materials and other related expenses. Applicants may also be able to borrow money to help cover living expenses.

Applicants may be employed, unemployed or self-employed. Applicants who have been out of work for three months or longer may be able to borrow 100% of course fees.

No repayments are made during the period of study or training and for up to a further month afterwards. The Department for Education and Skills pays the interest during this period. After this, repayments of the loan are payable at a fixed rate of interest over a period agreed with the bank.

In certain circumstances, a CDL recipient may apply to the bank to postpone the start of the loan repayments for up to a maximum of 17 months. This could apply, for instance, if one month after completing the training the CDL recipient is still unemployed and claiming related benefits, or is employed and receiving certain benefits, or is on a government-funded training scheme, or if the course is taking longer than expected due to special circumstances.

For further information

➤ **Career Development Loans Information Line** – freephone: 0800 585 505 (for a free information pack and application form); from 8am-10pm Monday to Sunday. www.lifelonglearning.co.uk/cdl

Studying on benefits or through government-funded programmes

Jobseeker's Allowance etc

The rules in this area are complex. Claimants should always check with their local Jobcentre Plus/Jobcentre or social security office on the most up-to-date rulings about studying whilst on benefit.

People in receipt of the **Jobseeker's Allowance** (JSA) may follow **part-time** courses of education or training, as long as they are still available for and actively seeking work. What constitutes part-time study will be decided in the client's Jobseeker's Agreement – usually up to 16 hours of guided study in further education; higher-education courses are assessed individually.

Whatever the level of the course they are following, JSA claimants must prove that they are continuing to actively seek work, and must be prepared to give up the course, or rearrange their hours of study, so that they are able to take up a suitable job offer. Clients are advised to keep records to show that they are actively seeking work, and have evidence from the course provider of the hours of study involved. They cannot turn down a job – or even a job interview – because it interferes with their course and still expect to receive JSA.

Students on Open University and other correspondence or distance-learning courses, which a full-time worker could fit in around work, can normally continue to claim JSA. If the course includes residential study weeks, or full-time blocks of study, clients should seek advice from the Students' Union or college counsellor. Unemployed students may be entitled to help towards OU course fees from the Open University's Financial Award Fund.

Full-time students are not normally eligible for JSA. However, students who have a partner and dependent child, where both adults are students, may claim JSA during the summer vacation.

Clients who are studying full-time cannot usually claim **Income Support** or **Housing Benefit**. Exceptions are lone parents or students with disabilities. Full-time students are usually exempt from paying **council tax**.

(N.B. Regulations differ slightly in Scotland and Northern Ireland. A booklet *Students and Benefits,* for students in Northern Ireland, can be downloaded from www.egsa.org.uk)

Work Based Learning for Adults

Work Based Learning for Adults (WBLA) is a training programme for those who are unemployed; eligibility and what it offers are described in more detail in *2:18 – Work Based Learning for Adults and other government-funded training.* Those who undertake WBLA receive a training allowance equivalent to their benefits plus an additional £10 a week. Help with travel costs and childcare costs may also be available. There are no fees payable for the training itself. (WBLA covers England; there are similar schemes in Wales, Scotland and Northern Ireland.)

New Deal

There are several programmes offered through New Deal e.g. for those aged **18-24, 25 plus** and **50 plus**; for **lone parents**; for **people with disabilities** and for people whose **partners** are claiming benefits. Those taking education and training options through New Deal will normally have their course costs paid, and may receive help towards books, equipment, transport, childcare etc. Most opportunities are part-time, short-courses or training in the workplace.

Within **New Deal for young people (18-24)** participants may be entitled to undertake full-time education or training. In this case, an allowance, equivalent to Jobseeker's Allowance, is paid.

If a client finds a job through the **New Deal 50 plus**, they may be able to claim the extra 50+ element of Working Tax Credit and an in-work training grant of up to £1500.

For those on the **New Deal for lone parents** programme, there is help with childcare and the costs incurred through participating in the scheme.

More detailed information about New Deal is given in *2:18 – Work Based Learning for Adults and other government-funded training.*

For further information

Ask at local Jobcentre Plus/Jobcentre offices for further details about studying on benefits or whilst on government-funded programmes.

For information on benefits, see: www.dwp.gov.uk

For further information on New Deal, view: www.newdeal.gov.uk

Welfare to Work Handbook 2004: Financial support and provision for adults of working age – published by the Centre for Economic and Social Inclusion, price £22.95 plus postage. Order via the website http://www.cesi.org.uk/or telephone for information: 020 7582 7221.

Further education (FE)

England

FE courses are those that go up to advanced level (i.e. level 3), such as AS/A levels, BTEC Nationals and SVQ/NVQ 3. They are offered mainly at FE colleges.

Students aged 19 and over on entry are normally liable for paying course fees. There are some circumstances where this may not apply; individual colleges have their own guidelines. Basic education is normally free, as are courses on English as a second language. Students on benefits, or dependent on others on benefits, may get full or partial fee remission. This should be checked with the college/adult education service offering the course. People in employment, taking work-related part-time courses, may have their fees paid by their employer.

The Government Skills Strategy White Paper proposal, that all adults who lack a level 2 qualification (equivalent to five GCSEs at A*-C) should be entitled to free learning to achieve this, is being phased in during 2004 and 2005. It may be extended to level 3 qualifications in some cases.

Currently, there are a number of ways that students may be able to get financial help.

- **Learner Support Funds** are administered by FE colleges for their own students. These funds are intended to help students who are on low incomes, or who are in hardship, and in the most need. Money from Learner Support Funds can be used towards any of the costs related to the student's course. Students should ask their FE college about their policy for allocating Learner Support Funds.

- Help towards **childcare** may be available. Colleges get funding so they can provide free or subsidised childcare places for students on benefits or low incomes.

- Students on low incomes who are studying on courses where they need to be resident may get help through the college towards their **residential costs.**

- Some colleges have **hardship funds** or bursaries to provide some additional funding to students in particular difficulties.

- **Adult Learning Grants** are currently being trialled in some areas. They are means-tested allowances of up to £30 a week for at least two years for over-19s who are studying full-time for their first, full, level 2 qualification, or 19- to 30-year-olds studying full-time for their first level 3 qualification. It is anticipated that the programme will be extended. The grant is intended to help meet the extra costs associated with learning, such as books and travel costs. Further information is available on: www.learndirect-advice.co.uk

When considering course costs, applicants should ensure they are aware of any costs additional to fees, such as registration and examination fees, and costs of any materials.

Other possible sources of assistance, which may apply to certain FE students (those on particular full- or part-time FE courses), include charities and trusts, Career Development Loans and Dance and Drama Awards.

Wales

Financial Contingency Funds in Wales are the equivalent of Learner Support Funds in England.

Further (and higher) education students in Wales can apply through their LEA for a means-tested **Assembly Learning Grant** of up to £1500 per year. This is targeted at people on low incomes who are taking full-time, or certain part-time, courses. The Grant provides help towards the costs of books, equipment, travel and childcare costs. For more information, see: www.learning.wales.gov.uk

Individual Learning Accounts Wales are also available for students with few or no qualifications. For details, see later in this section.

Scotland

Funding for FE students is closely aligned to that for HE students.

Tuition fees

Full-time FE students, who are resident in Scotland, and attending courses at Scottish FE colleges get their course fees paid through the Fee Waiver Scheme. Part-time students can also receive fee waiver if they are a registered jobseeker, on a low income, disabled or on benefits. Students should contact colleges direct for more information.

Student support

Students attending an FE college in Scotland can apply to that college's bursary officer for a means-tested bursary. Students should apply for support as soon as they find out they have a place on a course.

Student support can help towards:

- maintenance support

- Dependant's Allowance

- study and travel expenses

- Special Educational Needs Allowance (additional travel and study help for students with disabilities).

Hardship funds are provided to colleges by the Scottish Executive. Colleges can then allocate funds to students who, for whatever reasons, have financial difficulties which may prevent their access to FE.

In order to help students meet their study-related needs, **childcare support** is available through FE colleges. Although it is mainly aimed at part-time students, it may also be available to full-time students. Additional childcare funding particularly targets the needs of **lone parents**.

ILA Scotland offers up to £200 assistance towards training, initially targeted particularly at basic ICT skills. See later in this section for further details.

If a student lives in Scotland but wants to study outside Scotland, they might be able to get support from the education department of their local council. This funding is discretionary.

Full-time FE **students from outside Scotland** may be eligible for student support if they meet certain residency criteria.

Northern Ireland

Full-time students over the age of 19, who are taking eligible vocational courses up to NVQ level 3, do not pay fees. Students can apply for a means-tested Further Education Bursary of up to £2000 through their local Education and Libraries Board (see telephone numbers and websites under *NHS bursaries* later in this section). Students with dependants may be entitled to extra help.

Part-time students in receipt of benefits may be entitled to concessionary fees, at the discretion of individual colleges.

There are other forms of assistance, including College Support Funds for students in severe financial difficulties, for which the student applies directly to the college.

For further information

A DfES booklet *Money to Learn* (not updated since 2002 at the time of writing) can be obtained by phoning 0845 60 222 60 (quote reference MTLC). The booklet is aimed at those aged 19 and over in England. It can also be viewed on: www.lifelonglearning.co.uk/moneytolearn

For information about student funding in Northern Ireland: www.delni.gov.uk

For information about Wales: www.elwa.org.uk (the guide *Making Learning Work for You: Guide to Funding* can be accessed from this site)

For information about funding in Scotland: www.fundingforlearners.co.uk or email studentsupport@scotland.gov.uk

Further Education – the money guide for lone parents – published by One Parent Families (information applies to England and Wales). To order a copy, tel: 0800 018 5026. The first copy is free to lone parents, or £3.00 otherwise. See also: www.oneparentfamilies.org.uk

Individual college prospectuses and websites generally provide some information about student financial support, with details of relevant college contacts for further information.

Higher education

Higher education courses to which the information in this section applies are courses leading to:

- first degrees such as a BA, BSc, BEng or BEd

- Diplomas of Higher Education (DipHE)

- Higher National Diplomas (HND)

- foundation degrees

- other designated courses, including some courses leading to professional examinations at equivalent level.

Foundation years of designated courses are included, but Access or conversion courses leading to higher education are not.

If in doubt, LEAs can advise on which courses are designated.

Changes from 2006

As readers will be aware, funding for students in higher education in England is set to change from 2006 entry, following the passing of the Higher Education Act in July 2004. Outlined below is, first, information relevant to 2005 entry, followed by information about the changes being implemented from 2006 entry onwards.

Full-time students: 2005 entry (England and Wales)

Most people on full-time higher education courses in publicly-funded colleges or universities are financed mainly by the following sources:

- means-tested assistance towards the cost of tuition fees

- a student loan – to help with living expenses

- support from partners or parents

- earnings and savings

- Access to Learning Funds – administered by colleges and universities.

Eligibility

To qualify for assistance towards fees and loans, there are personal eligibility criteria, which include a **residence requirement**. The main stipulations are that students must have been living in the UK, Channel Islands or Isle of Man for the three years immediately prior to the start of the academic year in which the course begins. Students must also be living in England, Wales, Scotland or Northern Ireland on the first day of the academic year in which the course starts.

Others who may be eligible are EU citizens (for help with fees only). Those granted 'exceptional leave' to be in the UK who meet the three-year residence requirement, and asylum seekers who have been granted 'settled status' who meet the three-year residence requirement, may also be eligible for financial support.

Previous study at higher-education level, which included help from UK public funds, or if the college where the course was taken was publicly funded, may exclude students from entitlement to help with tuition fees. Previous study does not exclude students from applying for student loans and other funding. N.B. The entitlement to help with tuition fees of those who have previously received support and plan to take certain initial teacher training courses may not be affected. **It is important that applicants who have undertaken previous study at higher education level seek information and advice from their LEA, as the rules relating to previous study are complex.**

Tuition fees

A student's annual contribution to their course fees is means-tested. The maximum contribution for the academic year 2005/06 will be around £1200 (exact figures not yet released at time of writing). Students starting courses in 2005 are expected to pay any fee contribution directly to the institution at the start of the academic year. However, in the following years of their course (i.e. from September 2006), students who started their course in 2005 will have the option of taking out a **student loan** to match the level of their fee contribution. This loan only becomes liable for repayment once students have completed their course and earn more than £15,000 a year.

The amount of fees payable by the student will depend on their own income for that year, and that of their family, if applicable. If the student qualifies as an 'independent student' and is married, this means the husband's or wife's income.

To qualify for independent status, the student must meet one of the following conditions:

- be aged 25 or over before the start of the academic year for which they are applying

- have been married before the start of the academic year for which they are applying for support

- have supported themselves for at least three years before the start of the academic year of the course. This includes any time when registered unemployed, in receipt of certain benefits, caring for a dependant under 18, or on a state-funded training scheme.

For 'independent' students who are married, the husband/wife is expected to make some contribution to tuition fees, and possibly also living costs, if their *residual income* (i.e. the income remaining after certain deductions from gross income) is around £21,000 or more a year. For independent students aged over 25, their partner's income may similarly be assessed. For students who do not qualify as independent (and whose parents' income is therefore taken into account) the student/student's parents will be expected to make the contribution. Those whose parents or partners earn over around £32,000 a year will be liable for full fee contribution.

More information about student support is available from the DfES website. www.dfes.gov.uk/studentsupport

All students **must** apply to their **LEA** for assessment for tuition fee support, the student loan and other grants (see below).

Living costs

The main source of funding for living costs is through a **student loan.** These are government-funded loans administered by the Student Loans Company. 75% of the maximum loan will be available to all students under the age of 50, and to those aged 50-54 who are planning to return to work after studying. Entitlement to the remaining 25% of the loan is means-tested by the LEA. Students then decide how much loan they want, and inform the Student Loans Company.

The maximum loan available for 2004/5 for a student living away from home, and not studying in London, was £4095 or, for those living at home, £3240. Figures are slightly lower for the final year of study. These figures are likely to be revised slightly for 2005/06. There are extra amounts for courses with longer terms, or if study abroad is a necessary part of the course. Check with the LEA.

The loan has an interest rate linked to inflation, so that, in real terms, no one repays more than was borrowed.

Students are required to start to pay back the loan from the April after the course has finished. Payments are made automatically through the Inland Revenue, once the student's income rises above a certain threshold (£15,000 after April 2005). If their income falls below this level, repayments will be suspended.

Higher Education Grant: worth up to £1000 a year (2003/04 figures), this is a non-repayable grant, to help with the costs of living and studying. Students from households with incomes of £15,200 or below are entitled to the full amount, and those from households with incomes between £15,201 and £21,185 would qualify on a sliding scale.

N.B. **Medical and dental students** – for the first four years of a medicine or dentistry course, the above arrangements apply. From year five, students may be eligible for an NHS bursary and help with their tuition fees.

Other grants

Some students are entitled to extra help towards living costs, as outlined below. Amounts quoted are for the academic year 2004/05, as 2005/06 figures are not available at the time of updating.

- **Adult Dependants' Grant** – means-tested grants are available for full-time students with financially-dependant adults. The maximum grant is £2335 per year.

- **Childcare Grant** – means-tested help for full-time students of up to £114.75 per week for one child, or £170 per week for two or more children in registered and approved childcare.

- **Parents' Learning Allowance** – this is aimed at helping full-time students with dependent children with their course-related costs. The allowance is means-tested and more money is given depending on whether the student is a lone parent or not and how many children he or she has. The Allowance paid is a maximum of £1330 a year.

- **Child Tax Credit** – students with dependent children are eligible to claim this from the Inland Revenue. Tel: 0845 300 3900 (or 0845 603 2000 from Northern Ireland) or visit www.inlandrevenue.gov.uk/taxcredits for more details.

- **Students with disabilities** – Disabled Students' Allowances (DSAs) are available to help to pay for extra costs or expenses that students may have that arise because of their disability, and are available to full- and part-time students (undergraduates and postgraduates) taking at least 50% of a full-time course. DSAs include a Specialist Equipment Allowance, Non-medical Helper's Allowance, a General Allowance, which may cover other items, and extra travel costs. DSAs are not means-tested. A DfES leaflet *Bridging the Gap* is available from LEAs or from the DfES Student Support Information Line – listed at the end of this section.

All students in England and Wales must apply to their LEA for assessment for financial support – for help with fees and eligibility for a student loan and other grants. Forms can be downloaded from: www.dfes.gov.uk/studentsupport

Access to Learning Fund

In England, Access to Learning Funds provide extra financial support to students on a low income or who need extra money for their course and to stay in higher education.

Applications are dealt with by the institution attended, and help is given at the institution's discretion. Students are assessed according to their individual needs but, under current arrangements, certain groups of students are given priority e.g. lone parents, mature students with existing financial commitments, and students in their final year. Help through Access to Learning Funds does not have to be repaid.

Similar assistance is available in Wales through **Financial Contingency Funds**.

Part-time students: 2005 entry (England and Wales)

Part-time higher education students in England and Wales may be able to receive financial support if they are undertaking a course which is at least 50% of the equivalent full-time study. The support includes a **course grant** of £250, to meet the costs of items such as books, travel etc and a **fee grant**. From 2005 entry, the fee grant will be on a sliding scale, depending on the intensity of the course they are studying: a maximum of £590 for those studying the equivalent of 50% of a full-time course; £710 for 60% and £885 for 75% of a full-time course.

Entitlement is dependent on the student's income, and that of their wife/husband or partner. Full support is payable if their income is under around £14,900. Partial support may be available for students with income levels up to around £21,500.

The LEA is responsible for assessing eligibility.

Access to Learning Fund

Part-time students who are on a low income may also apply for help from the Access to Learning Fund. Those on some courses which are less than 50% of a full-time course may also be able to get help through this fund.

In Wales, students should check for eligibility for help from the Financial Contingency Funds.

Differences in the devolved areas of the UK (2005 entry)

Wales

Support for undergraduate higher education students living in Wales is broadly similar to the above, except that students who normally live in Wales and are studying at any publicly-funded institution in the UK can apply through their LEA for a means-tested **Assembly Learning Grant** of up to £1500 per year (2004/05 rates). The ALG is available to full-time students and to some part-time students. In Wales, the funds available through institutions to help students facing financial hardship are called **Financial Contingency Funds**.

Scotland

Scottish-domiciled students **do not pay tuition fees** if studying at Scottish institutions. However, they may have to contribute just over £2000 as a **Graduate Endowment** on successful completion of their course. Those who are classed as an independent student at the start of their course are not liable to pay the Endowment. This also applies to lone parents, or students with a disability who get DSA during the course.

Loans are available to help with living costs. Mature students studying in Scotland may apply to their college or university for support from the **Mature Student's Bursary Fund**, subject to eligibility criteria. The Bursary is intended to help students with things like childcare costs. **Supplementary grants** are available to help students with particular needs, such as lone parents and students with dependants.

The **Student Awards Agency for Scotland (SAAS)** administers financial support to higher education students.

Northern Ireland

Support for students living in Northern Ireland is currently broadly similar to England. However, students from low-income households can apply for a non-repayable, means-tested higher education **bursary** of up to £2000 per year (2004/05 rate).

The five regional **Education and Library Boards** administer financial support to higher education students (a list of telephone numbers and websites are listed under the heading *NHS bursaries* later in this section).

Changes from 2006 entry onwards (England)

The Higher Education Act 2004 brings in changes in tuition fees for students living in England and starting courses in 2006.

Tuition fees

Higher education institutions will be able to charge new students tuition fees ranging from £0 to a 'higher amount' **currently set at £3000** a year. Fees are likely to vary, therefore, between courses within institutions, and between institutions. At the time of writing, universities and colleges have yet to announce their intentions regarding the fee levels they intend to set for their courses.

Students will no longer be required to pay their fees 'upfront' i.e. while studying. Instead, they will be able to take out a loan to cover payment for fees. The loans available will exactly match the fees charged, and will be paid directly to the institution, on behalf of the student.

The loan for fees will be combined with loans taken out for living expenses (maintenance). Repayments start from the April after the student has completed their course, and only when they are earning more than a certain level – at present set at £15,000 a year. Any outstanding loans (fees or maintenance) which remain after 25 years will be written off.

Living expenses

Student loans for maintenance (living and study expenses), as described for 2005 entry, will continue to be available and be paid directly to the student. The Government has stated that, from 2006, the maximum loan rates will be raised above the rate of inflation. See previous paragraph above for repayment information.

New maintenance grant: non-repayable maintenance grants for full-time students from low-income families are being introduced from 2006. These are means-tested, and depend on the income of the student and their household. The maximum maintenance grant payable is £2700 a year. If the income of the student and their household is around £15,000 or less, the student is likely to eligible for the maximum grant. Monies will be paid in three termly instalments.

Bursaries: universities and colleges charging course fee levels of more than ' a basic amount' – currently set at £1200 – must satisfy the Office for Fair Access that they are making efforts to widen access and participation for students from under-represented groups, such as those from low-income backgrounds. As part of this, institutions must offer bursaries to students from low-income families. For example, institutions charging £3000 a year fees must provide at least £300 a year in non-repayable support, such as in bursaries, to students who are receiving the full £2,700 maintenance grant. It is expected that some institutions will make available to students bursaries worth more than £300.

Other financial help

Help for particular students will continue to be available, including the following which may be of particular interest to adults:

● **Childcare Grant** – for students with dependent children

● **Parents' Learning Allowance** – means-tested help for course-related costs for students with dependent children

● **Adult Dependants' Grant** –for students with adult dependants

● **Disabled Students' Allowance**

● **Access to Learning Fund.**

The above are described in more detail under the heading **Full-time courses: 2005 entry**, earlier in this section.

Application procedures

All students must continue to apply to their LEA for assessment to find out what loans (both for fees and maintenance) and grants they may be entitled to. Students may apply by application form, or online through www.studentfinancedirect.co.uk

Part-time students

Part-time study was not covered in the Higher Education Act. At the time of writing, no information has been announced about any changes from 2006 entry for financial support for part-time students. Information, as and when it becomes available, should be made available on: www.dfes.gov.uk/studentsupport

Wales – entry from 2006

The Higher Education Act 2004 only applies to England, and devolves responsibility to the Welsh Assembly for students who live in Wales. From 2006, the National Assembly will have the power, if it so chooses, to introduce higher fees, to create an access regulator and to determine student support arrangements. The National Assembly has ruled out variable fees for the lifetime of the present Assembly.

For the academic year 2006/07 there will be a fixed fee, to be set by the Assembly; loans will be available to cover payment of fees; a new means-tested maintenance grant of up to £2700 will be available, and a loan to cover living expenses will be available.

Decisions regarding the academic year 2007/08 and beyond will not be made until after a review has been completed, in April 2005.

Up-to-date information should be found at: www.learning.wales.gov.uk/students

Scotland – from 2006

No major changes to student funding for Scottish students studying in Scotland are anticipated.

For further information

Student Support Information Line – telephone 0800 731 9133 or textphone 0800 328 8988. Provides information about student support in higher education in England and Wales, and copies of the annually updated free booklet *Financial Support for Higher Education Students* – published by the DfES, which gives detailed information on tuition fee support, loans etc. Copies should be available at information, advice and guidance agencies, and information is also available on the DfES website: www.dfes.gov.uk/studentsupport

See also www.studentfinancedirect.co.uk

Financial support for part-time students in higher education – annually published booklet, available from the Student Support Information Line (see above) or through the DfES student support website.

Bridging the Gap – DfES guide on Disabled Students' Allowances – available from LEAs or via the Student Support Information Line.

Funding for Disabled Students in Higher Education – a booklet published by SKILL, The National Bureau for Students with Disabilities. Price £2.50. Individual disabled students, jobseekers and trainees can order up to five booklets free by calling the information service. Telephone 0800 328 5050 (Tuesday, 11.30am – 1.30pm; Thursday, 1.30pm – 3.30pm). The booklets can also be downloaded from the website: www.skill.org.uk/info

Into Higher Education 2005 – also published by SKILL, price £15 or £2.50 concessionary price for students, jobseekers or trainees with disabilities.

> **Student Loans Company** – 100 Bothwell Street, Glasgow G2 7JD.
> Tel: 0800 40 50 10.
> www.slc.co.uk

> **For students in Wales:** see www.learning.wales.gov.uk/students

> **For students in Scotland** – *Guide to Student Support* is a guide published by the
> Student Awards Agency for Scotland, Gyleview House, 3 Redheughs Rigg, South
> Gyle, Edinburgh EH12 9HH. Guides are available to download from the SAAS
> website, which also contains more detailed information on student support.
> Tel: 0845 111 1711.
> Email: saas.geu@scotland.gsi.gov.uk
> www.saas.gov.uk
> www.fundingforlearners.co.uk

> **For students in Northern Ireland** – *Financial Support for Higher Education Students* is
> a guide published annually. Available from Education and Library Boards or from the
> Student Support Branch, Department for Employment and Learning for Northern
> Ireland, Adelaide House, 39-49 Adelaide Street, Belfast BT2 8FD.
> Tel: 028 9025 7728.
> Email: studentsupport@delni.gov.uk
> www.delni.gov.uk/studentsupport

Students' Money Matters 2005 – published by Trotman, (annually updated – 2005 edition
available May 2005) £14.99.

Higher Education – the money guide for lone parents – published by One Parent Families
(relates to England and Wales). To order a copy, tel: 0800 018 5026. The first copy is free to
lone parents, or £3.00 otherwise.

Information is also available on the website www.oneparentfamilies.org.uk

Postgraduate funding

Fees and living costs have to be budgeted for – the average fee for a one-year Master's
course is around £3010. Living costs amount to several thousands of pounds a year,
depending on your circumstances. Postgraduate courses may require expensive
equipment and books. Printing and binding a thesis alone can cost £200. This is why so
many students study for postgraduate qualifications part-time whilst in paid employment.

Getting any finance for postgraduate study, particularly for non-vocational subjects, is not
easy, other than for PGCE students (see section on *Teacher training*).

Funding depends on a variety of factors, including:

● the class of degree; a research studentship usually requires a 2.1 honours degree

● the course subject

● place of residence

● reasons for wanting to do the course.

Research Councils

Most of the available funding for postgraduate qualifications comes from the government-funded Research Councils. Which body funds which course depends on the subject area in question. Awards offered by these bodies usually cover tuition fees and a contribution towards maintenance and expenses. Competition for this funding is very fierce, and there are not enough awards to go round. Awards are usually made on a competitive basis through the university or college concerned. Levels of funding offered through the various funding bodies vary. There are currently seven Research Councils and the Arts and Humanities Research Board (which is due to become a Research Council on the 1st April 2005):

> **Medical Research Council (MRC)** – biomedical sciences.
> Tel: 020 7636 5422.
> www.mrc.ac.uk

> **Biotechnology and Biological Sciences Research Council (BBSRC)** – non-medical life sciences.
> Tel: 01793 413200.
> www.bbsrc.ac.uk

> **Particle Physics and Astronomy Research Council (PPARC)** – particle physics, astronomy, solar system science and particle astrophysics.
> Tel: 01793 442000.
> www.pparc.ac.uk

> **Economic and Social Research Council (ESRC)** – economic and social studies.
> Tel: 01793 413000.
> www.esrc.ac.uk

> **Natural Environment Research Council (NERC)** – life, environmental and geological sciences.
> Tel: 01793 411500.
> www.nerc.ac.uk

> **Engineering and Physical Sciences Research Council (EPSRC)** – physical sciences and engineering.
> Tel: 01793 444000.
> www.epsrc.ac.uk

> **Council for the Central Laboratory of the Research Councils (CCLRC)** – science, research and engineering.
> Tel: 01235 445000.

> **Arts and Humanities Research Board (AHRB)** – a range of arts and humanities courses. (From 1st April 2005, the AHRB will become the Arts and Humanities Research Council.)
> Tel: 0117 987 6500.
> www.ahrb.ac.uk

Clients can complete application forms online on some of the websites listed.

Information on, and links to, all the above bodies can also be found on Research Councils UK's website: www.rcuk.ac.uk

Other possible sources of funding

Increasingly, students acquire portfolio funding whereby they put together a package of money from a range of difference sources. Apart from the Research Councils, there are several other postgraduate funding possibilities.

- Career Development Loans offer a way to finance certain postgraduate courses. CDLs are described in more detail earlier.

- The Association of MBAs administers the MBA Loan Schemes, financed via NatWest Bank.

- Certain banks run loan schemes for postgraduate students on particular courses, such as law.

- Full- and part-time postgraduate students may apply for help from Access to Learning Funds, with assessment criteria set nationally by the Government, and administered by the institution.

- Postgraduate students with disabilities can claim Disabled Students' Allowance, if they are not receiving awards from the Research Councils (which provide their own funding).

- NHS bursaries are available for graduates on some healthcare courses which lead to professional registration.

- Some grants from charitable trusts are available, but these are not likely to cover full costs.

- Employers may offer sponsorship as part of their employees' career development (generally undertaken on a part-time basis) and, in some cases, study leave.

- Some courses attract commercial sponsorship.

- Scholarships and bursaries for research may be offered by universities, with the money coming from contractual work for industry and commerce, or from university trust funds.

- Students can study part-time and support themselves through paid employment.

- Paid research/teaching assistant posts in higher education offer opportunities for postgraduate study.

- Students may choose to use their own savings, or receive financial support from partners or family, and regard it as an investment in their future that may repay dividends in the long term.

N.B. In **Scotland,** the Postgraduate Students' Allowances Scheme (PSAS) funds a limited number of awards (a 'quota') for places on certain vocational postgraduate courses. Students are nominated to receive the awards by the HE institution. There are also awards for some other non-quota postgraduate courses, in areas such as librarianship, IT and computer science and theology, and a limited number of awards are available for Scottish-domiciled students studying outside Scotland.

For further information

Information on postgraduate funding can also be found on: www.prospects.ac.uk

Residents of Northern Ireland seeking advice on finance should contact the Department for Employment and Learning. A booklet, *Awards for Postgraduate Study 2004-2005*, is also available:

> **The Department for Employment and Learning** – Student Support Branch, Adelaide House, 39-49 Adelaide Street, Belfast BT2 8FD.
> Tel: 028 9025 7757.
> Email: studentsupport@delni.gov.uk
> www.delni.gov.uk

> Residents of Scotland can see *Guide to Postgraduate Student Support 2004-2005* – available to download from the SAAS website, which also contains more detailed information.

> **Student Awards Agency for Scotland** – Gyleview House, 3 Redheughs Rigg, South Gyle, Edinburgh EH12 9HH.
> Tel: 0845 111 0244.
> Email: saas_4@scotland.gsi.gov.uk
> www.saas.gov.uk

Prospects Postgraduate Funding Guide – published by Graduate Prospects, price £4.99. Information about postgraduate funding is also available on the website: www.prospects.ac.uk

The Grants Register 2005 – published by Palgrave Macmillan, priced at £155.00. A complete guide to postgraduate funding worldwide.

Course providers and higher education institutions' careers services may be able to advise.

Dance and Drama Awards

The Dance and Drama Awards scholarship scheme offers financial assistance to students on approved dance, drama and stage management courses offered by 22 private training providers in England. The courses lead to Trinity College London National Diplomas or Certificates (which are level 4 qualifications; for explanation of levels see *2:6 – Qualifications*). Courses last from one to three years. There will be Awards for up to 525 students to enter training each year. Financial assistance can include the following.

● Help towards **tuition fees**: the award pays the majority of tuition fees, and students make a contribution. For 2004/2005, the student fee contribution is £1150. Students may also get help towards these fees also, depending on the student's financial circumstances.

● Help towards **living and learning costs** such as lodgings, travel and equipment, depending on the student's financial circumstances.

● Financial assistance towards childcare costs may also be available.

Students must audition for funded places, and course providers give the Awards to the most talented students. Students who have received financial help towards publicly-funded further or higher education in the past are still eligible to apply for an Award. Course providers supply application forms.

There is no upper age limit of eligibility for the scheme. Awards are open to students living in all parts of the UK and other EU countries. Eligibility includes a residence requirement.

For further information

The booklet *The Dance and Drama Awards* can be obtained by phoning the DfES publications line: 0845 60 222 60 – quoting reference D5.

See also, information at www.dfes.gov.uk/financialhelp/dancedrama

National Health Service bursaries

The NHS (and Scottish Executive Health Department) funds places on courses leading to registration for nursing and midwifery and many allied health professions. The arrangements cover full- and part-time diploma, degree and postgraduate-level courses, so long as they lead to professional registration in one of the following:

- nursing or midwifery (there are different arrangements for degree and diploma students)

- occupational therapy

- physiotherapy

- speech and language therapy

- radiography

- orthoptics

- chiropody

- dietetics

- prosthetics and orthotics (England only)

- dental hygiene

- dental therapy

- audiology/hearing therapy (if the course is recognised)

- operating department practice (diploma course)

The arrangements

- Course fees are paid for. No student contribution to course fees is required.

- Means-tested bursaries (or non means-tested bursaries for students on nursing and midwifery **diploma** courses, and operating department practice diploma courses).

- Access to student loans for the balance of the student's maintenance (living) costs (for undergraduates only).

The **bursary** is made up of a contribution towards day-to-day living costs, and there are allowances for particular circumstances including for extra weeks' attendance, dependants, single parents, and older students (payable to those who are aged 26 before the first academic year of the course).

N.B. In **Scotland**, students taking both degree and diploma courses in nursing or midwifery are eligible for a non-means-tested bursary under the Nursing and Midwifery Student Bursary Scheme. The bursaries are administered by the Student Awards Agency for Scotland.

Applying

Once the applicant has been offered an NHS-funded place, the institution will notify the NHS Student Grants Unit (in England – see below for contacts elsewhere in UK), who will send the applicant a bursary application pack. There are residence requirements.

N.B. While the majority of places on courses in the professions listed above will be NHS-funded, course providers may offer additional places on such courses which are not NHS-funded. For students recruited on non NHS-funded places, the financial arrangements will be the same as for undergraduates of all other subjects in full-time higher education.

Students on nursing and midwifery diploma courses

Basic rates of **non-means-tested bursaries** for full-time students on NHS-funded diploma places are £5695 or £6692 if studying in London (2004/5 rates). Extra allowances available include the older students' allowance, dependants' and practice placements costs allowances.

Medicine and dentistry courses

The arrangements for students entering undergraduate medical and dental courses will be the same as those for undergraduates on other higher education courses for the first four years of training. In year five and beyond, students will not have to pay tuition fees, and NHS non-repayable bursaries, assessed against family income, will be available towards maintenance.

For further information

The booklet *Financial Help for Health Care Students* (seventh edition published July 2004) is available from:

➤ **Department of Health** – PO Box 777, London SE1 6XH. Tel: 08701 555455, or by telephoning NHS Careers on: 0845 60 60 655
or can be viewed on: www.dh.gov.uk
(click on NHS Bursary Scheme in A-Z index)

For study in England:

> **The NHS Student Grants Unit** – 22 Plymouth Road, Blackpool FY3 7JS.
> Tel: 01253 655655.
> Email: nhs-sgu@ukonline.co.uk

For study in Wales:

> **NHS (Wales) Student Awards Unit** – 2nd Floor, Golate House, 101 St Mary's Street,
> Cardiff CF10 1DX.
> Tel: 029 2026 1495.
> Email: sau@wales.gsi.gov.uk
> www.hpw.org.uk

For study in Scotland:

> **The Student Awards Agency for Scotland** – Gyleview House, 3 Redheughs Rigg,
> South Gyle, Edinburgh EH12 9HH.
> Tel: 0845 111 0244.
> Email: saas.geu@scotland.gsi.gov.uk
> www.saas.gov.uk/healthcare.htm

For study in Northern Ireland:

Contact the relevant Education and Library Board:

> North Eastern area tel: 028 2565 5025 www.neelb.org.uk

> Belfast area tel: 028 9056 4000 www.belb.org.uk

> South Eastern area tel: 028 9056 6200 www.seelb.org.uk

> Southern area tel: 028 3751 2200 www.selb.org

> Western area tel: 028 8241 1411 www.welbni.org

If you live in other parts of the UK, and wish to study a health professional course in Northern Ireland, you should apply to the North Eastern Education and Library Board.

Teacher training

In recent years, various measures have been introduced to make teacher training and teaching an attractive option in areas of the country where there are teacher shortages. Trainee teachers who are not eligible for any of the funding described below – i.e. many students on undergraduate teacher-training courses – have the same funding arrangements as other undergraduates. The following are the main financial incentives available.

Students on full- and part-time **postgraduate** initial teacher training (ITT) courses in England and Wales (including those on certain full-time Certificate in Education courses for further education teaching) are paid a **training bursary/grant** of £6000 (tax-free for full-time students) during training, and have their **fees paid**. From August 2005, those training to teach secondary maths or science will be paid a training bursary/grant of £7000.

Those teaching certain shortage subjects in England and Wales receive a £4000 **'golden hello'** or **teaching grant** on starting their second year of teaching (in addition to the training bursary described above).

The **'fast track' scheme** programme offers accelerated career progression. It is open to qualified teachers and trainees. There are various eligibility criteria, including that applicants must hold at least a 2:1 degree, or the equivalent. The scheme carries a bursary of £5000. Eligibility depends on subject knowledge, communication skills, commitment and potential. See www.fasttrackteaching.gov.uk for more details.

Trainee teachers in England who are training to teach a shortage subject, i.e. maths, science/applied science, design and technology, engineering, manufacturing, modern foreign languages, ICT/applied ICT, religious education, geography and music, may be eligible for extra funding through the **Secondary Shortage Subject Scheme**. Awards, to a maximum of £6000 in any one year (£7500 for students aged over 25), are made on the basis of financial need. The maximum sums are rarely paid. Applications should be made to the individual teacher training institution. (N.B. The scheme is reviewed annually and subjects may change – subjects given relate to the 2004/05 academic year.)

The **Repayment of Teachers' Loans Scheme** is a three-year pilot in England and Wales, covering entrants to teaching in the three academic years up to 30 June 2005. Newly-qualified teachers have their student loans paid off over a period of time if they are employed to teach a shortage subject (maths, English – including drama, science, modern foreign languages, ICT, design and technology, engineering, construction and Welsh). The Scheme applies to teachers in schools and further education. Some specialist primary teachers are also eligible. At the time of updating, a decision as to whether the scheme is to be extended after June 2005 had not yet been announced. More information can be found on: www.teachernet.gov.uk/teachersloans

In Wales, those training for secondary teaching may be eligible for a **Secondary Undergraduate Placement Grant**. This offers £1000 to students on undergraduate teacher training courses in secondary shortage subjects, and £600 for those training to teach other subjects, to help pay for school-based placements. In addition, the **Assembly Learning Grant** is available to undergraduates; it is means-tested and offers payments of up to £1500 a year.

Certain students who start a secondary postgraduate teacher training course through the medium of Welsh are entitled to the **Welsh Medium Incentive Supplement**. This pays £1200 and there is an expectation that clients who benefit will look for a post in a Welsh medium school.

Trainees on **employment-based routes** have their training funded for them, and are paid by the employer.

In England, recruitment incentives (also known as 'golden hellos') have been introduced for new teachers in certain shortage subjects in **higher education**. They receive around £9000 spread over three years. See www.hefce.ac.uk for more information. A similar scheme already operates in **further education** where new lecturers in shortage subjects get up to £4000.

For further information

> **Teaching Information Line:** 0845 6000 991
> www.useyourheadteach.gov.uk

For a brochure on teaching in **Scotland** tel: 0845 345 4745
> www.scotland.gov.uk/education/teaching

Adult education bursaries

Adult education bursaries are available for students attending full-time courses of liberal adult education at one of the seven UK adult long-term residential colleges in England, Scotland and Wales.

The bursaries for English and Welsh residents are paid by the Learning and Skills Council, and administered by the residential colleges through their awards office.

The bursary includes:

- payment of tuition fees

- a maintenance grant, for living expenses, plus certain additional allowances

- in some cases, travelling costs in excess of £80 a year.

To be eligible, applicants must be recommended by the college for a bursary, be 20 years old or over before the start of the academic year in which the course begins, and satisfy residency criteria.

The personal maintenance grant is means-tested. The maintenance grant covers college term-time and the vacations between terms at Christmas and Easter. The rates of grant for full-time attendance of 30 weeks plus Christmas and Easter vacations for the academic year 2004/5 are:

- students living in college in the London area – £4225

- students living in college elsewhere – £3335

- students living in the parental home – £2520.

Each of the above includes £80 towards travelling expenses.

Other grants may be payable e.g. for students with dependants and students with disabilities.

For further information

For residents of England and Wales:

➤ The Awards Officer, **Adult Education Bursaries** – c/o Ruskin College, Walton Street, Oxford OX1 2HE. Provides copies of the booklet *Adult Education Bursaries* – annually published by the Residential Colleges Committee, which provides information for English or Welsh residents wishing to study at the English long-term residential colleges and at Newbattle Abbey College in Scotland.
Tel: 01865 556360.
Email: awards@ruskin.ac.uk

For applicants wishing to study at Coleg Harlech in Wales:

➤ The Student Grants Officer, **Coleg Harlech**, Harlech, Gwynedd LL46 2PU.
Tel: 01766 780363.
Email: bursary@harlech.ac.uk

For Scottish residents:

> **Student Awards Agency for Scotland** – Gyleview House, 3 Redheughs Rigg, South Gyle, Edinburgh EH12 9HH.
> Tel: 0845 111 0244.
> Email: saas.geu@scotland.gsi.gov.uk
> www.saas.gov.uk

There are no specific bursary schemes for residents of the Channel Islands or the Isle of Man wishing to study at the long-term residential colleges. Applicants from these areas should consult their LEAs concerning the possibility of financial assistance.

For further information about the adult residential colleges see *2:13 – Adult residential colleges*.

Individual Learning Accounts

The Individual Learning Account (ILA) programme, launched nationally in September 2000, was shut down in November 2001.

In Wales, ILAs were relaunched in February 2003. An ILA Wales can provide from £100 to £200 towards the cost of a course, depending on a client's personal circumstances and the cost of the course. The ILA Wales programme is targeted at people aged 18 and over living in Wales with no qualifications or with level 2 qualifications or below. For more details contact learndirect, tel: 0800 100 900 or see www.ilawales.com

In England, the Government decided not to introduce a successor scheme to the ILA programme. New arrangements for financial support are now being considered – an Adult Learning Grant is being piloted (see the earlier section above on further education) and the Government's Skills Strategy White Paper proposes that all adults who lack a level 2 qualification should be entitled to free learning to achieve this.

In Scotland, ILAs are being relaunched. Individuals will be able to claim up to around £200 towards the cost of a course, initially only if their income is less than £15,000. In Spring, 2005, this income limit will be removed. ILAs will be especially targeted at basic ICT skills. For details, telephone 0808 100 1090, or see: www.ilascotland.org.uk/

See www.my-ila.com for more information on the history of the ILA programme.

Sponsorships and scholarships

Sponsorships

Sponsorships for students on full-time courses (usually a degree) are offered by a number of employers and related organisations. Sponsorships vary considerably, but typically could include:

- a bursary (which would be additional to the normal available financial support)

- guaranteed vacation work

- spending work experience placements at the company, for students on sandwich courses.

Students rarely enter into a formal agreement to work for the sponsor on graduation, but the intention is that sponsorship allows employers to introduce prospective graduates into the company, and that this will lead to a job offer on graduation.

Most sponsorships are in vocational subjects, such as engineering, construction and business-related fields. Competition is strong for sponsorships.

Scholarships

There are some scholarships and bursaries for students awarded by individual universities and colleges. These are awarded on a competitive basis, and competition is fierce. Some scholarships are open to undergraduates of any subject. Others are for particular subject areas. Scholarships are likely to provide no more than a small financial supplement to funding from other sources.

For further information

University Scholarships and Awards – published by Trotman, 2004 edition, £19.99. Lists university and other awards available to students.

Everything You Wanted to Know about Sponsorship, Placements and Graduate Opportunities – published annually by the British Council in association with Amoeba Publications, available from Trotman, £14.95.

The Student Money website offers a free, searchable database of undergraduate and postgraduate bursaries, awards and scholarships from academic institutions, professional bodies and charities: www.studentmoney.org

Also, consult course prospectuses and course providers.

Charities and trusts

There are some charities and trust funds which make payments to students. Any grant is usually small. Support may be aimed at a particular age group, often under 25, is sometimes restricted to people living in a particular locality, or is aimed at those studying a particular subject area – but such assistance is worth looking into. Assistance may be available for students experiencing financial hardship during a course, but funding for a whole course is rare. Sometimes the help is in the form of a loan. Any financial assistance available is in demand and not easy to get. An example of available assistance is the Elizabeth Nuffield Educational Trust, which gives grants to help with the childcare costs of student mothers in higher education.

It is extremely difficult for undergraduate students who are already benefiting from statutory funding (through assistance with tuition fees, loans etc) to find additional funding through charitable bodies. Funding for postgraduate students is also limited.

For further information

Contact course providers, who may be aware of possible charities or trusts.

Some **LEAs** keep lists of local educational charities and trusts.

Local **adult information, advice and guidance services** may hold relevant information.

The Educational Grants Directory – published by the Directory of Social Change (tel: 020 7209 5151), price £22.95 for 2004-05 edition. A guide to the sources of funding available to students in need, listing trusts and foundations. Covers courses up to and including degree level. This and other similar directories are usually available in public reference libraries.

Educational Grants Advisory Service (EGAS)

The Educational Grants and Advisory Service offers guidance and advice to students who are over 16. EGAS is primarily concerned with helping disadvantaged students, giving priority to lone parents, people with disabilities, refugees and people from low-income backgrounds. Student Advisers can provide information on sources of financial assistance for learning, including loans, grants, access/hardship funds, benefits, bursaries and charitable trusts. Services are provided free to individual students.

➤ **EGAS** – 501-5 Kingsland Road, London E8 4AU. Send a stamped addressed envelope, and a student enquiry form will be sent. Alternatively, print off a student questionnaire from their website.
Tel: 020 7254 6251 (helpline open Mondays, Wednesdays and Fridays from 10am – 12noon and 2pm – 4pm).
www.egas-online.org.uk

Employers

Employers may financially assist their employees' learning in various ways:

● contributing to course fees and/or other costs, such as examination fees

● through allowing paid time off to study.

In general, financial assistance is only considered for courses relevant to the employee's work, although some large employers have established employee development programmes which may include providing support towards learning across a wide range of subjects.

It is always worthwhile for employees to approach their employers for assistance.

Some employers, such as the Armed Forces, may allow employees to undertake full-time study while retaining their salary.

Some employers offer assistance in the form of sponsorships for higher education courses – see *Sponsorships and scholarships* section.

Trade unions

Trade unions may offer some assistance; anyone in a trade union should enquire.

The Union Learning Fund has been set up to promote the activity of trade unions in helping to achieve a 'learning society'. The Fund helps support various union projects such as the provision of basic and key skills courses through to opening workplace learning centres. See www.learningservices.org.uk for more information.

The General Federation of Trade Unions Educational Trust makes small grants for full-time and Open University students. However, there are limiting criteria. People must be studying subjects within economic theory and history, industrial law, history and principles of industrial relations. Industrial trade unions may have other schemes.

> **The General Federation of Trade Unions Educational Trust** – Central House, Upper Woburn Place, London WC1H 0HY.
> Tel: 020 7387 2578.
> Email: gftuhq@gftu.org.uk
> www.gftu.org.uk

For further information about learning and trade unions see *2:19 – Learning in the workplace.*

Further information

> **learndirect** can provide information on financing a wide range of learning.

> **learndirect advice line** tel: 0800 100 900.
> www.learndirect-advice.co.uk

> **learndirect Scotland** tel: 0808 100 9000.
> www.learndirectscotland.com

2:8

Further and adult education

Topics covered:

- Further education provision
- Adult education provision
- Relevant organisations

Some adult clients may not realise the extent of adult participation in further and adult education, feeling that colleges are mainly for 'young' people. But many adults undertake vocational courses related to business and industry, as well as learning for leisure courses. For example, over three quarters of students in further education colleges are over 21, and around 38% of all adults have undertaken some form of learning in the last three years.

The majority of adults attend on a part-time basis, but there are also many adults in full-time further education, including those on Access to higher education courses.

The Government is keen to increase the number of adult participants in learning.

Further education provision

In England, the Learning and Skills Council is responsible for the delivery of all post-16 education and training (excluding higher education). This responsibility includes funding colleges, and developing arrangements for adult and community learning. (See under 'Relevant organisations' for full details of the LSC's responsibilities.)

In Wales, ELWa has responsibility for funding, planning and promoting all post-16 education and training in Wales, with the exception of higher education.

In Scotland, the Scottish Executive's Enterprise, Transport and Lifelong Learning Department provides the main source of funding for the 46 colleges across Scotland, through the Scottish Further Education Funding Council (SFEFC). The SFEFC works closely with the Scottish Higher Education Funding Council (SHEFC).

In Northern Ireland, responsibility for provision, policy, strategic development and financing of statutory further education and adult lifelong learning, including essential skills, comes under the Department for Employment and Learning. The Department also supports a small number of non-statutory further education providers.

Adult clients may have little knowledge or experience of further education. For instance, they may not know that:

- with the advent of modular courses and open learning – including learning delivered through computer packages and the internet – there is much more flexibility than in the past, and courses can be better tailored to meet the needs of the individual student

- having said the above, many full-time and part-time further education courses still start in September and last 36–38 weeks, until June or July

- colleges offer day-release, block-release and sandwich courses to fit in with the needs of local employers and employees

- most further education courses lead to recognised qualifications: GCSEs/Standard Grades/Highers and Advanced Highers, A and AS levels, and a range of vocational courses leading to NVQs, City & Guilds and BTEC National and Higher National qualifications

- qualifications offered by various professional bodies, such as in accountancy and marketing, may be gained through study at a local FE college

- the range of subjects is enormous and, increasingly, further education colleges are offering degree and foundation degree courses in partnership with universities and colleges of HE. Clients can, therefore, often find a complete progression route from level 1 through to level 4/5 in one local college.

To find out what is available, adult clients should:

- consult directories, databases or the learndirect helpline (see later under 'Relevant organisations') about the availability of courses

- obtain a prospectus, which should give details of courses, describe the resources and expertise of the college, fee remission policies and student financial support arrangements

- ask for information leaflets which give more detail about the individual courses; leaflets should cover course subjects and teaching and assessment methods, hours of attendance at college and anticipated study-time required at home

- check the availability of courses/learning support in study skills, IT, basic maths, etc – or 'return to learn' courses, if needed

- request information on the success rates and destinations (into employment and higher education) of previous students

- ask for information about childcare facilities, including opening hours, demand and availability, and about any financial support for childcare, if needed

- having decided on a course, obtain an application form.

Colleges normally have marketing, student services or admissions officers whose remit is to provide information and advice to prospective students.

Adult education

Adult education is a very broad term. In this context, the term is used to cover the range of non-vocational courses available to adults on a part-time basis. Although non-vocational, adult education provides a starting point for many adults wishing to return to learning, update their skills and improve their qualifications.

In England, adult and community learning is the responsibility of the Learning and Skills Council, operating through its network of 47 local Learning and Skills Councils. How adult education is provided, however, varies considerably from one local education authority (LEA) area to another. In some areas adult education is delivered by the LEA through its adult or community education service, through a network of adult education centres, FE colleges, community colleges and voluntary and community providers. In other LEA areas, local arrangements result in delivery mainly through FE colleges, rather than through an adult education service, complemented by classes offered by voluntary organisations.

In Scotland, community education departments of local authorities, colleges, universities and voluntary organisations mainly deliver adult education. Funding comes from a variety of sources.

Whatever the mode of provision, adult education offers mainly part-time courses, often for two to three hours per week. Subjects include study skills, assertiveness and time management as well as a wide range of recreational and leisure subjects. Some craft and office-skill courses may be a useful introduction to possible career areas, or may be specifically targeted at preparing unemployed people for a return to work. Courses may be offered through a variety of means: traditional evening classes, daytime classes and, increasingly, summer schools, distance learning and weekend schools. There are a number of short-term adult residential colleges, mainly offering courses for leisure, a number of which are run by local authorities. N.B. These are not to be confused with the long-term adult residential colleges offering academic study opportunities (see *2:13 – Adult residential colleges*).

Classes tend to be more flexible if there is no examination syllabus to follow, and may be student-led. Practical courses such as woodwork and upholstery may allow students to suggest a project of their own and get tuition and help to complete it. Often people attend the same class for a number of years as they enjoy the hobby and want tuition as they go along. Beginners as well as more experienced people are welcome at all these classes.

Providers of adult/community learning

Providers include:

- LEA adult or community education/learning services

- colleges of further education

- community colleges or community schools, which are schools also offering a range of community facilities such as adult education, youth work, use of school premises and equipment by community groups

- secondary schools which may offer adults access to classes to study for GCSEs, A and AS levels etc.

- voluntary organisations e.g. Workers' Educational Association, The University of the Third Age (U3A)

- extra-mural departments of universities which aim to provide education accessible to the community, which is not part of longer degree courses.

See *2:10 – Learning for leisure* for further information about non-vocational/recreational courses.

Money

Fees for further and adult education courses vary tremendously. Full or partial fee remission is generally available for certain categories of students (such as those on benefits) and for certain kinds of courses, particularly basic skills. Financial support may be available towards expenses such as transport and childcare, but the situation is complicated and varies across the UK. Many adult education courses have to be self-financing.

Clients should talk to an adviser at the college or centre where they wish to study before enrolling to enquire about any fee remission and financial support available.

See *2:7 – Money* for information on financial support arrangements.

Relevant organisations

England: Learning and Skills Council

The LSC is responsible for all post-16 education and training in England, including further and adult learning (but excluding higher education). There is a National Office, and a network of nine regional and 47 local Learning and Skills Councils. The LSC's responsibilities include:

- funding colleges

- developing arrangements for adult and community learning

- providing information, advice and guidance to adults

- funding workforce development and government-funded training programmes, other than those for adults

- working with the pre-16 sector to ensure coherence across all 14–19 education.

➤ **Learning and Skills Council National Office** – Cheylesmore House, Quinton Road, Coventry CV1 2WT.
Tel: 0845 019 4170.
Email: info@lsc.gov.uk
www.lsc.gov.uk

Wales: ELWa

ELWa – Education and Learning Wales – is more formally known as the National Council for Education and Training for Wales. It incorporates the Further Education Funding Council for Wales, and is sponsored by the Welsh Assembly. ELWa is responsible for funding, planning and promoting all post-16 education and training in Wales (with the exception of higher education). ELWa operates through a network of four regional offices, which are listed in the Gazetteer, or can be accessed through its website: www.elwa.org.uk

Scottish Executive: Enterprise, Transport and Lifelong Learning Department

The ETLLD's responsibilities include economic and industrial development, further and higher education, skills and lifelong learning in Scotland. The Department also funds the Scottish Further Education Funding Council.

> www.scotland.gov.uk/

> www.sfefc.ac.uk

Community education also comes under the jurisdiction of **Communities Scotland**, an agency of the Scottish Executive. See www.communitiesscotland.gov.uk

Northern Ireland: Department for Employment and Learning

Information about the Department, which is responsible for further education, lifelong learning, training and employment measures, can be accessed through www.delni.gov.uk

National Institute of Adult Continuing Education (NIACE)

NIACE aims to advance the interests of adult learners and potential learners. It works to increase the numbers of adults undertaking learning, to widen access and to improve opportunities. Its remit covers England and Wales.

NIACE is a membership organisation for all those working in the field of adult education. It undertakes projects and research in all aspects of education for adults and publishes handbooks, guides and project reports. NIACE organises Adult Learners' Week in England and Wales.

> **NIACE** – 21 De Montfort Street, Leicester LE1 7GE.
> Tel: 0116 204 4200.
> Email: enquiries@niace.org.uk
> www.niace.org.uk

> **NIACE Dysgu Cymru** – Ground Floor, 35 Cathedral Road, Cardiff CF11 9HB.
> Tel: 029 2037 0900.
> Email: enquiries@niacedc.org.uk
> www.niacedc.org.uk

National Open College Network (NOCN)

The National Open College Network (NOCN) provides accreditation services for adult learning. NOCN is a recognised national qualification-awarding body and is the central organisation for 28 Open College Networks (OCNs) based across the UK. NOCN seeks to widen participation in learning and increase access to high quality and flexible education, through a comprehensive framework of accreditation and qualifications. For details of the local OCNs licensed by the NOCN, see *2:12 Access and other adult routes.*

> **National Open College Network (NOCN)** – 9 St James Court, Friar Gate, Derby DE1
  1BT.
  Tel: 01332 268080.
  Email: nocn@nocn.org.uk
  www.nocn.org.uk

ContinYou

ContinYou is a community learning charity, formed by the coming together of CEDC and Education Extra. ContinYou publishes regular journals, including *Extra Community*, and provides programmes to encourage people of all ages and backgrounds to take up opportunities for learning. It carries out demonstration projects, undertakes consultancies, provides training and runs conferences. ContinYou aims to help build strong communities, supportive families and confident individuals.

> **ContinYou** – Unit C1, Grovelands Court, Grovelands Estate, Longford Road, Exhall, Coventry CV7 9NE.
  Tel: 024 7658 8440.
  Email: info.coventry@continyou.org.uk
  www.continyou.org.uk

Educational Centres Association

ECA is a membership organisation which aims to promote adult education and works in England and Wales through affiliated centres, as a partnership between organisers, teachers and students. It organises national and regional conferences, seminars and campaigns, produces publications and responds to consultations from Government, the LSC and related bodies.

> **ECA** – 21 Ebbisham Drive, Norwich NR4 6HQ.
  Tel: 0870 161 0302.
  Email: info@e-c-a.ac.uk
  www.e-c-a.ac.uk

Learning and Skills Development Agency

The LSDA (previously known as the Further Education Development Agency) is a national (across England, Wales and Northern Ireland) resource for the development of policy and practice in post-16 education and training. Among its many publications is the free monthly journal *Briefing*.

> **Learning and Skills Development Agency** – Regent Arcade House, 19-25 Argyll Street, London W1F 7LS.
  Tel: 020 7297 9000.
  Email: enquiries@lsda.org.uk
  www.lsda.org.uk

learndirect

The national learning helpline, learndirect provides information on further and adult education courses offered on a part-time, full-time, distance learning and open learning basis. It also offers a range of open learning courses, which can be accessed at home, in the workplace and through a network of learndirect centres.

Tel: 0800 100 900 from 8am to 10pm seven days a week in England for general advice and information (0800 101 901 for learndirect's own courses and centres) – slightly different hours in Wales and Northern Ireland.

> www.learndirect-advice.co.uk

> www.learndirect.co.uk

learndirect Scotland

For information and advice on courses, childcare, funding etc

> Tel: 0808 100 9000 from 7.30am to 11pm Monday to Friday; 9am to 6pm weekends
> www.learndirectscotland.com

See *2:17 – Open/distance and other independent learning* for more information about learndirect centres.

Scottish Adult Learning Partnership

The Scottish Adult Learning Partnership (SALP) is a multi-agency partnership open to all adult learning providers and learners who can sign up to its mission:

'To support and encourage those adults who do not traditionally participate within our education system to become involved in community-based learning in Scotland.'

SALP is also responsible for six annual campaigns in Scotland, which promote access to learning: Adult Learners' Week, Sign Up Now, Signed Up Yet?, Family Learning Week, One Hour A Day for Learning and Bite Sized.

> **Scottish Adult Learning Partnership** – 22 Hill Street, Edinburgh EH2 3JZ.
> Tel 0131 220 5567.
> www.salp.org.uk

See also www.ceg.org.uk – the **Continuing Education Gateway** which offers all-age vocational and educational guidance. Its PlanIT Plus website contains information about opportunities in Scotland, including links to FE colleges. There is also a Careersline, which offers advice about education and training: 0800 44 22 22.

Further information

Further Education in Scotland – annual reference guide to full-time courses available at Scottish institutions, up to Higher National level. Published by Continuing Education Gateway, £7.00.

Study Gap – published by ISCO, £7.95 plus £1 postage. Aimed at gap-year students, but contains relevant information on the range of vocational and academic short courses in the private sector.

Time to Learn – published twice a year by City & Guilds, 1 Giltspur Street, London EC1A 9DD. Tel: 020 7294 2850. The summer edition covers April to September, the winter edition October to March. Each edition contains about 2000 entries. £4.95 plus £1.50 p&p. You can view the information on: www.timetolearn.org.uk

Directory of Vocational and Further Education – published by Pearson Education. 2004/2005 edition priced at £90.00. Lists all courses offered at sixth form and FE colleges across the UK.

Adult Learning Yearbook – published annually by NIACE; 2004/2005 edition priced at £21.95. Comprehensive information on adult education organisations and providers. Includes lists of short-term residential colleges and adult and community education organisations.

Adults Learning – journal published by NIACE ten times a year. Subscription rates are £34 for individuals; £18 for students and part-time tutors; £56 for institutions.

2:9

Basic skills

Topics covered:

- Basic skills provision
- Qualifications
- English for speakers of other languages
- Getting what the client needs
- Relevant national agencies

The Basic Skills Agency (the national agency for basic skills in England and Wales) defines basic skills as:

'the ability to read, write, and speak in English (or Welsh) and to use mathematics at a level necessary to function and progress at work and in society in general.'

In our rapidly changing world, good communication skills are essential – both within the workplace and in everyday life. Basic skills – reading, writing, speaking, listening and basic maths – underpin all education and training. It has been estimated that up to seven million adults in the UK have problems with basic skills, and there is a variety of initiatives nationally to combat this.

- Sir Claus Moser's report on literacy and numeracy in 1999 *(A Fresh Start – Improving Literacy and Numeracy),* called for an improved framework for the delivery of basic skills education, including national standards for adult literacy and numeracy.

- *Skills for Life,* the Government's response to the Moser report, was published in 2001, setting out plans for tackling the problem. This led to the creation of the Adult Basic Skills Strategy Unit, see: www.dfes.gov.uk/readwriteplus The website includes access to *Skills for Life,* for further information about the national strategy in England and Wales.

- From September 2001, national qualifications in adult literacy and numeracy became available for the first time. The accreditation of these qualifications gives assurance to users that they are based on the national standards ensuring consistency in terms of level, demand, content and outcomes, see: www.qca.org.uk/qualifications

- The DfES's current *Get On* campaign (www.dfes.gov.uk/get-on) aims to encourage as many adults as possible to take action to improve their basic skills.

- In Wales, the National Strategy for Basic Skills, which is overseen and implemented by the Basic Skills Agency, (www.basic-skills-wales.org), has similar aims.

The Government is on target for 1.5 million adults to improve their basic skills by 2007, with the 2004 benchmark of 750,000 adults with improved literacy and numeracy reached.

For general information on adult literacy campaigns, research and initiatives, see www.literacytrust.org.uk (the website of the National Literacy Trust).

Basic skills provision

Basic skills courses aim to build up skills and confidence in literacy, numeracy, speaking, reading and writing. They are run in colleges of further education, adult education and community centres, libraries and other centres.

As well as basic literacy and numeracy, some centres offer courses in English and maths for improvers, and pre-GCSE courses for those not quite ready to be launched straight into a GCSE in English or maths.

Further education colleges/adult education services

Adult basic education is provided through a great variety of classes run by adult/community education services and further education colleges. Basic skills education is also provided on an individual basis, through drop-in centres, or planned individual sessions. These may be open to those who cannot attend a regular class, and to students on other college courses wishing to improve their basic skills. Tuition may be one or two hours a week, or it could be more. It's partly up to the individual student, but it also depends on what's available. Basic skills courses are normally provided free of charge to the learner.

Open learning

With the increase in open learning opportunities, it is possible to follow basic maths and English courses as an independent learner, either at home, in the workplace or at an open learning centre. Back-up tutorial support may be provided.

learndirect courses

Courses run through learndirect can be accessed at home, within the workplace or at one of the learndirect centres across the UK. The learning packages available include a range of basic skills courses. These are mainly courses at entry level (see *2:6 – Qualifications* for further information about levels within the National Qualifications Framework) and range in duration from two-hour packages to 40 hours, covering basic word and number skills, as well as some English courses for those whose first language is not English. Fees are not charged for basic skills learning packages.

> **learndirect advice line** tel: 0800 100 900
> www.learndirect-advice.co.uk

> **learndirect** (for courses and centres) tel: 0800 101 901
> www.learndirect.co.uk

> **learndirect Scotland** tel: 0808 100 9000
> www.learndirectscotland.com

The National Extension College (NEC)

The NEC is a non-profitmaking trust, providing a range of distance learning courses. It offers the following basic skills courses:

Back to Basics – four short courses, which can be taken individually or together, in grammar, spelling, punctuation and reading (price £115 per course)

Develop Your English – a preparation course for the level 2 Certificate in Adult Literacy (price £195 or £75 per module)

Develop Your Maths – a preparation course for the level 2 Certificate in Adult Numeracy (price £195 or £75 per module).

Discounts are available for those on benefits, state pension etc. From time-to-time, specific NEC courses carry special offers (see website below for details).

➤ **National Extension College** – Student Advisers, The Michael Young Centre, Purbeck Road, Cambridge CB2 2HN.
Tel: 0800 389 2839.
Email: info@nec.ac.uk
www.nec.ac.uk

See *2:17 – Open/distance and other independent learning* for more information about learndirect and the NEC.

Government-funded initiatives

The Government is involved in supporting and funding a range of initiatives and training programmes related to basic skills, both within the community and in the workplace. Some are outlined below.

● Programmes for unemployed people, such as **Work Based Learning for Adults** and the **New Deal**, provide help to improve literacy and other basic skills. Details are available at the Jobcentre Plus/Jobcentre. See also *2:18 – Work Based Learning for Adults and other government-funded training* for further information.

● Most local Learning and Skills Councils and equivalent organisations elsewhere in the UK are playing a key role in encouraging **local employers** to provide basic skills training for employees. For further information, see the employer toolkit and workplace sections of www.dfes.gov.uk/readwriteplus and the website of the Workplace Basic Skills Network (which works with training providers, employers, trade unions and others to extend and enhance basic skills training in the workplace) www.lancs.ac.uk/wbsnet

● In 20 Learning and Skills Council areas, pilot schemes are under way to enable thousands of low-skilled employees to be **released during work time** to improve their skills, including basic skills. See *2:19 – Learning in the workplace* for more information.

● **Family literacy, language and numeracy** programmes have been designed to help parents and their children to improve their skills separately and together. The Basic Skills Agency produces annual guidelines on the types of programmes and supporting material for local Learning and Skills Councils/LEAs. Funding is focused on the most deprived English areas and LEAs work in partnership on some programmes e.g. with the voluntary sector. The websites www.familyprogrammes.org and www.skillsfor families.org provide more information.

- **Prisons** make extensive basic skills provision, and many probation services provide help with basic education for offenders and ex-offenders in the community. The Government is currently making prisoner education a higher priority by setting ambitious targets to raise standards and increasing the prison education budget.

Voluntary services

As well as local authority and college provision, there are various voluntary literacy schemes. Libraries, volunteer centres, Citizens Advice Bureaux or adult information, advice and guidance services should have details.

Qualifications

City and Guilds qualifications

Basic skills qualifications offered by City and Guilds include:

- *Communication Skills (Wordpower)* – there are four levels: entry level and levels 1, 2 and 3. The certificate covers reading, writing, listening and speaking

- *Numeracy (Numberpower)* – there are three levels: entry level, and levels 1 and 2. The certificate covers applying number skills, measuring and handling data. Candidates learn to work with units of measurement, charts, tables, graphs, money and time

- *Wordwise* and *Numberwise* – these schemes are assessed through a portfolio of evidence. They are available at entry level (entry 1, entry 2 and entry 3) and at levels 1 and 2.

- ➤ **City and Guilds** – Customer Services Enquiries Unit, 1 Giltspur Street, London EC1A 9DD.
  Tel: 020 7294 2800.
  Email: enquiry@city-and-guilds.co.uk
  www.city-and-guilds.co.uk

OCR qualifications

At entry level: OCR offers basic skills qualifications, including:

- *OCR Entry Level Certificate in Adult Literacy (including Spoken Communication)*

- *OCR Entry Level Certificate in Adult Numeracy.*

Each provides accreditation at entry 1, entry 2 and entry 3. Other entry level qualifications offered by OCR include work-related learning qualifications.

National Basic Skills Tests: available at levels 1 and 2, the National Basic Skills Tests provide an accreditation route for adults wishing to have their achievement recognised. Candidates passing the tests will be awarded the Certificate in Adult Literacy or Adult Numeracy at levels 1 or 2 as appropriate. The tests are available as paper-based tests and online via the OCR website.

OCR National Skills Profile: has been developed to provide recognition of the skills of those working at entry level and those for whom existing qualifications frameworks are inappropriate. The scheme offers a flexible profiling framework, which allows centres to select modules appropriate to the needs of their students. It is designed to create a bridge into mainstream national qualifications such as Key Skills units or NVQs, or as an achievement in its own right. It incorporates six 'essential skills', including communication and numeracy, and personal and practical work skills, and 13 vocational areas, including care, catering, motor vehicles and office practice.

➤ **OCR** – Progress House, Westwood Way, Coventry CV4 8JQ.
  Tel: 024 7647 0033.
  Email: helpdesk@ocr.org.uk
  www.ocr.org.uk

Edexcel qualifications

Edexcel adult literacy and numeracy qualifications are aimed at adults wanting to improve their literacy or numeracy qualifications, in order to progress their learning and/or their employment opportunities. Edexcel also offers qualifications to those for whom English is a second language.

The qualifications are available at entry level (entry 1, entry 2 and entry 3), level 1 and level 2.

➤ **Edexcel** – One90 High Holborn, London WC1V 7BH.
  Tel: 0870 240 9800.
  Email: enquiries@edexcel.org.uk
  www.edexcel.org.uk

English for speakers of other languages

Classes or one-to-one tuition in English for Speakers of Other Languages (ESOL), Spoken English for Speakers of Other Languages (SESOL), English as a Second Language (ESL) or English as Another Language (EAL) are available for residents of the UK whose first language is not English. These are similar to basic skills courses, but take into account the particular needs of those whose native language is not English. Learners develop their language skills on these courses so they can:

● become familiar with the laws and customs of the UK

● participate and progress in the labour market

● access further education and training

● support their children's education.

Such courses are provided by:

- local authorities in adult education centres or community centres

- local colleges which may have specific classes in areas where demand is high; in other areas they may offer general adult literacy courses but will take into account the needs of ESOL students

- training providers who may offer ESOL programmes alongside other government-funded adult training programmes which are primarily to train people for employment.

Most LEAs provide free basic ESOL tuition – although some will make a charge for courses at a higher level.

A new set of ESOL skills for life qualifications, developed by the QCA, are now available, see www.qca.org.uk. These will soon become the only ESOL qualifications that count towards the Governments *Skills for Life* targets. The following bodies will be providing these qualifications:

- Cambridge ESOL – see www.cambridgeesol.org

- City and Guilds (Pitmans) – see www.pitmanqualifications.com

- Edexcel – see www.edexcel.org.uk

- National Open College Network – see www.nocn.org.uk

- Open College of the North West – see www.ocnw.com

- Trinity College London – see www.trinitycollege.co.uk

Radio and television: from time to time there will be programmes aimed at teaching English to speakers of other languages. Broadcasters' websites also contain teaching materials including audio clips.

Open learning courses: open learning/self study courses are available (including learndirect courses) for those whose first language is not English and who wish to improve their reading and writing skills.

Getting what the client needs

With basic education and ESOL courses readily available in nearly all areas, there is a wide variety in the type and quality of provision. It is important to have an idea of the aims of the learner – does he/she need numeracy skills in order to learn measuring and estimating skills for employment purposes, for example, or do they need to gain numeracy skills for other reasons? It is necessary to shop around to find the learning opportunity that offers the most appropriate tuition.

Basic skills assessment

Initial assessment, which provides information on the strengths and needs of an individual in relation to their basic skills, is crucial. The Basic Skills Agency publishes the following assessment materials:

- *Fast Track* – a screening test that takes 10 minutes to administer, which can be used in one-to-one interviews, and can be used by non-specialists

- *Initial Assessment* – assesses an adult's level of literacy and/or numeracy skills. Scores are aligned to national levels. Each test takes about 20 minutes and they can be administered and marked by non-specialists.

These assessments can be obtained from Basic Skills Agency Publications. Tel: 0870 600 2400. Email: basicskills@twoten.press.net

For more information on the Basic Skills Agency, see *Relevant national agencies* below.

As part of the Government's *Skills for Life* strategy (mentioned previously), a suite of diagnostic assessment materials, which provide detailed assessment, is also available. All tools produced have been matched to the national standards, the adult core curricula for literacy and numeracy, the pre-entry curriculum and the ESOL curriculum. The materials cover the range from pre-entry to level 2 and include materials to assess literacy and numeracy, in addition to materials for use with ESOL learners and learners who have either already undertaken an assessment for dyslexia or who demonstrate potential dyslexia indicators.

To view a full list of contents, see www.dfes.gov.uk/readwriteplus

Questions to ask

Clients should ask the course provider:

- if they offer guidance on what's the best course for them

- how progress is reviewed

- if the teaching is one-to-one, in a group or through open/distance learning

- if it's possible to have the teaching at home

- about any costs involved (normally, fees are not charged for adult basic education and basic ESOL courses).

As with all studying it may be very hard work and the client may not be as successful as they hope – not necessarily through their own fault. Success at this level can sometimes depend on how the student gets on with the tutor.

So if there are problems at first, it may just be a question of changing tutor or class.

Clients with a disability

Most basic education providers will do their best to help. For example, they may be able to arrange for a tutor to visit the client at home. See *3:26 – People with disabilities* for general information on support for those with disabilities.

Relevant national agencies

England and Wales

The Basic Skills Agency

The Basic Skills Agency is the national agency for basic skills in England and Wales, funded primarily by the DfES and the Welsh Assembly Government. It is an independent not-for-profit organisation; a company limited by guarantee and a registered charity.

In 2004, the board of the Basic Skills Agency approved three key priorities. These are:

- improving the speaking and listening skills of children, young people and adults

- improving basic skills at transition points in a child's, young person's or adult's life

- engaging disengaged children, young people and adults in improving basic skills.

There is a Basic Skills Agency Resource Centre, where materials can be viewed:

> **Basic Skills Agency Resource Centre** – The Institute of Education Library, University of London, 20 Bedford Way, London WC1H 0AL.
> Tel: 020 7612 6069.
> Email: b.sakarya@ioe.ac.uk
> www.ioe.ac.uk/library/bsa

A publications catalogue is available from The Basic Skills Agency Publications, tel: 0870 600 2400. The Agency publishes a magazine *Basic Skills*, available free on a termly basis – contact using the Publications number above.

> **The Basic Skills Agency (BSA)** – Commonwealth House, 1-19 New Oxford Street, London WC1A 1NU.
> Tel: 020 7405 4017
> Email: enquiries@basic-skills.co.uk
> www.basic-skills.co.uk

Wales

The Basic Skills Agency is overseeing the implementation of the National Basic Skills Strategy on behalf of the Welsh Assembly Government. The National Basic Skills Strategy for Wales was launched in April 2001. The Strategy aims to provide a coherent approach to raising standards of literacy and numeracy in children, young people and adults. It involves a number of specific measures and partnership with a range of organisations. See www.basic-skills-wales.org for more information.

Scotland

In July 2001, the Scottish Executive published the *Adult Literacy and Numeracy in Scotland* report, which made a number of recommendations to raise the levels of adult literacy and numeracy in Scotland. The report can be accessed at www.scotland.gov.uk

There is no direct equivalent to the Basic Skills Agency in Scotland, but a development unit, to drive the creation of quality adult literacy and numeracy, has been created within

Communities Scotland. Current developments under way include 12 pathfinder projects, a new curriculum and a training programme.

In Scotland, the Scottish Executive Enterprise Transport and Lifelong Learning Department's responsibilities include further education, skills and lifelong learning.

See also www.planitplus.net – the PlanIT Plus website, which contains information about opportunities in Scotland, including links to adult basic education providers.

Northern Ireland

The Essential Skills for Living Strategy is a new approach to adult literacy and numeracy in Northern Ireland. As part of the Strategy, a regional curriculum has recently been introduced. There is now accreditation for adult learners and improved tutor qualifications. Targets have been set for engaging new learners.

➤ **The Department for Employment and Learning** – Brendan Murray, Room 106, Essential Skills Branch, Adelaide House, 39-49 Adelaide Street, Belfast, Co. Antrim BT2 8FD.
Tel: 028 9025 7443
Email: brendan.murray@delni.gov.uk
www.delni.gov.uk

2:10

Learning for leisure

Topics covered:

- Opportunity providers
- Ideas for learning topics

Learning for leisure can include just about anything that is not for immediate vocational purposes. There is an enormous choice of leisure activities and classes for those who wish to devote more time to an existing interest, or try their hand at something new – from 'exploring local history' to 'an introduction to watercolour painting'. Many people, of course, also join academic, certificated courses, such as for a GCSE or A level, solely for personal interest and pleasure. This section focuses particularly on those courses that are non-vocational, do not lead to a full qualification (although some may offer some form of accreditation) and are intended to be undertaken for general interest.

As well as for its own sake – for recreation, enjoyment or personal fulfilment, learning for leisure has a number of practical uses:

- as an introduction to study on a part-time basis, or a return to study after a break

- as evidence of being able to study, which is often an entry requirement for higher education

- as a way of keeping mind and body active, in times of enforced leisure, such as unemployment

- as a way of learning skills (e.g. motorcycle maintenance, French, jewellery making) including those that might offer the potential of earning money

- to explore a new subject before making a commitment to undertake a more advanced course

- to gain qualifications, if the course leads to certification by a recognised awarding body.

Opportunities are provided by a range of organisations, such as: adult or community education services, further education colleges, university extra-mural departments, recreation and leisure centres, independent learning providers, voluntary organisations and distance learning providers.

Classes are held in:

- colleges – both at main college sites and at outreach locations in the community

- adult education centres

- community centres and village halls

- sports and leisure centres

- schools

- pubs and other places.

Or there are many opportunities for learning independently at home, by taking a distance/open learning course.

Opportunity providers

Local education authorities and further education colleges

Part-time adult education, also called community education, offers a range of recreational learning opportunities. The variety of subjects available is huge – from arts and crafts or courses related to food and drink, through to foreign languages, history or health and fitness. Adult/community education is provided by local education authorities, and delivered through their adult education or community education services, community colleges and other community and voluntary providers, and/or by local further education colleges, depending on local LEA arrangements.

Enrolment arrangements vary; some courses have to be booked well in advance, for others, it may be possible to leave enrolling until the first class. Fees vary from area to area; adults may be entitled to reduced fees if they are retired or receiving benefit. Published course information should give details, or contact the organiser. Many courses have to be self-financing. That means students have to pay enough in fees to cover all the costs. Clubs and associations may organise their own classes and get special rates.

How to find out more

Information about local courses may be accessed, in paper format or through local databases:

- in local libraries

- from the adult or community education department (if there is one) of the local authority

- at adult education/community centres

- from local colleges

- through the local press – in particular in August and September

- at local adult information, advice and guidance services.

The national telephone helpline, learndirect, also holds information about such courses – tel: 0800 101 901 or, in Scotland, 0808 100 9000. Or their course databases can be searched online: www.learndirect.co.uk or www.learndirectscotland.com

University extra-mural departments

With the aim of taking higher education to the people, a number of universities and other higher education establishments have extra-mural departments, departments of adult education, or centres of continuing education, offering courses to the general public. They are usually concerned with the arts and sciences in general and with local interests. However, they do not restrict themselves to this sort of work; increasingly they are offering courses relevant to local needs.

Courses may be held at the university or college itself, or elsewhere – sometimes over quite a wide area. Some universities have a separate college or base for their extra-mural work. The departments offer evening classes, part-time classes, short courses, weekend events, summer schools and public lectures. They are often at a high academic level, and taught by higher education lecturers. They're open to absolutely everyone – no previous academic knowledge or experience is expected.

Details of what is on offer can be obtained by contacting the university department concerned. Courses will probably also be advertised at the public library. Prospectuses are usually published every year in August/September, or every term. Some also have short course information, mainly for the summer.

Distance and open learning providers

There are many opportunities for learning for leisure through distance learning. Providers of such courses, which can range from understanding antiques or learning a language to creative writing, include:

- the Open College of the Arts

- colleges accredited by the Open and Distance Learning Quality Council – including the National Extension College

- colleges who are members of the Association of British Correspondence Colleges

- the Open University.

Open learning centres, such as learndirect (where you can learn at a time and pace to suit yourself), offer courses that are primarily related to developing work-related skills. However, there are also many introductory IT and basic skills courses which are very suitable for anyone wishing to develop such skills for their own self-development.

See *2:16 – The Open University* and *2:17 – Open/distance and other independent learning* for more information about the above organisations.

Voluntary organisations

Voluntary organisations offer many opportunities for learning for leisure. Examples are:

- the Workers' Educational Association (WEA), which offers a variety of courses through its branch network

- The Women's Institute (WI), which offers adult education in local institutes, through a travelling tutor scheme, on study tours abroad or at the WI's own Denman College

- national voluntary organisations related to particular interests, such as those concerned with wildlife conservation and the environment, which may organise short courses, including residential courses, seminars and workshops

- local societies, clubs and interest groups which may arrange short courses, workshops and lectures on topics relating to their particular area of interest

- groups run through NASO (see below)

- University of the Third Age (U3A) – a self-help movement for people no longer in full-time employment, which offers a wide range of educational, creative and leisure activities, through a network of local groups.

These organisations advertise their courses in the same way as other adult education providers – through libraries, the local press and so on.

For more information, see *2:11 – The Workers' Educational Association; 2:21 – Volunteering; 3:24 – Women* (for further details on the WI) and *3:25 – Third age* (for further information on U3A).

National Adult School Organisation (NASO)

This is a national voluntary adult education movement, which has existed for over 200 years. NASO 'friendship through study' groups meet throughout the country, to discuss a wide range of topics based on the NASO handbook. Regional activities include residential weekends, studying a particular subject in some depth and social outings to visit a place of interest.

The national office publishes discussion leaflets, the annual study handbook to help groups with their discussion programme, and a monthly magazine, *One and All.*

The national office also organises study tours abroad, residential courses at home and abroad and activity weekends to complement studies in the handbook. Groups vary from five to 25 people and each group finds its own meeting place, for example a community centre, church hall or a member's home.

There is a small national membership fee.

> **NASO** – Riverton, 370 Humberstone Road, Leicester LE5 0SA.
> Tel: 0116 253 8333.
> Email: gensec@naso.org.uk
> www.naso.org.uk

Residential course providers

A number of learning providers offer weekend, half-week or longer residential courses in a wide range of activities and subjects. Organisations offering residential courses for leisure include:

- independent learning providers – from very small businesses offering e.g. residential art courses, through to large independent residential colleges, such as those which are members of ARCA (see below)

- local authorities – through their own residential centres

- universities and larger independent schools – which may run public summer schools

- voluntary organisations – such as the Field Studies Council, BTCV, and The Women's Institute (which operates Denman College, a residential adult education college)

- specialist tour operators, which may offer study tours and trips locally and abroad, with a learning focus.

Many of these are courses for the whole family and make ideal short holidays for people who like studying for relaxation. Course costs vary enormously, depending on the sort of accommodation and level of catering. Courses are advertised in the press, special interest magazines or in local libraries; a few directories and lists of residential courses are available. See also the ARCA website.

More about voluntary organisations can be found in *2:21 – Volunteering,* and about Denman College in *3:24 – Women.*

Adult Residential Colleges Association (ARCA)

ARCA is an association of over 30 colleges – some of which are historic houses in countryside settings – specialising in short-stay residential adult education courses. Members include colleges run by local authorities as well as independently run colleges. ARCA's website provides links to member colleges.

> **Adult Residential Colleges Association** – 6 Bath Road, Felixstowe, Suffolk IP11 7JW.
> Email: arcasec@aol.com
> www.aredu.org.uk

Other independent providers

Besides those independent learning providers offering distance learning or residential courses as previously mentioned, there are many privately-run organisations/businesses – perhaps run by one person with a particular skill – offering regular weekly classes or private tuition, aimed at learners based locally. Typical subjects could be arts and crafts, learning a musical instrument etc.

Broadcast media

The BBC, commercial TV channels and radio stations broadcast programmes that provide opportunities for learning. The BBC, in particular, is well known for its educational broadcasting. See *2:17 – Open/distance and other independent learning* for more information about opportunities for learning through the broadcast media.

Ideas for learning topics

The arts

A huge variety of classes and courses are held in:

- residential colleges

- university extra-mural departments

- adult education classes

- art colleges

- arts centres

- museums and galleries

- community centres.

The Arts Councils (the national bodies for the arts) aim to encourage popular access to the arts.For example, they may operate 'artists in residence' schemes – artists, dancers, photographers, writers, storytellers, actors, film makers or musicians who work with, and give support to, community or education groups.

> **Arts Council England** – 14 Great Peter Street, London SW1P 3NQ.
> Tel: 0845 300 6200.
> Email: enquiries@artscouncil.org.uk
> www.artscouncil.org.uk

> **The Arts Council of Northern Ireland** – MacNeice House, 77 Malone Road, Belfast BT9 6AQ.
> Tel: 028 9038 5200.
> Email: info@artscouncil-ni.org
> www.artscouncil-ni.org

> **The Arts Council of Wales** – 9 Museum Place, Cardiff CF10 3NX.
> Tel: 029 2037 6500.
> Email: info@artswales.org.uk
> www.artswales.org.uk

> **The Scottish Arts Council** – 12 Manor Place, Edinburgh EH3 7DD.
> Tel: 0131 226 6051.
> Email: help.desk@scottisharts.org.uk
> www.scottisharts.org.uk

Details of short courses, in particular arts and crafts, are likely to be found in special interest magazines, or in the weekend supplements of broadsheet newspapers. Local museums and art galleries will publicise local events. Many adult education classes organised through the LEA or local colleges relate to the arts.

The environment and conservation

Some environmental organisations which offer learning opportunities are listed in *2:21 Volunteering*. Local adult education provision may include classes related to the environment and conservation. The following also provide learning opportunities.

Centre for Alternative Technology

The Centre is open to the public most days of the year, and has a wide range of displays and information on renewable energy, organic growing and all aspects of sustainable living. As part of its activities, the Centre runs short residential courses for the public (usually at weekends) on a variety of topics. These are listed and described in its *Residential Courses Programme*, or on the website.

> **Centre for Alternative Technology** – Machynlleth, Powys SY20 9AZ.
> Tel: 01654 705981.
> Email: courses@cat.org.uk
> www.cat.org.uk

The Soil Association

The Soil Association is a charity that promotes organic food and farming. Members receive the *Living Earth* magazine three times a year.

> **The Soil Association** – Bristol House, 40-56 Victoria Street, Bristol BS1 6BY.
> Tel: 0117 314 5000.
> Email: info@soilassociation.org
> www.soilassociation.org

HDRA, the organic organisation

The organisation researches and promotes organic gardening, farming and food. HDRA runs regular workshops, courses and events.

> **HDRA, the organic organisation** – Ryton Organic Gardens, Coventry, Warwickshire CV8 3LG.
> Tel: 024 7630 3517.
> Email: enquiry@hdra.org.uk
> www.hdra.org.uk

Sport

Much part-time and recreational education involves sport. Sport and keep-fit classes are always among the most popular in adult education. There is also likely to be an extensive range of sport and fitness courses on offer at recreation and leisure centres run by local authorities, and at privately-run gyms, health and fitness studios and sports clubs.

Sports Councils

The national bodies for sport have information about all sports as well as where to contact for details of the various coaching, refereeing and instructing courses available. The Sports Councils can give out governing body contacts for courses, but do not hold specific details.

> **Sport England** – 3rd Floor, Victoria House, Bloomsbury Square, London WC1B 4SE.
> Tel: 0845 8508 508.
> Email: info@sportengland.org
> www.sportengland.org

> **sportscotland** – Caledonia House, South Gyle, Edinburgh EH12 9DQ.
> Tel: 0131 317 7200.
> Email for general enquiries: library@sportscotland.org.uk
> www.sportscotland.org.uk

> **Sports Council for Northern Ireland** – The House of Sport, 2a Upper Malone Road, Belfast BT9 5LA.
> Tel: 028 9038 1222.
> Email: info@sportni.net
> www.sportni.net

> **Sports Council for Wales** – Sophia Gardens, Cardiff CF11 9SW.
> Tel: 029 2030 0500.
> Email: scw@scw.co.uk
> www.sports-council-wales.co.uk

For information about learning to be a sports coach, see also the **sportscoach UK** website: www.sportscoachUK.org or email: coaching@sportscoachuk.org

Personal development

The last 20 years have seen a rapid expansion of activities in holistic education, for example: assertiveness training, counselling, life-planning, stress management and a host of others. They deal with the whole person – spiritual, physical, emotional, social and intellectual. There are many courses to help people to develop self-confidence, as well as new skills and insights. Many of these are run through local adult education classes; there are also private practitioners who may advertise locally or nationally.

Alternative lifestyles

Some people experiment with a wide variety of alternative ways of living. Alternative community living often means sharing, working and playing together, sometimes pooling personal resources, sometimes not. Some communities offer educational programmes and invite people to participate in them.

Politics

Participation in politics provides an opportunity to learn about different topics. Organisations hold meetings, discussions or workshops on a variety of political issues. These events can be a chance to learn and share ideas with people from politics and education.

Some university extra-mural departments run courses related to politics.

> **Conservative Central Office** – 25 Victoria Street, London SW1H 0DL.
> Tel: 020 7222 9000.
> Email: correspondence@conservatives.com
> www.conservatives.com

> **Labour Party Headquarters** – 16 Old Queen Street, London SW1H 9HP.
> Tel: 0870 5900 200.
> Email: info@new.labour.org.uk
> www.labour.org.uk

> **Liberal Democrat Headquarters** – 4 Cowley Street, London SW1P 3NB.
> Tel: 020 7222 7999.
> Email: info@libdems.org.uk
> www.libdems.org.uk

> **Trades Union Congress** – Congress House, Great Russell Street, London WC1B 3LS.
> Tel: 020 7636 4030.
> Email: info@tuc.org.uk
> www.tuc.org.uk

Learning opportunities abroad

There are many opportunities for learning for leisure abroad – such as taking a foreign language course in the country concerned, going on discovery and adventure holidays, and so on. The WEA, The Women's Institute, some ARCA member colleges and many higher education institutions and other organisations offer study tours abroad. See also under the NASO details above. Opportunities are often advertised in the press and are included in some of the publications listed below.

Further information

National Institute of Adult Continuing Education (NIACE)

NIACE aims to advance the interests of adult learners and potential learners. It works to increase the numbers of adults undertaking learning, to widen access and to improve opportunities. It publishes handbooks, guides and project reports.

> **NIACE** – Renaissance House, 20 Princess Road West, Leicester LE1 6TP.
> Tel: 0116 204 4200.
> Email: enquiries@niace.org.uk
> www.niace.org.uk

> **NIACE Dysgu Cymru** – 3rd Floor, 35 Cathedral Road, Cardiff CF11 9HB.
> Tel: 029 2037 0900.
> Email: enquiries@niacedc.org.uk
> www.niacedc.org.uk

Time to Learn – published twice a year by City and Guilds, 1 Giltspur Street, London EC1A 9DD. Tel: 020 7294 2850. The summer edition covers April to September, the winter edition October to March. Each edition contains about 2000 entries for day schools, learning breaks and study tours. Price £4.95 plus £1.50 p&p. A searchable online version can be accessed at www.timetolearn.org.uk

Study Gap – published by ISCO. Price £7.95 (2004 edition). A guide to a wide range of short courses, including those that can be built into a year off.

FSC Natural History Courses, FSC Arts Courses – two free guides to courses run by the Field Studies Council, Head Office, Montford Bridge, Preston Montford, Shrewsbury SY4 1HW. Tel: 01743 852100. Email: fsc.headoffice@field-studies-council.org or see www.field-studies-council.org

BTCV Holidays and *BTCV Training* – brochures available free from BTCV, Conservation Centre, Balby Road, Doncaster DN4 0RH. Tel: 01302 572244. Email: information@btcv.org.uk or see www.btcv.org/shop

A Year Off ... A Year On? – published by Lifetime Careers Publishing. Price £10.99. Contains information about opportunities for studying in the UK and abroad, as well as other ways of spending a career break.

Good Non Retirement Guide 2004 – published by Kogan Page. Price £14.99. Whilst this guide is primarily aimed at older people it incorporates a useful directory of organisations offering leisure activities and holidays.

Leisure and Learning – Factsheet No.30 published by Age Concern, available free through their information line: 0800 00 99 66.

Adult Learning Yearbook – published annually by NIACE; 2004/2005 edition priced at £21.95. Includes lists of short-term residential colleges and adult and community education organisations.

Kindred Spirit – magazine featuring articles on body, mind and spirit. The resources directory section advertises a wide range of courses, centres, retreats, places to go etc. Annual subscription £21, for six issues a year. Two years' subscription: £37. Three years' subscription: £51. Available from specialist shops and some large newsagents at £3.50; or £4 including p&p from Kindred Spirit, Foxhole, Dartington, Totnes TQ9 6EB. Tel: 01803 866686. Email: subs@kindredspirit.co.uk or see www.kindredspirit.co.uk

2:11

The Workers' Educational Association (WEA)

Topics covered:

- The background and structure of the WEA
- The types of course available
- Addresses of regional offices

The Workers' Educational Association (WEA) is a major voluntary adult education organisation offering classes to adults countrywide. It is an organisation that anyone can join and be involved in planning the local programmes – it is governed by its members. Classes and courses are run everywhere – in schools, adult education centres, local halls, members' houses and so on. It uses other organisations' premises but remains separate and independent, and tries to reach people where they live and work.

How it works

- Despite its name, the WEA is not restricted to any one kind of worker – it is **open to all adults** from every walk of life.

- It was established in 1903 to overcome the disadvantages of workers who didn't have access to established channels of education.

- It provides over **10,000 courses** each year to over 100,000 students.

- It has over **650 local branches,** each with its own officers (secretary, treasurer, chairperson), who plan the local programme in consultation with their regional office. Anyone can join the WEA and become a member of the local branch. People joining a WEA class promoted by a branch become members automatically.

- The branches make up **nine regions in England,** each with a regional secretary (listed below). In each region, there are staff who help branches to organise their programme, work with affiliated societies and recruit suitable part-time tutors. Others concentrate on regional provision, for example pre-retirement education, trade union and industrial studies. The WEA also operates in **Scotland, Wales** and **Northern Ireland** (see contact points listed below).

- Classes may be during the day or evening. There may be crèche facilities attached to daytime classes.

- The WEA runs activities in co-operation with local education authorities, other voluntary and community organisations, and has a particularly close relationship with some university extra-mural departments.

- WEA classes are designed to develop understanding and some may lead to formal qualifications. Students often take up other work or take further or higher education courses as a result.

- Increasingly, accreditation is available to students who want it.

What it does

The WEA's activities vary from area to area because branches have their own ideas about local needs, and the professional staff who help them have their own interests and expertise. Broadly its work includes:

- **community learning** – for people in deprived areas, or who suffer from social or educational disadvantage (for example elderly people, people with special needs and unemployed people). Tackling social exclusion this way involves a range of other organisations

- **workplace learning** – organised in partnership with UNISON at or through the workplace, providing an opportunity to return to learn. The WEA also organises workplace learning courses – with a range of trades unions – on such issues as health and safety at work, employment law and equal opportunities

- **general programme of education** – the traditional WEA class, in subjects like ICT, philosophy, art, literature, and also preparation for higher education.

More information about courses is available from the WEA. The WEA website includes a searchable database of courses.

➤ **WEA** – Quick House, 65 Clifton Street, London EC2A 4JE.
  Tel: 020 7375 3092.
  Email: national@wea.org.uk
  www.wea.org.uk

What the courses cost

If it's a trade union course, it's likely to be free. Courses for unemployed people and other disadvantaged groups are often free, but it is up to the local branch. Fees usually have to cover all costs.

How to find out more

The local library should have the names of local branch secretaries; otherwise the region organisers at the addresses below will have details.

Regional offices

England

➤ **Eastern** – Botolph House, 17 Botolph Lane, Cambridge CB2 3RE.
Tel: 01223 350978.
Email: eastern@wea.org.uk

➤ **East Midlands** – 39 Mapperley Road, Nottingham NG3 5AQ.
Tel: 0115 962 8400.
Email: eastmidlands@wea.org.uk

➤ **London** – 4 Luke Street, London EC2A 4XW.
Tel: 020 7613 7550.
Email: london@wea.org.uk

➤ **North East** – First Floor, Unit 6, Metro Riverside Park, Delta Bank Road, Gateshead NE11 9DJ.
Tel: 0191 232 3957.
Email: northeast@wea.org.uk

➤ **North West (Liverpool)** – 7-8 Bluecoat Chambers, School Lane, Liverpool L1 3BX.
(Due to change address – date and location yet unknown)
Tel: 0151 709 8023.
Email: northwest@wea.org.uk

➤ **North West (Manchester)** – 4th Floor, Crawford House, University Precinct Centre, Oxford Road, Manchester M13 9GH.
Tel: 0161 277 5400.
www.nw.wea.org.uk
Email: northwest@wea.org.uk

➤ **Southern** – Unit 57, Riverside 2, Sir Thomas Longley Road, Rochester, Kent ME2 4DP.
Tel: 01634 730101.
Email: southern@wea.org.uk

➤ **South West** – Bradninch Court, Castle Street, Exeter EX4 3PL.
Tel: 01392 474 330.
Email: southwest@wea.org.uk

➤ **West Midlands** – 78-80 Sherlock Street, Birmingham B5 6LT.
Tel: 0121 666 6101.
Email: westmidlands@wea.org.uk

➤ **Yorkshire and Humber** – 6 Woodhouse Square, Leeds LS3 1AD.
Tel: 0113 245 3304.
Email: yorkshumber@wea.org.uk

➤ **Yorkshire and Humber (South Yorkshire Office)** – Chantry Buildings, 20 Corporation Street, Rotherham S60 1NG.
Tel: 01709 837001.
www.ys.wea.org.uk
Email: yorkshumber@wea.org.uk

Scotland

➤ **WEA Scotland** – Riddles Court, 322 Lawnmarket, Edinburgh EH1 2PG.
Tel: 0131 226 3456.
Email: hq@weascotland.org.uk

Wales

➤ **WEA South Wales** – 7 Coopers Yard, Curran Road, Cardiff CF10 5NB.
Tel: 029 2023 5277.
Email: weasw@swales.wea.org.uk

➤ **WEA North Wales** – for residential learning, contact: Coleg Harlech WEA, Harlech,
Gwynedd LL46 2PU.
Tel: 01766 781900.
Email: info@harlech.ac.uk
www.harlech.ac.uk – for community learning courses, contact local offices listed on
www.harlech.ac.uk

Northern Ireland

➤ **WEA Northern Ireland Head Office** – 1-3 Fitzwilliam Street, Belfast BT9 6AW.
Tel: 028 9032 9718.
Email: info@wea-ni.com

2:12

Access and other adult routes

Topics covered:

- Different ways of returning to education at various levels
- Access to higher education courses
- Providers of Access and equivalent courses
- Information on accreditation of prior learning and credit accumulation and transfer schemes

There are many courses designed to encourage adults to re-enter the education system and to participate in lifelong learning. The Government is keen to widen access to further and higher education and is actively encouraging institutions to recruit students from social and ethnic groups, which have been under-represented in the past.

Adults thinking of returning to learning after a break could consider:

- starting with a short part-time course, such as an evening class, perhaps in a leisure or recreation subject. As their interest in the subject grows, they may consider working towards qualifications, or changing to study something 'more serious'

- attending a full- or part-time course at a further education college, perhaps studying alongside young people.

- some schools (often those calling themselves community colleges) which accept mature people to study alongside their younger pupils, usually for GCSEs, A levels or other traditional academic qualifications

- using open or distance learning to gain A level or equivalent qualifications quickly, if already of a sufficient educational standard.

Adult routes

The traditional routes are not for everyone, particularly if their first experience of learning was not positive. Courses geared specifically to give adults a 'second chance' help to build up the individual's confidence and are designed to take into account the fact that most people need a lot of encouragement to start learning after a break.

Skills updating

There are professional updating courses, for those who have been away from the workplace for a number of years. Many of these courses are for those who have been raising a family. For example, there are courses for returning to teaching or nursing, re-entry to General Practice (medicine), and updating in information technology and office skills.

Starting afresh

There are many courses for those who have no qualifications or who want to start afresh. They include:

- entry level courses

- pre-Access courses

- Access to higher education courses

- short 'taster' courses at universities

- foundation courses

- local study skills and refresher courses with a variety of names

- women returners' courses. See also *3:24 – Women.*

What are courses like?

- Courses are usually structured, with as much support as possible. Tutors are there not only to teach but also to counsel and give advice on any type of problem encountered in doing the course – whether it's difficulties with studying, financial or childcare matters. Educational guidance is an essential part of the course. Tutors will analyse what the student has done prior to the course and, by going through available options, advise on the next move.

- Courses are student-centred; designed and adjusted in response to what people want.

- The aim of these courses is to give students the study skills and the confidence they need to make the most of the education system. Students have the opportunity to investigate different higher education subject options.

- For some students, these courses provide a fast route to qualifications and higher education.

- Some classes start and finish so that children can be dropped off and picked up from school; many courses are part-time and available in the evenings or during the day.

- Often, courses can be adapted to help people with any special requirements they may have due to age, gender, race or disability. Some are designed for women, people from specific minority ethnic groups and people with disabilities.

- Extra English language support may be available.

What is available?

Provision varies from one place to another. In areas with long-established courses, a wide variety of subjects is often available, particularly for learning to use new technology. In other areas, there may be less choice with only general courses on offer.

Although all the courses are for adults coming back into education, they are not all at the same academic level. They range from basic literacy and numeracy courses to higher education preparation courses. Usually, no formal entry qualifications are needed; it's up to the individual student and tutor to decide which course is appropriate. Names can be misleading: for example, 'access' is sometimes used for courses other than those preparing students for higher education. Students and their advisers should always check the level of the course.

Access to higher education courses

Students on the courses may have difficulties in returning to education but have shown that they have the potential to succeed in higher education. Access courses have been called the third route into higher education – alongside A levels/Advanced Highers and vocational A levels.

Access courses are designed to provide the skills and understanding needed to succeed on a degree course. They are open to 'mature' people, that is aged 19 and over, but in reality the average tends to be in the 25 to 35 age bracket. Usually, there are no formal entry requirements, but students should check individual course details. Competence in English and maths may need to be assessed; many Access courses have these subjects built into their programme.

Typical subject areas are: humanities, social sciences, health studies, science, business, performing arts, information technology, art and design. Some Access courses, such as nursing and teaching, prepare students for higher education courses that lead to a particular career. Access courses are validated on behalf of the Quality Assurance Agency by Authorised Validating Agencies, most of which are members of the National Open College Network.

The majority of Access students stay in their own area to study. Most courses last one or two years. They may be gained by full-or part-time college attendance or through distance learning. Some are directly linked to a particular degree course, so that success on the Access course gives automatic entrance to that degree. Otherwise, entry to a degree course is not always guaranteed, but admissions tutors usually welcome students from Access courses because of their motivation and their good grounding in study skills.

The Scottish Wider Access Programme (SWAP)

This programme is for students aged 21 and over and works to create new ways into higher education through the design of Access courses and of individual programmes guaranteeing entry to higher education, and through credit transfer and flexible study plans. It has three regional consortia established to develop and coordinate access to higher education in Scotland. Many of the Access programmes are offered in further education colleges, mostly on a full-time basis but with some part-time or open learning provision. Individual colleges have funds allocated which they may use to help support students on the programmes. Students on social security benefits may be entitled to a remission of fees.

> **SWAP**
Tel: 0800 731 0949.
Email: enquiries@swap2highereducation.com
www.swap2highereducation.com

> **SWAP North** – Faculty of Education, University of Aberdeen, Milton Place, Aberdeen AB24 2FA.
Tel: 01224 572796.
Email: swapnorth@abdn.ac.uk

> **SWAP East** – 25 Buccleuch Place, Edinburgh EH8 9LN.
Tel: 0131 650 6861.
Email: swapeast@ed.ac.uk

> **SWAP West** – Charles Oakley Building, Central College of Commerce, 300 Cathedral Street, Glasgow G1 2TA.
Tel: 0141 553 2471.
Email: swapwest@btconnect.com

National Open College Network (NOCN)

The National Open College Network (NOCN) provides accreditation services for adult learning. NOCN is a recognised national qualification awarding body and is the central organisation for 28 Open College Networks (OCNs) based across the UK. NOCN seeks to widen participation in learning and increase access to high quality and flexible education, and works to promote social inclusion through learning.

> **National Open College Network (NOCN)** – 9 St James Court, Friar Gate, Derby DE1 1BT.
Tel: 01332 268080.
Email: nocn@nocn.org.uk
www.nocn.org.uk

Open College Networks

Open College Networks (OCNs) are licensed by NOCN. They are locally managed, not-for-profit partnerships providing a flexible and responsive local accreditation service for a wide range of learning activities.

All NOCN- and OCN-accredited learning is delivered within a credit-based unitised framework. This allows employers and providers to customise and design provision according to their individual needs.

3900 organisations are members of OCNs nationally, including: adult and community education centres; further education and sixth form colleges; voluntary and community organisations; universities and higher education institutions; trade unions and employers; local education authorities; and training organisations.

➤ **Anglia South Open College Network** – University of Essex, Wivenhoe Park, Colchester CO4 3SQ.
Tel: 01206 873023.
Email: ocn@essex.ac.uk
www.asocn.co.uk

➤ **Open College Network Oxford and Chiltern Region** – Maybrook House, 224 Queensway, Bletchley, Milton Keynes MK2 2GE.
Tel: 01908 361520.
Email: ocnocr@ocnocr.com
www.crocn.org.uk

➤ **Greater Manchester Open College Network** – 4th Floor, Mauldeth House, Nell Lane, Chorlton, Manchester M21 7RL.
Tel: 0161 860 2710.
Email: gmocn@gmocn.ac.uk and info@gmocn.ac.uk
www.gmocn.ac.uk

➤ **London Open College Network** – 15 Angel Gate, City Road, London EC1V 2SF.
Tel: 020 7278 5511.
Email: locn@locn.org.uk
www.locn.org.uk

➤ **Merseyside Open College Network** – Suite 304-306, The Cotton Exchange Building, Old Hall Street, Liverpool L3 9LQ.
Tel: 0151 255 0515.
Email: ocn@mocn.co.uk
www.mocn.co.uk

➤ **North Anglia Open College Network** – St Andrews Street, Norwich NR2 4RB.
Tel: 01603 697640.
Email: naocn@naocn.org.uk
www.naocn.org.uk

➤ **North East Midlands Open College Network** – Unit G, Long Eaton Trade Centre, 52-56 Nottingham Road, Long Eaton, Nottingham NG10 3AU.
Tel: 0115 946 1118.
Email: nemocn@nemocn.org.uk
www.nemocn.org.uk

➤ **North East Open College Network** – Lloyds Bank Chambers, 1 Heaton Road, Byker, Newcastle-upon-Tyne NE6 1SA.
Tel: 0191 224 3434.
Email: neocn@neocn.co.uk
www.neocn.co.uk

➤ **North Wales Open College Network** – Uned/Unit 2, Llys y Fedwen, Parc Menai, Bangor, Gwynedd LL57 4BF.
Tel: 01248 670011.
Email: croeso@nwocn.org.uk
www.nwocn.org.uk

> **Northern Ireland Open College Network** – University of Ulster, Art and Design, 1-51 York Street, Belfast BT15 1ED.
> Tel: 028 9032 0511.
> Email: info@niocn.co.uk
> www.niocn.co.uk

> **Open College Network (North and East London and Hertfordshire)** – 14 Ladysmith Road, Enfield, Middlesex EN1 3AA.
> Tel: 020 8342 2922.
> Email: enquiries@ocnetwork.co.uk
> www.ocnetwork.co.uk

> **Open College Network (South Yorkshire and Humber Region)** – Sheffield Hallam University, 37 Broomgrove Road, Sheffield S10 2BP.
> Tel: 0114 225 2585.
> Email: ocn@shu.ac.uk
> www.shu.ac.uk/ocn

> **Open College Network (TROCN)** – PO Box 310, Middlesbrough, TS4 3YH.
> Tel: 01642 296830.
> Email: admin@trocn.co.uk
> www.trocn.co.uk

> **Open College Network for Central England** – The Gatehouse, Westwood Campus, University of Warwick, Coventry CV4 7AL.
> Tel: 024 7652 4728.
> Email: ocnce@warwick.ac.uk
> www.ocnce.warwick.ac.uk

> **Open College Network Kent and Medway** – Rooms Hg 1-3, Keynes College, University of Kent at Canterbury, Canterbury CT2 7NP.
> Tel: 01227 827823.
> Email: ocn-km@ukc.ac.uk
> www.ocnkm.ac.uk

> **Open College Network North West Midlands** – Winton Chambers, Staffordshire University, College Road, Stoke-on-Trent ST4 2DE.
> Tel: 01782 292712.
> Email: ocnnwm@staffs.ac.uk

> **Open College Network of the South West** – University of Plymouth, Drake Circus, Plymouth PL4 8AA.
> Tel: 01752 232381/232385.
> Email: ocnsw@plymouth.ac.uk
> www.ocnsw.org.uk

> **Open College Network West Midlands** – Wolverhampton Science Park, Glaisher Drive, Wolverhampton WV10 9RU.
> Tel: 01902 824212.
> Email: ocnwm@wlv.ac.uk

> **Open College Network South East Midlands** – 249 Derby Road, Loughborough LE11 5HJ.
> Tel: 01509 211881.
> Email: ocnsem@ocnsem.com

- **Western Region Open College Network** – 53 Oxford Street, Weston-super-Mare, Somerset BS23 1TR.
  Tel: 01934 612727.
  Email: info@wrocn.co.uk

- **Western Region Open College Network (Gloucester Office)** – 122 Bath Road, Cheltenham, Gloucester, GL53 7XJ.
  Tel: 01242 225511.
  Email: info@wrocn.co.uk

- **Open College Network: South Central** – Eastpoint Centre, Burgoyne Road, Thornhill, Southampton SO19 6PB.
  Tel: 023 8036 3413.
  Email: admin@hocn.co.uk

- **South East Wales Open College Network** – Forgemasters' Site, Garth Estate, Taff's Well CF15 7YF.
  Tel: 029 2081 1233.
  Email: croeso@sewocn.co.uk

- **South of England Open College Network** – University of Brighton, A Block, Lewes Road, Brighton BN2 4GJ.
  Tel: 01273 642930.
  Email: seocn@brighton.ac.uk
  www.brighton.ac.uk/seocn

- **South West Wales Open College Network** – The Stebonheath Centre for Enterprise, 'The Old School', Stebonheath Terrace, Llanelli SA15 1NF.
  Tel: 01554 747980.
  Email: croeso@swwocn.org.uk
  www.swwocn.org.uk

- **Surrey and Region Open College Network** – Runnymede Centre, Chertsey Road, Addlestone, Surrey KT15 2EP.
  Tel: 01932 569894.
  Email: socf@surreycc.gov.uk
  www.nocn.org.uk/srocn

- **Thames Region Accrediting Consortium Open College Network** – Thames Valley University, Walpole House, 18-22 Bond Street, Ealing W5 5AA.
  Tel: 020 8567 6678.
  Email: TRAC@tvu.ac.uk
  www.tracocn.co.uk

- **West and North Yorkshire Open College Network** – No 4 College Close, Leeds Metropolitan University, Beckett Park Campus, Leeds LS6 3QS.
  Tel: 0113 283 7460.
  Email: open.college.network@lmu.ac.uk
  www.wnyocn.org.uk

Alternatives to Access courses

If there are no specific Access courses running locally, there may be a similar course available designed by the college itself with a special arrangement with a higher education institution.

Some higher education institutions accept the completion of an Open University course for entry to certain degrees. Individual institutions can provide information.

National Vocational Qualification (NVQ) at level 3, which may be gained in the workplace, may be accepted for entry to some vocational degree, foundation degree or Higher National Diploma or Certificate courses. NVQs can include an element of Accreditation of Prior Learning (see below), so may be particularly relevant to adults wishing to use their knowledge and experience to return to education.

Foundation courses

A number of higher education courses incorporate a foundation year, mainly intended for students leaving school with the 'wrong' A level subjects – e.g. arts A levels for entry to an engineering or science degree course. These courses may also be appropriate for mature students without the usual entry qualifications. There are also some freestanding foundation courses.

Summer schools at universities

There are a number of summer schools aimed to encourage non-traditional entrants to higher education, including mature students. Students should enquire at individual universities.

Accreditation of Prior and Experiential Learning APL/APEL

This is the process which enables people to gain certification for their past achievements, often outside the formal education system, for example in work, leisure or community activities. Identified learning can be matched against nationally recognised qualifications at various levels.

Many universities and colleges of higher education subscribe to credit accumulation and transfer schemes (CATS). These allow accumulation of academic credits towards awards (undergraduate or postgraduate degrees) through the process of APL (or APEL). See also *2:14 – Higher education – first degrees.*

Further information

More information about Access courses is available on the Quality Assurance Agency website: www.qaa.ac.uk/crntwork/access

You can search for Access courses, starting from a keyword, a subject area, a region etc on the UCAS website: www.ucas.com/access

UCAS/Trotman Complete Guides Series 2005 – published by UCAS/Trotman. Price £17.99 each. There are seven guides, each on a different subject area. The guides include information about degree courses, including those that incorporate a foundation year.

The Mature Students' Directory 2005 – published by Trotman. Price £19.99. Contains information on further and higher education institutions and includes information about various issues that adults face when choosing and applying for courses.

Coming Back to Learning – published by Lifetime Careers Publishing. Price £11.99. Covers all learning opportunities for adults.

Returning to Education – published by How To Books. Price £9.99 (£8.49 if bought online). Handbook to help adults identify opportunities and make decisions about their learning.

2:13

Adult residential colleges

Topics covered:

- Details of the adult residential colleges at which students receive adult education bursaries
- Courses offered by these colleges
- Student eligibility
- Where to find out about other adult residential education provision

What are they?

The long-term colleges for residential adult education in the UK provide educational opportunities for adults whose full-time studies stopped when they left school. The colleges are designated for support by the Learning and Skills Council (LSC), which means that nearly all the students attending are funded for up to one year, full-time by a special bursary. The education they offer is mainly academic.

How they work

The colleges have a number of things in common.

- Whilst often vocationally orientated, they offer mainly academic education rather than training.
- They are mainly residential (with non-residential courses at some).
- Few, if any, qualifications are required for entry.
- Selection is normally by interview. Applicants may also have to write an essay and usually have to give the names of referees.
- Most of the colleges offer an Access to higher education qualification, which may also be suitable for entry to some professions.
- The teaching is geared to the learning needs of each student; there are regular individual or small group tutorials with lectures and seminars and a lot of individual study.
- Terms are usually September to December, January to Easter, Easter to June.

Money

Adult education bursaries are available for one-year, full-time diploma and certificate courses – provided the applicant has not previously received a bursary or state funding for higher education. Bursaries cover a grant for living expenses, tuition fees and some travelling expenses. They are not available for courses leading to professional qualifications. See *2:7 – Money* for details of how to apply for a bursary.

Applications

There is no central admissions system. Applicants can obtain prospectuses and application forms directly from the colleges.

Overseas students, in limited numbers, are accepted by most of the colleges. Some have specific charitable trusts for this purpose. However, fees are normally higher than for UK students. Application is normally through the British Council.

The Colleges and the courses they offer

Coleg Harlech

Courses

The college runs an Access programme leading to a University of Wales Foundation Certificate, which satisfies university entry requirements. The full-time, one-year courses include social studies (including Access to nursing option), art and design, music technology and information technology.

Entry requirements

Minimum age 20 and over. Must have been resident in the UK for at least three years. No formal qualifications are needed.

Notes

The college has about 120 students – both men and women. It has its own audio-visual studio, radio station, IT suite, theatre and arts centre.

Bursaries and accommodation are available to all eligible students.

➤ **Coleg Harlech** – Student Admissions, Coleg Harlech, Harlech, Gwynedd LL46 2PU.
Tel: 01766 781900.
Email: info@fc.harlech.ac.uk
www.harlech.ac.uk

Fircroft College

Courses

The college offers a one-year, full-time residential or non-residential programme resulting in an Access qualification, making students eligible for higher education. Examples of subjects covered are social policy, sociology, African and Caribbean studies, race and ethnic studies, literature, mathematics and information technology.

Short residential courses are also available, aimed at personal, professional and political development.

Entry requirements

Minimum age 20 and over, but no upper age limit.

Entry to Access courses is by application form and interview. Apply at any time, preferably before the end of May for the following September.

Entry to short courses is by completion of an application form.

Notes

There are 20 residential places for Access courses each year. Facilities are available for people with sensory impairment and for wheelchair users.

A grant covers tuition and accommodation fees for eligible students.

➤ **Fircroft College of Adult Education** – The Registrar, 1018 Bristol Road, Selly Oak, Birmingham B29 6LH.
Tel: 0121 472 0116.
Email (Short courses): shortcourses@fircroft.ac.uk
Email (Access courses): alex.miles@fircroft.ac.uk
www.fircroft.ac.uk

Hillcroft College (the national residential college for women)

Courses

Full- and part-time programmes of study (validated by the Open University), leading to university entry.

There are business and management courses for women seeking to enter or return to the job market, or who wish to boost skills and gain management qualifications.

They also run assertiveness courses, courses for carers and family learning programmes.

Entry requirements

Minimum age 19 and over. Must usually have been resident in the UK for at least three years. No qualifications are needed.

Notes

Grants are available to most students.

➤ **Hillcroft College** – South Bank, Surbiton, Surrey KT6 6DF.
Tel: 020 8399 2688.
Email: enquiry@hillcroft.ac.uk
www.hillcroft.ac.uk

Newbattle Abbey College

Courses

37-week residential/non-residential courses are offered leading to a nationally-validated award at level 6 in the Scottish Credited Qualifications Framework. This is recognised as an Access qualification for entry to universities and colleges all over the UK. The college also offers a variety of short courses throughout the year.

Entry requirements

Minimum age 20 and over. Entry is based on interview and the only requirements are enthusiasm and aptitude as the course is quite intensive. Two referees are requested.

Notes

The college is situated seven miles south of Edinburgh. There are 80 study bedrooms available to the 60 full-time students plus those on short courses, and an IT learning centre. Full-time bursaries (not loans) are available.

> **Newbattle Abbey College** – Jackie Kane, Dalkeith, Midlothian EH22 3LL.
> Tel: 0131 663 1921.
> Email: office@newbattleabbeycollege.ac.uk
> www.newbattleabbeycollege.ac.uk

Northern College

Courses

A full-time, nine-month diploma course is offered, which is recognised as a valid university entrance qualification. There are some part-time places. Bursaries are available for diploma students. These courses cover a number of basic disciplines and study skills. Optional subjects include: psychology, sociology, history, European studies, information and communications technology, environmental studies, women's studies and literature and cultural studies. The course starts in September.

Many free, short courses are offered throughout the year; most last for two to three days.

Entry requirements

Admission to the diploma course is by application form and interview. Minimum age 21 and over.

Notes

Residential accommodation is provided in single and shared study bedrooms. Non-residential places are available. There is a children's centre on campus for children aged over six months and under 14 years – limited places are available. Support is provided by a personal tutor and student services. The library and learning resource centre includes access to email and internet facilities.

> **Northern College** – Registry, Wentworth Castle, Stainborough, Barnsley S75 3ET.
> Tel: 01226 776010.
> Minicom: 01226 776026.
> Email: registry@northern.ac.uk
> www.northern.ac.uk

Plater College Oxford

Courses

One-year courses leading to the Certificate of Higher Education, a modular, continuously-assessed course, accredited by the Open University with 120 CATS points. There are four pathway options: legal studies, social administration, theology and religious studies and business with business ethics.

A variety of weekend and mid-week short courses are available.

Entry requirements

No formal entrance qualifications are required for the Certificate of Higher Education course. Admission is via an application form giving two referees and a covering letter followed by an interview.

Notes

There are approximately 80 full-time, residential students. Students have access to libraries in the University of Oxford and Oxford Brookes University. Most students qualify for a bursary that covers living costs and fees. The college actively encourages enquiries from people with disabilities and people from a wide range of socially excluded and deprived backgrounds including the homeless and ex-forces personnel. Although Plater is a Catholic college, it welcomes applications from students of any faith or belief.

➤ **Plater College Oxford** – The Registrar, Pullens Lane, Oxford OX3 0DT.
  Tel: 01865 740500.
  Email: admissions@plater.ac.uk
  www.plater.ac.uk

Ruskin College

Courses

One-year courses leading to the Certificate of Higher Education in the following subjects: computing, creative writing and English studies, history, labour relations, law, studying society and women's studies.

There is also a three-year degree in social work, a two-year foundation degree in youth and community work, a one-year Diploma of Higher Education in social change and two-year, part-time MAs in women's studies and in public history. There are also part-time and short courses in a wide variety of subjects.

Entry requirements

No formal academic qualifications are required for the Certificate of Higher Education course, but an interest in learning and life experience are important. Minimum age 19 and over. Entrance via a piece of writing about yourself and personal or telephone interview.

Notes

There are approximately 150 resident students and around 40 non-resident 'external' students on long courses. Limited family accommodation is available. There is a small nursery.

➤ **Ruskin College** – The General Secretary, Walton Street, Oxford OXI 2HE.
  Tel: 01865 310713.
  Email: enquiries@ruskin.ac.uk
  www.ruskin.ac.uk

Other residential colleges

There are many other residential colleges, which offer mostly short-term leisure courses, but some lead to qualifications. See *2:10 – Learning for leisure*. Some specialise in music, art or creative writing for example, while others offer a wide range of studies. There is even a college especially for WI members. Many of these are listed in:

Adult Learning Yearbook 2004/5 – published annually by NIACE, £21.95.

City and Guilds also provides a facility for searching for short residential courses. See www.timetolearn.org.uk

2:14

Higher education – first degrees

Topics covered:

- The choice of qualifications and courses in higher education
- Entry requirements for mature students
- Applying for higher education
- Different ways of studying for a degree
- Accreditation for previous work and study

Higher education is traditionally associated with study after A level or equivalent at the age of 18. However, with the recent expansion in the number of places, universities now recruit a high proportion of mature students and are being encouraged to widen access to HE for previously under-represented groups.

Adults considering higher education should be aware of:

- the choice of courses on offer – degrees such as BA, BSc, BEd etc (some are called MSci or MA in Scotland), HNC/HND, DipHE etc

- the variation in length of course (two years for HND; three to four years for most degrees or longer for courses such as medicine)

- availability of part-time and sandwich courses as well as standard full-time courses

- foundation degrees which may take two years full-time or can be studied over a longer period while working

- the availability of HE courses of one or more years at some further education colleges

- the need for self discipline; clients may not be aware of the amount of private research and background reading involved.

Entry requirements for mature students

The entry requirements for each course vary enormously. Although for degrees the minimum requirements are generally accepted as five GCSE and two A level passes (or equivalent), popular courses at popular universities will be more demanding. But most of the information published applies to 18-year-old school leavers; mature applicants are often treated very differently. They may not be asked for such specific qualifications. Access courses designed especially for mature students, or even evidence of recent advanced level study, are often accepted for entry. Most institutions will interview their mature applicants to ascertain:

- at what level they have studied recently, and how successfully

- what success they achieved at school (if appropriate)

- what employment they have had, whether paid or voluntary, and the level of responsibility held – as supervisor or manager, for example

- any professional or vocational qualifications held or being studied

- key skills gained during their career

- any hobbies and interests which may be relevant to the course.

In most cases, universities will look favourably on mature applicants, provided that they can satisfy the admissions tutor that they have:

- the ability to complete the course

- the self discipline required to cope with degree-level study

- sufficient interest in and understanding of the subject.

Mature students are advised to contact the department of the university or college they wish to apply to direct, to discuss their qualifications and experience.

For information on adult entry to higher education, see *2:12 – Access and other adult routes* and *2:7 – Money* for details about student finance.

Choosing a course of study

With more than 55,000 higher education courses on offer and over 300 universities and colleges throughout the UK, choosing the right course can be difficult.

To assist in this search, clients can:

- use some of the computer programs widely available, such as *Course Discover* (published by Trotman), or the handbooks and general guides to higher education, some of which are listed at the end of this section

- use prospectuses, video prospectuses and the institution's website (given in the UCAS publication *The Big Guide: The Official Universities and Colleges Entrance Guide* and on the UCAS website: www.ucas.com) to find out more about the course, the methods of course delivery and assessment and the university or college itself

- visit the institution, either individually or on publicised open days – several universities and colleges now run virtual open days.

In choosing a course subject, clients should consider:

- whether the subject is one they really want to devote three or four years of their lives to

- whether they want to study a specific subject, or to take a course that will qualify them for a job – such as a physiotherapy degree or a degree offering qualified teacher status

- if they prefer to take a single subject or to make up a degree from a number of major and minor subjects

- whether they would value a year's work experience in industry, which may be available on some vocational courses

- whether, if studying a foreign language, it is practical for them to spend a term or a year abroad as part of the course.

There is no right or wrong choice. It is simply a matter of individual preference.

Applying for higher education

Applicants for full-time and sandwich first degrees – including teaching, medicine and art and design courses, DipHE and HND courses at all UK universities and most colleges of higher education will go through the Universities and Colleges Admissions Service (UCAS) system. UCAS acts as a central clearing house for all applications. Art and design students should be aware of the two different application routes.

For 2005 entry, application forms – and instructions for their completion – are available direct from UCAS, local colleges or from local adult information, advice and guidance agencies. Electronic and online application systems are also available to clients via institutions such as colleges and guidance services. From 2006 entry, UCAS is moving to an all electronic entry system, through the online application system, ucasapply. Applicants who are applying independently (i.e. not through a college) will also be able to apply through this system, from wherever there is access to the internet.

➤ **UCAS** – Rosehill, New Barn Lane, Cheltenham GL52 3LZ.
   Tel: 0870 1122211 (for applicant materials and enquiries).
   Email: enquiries@ucas.ac.uk (gives an automated response with useful information)
   www.ucas.com

Some useful questions

- Will they accept students with other qualifications?

- Does the university have any linked Access courses, and what success level do they require?

- Are there any taster courses? Is there the opportunity to sit in on some lectures beforehand?

- Do they have any special mature student accommodation, for example for families?

- Is there a mature entry exam? A few universities will allow applicants with no qualifications to sit their entrance exam to determine whether they have the ability to do the course. What help do they offer students wishing to take this route, and what form does it take?

Some colleges of higher education and specialist colleges operate outside the UCAS system. Applicants need to make direct contact with these institutions.

Part-time study

Some mature applicants find full-time study is impossible because of financial constraints. Giving up a job in order to study is not always an option. Educational institutions are introducing an increasing number of part-time courses. Birkbeck College in London specialises in part-time evening courses for those who have other responsibilities or activities during the day.

Some part-time degree courses are offered largely as distance-learning packages, such as those offered by the Open University. Others will offer a mix of Saturday, weekday and evening lectures. Some courses assume limited attendance during the day alongside full-time students. Potential students should contact the institutions of their choice for further information.

Foundation degrees

Foundation degrees, which are employment-related qualifications, were developed by universities and colleges, together with employers. They can be taken on a part-time basis and are delivered in different ways, for example, through distance learning or at a local further education college. Foundation degrees enable progression to an honours degree. See www.foundationdegree.org.uk/ for more information.

Open University

The Open University was created specifically for mature students – although since the introduction of tuition fees it now also attracts more young people. It allows students to work from home with only the minimum amount of attendance at seminars and, for some courses, summer schools. There are no formal entry requirements for most courses. For further information, see *2:16 – The Open University*.

learndirect – Learning through Work

This is an innovative scheme to enable people to achieve higher education qualifications, including first degrees, whilst staying in employment. Students design their own programme of study based on their work, career aspirations and personal development to date. Participating higher education institutions offer these work-based qualifications using online technology. For more details refer to *2:19 – Learning in the workplace*.

Accreditation for previous work and study

Credit accumulation and transfer schemes

The increase of modular courses and a variety of government and European Union initiatives have led to much greater flexibility in the provision of higher education. Many universities and colleges operate credit accumulation and transfer schemes (CATS), which means that students can collect credits from a number of different courses and use them towards their final qualification.

CATS enable students to:

- transfer across subject boundaries within one institution

- transfer within a subject but across different institutions in both the UK and abroad

- gain part exemption from examinations of professional bodies – or use professional body qualifications as credit towards an academic course

- combine periods of full-time and part-time study

- continue studying after a break.

In Scotland, the Scottish Credit and Qualifications Framework (SCQF) shows how different learning programmes relate to each other. The Framework gives each qualification SCQF credit points, where one point represents a notional ten hours of learning. Most mainstream qualifications will be in the Framework by 2006. For further information, visit the SCQF website at www.scqf.org.uk

Wales has a similar credit framework, called the Credit and Qualifications Framework for Wales (CQFW). More details are available on the following website: www.elwa.org.uk/creditframework

Accreditation of prior learning or experience

The process of gaining credit for previously certificated qualifications or learning is usually known as the Accreditation of Prior Learning (APL) or, sometimes, the Accreditation of Prior Certificated Learning (APCL) or Accreditation of Prior Learning and Achievement (APL&A). It is particularly valuable to mature learners wishing to re-enter education or training, or reduce the overall time of the study programme. Sometimes qualifications are given an equivalence, but if not, clients may go through an assessment process in order to gain credit for modules or units of a course they intend to study in higher education. Universities and colleges may charge for this assessment.

Through the process of the Accreditation of Prior Experiential Learning (APEL), it is also possible for work or voluntary experience to count towards a higher education course. In Scotland, this process is also known as the Recognition of Prior informal Learning (RPL). Guidelines on recognising prior informal, or experiential, learning within the SCQF are currently being developed (visit www.scqf.org.uk/rpl). These guidelines will be aimed at colleges, universities and other learning and training providers in Scotland.

APEL, or RPL, can help people to build upon the knowledge and skills they have already gained through their experience. Recognising prior informal, or experiential, learning can enable adults without formal qualifications to gain access to further learning at all levels. It can also be used to gain credit within academic programmes. In order to gain credit, clients have to reflect upon the skills and knowledge gained during their work experience and put together evidence of this learning. Some colleges and universities actually offer a module to help students identify and present evidence of relevant learning and experience. Once again, a charge may be made, but it is worth it if credit is awarded.

Universities and colleges of higher education will be able to advise on whether a client's previous qualifications, learning or experience could count. The best approach is to ask several higher education institutions, as their answers may vary.

Further information

Degree Course Offers 2005 Entry – published by Trotman, price £26.99. Lists all the different courses available at universities and other HE institutions, and the qualifications likely to be needed for entry.

Choosing your Degree Course and University – published by Trotman, price £21.99. Compares the content of different degree courses and the ranking of institutions according to teaching and research.

CRAC Degree Course Guides 2003/04 and 2004/05 – published by Trotman, price £9.99 each. There are 20 guides covering one or more related subject areas.

UCAS/Trotman Complete Guides Series 2005 – published by UCAS/Trotman, price £17.99 each. There are seven guides, each on a different subject area. The guides include information on course characteristics, employment prospects and case studies.

Directory of University and College Entry (DUCE) 2005/06 – published by Trotman, price £39.99. Lists groups of similar higher education courses together so users can compare entry requirements.

UCAS/Universities Scotland: Entrance Guide to Higher Education in Scotland 2005 Entry – published by UCAS, price £9.95. Lists entry requirements for courses available in Scotland and gives advice on how to apply for them.

The Big Guide: The Official Universities and Colleges Entrance Guide 2005 Entry – published by UCAS, price £27.50. Lists entry requirements for all courses entered via UCAS. Information is also available on www.ucas.com

The Mature Students' Guide to Higher Education – published by UCAS. Free.

The Mature Students' Directory 2005 – published by Trotman, price £19.99. Contains information on further and higher education institutions and includes information about various issues that adults face when choosing and applying for courses.

Coming Back to Learning – published by Lifetime Careers Publishing, price £11.99. Covers all learning opportunities for adults.

Initial Teacher Training Handbook 2005 – published annually by UCAS, price £9.99.

Net that Course – published by Kogan Page, price £8.99. Demonstrates how to use the internet to find out about degree courses, including overseas study and 'virtual' visits to institutions.

The Ultimate University Ranking Guide 2005 – published by Trotman, price £14.99. Ranks universities in a number of ways including quality of teaching and employment prospects, and gives the top ten universities for mature students.

2:15

Higher education – higher degrees

Topics covered:

- Reasons for postgraduate study
- Courses and qualifications available
- Methods of postgraduate study
- How to apply
- Postgraduate funding

Why do people study for a higher degree?

Each year, around 12% of graduates go on to further study. People decide to undertake a higher degree for a variety of reasons, including:

- to change career direction
- to gain specific practical skills, or analytical skills through academic research
- to improve employment prospects – postgraduates are less likely to be unemployed than graduates
- because of a desire to study a particular subject in greater depth
- to update existing skills or knowledge of the subject taken as a first degree.

Traditionally, graduates studied for a higher degree immediately after a first degree, but increasingly postgraduate opportunities are being used as a form of career development. Some postgraduate courses are open to people other than graduates.

Courses and qualifications available

A range of postgraduate courses and qualifications exists – some are described below.

- Vocational courses leading to qualifications which are required for particular professions, for example Postgraduate Certificate of Education (PGCE) for would-be teachers, postgraduate Diploma in Law and the Legal Practice Course for those wanting to become barristers or solicitors.

- Vocational courses which are not compulsory but which may help entry to particular occupations, for example the qualifications of the Chartered Institute of Personnel and Development or journalism courses.

- Skills courses which add practical abilities to academic knowledge, such as computer programming, languages and secretarial skills.

- Academic courses leading to Certificates, Diplomas, Masters degrees or Doctorates in virtually every subject imaginable.

The number of postgraduate courses has increased in recent years, with the major growth being in subjects such as business administration, computing, social sciences, humanities and courses related to medicine.

Who awards higher degrees?

Like first degrees, higher degrees are awarded by universities. All universities in the UK, including the Open University, award higher degrees of some kind; the exact kinds of degree vary with the institution.

Where to study

Most universities offer research degrees. Some specialise in taught programmes; others have expertise or facilities for particular research topics. Universities often have highly specialised facilities for research into scientific or medical subjects; competition is very fierce for places at these universities. As higher degrees are awarded by the universities themselves, it is usually possible for the scheme of research to change and develop as it progresses.

Colleges and institutes of higher education may offer higher degrees. There are also business schools, which may be independent or attached to higher education institutions. Higher degrees from these bodies may be awarded by a nearby university.

Entry requirements

Most institutions expect a good academic background for entry to a postgraduate course. Exact requirements vary according to the popularity of the course. Higher qualifications (such as a 2.1 honours degree) are likely to be demanded for a research degree than for a taught course.

Many institutions are willing to accept qualifications other than the usual first degree, if they think the applicant will add something to the study group and/or can fund themselves through the course. Some courses, such as Masters in Business Administration (MBA), require relevant work experience as well.

Applicants should contact the admissions tutor for the course they are considering to check entry requirements.

Overseas study

British university graduates are held in high regard abroad, so postgraduate work is available, especially in the USA and Canada. Scholarships may be available for study abroad. See *2:22 Learning opportunities abroad* for more information.

Credit accumulation and transfer schemes (CATS)

It is possible to accumulate credit for previous study and experience, and use it towards gaining a postgraduate qualification. See *2:14 Higher education – first degrees* for more details.

Methods of study

Postgraduate qualifications can be gained in a variety of ways, including through:

- taught courses

- research degrees

- part-time study

- modular programmes

- open and distance learning.

Taught courses

These courses usually last a year, which is longer than the normal academic year, or occasionally two years. A Master's degree course is made up of lectures and examinations, followed by months of private research for a thesis or dissertation. A Certificate or Diploma course is shorter and does not usually include the research element. Sometimes there is a system of continuous assessment to measure progress throughout the course.

Certificates and Diplomas are usually awarded after vocational courses in specific fields, such as teaching. Degrees may be Master of Arts (MA); Master of Education (MEd); Master of Science (MSc); Master of Business Administration (MBA). There are also some taught doctorates, such as Doctor of Business Administration (DBA) or Doctor of Engineering (DEng).

Research degrees

The research begins with the student deciding what he or she wants to study, why, where and under the supervision of whom. They should look at the record of different institutions and the individual academics they would be working under. Research degrees include a Master of Philosophy (MPhil) which usually takes one or two years and a doctorate (PhD) which takes at least three years – usually longer – if studied full-time.

It is possible to study for a one-year Master's degree before converting to a PhD. Some universities offer a one-year Master of Research (MRes) programme of study. This provides research training, with strong links with industry, which will help students who wish to go on to a PhD.

Research degrees are awarded by thesis – an extended written account of the research and its findings. Usually this will be about as long as the average novel. The advantage of a degree by research is that only the topic of study is fixed. How it is studied is up to the student to decide, in consultation with their supervisor. This can be exciting, but it can also be daunting to those used to studying set syllabuses. Self-motivation is vital.

Students need to check the entry requirements of individual institutions. If hoping for Research Council funding (see later), students should choose and apply for a course as early as possible.

Part-time courses

Many postgraduate courses are now available on a part-time basis. Arrangements for part-time study vary enormously. Courses by instruction often require one full day's attendance a week at university or college for two or three years. Degrees by research, when experimental work is not necessary, may be achieved through evening attendance only. It takes about two to four years for an MPhil, and four, five or more for a PhD.

The advantage of studying part-time is that study can be undertaken alongside employment. However, students should think carefully about the various demands on their time, which might make it difficult to follow a part-time course. Once again, motivation is vital.

learndirect – Learning through Work

This is an innovative scheme to enable people to achieve higher education qualifications, including postgraduate qualifications, whilst staying in employment. Students design their own programme of study based on their work, career aspirations and personal development to date. Participating higher education institutions offer these work-based qualifications using online technology. For more details refer to *2:19 Learning in the workplace.*

Modular courses

More and more taught courses are being offered on a modular basis – the mix and match method of study. Courses are divided into a number of units, some compulsory and some optional. Postgraduate qualifications are awarded when a particular number of credits or units are obtained. The main benefit of this type of study is that the student can concentrate on areas that they enjoy, but they should be careful not to exclude the fundamentals in which employers may be interested.

Open and distance learning

The Open University, and other open learning colleges, offer a range of higher degrees, research degrees etc which may be a more flexible way to study. See *2:16 The Open University* and *2:17 Open/distance and other independent learning.* Many universities also now offer their courses by open or distance learning.

How to apply

There is no central application scheme, like that for first degrees. Applicants should:

- use directories and databases such as those listed at the end of this chapter to discover which institutions offer programmes in their areas of interest

- obtain and read prospectuses or view video prospectuses

- visit the institution's website

- find out who the admissions tutor is for the course, and where possible arrange to see them in person; alternatively write or telephone

- apply directly to the individual institution in the autumn of the final undergraduate year, if still a student (candidates who are seeking funding should make it clear that they want to apply for an award).

Applicants should be advised to take time, care and trouble over the presentation of their application. A covering letter and/or CV may help to persuade admissions tutors of their enthusiasm and suitability. Applicants for research degrees will have to submit a fairly detailed scheme, outlining what they intend to study and how they intend to approach it. They should be prepared for some searching questions on this and will almost certainly be interviewed before being offered a place.

Postgraduate funding

There is no single source of financial support for postgraduate education and training. It is much easier to find a place on a postgraduate course than it is to find the funding for it.

Most of the available funding for postgraduate qualifications comes from government-funded Research Councils. However, there are many other sources of funding a potential postgraduate student can access.

For more detailed information on financing postgraduate study, see *2:7 – Money*.

Further information

Broadsheet newspapers, specialist journals and the educational press, such as *Times Higher Education Supplement*, carry details of postgraduate opportunities.

Clients who are still studying could see an advisor at their university careers service or at their student union welfare office to discuss postgraduate opportunities.

CRAC Prospects Postgraduate Directory 2005 – available from Graduate Prospects, price £105.50. Provides information on over 19,000 full- and part-time UK postgraduate courses.

The CRAC *Prospects Postgraduate Directory* is also available in separate volumes:

Volume 1 – Arts and Humanities – price £33.50

Volume 2 – Science and Engineering – price £38.50

Volume 3 – Business and Social Science – price £33.50.

Postgraduate Courses Series 2005/6 – published by Trotman, £9.99 each. There are three guides, each on a different subject area:

Art and Design Postgraduate Courses

Engineering Postgraduate Courses

Physical Sciences Postgraduate Courses

Hobsons Graduate Career Directory 2005 – available from Trotman, price £24.99. Lists more than 60,000 vacancies and graduate courses.

Postgraduate Study and Research – available from Graduate Prospects, price £3.30. May be available for reference in Connexions/careers libraries.

The following websites provide information about postgraduate study: www.prospects.ac.uk www.postgrad.hobsons.com

The Association of Business Schools' website has a facility to search for information about postgraduate business courses: www.abs.bized.ac.uk

2:16

The Open University (OU)

Topics covered:

- The range and level of courses offered by the Open University
- Learning methods and support provided
- Assessment methods
- Provision for students with disabilities or living in remote areas
- The costs involved and financial support
- The value of an OU degree

With over 200,000 students, the Open University (OU) is the UK's largest university. 22% of all part-time higher education students in the UK study with the OU. It is also the only university that caters particularly for mature students. Its approach takes into account the problems adults have in returning to study (although an increasing number of school-leavers are turning to the OU as an alternative to full-time university study). As well as taking students who want to study for degrees, it has developed a wide range of non-degree courses to cater for the education of the community. People choose to study with the OU for many different reasons – some want to develop their careers, many want to make more of a personal interest and others want to achieve an ambition.

Listed below are some of the ways the OU differs from other universities.

- Most courses have no minimum entry requirements.
- About two-thirds of all OU students are between the ages of 25 and 44; all students are 18 or over.
- The vast majority of students are part-time.
- Most of the work is by distance learning supported by personal contact with tutors.
- Courses may include residential schools.
- Some courses have BBC radio and TV programmes associated with them.
- With a few exceptions, OU courses are open to residents of EU countries and of certain other counties outside the EU.

- Rather than following the usual academic year, most undergraduate courses start in February and run continuously for nine months (applications should be in by the October in the year prior to a course starting).

- Qualifications can be taken over many years, with breaks in between if required.

- Students can start at any level suitable and take as many or as few courses as they like.

Courses available

Diplomas and first degrees

These are modular, combining different courses. Each course completed successfully earns points towards a diploma, or a degree with or without honours. People who have not studied at degree level before should start at level 1 or with an Openings short course. It is not necessary to specialise in one subject; a degree can be made up from a very wide spectrum. However, specialist degree profiles may also be studied to gain recognition by most professional institutes. Most people study just one course each year.

A 60-point course takes around 16 hours of study per week (sometimes longer). A 30-point course takes approximately 8 hours a week. Although each course has to be completed within a set time, there is usually no limit on the time taken to gain a degree.

Students need 120 points to achieve a diploma and 360 points to achieve an honours degree. Whether a degree is a BA or BSc will depend on the balance of courses taken.

Further information can be found in the OU's *Undergraduate Courses Catalogue* and the accompanying *Undergraduate Certificates, Diplomas and Degrees Prospectus* and on the website at www3.open.ac.uk/stepforward

Higher degrees and research degrees

Higher degrees

The OU also offers a programme of taught higher degrees. A range of Master's degrees is available, including an MA in Education, an MBA and MSc courses in mathematics and science subjects.

For more information see the *Higher Degrees Prospectus,* or look at: www.open.ac.uk/brochure/higherdegrees

Research degrees

It is possible to take a research degree such as a BPhil, MPhil or PhD full- or part-time internally (at Milton Keynes or at the Oxford Research Unit) or externally part-time.

For more information see the *Research Degrees Prospectus* or look at: www.open.ac.uk/research-school

Non-degree courses

For students who don't want to take a full diploma or degree, or who would like a taste of

OU study, there is a range of options, including those listed below. Remember that single undergraduate courses can be taken without aiming to complete a full degree.

Short courses

There are an increasing number of short courses on offer by the OU. These range from eight- or twelve-week courses to one-week residential schools. They range in credit from 10 to 15 points, depending on the amount of study required.

Certificates

Certificates are usually the first step on the ladder to undergraduate-level study. However, certain ones e.g. the Specialist Teacher Assistant Certificate and the Certificate in Accounting, are designed for professional purposes.

Study packs

The OU offers a wide range of self-contained study packs for those interested in a particular field but who do not wish to enrol on a course.

Preparing for degree-level study

The OU provides its own preparatory packages for prospective undergraduate students. In addition, courses are available to specifically prepare people for degree-level study. Through an Openings course, lasting approximately 14 weeks, students complete three short pieces of written work. These assignments are designed to help develop a student's study skills, develop their confidence and provide a taste of what OU study is really like. By completing an optional extra assignment at the end of an Openings course, a student will gain 10 credit points towards a qualification.

Clients should remember that preparation for a course is worthwhile; an OU degree is hard work.

How it's done

The correspondence material

Students are sent their materials by post. These may include specially written teaching texts, computer software, CD-ROMs, home experiment kits (for science and technology courses), audiocassettes, slides and videos. Students may also be sent exercises, self-assessment tests and assignments.

Broadcasts

Some courses include radio and television programmes on the national BBC network. These make the course more immediate or help to reinforce some of the more difficult ideas in the texts. For students outside the UK, these programmes may be sent on video or cassette. www.open2.net provides listings of OU broadcasts.

Support from tutors

Course tutors usually hold regular tutorial meetings at local study centres. Tutorials provide a valuable chance to talk to fellow students and, in addition, informal study groups are often set up. Tutorial support is also offered by post and possibly by telephone, computer conferencing, fax and email. Whether a student's tutor will be able to provide tuition in person will depend on the number of students in the area.

Residential schools

Some courses, particularly those in science, technology and languages, include a one-week residential course, usually in the summer. These are held at a university and provide a chance for students to experience the traditional university atmosphere, use equipment (e.g. laboratories and university libraries) and meet fellow students and staff. They also allow for the discussion of ideas and for participation in group activities.

> **Open University Residential Schools Student Office**
> Tel: 01908 653235.
> Email: res-schools-student-enquiries@open.ac.uk
> www.open.ac.uk/residential-schools

How it's assessed

Continuously

The degree is not achieved purely on the strength of passing an exam. Students are assessed continuously. At intervals throughout the course, computer-marked and tutor-marked assignment results are recorded and assessments are combined with the final exam result to produce an overall grade for the course.

By exam

At the end of most courses there is a three-hour exam at a local centre which contributes to the total marks. Alternatively, there may be an end of course assessment – a project or extended essay – completed from home and submitted by a set date.

Transferability

If a potential student has already successfully completed some higher education-level study, they may be able to count it towards an OU qualification by applying for transferred credit. Further information is available on the website below and there is also a facility to download a credit claim form. Alternatively, the Credit Transfer Centre can provide advice.

> **Credit Transfer Centre** – The Open University, PO Box 80, Milton Keynes MK7 6AS.
> Tel: 01908 653077.
> Email: credit-transfer@open.ac.uk
> www3.open.ac.uk/credit-transfer

Students with disabilities

The OU has developed a wide range of services for students with disabilities. These are coordinated by the Office for Students with Disabilities as well as at Regional Centres and central departments.

OU courses are taught through a range of media and materials can often be produced in alternative formats to suit the needs of individual students. For instance, the OU may be able to provide students with transcripts of broadcasts, or audiocassettes instead of printed course materials. The website shown below gives information about the range of services available and course materials offered in alternative formats.

➤ **The Office for Students with Disabilities** – The Open University, PO Box 79, Milton Keynes MK7 6AA.
Tel: 01908 653745.
Textphone: 01908 655978
Email: osd-wh@open.ac.uk
www3.open.ac.uk/learners-guide/disability

Studying in remote areas

In some remote areas, extra telephone and perhaps email tuition is available for students who are far away from a study centre.

Students who live in an area of Scotland too far away from a study centre to attend regularly, if at all, will be supported by the Regional Centre (see contact details under further information). They will also be allocated a course tutor who may be able to provide support by post, telephone, email or occasional meetings.

What it costs

The cost of an OU course depends on the nature and level of the course itself. The course fee usually includes the cost of residential schools (if applicable), most learning materials, tuition and assessment. Clients will have to pay for their own study materials. They may need to purchase equipment needed for certain courses, buy set books or pay for travel to residential schools, exam centres etc.

If students cannot afford to pay their fees in one go, they may pay course fees by instalments by charging the fees to an Open University Student Budget Account (OUSBA).

➤ **OUSBA** – The Open University, PO Box 508, Walton Hall, Milton Keynes MK7 6HX.
Tel: 0845 769 7937.
www.open.ac.uk/ousba

Financial support

The OU has a Financial Award Fund and receives additional funding from the Government to help some students (e.g. the unemployed, those receiving certain state benefits and those on a low income) who would otherwise find it difficult to pay their fees. Other means of financial support are also available for people who meet certain eligibility criteria. Clients should ask at their Regional Centre for further information about help with fees and study costs.

Sponsorship

Some employers are generous and sponsor employees for all or part of an OU course. Students should apply to their employers' personnel or training department. The OU can send information, and a sponsorship form is included in registration packs.

Is it worth it?

Are OU degrees as good as others?

The OU type of modular degree is getting more common. Employers and others are becoming more familiar with the idea of a degree that shows students have worked hard for some years at several subjects rather than studying one or two subjects in greater depth. Most British universities accept OU credits for entry to later years of their own courses and also accept OU degrees for postgraduate study. Most professional institutions and bodies recognise OU degree profiles.

Students

'They give a good indication of its worth. When they've done an OU degree they're often hooked, and keep on doing other OU courses for years.'

Open University Students' Association (OUSA)

Membership of the OUSA includes all currently registered students of the OU and does not carry a subscription.

The OUSA provides the support services necessary for the effective representation of students' views, both within the OU and outside. It also offers help with educational and welfare problems, sponsors weekend schools, organises self-help study groups, encourages the formation of societies for special interest groups, operates a marketing service, and provides a range of social activities for members and their families through its branches.

The governing body is the annual Conference attended by representatives from all study centres and affiliated societies. An Executive Committee has responsibility for implementing the policies determined by the Conference.

➤ **OUSA** – PO Box 397, Walton Hall, Milton Keynes MK7 6BE.
  Tel: 01908 652026.
  Email: ousa@student.open.ac.uk
  www2.open.ac.uk/ousa

Further information

To buy OU publications

➤ **Open University Worldwide Ltd** – Walton Hall, Milton Keynes MK7 6AA.
  Tel: 01908 858785.
  Email: ouwenq@open.ac.uk
  www.ouw.co.uk

General enquiries and course information

> **Course Information and Advice Centre** – The Open University, PO Box 724, Milton Keynes MK7 6ZS.
> Tel: 01908 653231.
> Course reservations: 0845 300 6090.
> Email: general-enquiries@open.ac.uk
> www.open.ac.uk

The website www3.open.ac.uk/learners-guide provides advice and guidance to help students and potential OU students make informed decisions about their study. It also includes information on support for learning.

OU Regional Centres

Advisory staff based at each of the OU's Regional Centres can answer queries about course or qualification choice and all aspects of studying with the OU.

> **London 01** – The Open University in London, 1-11 Hawley Crescent, Camden, London NW1 8NP.
> Tel: 020 7485 6597.
> Email: london@open.ac.uk

Area covered: Greater London.

> **South 02** – The Open University in the South, Foxcombe Hall, Boars Hill, Oxford OX1 5HR.
> Tel: 01865 327000.
> Email: south@open.ac.uk

Area covered: Berkshire, Buckinghamshire, Channel Islands, Dorset, Hampshire, Isle of Wight, Oxfordshire, part of Wiltshire.

> **South West 03** – The Open University in the South West, 4 Portwall Lane, Bristol BS1 6ND.
> Tel: 0117 929 9641.
> Email: south-west@open.ac.uk

Area covered: Bristol and its neighbouring unitary authorities, Cornwall, Devon, Gloucestershire, Somerset, Scilly Isles, most of Wiltshire.

> **West Midlands 04** – The Open University in the West Midlands, 66 High Street, Harborne, Birmingham B17 9NB.
> Tel: 0121 426 1661.
> Email: west-midlands@open.ac.uk

Area covered: Herefordshire, Worcestershire, Shropshire, most of Staffordshire, Warwickshire, West Midlands.

> **East Midlands 05** – The Open University in the East Midlands, Clarendon Park, Clumber Avenue, Sherwood Rise, Nottingham NG5 1AH.
> Tel: 0115 962 5451.
> Email: east-midlands@open.ac.uk

Area covered: most of Derbyshire, Leicestershire, Lincolnshire, Northamptonshire, Rutland, Nottinghamshire, part of Staffordshire (Burton-on-Trent area).

➤ **East of England 06** – The Open University in the East of England, Cintra House, 12 Hills Road, Cambridge CB2 1PF.
Tel: 01223 364721.
Email: east-of-england@open.ac.uk

Area covered: Bedfordshire, Cambridgeshire, Essex, Hertfordshire, Norfolk, Suffolk.

➤ **Yorkshire 07** – The Open University in Yorkshire, 2 Trevelyan Square, Boar Lane, Leeds LS1 6ED.
Tel: 0113 244 4431.
Email: yorkshire@open.ac.uk

Area covered: North, South and West Yorkshire, East Ridings of Yorkshire.

➤ **North West 08** – The Open University in the North West, 351 Altrincham Road, Sharston, Manchester M22 4UN.
Tel: 0161 998 7272.
Email: north-west@open.ac.uk

Area covered: Cheshire, part of Derbyshire, Isle of Man, Lancashire, Greater Manchester, Merseyside.

➤ **North 09** – The Open University in the North, Eldon House, Regent Centre, Gosforth, Newcastle upon Tyne NE3 3PW.
Tel: 0191 284 1611.
Email: north@open.ac.uk

Area covered: Cumbria, Durham, Northumberland, Tyne and Wear, Teeside.

➤ **Wales 10** – The Open University in Wales, 24 Cathedral Road, Cardiff CF11 9SA.
Tel: 029 2066 5636.
Email: wales@open.ac.uk

Area covered: Wales.

➤ **Scotland 11** – The Open University in Scotland, 10 Drumsheugh Gardens, Edinburgh EH3 7QJ.
Tel: 0131 226 3851.
Email: scotland@open.ac.uk

Area covered: Scotland.

➤ **Ireland 12** – The Open University in Ireland, 40 University Road, Belfast BT7 1SU.
Tel: 028 9024 5025.
Email: ireland@open.ac.uk

Area covered: Northern Ireland, Republic of Ireland.

➤ **South East 13** – The Open University in the South East, St James' House, 150 London Road, East Grinstead RH19 1HG.
Tel: 01342 327821.
Email: south-east@open.ac.uk

Area covered: Kent, Surrey, East Sussex, West Sussex.

2:17

Open/distance and other independent learning

Topics covered:

- A description of open and distance learning

- How to choose a course

- Information about providers of open and distance learning

- Other resources for independent learning, such as books, CDs, computer programs, TV and radio broadcasts, the internet etc

What is open or distance learning?

Open learning is a broad definition of flexible learning, which can include using a resource centre, some face-to-face tuition as well as studying at home from prepared materials. The student has control of the learning situation. Distance learning is literally learning at a distance from the provider, where any personal tuition that accompanies the course materials is likely to be by post, telephone or computer link.

- Individuals can learn at a

    - time

    - place

    - and pace

    to suit themselves.

- Student-centred learning methods and appropriate media, such as video, text, audio, websites and computer packages are used.

- Typically an open learning course comprises:

    - a pack of learning materials

    - arrangements for tutorial support as and when required.

- Many producers of open and distance learning materials align their materials with national qualifications.

- Few courses impose entrance qualifications.

- As a method of learning, open or distance learning can be lonely and hard, requiring a great deal of self-discipline.

- Open and distance learning courses are a way of getting qualifications, gaining knowledge, and refreshing old skills, as well as learning new ones.

- Many universities and colleges offer open and distance learning as an alternative means of accessing their courses; the UHI Millennium Institute in Scotland links various scattered sites through distance learning facilities.

How much do the courses cost?

Prices vary greatly, depending on how much tutorial support is included. Students can send for several prospectuses and compare prices.

Choosing a course

Accreditation

Open and Distance Learning Quality Council (ODL QC)

As most open colleges are private enterprises outside government control, the Open and Distance Learning Quality Council (ODL QC) was formed to develop a system of accreditation approved by the Department for Education and Skills (DfES). ODL QC is an independent body, and has been operating since 1968. Its independent assessors, drawn from the professions and universities, inspect every aspect of a college and give approval if the Council criteria are being met.

If a student wants information about where to find a particular course at an accredited college, or whether a college is accredited (and if not, whether the course is available at one which is) ODL QC has an advisory service. Colleges accredited by the ODL QC are listed under the later heading of 'Open learning providers'.

➤ **ODL QC** – 16 Park Crescent, London W1B 1AH.
Tel: 020 7612 7090.
Email: info@odlqc.org.uk
www.odlqc.org.uk

Non-accredited colleges

There are many colleges that are not accredited. They offer courses in anything you can think of – photography, languages, drawing, piano playing, aromatherapy, journalism, religion, to name a few. Some offer value for money, but there is no easy way of knowing. Prospective students can try to contact people who have completed the course to find out whether they found it satisfactory.

Selecting a college

There are a few big colleges that offer a range of courses including professional subjects, for example banking or accountancy, or GCSE courses. The others tend to be more specialist.

It's very hard to judge in advance how good the colleges really are. Accreditation helps, but not in the choice between two accredited colleges, or if a college which offers an apparently tailor-made course is not accredited.

Students should try to compare courses offered by different providers. They should also try to ask the colleges the following kinds of questions, some of which reflect the issues that concern the ODL QC when its inspectors assess a college.

- Is it possible to look at course materials, attend an open day or take a trial period prior to enrolling?

- Is there a refunds policy? If so, for what?

- Is the course pitched at the right level and does it use the right kind of learning methods?

- Has the course been written or adapted especially for the purpose of open or distance learning?

- Has the course already been written? If so, when was it last thoroughly revised?

- How much support is there? For example, is there access to tutors by email, fax, telephone or post?

- Is there any face-to-face training or is the course completed entirely at home?

- Is it possible to talk to former students?

- Have former students been successful?

Association of British Correspondence Colleges (ABCC)

ABCC is an association representing around 25 colleges. It produces a free broadsheet and will offer advice to potential students. Its members also have an agreed code of ethics designed to maintain standards and integrity.

➤ **Association of British Correspondence Colleges** – The Secretary, PO Box 17926, London SW19 3WB.
Tel: 020 8544 9559.
Email: info@homestudy.org.uk
www.homestudy.org.uk

Complaints

Dissatisfied students can:

- contact ODL QC (see above) – they will take it up with the college if the complaint is about one of their accredited colleges

- contact ABCC (see above) if the complaint is about one of their member colleges.

Open learning providers

Open University

For details of opportunities available through the university: see *2:16 – The Open University (OU)*.

Open College of the Arts (OCA)

The OCA was set up in 1986 as an educational trust, on the premise that everyone has an artist inside them, if given the skills they need to achieve their creative potential. Structured home-study courses are offered in a wide range of subject areas, supported by tutors who are themselves practising artists. There are almost 40 courses, most of which are university-accredited. Subjects available include: sculpture, drawing, singing, textiles, interior design, calligraphy, photography, creative writing, garden design, dance and music.

Course costs range from £365 to £485. Students can start at any time of the year. No previous experience is needed and they can study at their own pace. Credits can be gained towards higher education qualifications.

> ➤ **Open College of the Arts** – Unit 1B, Redbrook Business Park, Wilthorpe Road, Barnsley S75 1JN.
> Tel: 01226 730495 or Freephone: 0800 731 2116.
> Email: open.arts@ukonline.co.uk
> www.oca-uk.com

National Extension College (NEC)

The NEC is a non-profitmaking trust established in 1963, dedicated to widening access to education for adults through distance learning. It enrols around 10,000 learners each year.

The NEC provides over 100 home study courses designed to appeal to learners from all walks of life, whether they are looking to develop learning skills, wanting to gain a recognisable qualification, seeking to extend expertise in a chosen field or studying purely for pleasure. All courses are accredited by the Open and Distance Learning Quality Council (ODL QC).

Gaining a qualification is optional, but provision exists for the learner to achieve a wide range of GCSEs and A levels, as well as professional and vocational qualifications including those of the Association of Accounting Technicians (AAT), the Chartered Institute of Marketing (CIM), the Chartered Management Institute (CMI) and the Council for Awards in Children's Care and Education (CACHE).

NEC students set the pace of their own study, enrolling at any time and working as many or as few hours as they choose. All tutoring is by phone, fax, email and post and there is no need to attend a college or any other institution except for sitting examinations. Advice and feedback is available from expert personal tutors assigned to each student on enrolment. Students can use the NEC's online community to share ideas and experiences with other students. NEC's advisers welcome telephone calls from prospective and existing students seeking guidance and help in their choice of studies.

A free *Guide to Courses* is available on request.

> **National Extension College** – The Michael Young Centre, Purbeck Road, Cambridge CB2 2HN.
  Tel: 0800 389 2839.
  Email: info@nec.ac.uk
  www.nec.ac.uk

learndirect

Set up by University for Industry, learndirect is a source of information about over 600,000 courses offered by colleges and training providers throughout the UK. See *1:4 – Sources of information, advice and guidance*. However, learndirect is also a major provider of courses, more than 80% of which are online. Around 500 courses are available in the following categories: home and office IT, specialist IT, business and management, languages and skills for life (e.g. literacy, numeracy and ESOL). Many courses are designed with the training needs of businesses of all sizes in mind.

There are over 2,200 learndirect centres across the UK, in venues that range from workplaces to sports clubs, libraries to supermarkets and churches to pubs. There are people at the learning centres to help, if new learners are not confident with computers. Students can also study at home via the learndirect website and through distance-learning packages. Courses are supported by a network of tutors.

Course costs vary, for example, a basic literacy course is likely to be free, while a 30-hour advanced computer course may cost students around £240 if they are not eligible for funding. The website or helpline can advise on possible financial help towards course costs.

> **learndirect**
  Tel: 0800 100 900 (national learning advice line)
  www.learndirect-advice.co.uk (offers a national course search facility)
  Tel: 0800 101 901 (information on learndirect courses and centres)
  www.learndirect.co.uk (offers a learndirect course search facility)

> **learndirect Scotland** – Tel: 0808 100 9000 (helpline)
  Email: info@learndirectscotland.com
  www.learndirectscotland.com (offers a national course search facility)

The Co-operative College

The Co-operative College provides learning, education, training, consultancy and research for the co-operative, social enterprise and mutual sectors in the UK and internationally. It offers tailored workshops and qualifications for members, directors, staff and managers within these sectors.

> **Co-operative College** – Holyoake House, Hanover Street, Manchester M60 0AS.
  Tel: 0161 246 2902
  Email: enquiries@co-op.ac.uk
  www.co-op.ac.uk

Lifelong learning in Scotland

Public libraries in Scotland have continued to expand their open learning provision. Further financial commitments from the Government via the New Opportunities Fund will allow libraries to develop these services into Lifelong Learning centres, in cooperation with a range of partners. A key element of the centres will be access to electronic resources, internet and distance learning packages. Public libraries have been described as 'street corner universities', reaching the heart of the community and supporting independent learners. They will now offer opportunities to follow more formal education routes in an informal environment.

> **Chartered Institute of Library & Information Professionals in Scotland (CILIPS), Scottish Library and Information Council (SLIC)** – 1st Floor, Building C, Brandon Gate, Leechlee Road, Hamilton ML3 6AU.
> Tel: 01698 458888.
> Email: slic@slainte.org.uk
> www.slainte.org.uk

Colleges accredited by the ODL QC (2004)

> **Advance Training** – PO Box 594, Hull HU5 3YA.
> Tel: 0845 4588 999.
> Email: info@adv.co.uk
> www.adv.co.uk

> **The BSY Group** – Stanhope Square, Holsworthy, Devon EX22 6DF.
> Tel: 0800 731 9271.
> Email: info@bsygroup.co.uk
> www.bsygroup.co.uk

> **Caltrop College** – PO Box 6, Llanfyllin, Powys SY22 5WP.
> Tel: 01691 649102.
> Email: training@caltrop.co.uk
> www.caltrop.co.uk

> **Cambridge International College** – College House, Leoville, St Ouen, Jersey JE3 2DB.
> Tel: 01534 485485.
> Email: learn@cambridgetraining.com
> www.cambridgecollege.co.uk

> **Cheltenham Tutorial College** – 292 High Street Cheltenham, GL50 3HQ.
> Tel: 01242 241279.
> Email: info@cheltenhamlearning.co.uk
> www.cheltenhamlearning.co.uk

> **Computeach International** – University House, PO Box 51, Dudley DY3 2AG.
> Tel: 0800 083 1255.
> Email: info@computeach.co.uk
> www.computeach.co.uk

> **Diplomatic Council** – Belsyre Court, 57 Woodstock Road, Oxford OX1 6HJ.
> Tel: 01865 292008.
> Email: registrar@diplomatic-council.com
> www.diplomatic-council.com

> **Ethos Associates** – 1 Winnington Court, Winnington Street, Northwich, Cheshire CW8 4DE.
> Tel: 08707 550 028.
> Email: info@ethosdirect.com
> www.ethosdirect.com

➤ **Forensic Linguistics Institute** – Bryntirion Mawr, Llanfair, Caereinion, Powys SY21 0BL.
Tel: 01938 811192.
Email: prov@thetext.co.uk
www.thetext.co.uk

➤ **Greenwich School of Theology** – 8 Foxdale Avenue, Thorpe Willoughby, Selby YO8 9NW.
Tel: 01757 702191.
Email: woody.gst@btopenworld.com
www.gschooltheol.com

➤ **Henley College Homestudy Unit** – Henley, College, Henley Road, Bell Green, Coventry CV2 1ED.
Tel: 02476 626 300 ext.511.
info@henley-cov.ac.uk
www.henley-cov.ac.uk

➤ **Highflyers Distance Tuition** – Walton House, 27 Banbury Park, Shiphay, Torquay TQ2 7HN.
Tel: 01803 551636.
Email: marie@highflyers00.freeserve.co.uk
www.highflyers-dl.co.uk

➤ **Horticultural Correspondence College** – Freepost, Notton, Chippenham, Wiltshire SN15 2BR.
Tel: 01249 730326 or 0800 378918.
Email: info@hccollege.co.uk
www.hccollege.co.uk

➤ **i-to-i** – Woodside House, 261 Low Lane, Leeds LS18 5NY.
Tel: 0870 333 2332 or 0113 2054635.
Email: info@i-to-i.com
www.i-to-i.com

➤ **Institute of Chartered Shipbrokers** - Tutorship – 85 Gracechurch Street, London EC3V 0AA.
Tel: 020 7623 8008.
Email: tutorship@ics.org.uk
www.ics.org.uk

➤ **Institute of Chiropodists and Podiatrists** – 27 Wright Street, Southport, Merseyside PR9 0TL.
Tel: 01704 546141.
Email: secretary@inst-chiropodist.org.uk
www.inst-chiropodist.org.uk

➤ **Institute of Heraldic & Genealogical Studies** – Northgate, Canterbury, Kent CT1 1BA.
Tel: 01227 768664.
Email: education@ihgs.ac.uk
www.ihgs.ac.uk

➤ **The International Graphology Association** – Stonedge, Dunkerton, Bath BA2 8AS.
Tel: 01761 437809.
Email: educ@graphology.org.uk
www.graphology.org.uk

➤ **The International Institute of Reflexology** – 146 Upperthorpe, Walkley, Sheffield S6 3NF.
Tel: 01142 812100.
Email: info@reflexology-uk.net
www.reflexology-uk.co.uk

➤ **The International School of Navigation** – 135 Sandyford Road, Newcastle upon Tyne NE2 1RG.
Tel: 07779 289631.
Email: admin@harbourlights.nu
www.harbourlights.nu

➤ **Kevala Centre** – Hunsdon Road, Torquay TQ1 1QB.
Tel: 01803 215678.
Email: information@kevala.com
www.kevala.com

➤ **KLC School of Design** – Unit 503, The Chambers, Chelsea Harbour, London SW10 0XF.
Tel: 020 7376 3377.
Email: openlearning@klc.co.uk
www.klc.co.uk

➤ **The Learning Institute** – Honeycombe House, Bagley, Wedmore, Somerset BS28 4TD.
Tel: 01934 713 563.
Email: courses@inst.org
www.inst.org

➤ **London Management Centre** – 92 Seymour Place, London W1H 2NJ.
Tel: 020 7724 6007.
Email: lmc.uk@btinternet.com
www.lmcuk.com

➤ **London School of Classical Homoeopathy** – 94 Green Dragon Lane, Winchmore Hill, London N21 2NJ.
Tel: 020 8360 8757.
Email: registrar@homeopathy-lsch.co.uk
www.homeopathy-lsch.co.uk

➤ **The London School of Journalism** – 126 Shirland Road, Maida Vale, London W9 2BT.
Tel: 020 7432 8140.
Email: chances@lsjournalism.com
www.home-study.com

➤ **MOL** – D9 Moston Campus, Ashley Lane, Manchester M9 4WU.
Tel: 0161 203 2103.
Email: enquiries@mol-openlearning.co.uk
www.mol-openlearning.co.uk

➤ **Maple Academy** – Freepost, HA4446, Southall, Middlesex UB1 3BR.
Tel: 0870 011 5000.
Email: mapleco@aol.com
www.mapleacademy.co.uk

> **Modern Montessori International** – 142 Mitcham Lane, London, SW16 6NS.
Tel: 0208 769 5555.
Email: modernmontessori.intl@btinternet.com
www.modernmontessori-intl.com

> **Montessori Centre International** – 18 Balderton Street, London W1K 6TG.
Tel: 020 7493 0165.
Email: mci@montessori.ac.uk
www.montessori.ac.uk

> **Music for the Media** – Atlantic House, 65 Jeddo Road, London W12 9ED.
Tel: 0208 740 7727.
Email: info@musicforthemedia.co.uk
www.musicforthemedia.co.uk

> **National Council for the Training of Journalists** – Latton Bush Centre, Southern Way, Harlow, Essex CM18 7BL.
Tel: 01279 430009.
Email: info@nctj.com
www.nctj.com

> **National Extension College (NEC)** – The Michael Young Centre, Purbeck Road, Cambridge CB2 2HN.
Tel: 0800 389 2839.
Email: courses@nec.ac.uk
www.nec.ac.uk

> **The National IT Learning Centre** – The Bearings, Bowbridge Road, Newark, Nottinghamshire NG24 4BZ.
Tel: 01636 612226.
Email: enquiries@nitlc.com
www.nitlc.com

> **NIG Academy of Professional Investigation** – 141 Western Road, Haywards Heath, West Sussex RH16 3LH.
Tel: 01444 441111.
Email: sales@pi-academy.com
www.pi-academy.com

> **Open Learning Centre International** – 24 King Street, Carmarthen SA31 1BS.
Tel: 0800 393 743.
Email: info@olci.info
www.olci.info

> **The Projects Group plc** – Windsor House, Lodge Place, Sutton, Surrey SM1 4AU.
Tel: 020 8770 9393.
Email: info@theprojectsgroup.plc.uk
www.TPGAcademy.com

> **The Publishing Training Centre** – Book House, 45 East Hill, London SW18 2QZ.
Tel: 020 8874 2718.
Email: publishing.training@bookhouse.co.uk
www.train4publishing.co.uk

> **The Regent Academy** – 6 John Street, London WC1N 2ES.
> Tel: 0800 378 281.
> Email: info@regentacademy.com
> www.regentacademy.com

> **Rhodec International College of Interior Design** – 35 East Street, Brighton BN1 1HL.
> Tel: 01273 327476.
> Email: contact@rhodec.edu
> www.rhodec.edu

> **RRC Business Training** – 27-37 St George's Road, London SW19 4DS.
> Tel: 020 8944 3100.
> Email: info@rrc.co.uk
> www.rrc.co.uk

> **The School of Homoeopathic Medicine** – 74 Clonard Street, County Dublin, Ireland.
> Tel: 00 353 1 841 4274.

> **Stratford Business School** – Bridge House, PO Box 1754, Stratford upon Avon CV37 6TW.
> Tel: 01789 766123.
> Email: study@stratbiz.co.uk
> www.stratbiz.co.uk

> **Tactics for Exam Success** – Thornton Chenie House, 27 Bloomfield Road, Bromley BR2 9RY.
> Tel: 020 8313 9317.
> Email: enquiries@tactics.demon.co.uk
> www.tacticsforexamsuccess.co.uk

> **Top Cat Cruising School** – Whimbrels, Southdown, Millbrook, Torpoint, Cornwall PL10 1EZ.
> Tel: 01752 823360.
> Email: jim@multihull.tv
> www.multihull.tv

> **UNISON Open College** – 1 Mabledon Place, London WC1H 9AJ.
> Tel: 0845 355 0845.
> Email: open.college@unison.co.uk
> www.unison-education.org.uk

> **Writers Bureau** – Sevendale House, 7 Dale Street, Manchester M1 1JB.
> Tel: 0161 228 2362.
> Email: studentservices@writersbureau.com
> www.writersbureau.com

Other independent learning

There are hundreds of books, tapes, CDs, videos and computer programs that enable people to study many subjects. They are different from distance and open learning courses primarily because they offer no tutorial support. Like open learning methods, these systems are useful for those who cannot travel to a course centre or have limited time available for study.

Books

Publications in the *Teach Yourself* and *How To* books series are well known. Similar to these, there are also cheaper, shorter learning guides, as well as DIY books, car manuals, computer handbooks and others. The subject range is wide – anything from aromatherapy to writing science fiction.

Advantages

- They can be an introduction to a subject, before deciding whether to study it further.

- There is a wide subject range available from libraries and bookshops – especially those that specialise in educational books. Sometimes books are advertised in magazines or in connection with a television series. Specialist magazines sometimes advertise self-tuition books on their subject.

- The books are very accessible, and students can dip into them as and when they choose to.

- Many manuals are useful as a source of updating on subjects that the student may already be familiar with.

Disadvantages

- It can be difficult to learn a subject from scratch using a book, especially if it is a practical skill, with no assistance.

- It requires patience to find the information needed for a specific purpose.

- Reference books can be quite expensive.

Tapes and CDs

These usually teach languages, as students benefit from listening to the spoken word. They are also popular for management techniques and self-development, as they are aimed at busy people who perhaps find listening in the car convenient. They may be expensive, as a large number of CDs or tapes are sometimes needed to cover the course, but this may compare favourably with the cost of evening classes and related transport.

Computers

Computers can be used at home in two ways:

- to learn about a wide range of subjects using educational programs and the internet

- to learn IT skills and how to use various software packages.

Most educational software is written for schools, and often the learning can be achieved as easily through more traditional methods. However, with lifelong-learning initiatives and more sophisticated technology, more programs for adults are becoming available. Specialist software designed to teach people with disabilities has been used successfully with, for example, people who are visually impaired, autistic, dyslexic or who have other learning difficulties. Most packages are for IBM-compatible computers. It may be possible to sample materials before purchasing.

The internet is a major source of information. If students do not have access on their home computers, there are many sites where the internet can be used, such as in further education colleges, internet- or cyber-cafes or public libraries and community centres. Some educational websites are for subscribers only, but a lot of information is open to anyone. Internet novices can take short courses to acquire the necessary 'surfing' skills.

To find out what is available, students can:

- browse through computer magazines available from newsagents and in libraries

- ask at local further education colleges, community schools or adult education centres as they often use educational packages.

The National Grid for Learning website is a good introduction to learning opportunities on the internet. See www.ngfl.gov.uk

Learning computing skills and how to use software packages

It's possible to gain IT skills using magazines and books with a home computer. Software usually comes with a manual and an on-screen 'tutorial' facility. Even those attending a computing class will benefit from also working at home. The quality of user manuals and books teaching programming can vary widely in standard, so students should examine products before buying.

The British Computer Society offers distance learning packages leading to their own professional degree-equivalent qualification and to the internationally recognised European Computer Driving Licence (ECDL).

> **British Computer Society** – 1 Sanford Street, Swindon SN1 1HJ.
> Tel: 01793 417417.
> Email: examenq@hq.bcs.org.uk
> www.bcs.org.uk
> www.ecdl.co.uk

Broadcasting

BBC TV, radio and online

BBC Education offers an integrated multi-media approach to adult learning, using broadcast media, online and off-screen support. Areas of special focus include learning about the modern workplace, work and life skills (including IT), health and parenting education, language courses and programmes that encourage a hands-on interest in history and science.

Major recent and continuing initiatives include *Computers don't Bite*, *Becoming Webwise*, *History 2000*, *Fighting Fat, Fighting Fit*, *Skillswise* and *Get Writing*. The BBC is also developing the idea of 'learning journeys', based on documentaries such as *Walking with the Beasts* and *Restoration*, featuring online opportunities for viewers to take their interest further.

The overnight service – *The Learning Zone* – on BBC 2 is provided throughout the year in partnership with the Open University. Programmes cover a wide range of topics, aimed at varying levels of learning need, from supporting accredited learning through to degree-level, training for work from retail to nursing, through to basic skills like getting started with computers. Language learning is one of the most popular offerings for business, travel and leisure learning. Learning Zone programme schedules can be viewed on: www.bbc.co.uk/learningzone or leaflets are available in most public libraries.

There is a growing range of long-term learning resources available, such as the *Webwise* CD-ROM and *Becoming Webwise* and *Skillswise* online courses. Also, pioneering work incorporating on-demand video and multimedia applications via broadband networks is being progressed as fast as the technology allows.

The BBC has a team of education officers who welcome comments or suggestions about BBC Education's programming, who can be contacted at the following offices:

➤ England: 020 8752 5650

➤ Northern Ireland: 028 9033 8435

➤ Scotland: 0141 338 3422

➤ Wales: 029 2057 288.

Most BBC local radio stations have a producer responsible for education who can give information and advice about programmes. Local radio addresses and programmes are listed in local editions of *Radio Times*. The BBC also publishes information centrally about local radio.

For other enquiries:

➤ **BBC Information** – PO Box 1922, Glasgow, G2 3WT.
  Tel: 08700 100 222.
  www.bbc.co.uk/learning

There is a dedicated learndirect phone number for information about BBC-related courses. Tel: 08000 150 950.

Independent television

Ofcom is the regulator for the UK communications sector and its duties include licensing and regulating commercial television. It looks after viewers' interests by setting and maintaining the standards for programmes, advertising and technical quality. It monitors the education and social action output of its licensees. It is independent of the Government and of the broadcasters, and is funded from fees that its licensees have to pay.

S4C is a commissioning broadcaster in Wales and delivers programmes in the Welsh language. S4C does not produce programmes itself – of the 30 hours per week of Welsh language programmes, 10 are from BBC Wales and the remainder from independent, Welsh television producers. All the English output is received from Channel 4 and rescheduled on S4C.

Some cable and satellite programme services also have an educational purpose or component.

➤ **Channel 4 Television** Commissioning Editor (Education) – 124 Horseferry Road,
  London SW1P 2TX.
  Tel: 020 7396 4444.
  Email: viewerenquiries@channel4.co.uk
  www.channel4.com

> **S4C** Commissioning Editor (Factual Programming) – Parc Tw Glas, Llanishen, Cardiff CF14 5DU.
> Tel: 029 2074 7444.
> Viewers' hotline: 0870 600 4141.
> Email: hotline@S4C.co.uk
> www.S4C.co.uk

> **Ofcom** – Riverside House, 2a Southwark Bridge Road, London SE1 9HA.
> Tel: 020 7981 3000.
> Email: contact@ofcom.org.uk
> www.ofcom.org.uk

Languages

There are many programmes on TV and radio to help teach yourself foreign languages and introduce you to the culture. All have related packs containing books and cassettes or CDs to support the series, but these can be used as courses in themselves.

Local and regional radio

Local radio sometimes publicises adult education opportunities. If not, stations may be open to suggestions for future programmes. Scotland, Wales and Northern Ireland have radio services, which include programmes in Welsh and Gaelic.

Commercial radio

Commercial radio is licensed and regulated by Ofcom. Commercial radio is not required by legislation to provide educational programmes, although many such programmes are produced. There are around 270 radio stations. 47 digital radio multiplexes produce a variety of formats.

There are also 14 pilot community radio stations broadcasting at the moment. This not-for-profit sector of commercial radio seeks to use radio to assist in broader aspects of education, social inclusion and innovation, and enable public access to radio in new and imaginative ways.

> **Ofcom** – see under 'Independent television' above.

Broadcasting Support Services (bss)

Back-up support (such as advice, helplines, websites and publications) to specific radio and TV programmes on both BBC and independent stations, usually for programmes that have just been broadcast, is provided by bss.

> **Broadcasting Support Services** – International House, 7 High Street, Ealing, London W5 5DB.
> Tel: 0845 600 1317.
> Email: marketing@bss.org
> www.bss.org

Further information

Information on open learning courses and products (some of it geared to companies rather than to individuals) can be viewed on the website of the British Learning Association (click on BLA Direct): www.british-learning.com

Useful information can also be found on www.distancelearning.hobsons.com

The ODL QC Buyer's Guide to Distance Learning – available free from ODL QC by post or downloadable from their website (click on 'buyers guide').

Improve Your Written English, Book-Keeping & Accounting for the Small Business, Learning to Read Music, The Complete Guide to Learning a Language, and *Touch Typing in Ten Hours* are just a few of the titles available from How To Books (address in *Section 4 – Publishers' contact details*), mostly priced from around £4.99 to £12.99 (less if bought online).

The *Teach Yourself* series of titles includes *Photography, Internet, Classical Music* and a range of modern and classical languages. All available from Bookpoint Ltd – 130 Milton Park, Abingdon, Oxfordshire OX14 4SB. Tel: 01235 400414. Books are mostly priced between £7.99 and £14.99. Language CDs/cassettes and packs of books and cassettes cost from around £12.99. You can find out more about what's available on Hodder Headline's website: www.madaboutbooks.com (type 'Teach Yourself' in the quick search box). Alternatively, order through: www.teachyourself.co.uk

Kogan Page (address in *Section 4 – Publishers' contact details*) publishes a number of 'self-help' titles relating to acquiring business and communication skills.

Most of these materials can be ordered through local bookshops, and there are also online bookshops at websites such as:

➤ www.blackwell.co.uk

➤ www.uk.bol.com

➤ www.whsmith.co.uk

➤ www.amazon.co.uk

2:18

Work Based Learning for Adults and other government-funded training

Topics covered:

- Work Based Learning for Adults in England, and similar programmes in Wales, Scotland and Northern Ireland
- Full-time education and training under the New Deal
- Apprenticeships

Work Based Learning for Adults in England

The WBLA programme in England aims:

- to help adults who are not in work, and who may lack employability skills, to move into sustained employment

- to help long-term unemployed people to gain occupational skills relevant to local labour market skill shortages

- to help long-term unemployed people to move into self-employment

- to provide 'basic employability training' to people whose basic literacy and numeracy skills provide a barrier to employment.

WBLA is a voluntary programme, aimed mainly at those aged 25 and over who have been unemployed for at least for six months and are claiming Jobseeker's Allowance or certain other benefits. Others who are disadvantaged in the labour market may move into WBLA earlier.

WBLA programmes are accessed and delivered by Jobcentre Plus.

- Jobcentre Plus contracts with approved training providers to deliver the training. Programmes are developed to meet the need of the local labour market, so the occupational training available through WBLA will vary from area to area.

- Training providers can be private training companies, further education colleges, companies offering in-house training, Chambers of Commerce, local authorities or any other body deemed suitable.

- Jobcentre Plus/Jobcentre advisers check the eligibility of those wishing to enter the programme.

- On joining WBLA, each participant will have an agreed training plan, to meet the entrant's specific needs.

The programmes available

Basic Employability Training

Basic Employability Training (BET) consists of a package of provision lasting up to 26 weeks. It aims to address the barriers to work faced by people who have been out of work for a minimum of 26 weeks, and who are finding it particularly difficult to find work, and are in real danger of becoming permanently detached from the labour market. It includes support which is tailored to individual needs, to help participants combat any barriers that they may have to getting a job. BET is particularly focused on people who need assistance in overcoming severe basic skills needs, and those whose first language is not English who may have ESOL (English for Speakers of Other Language) training needs.

Eligibility

- People who have been unemployed for six months who are claiming Jobseeker's Allowance or another qualifying benefit.

- Those who are disadvantaged in the labour market, who may enter earlier than six months:

  – people with a disability

  – lone parents

  – those with basic skills needs

  – those whose first language is not English

  – labour market returners (those who have been out of the labour market for domestic reasons for two years or more)

  – people who have been involved in a large-scale redundancy

  – refugees (who have been granted permission to stay and claim JSA)

  – homeless people

  – those recovering from substance abuse (who have successfully completed a drug rehabilitation programme)

  – those who have been referred at the discretion of their Jobcentre Plus/Jobcentre adviser.

Entrants must take a Basic Skills Assessment and be assessed at below entry level in any of the three literacy elements (reading, spelling, and punctuation) or in numeracy.

Short Job-Focused Training

This offers up to six weeks' training. Examples of what training could be included are: fork lift truck driving, IT skills, intruder alarm installation, call centre work – but this depends on local labour market needs.

Eligibility

- People who have been unemployed for six months who are claiming Jobseeker's Allowance or another qualifying benefit.

- Those who are disadvantaged in the labour market, as specified above, who may enter earlier than six months.

Longer Occupational Training

This offers a package of training, which can last between seven and 52 weeks, tailored to the needs of the participant. For example, it may include work placements, basic skills or focused training leading to vocational qualifications.

Eligibility

- People who have been unemployed for 12 months who are claiming Jobseeker's Allowance or another qualifying benefit.

- Those who are disadvantaged in the labour market, as specified above, who may enter earlier than 12 months.

Self-employment

Offers initial support and advice, help to develop business plans, appropriate skills training and ongoing mentoring.

Eligibility

- People who have been unemployed for six months who are claiming Jobseeker's Allowance or another qualifying benefit.

- Those who are disadvantaged in the labour market, as specified above, who may enter earlier than six months.

Other aspects

Part-time attendance

Most participants in WBLA will be training on a full-time basis, but those whose personal circumstances do not allow them to train full-time may attend part-time.

Training allowances

While undertaking WBLA, trainees receive an allowance which is equivalent to any benefit to which they are entitled, plus £10 a week, and may be able to receive help with expenses such as childcare or travel.

People with disabilities

People who need specially adapted equipment or special aids may be provided with this by their training provider.

Employed status

It is possible to follow Work Based Learning for Adults as an employee. This involves training in addition to that normally provided by the employer. In these circumstances, an allowance will not be payable.

For further information, contact the local Jobcentre Plus/Jobcentre.

➤ www.jobcentreplus.gov.uk contains information about WBLA.

Skill Build in Wales

Skill Build operates in Wales, providing quality-assured training opportunities for people who have been out of work for at least six months. Certain people, such as those with a disability, lone parents, those who need help with English, computer skills or basic education, can access the scheme immediately. Participants normally continue to receive their benefits, plus a top-up and help with expenses. There are two options for those who are unemployed, depending on the needs of the individual:

● Skill Build – identifies learning barriers and basic skills needs, and provides learning opportunities to develop skills.

● Skill Build+ – provides occupational learning leading to NVQs in a broad range of work areas.

Each individual will have an agreed training plan to meet their specific needs. The plan might involve job specific training, work towards an NVQ or a work experience placement. In certain cases, it could be a mixture of all of these.

For up-to-date information about eligibility criteria and what Skill Build offers in Wales, contact the local Jobcentre Plus /Jobcentre, Careers Wales centres or visit www.elwa.org.uk

Training for Work in Scotland

Training for Work (TfW) is the Scottish counterpart to WBLA, very much focused on getting participants into jobs. It is the responsibility of Scottish Enterprise and Highlands and Islands Enterprise. TfW is organised locally through Local Enterprise Companies (LECs).

Courses offered through Training for Work vary in length, depending on the type of occupational training involved and the participant's needs; most courses are of between six and 26 weeks' duration, but could be longer. Training is provided by a range of approved training providers. For example, in Glasgow, there are around 40 training providers, who run over 100 training courses, in a wide range of occupational areas. Training can lead to certification at national standards. Training may include work experience placements.

Eligibility

Training for Work is open to adults aged 25+, who have been unemployed for at least six months over the last year. Those who may be eligible to start with less than six months' unemployment include:

- lone parents

- people with disabilities

- those who have been involved in large-scale redundancy

- people aged 50+

- Social Inclusion Partnership (SIP) Area Residents.

N.B. Other groups may also be eligible; check at the Jobcentre Plus/Jobcentre office.

While on the programme, participants receive their benefit entitlement plus £10 a week.

Clients should find out about opportunities through their local Jobcentre Plus/Jobcentre, Local Enterprise Company or directly from a training provider. Alternatively, ring the Scottish Enterprise helpline: 0845 607 8787 or view www.scottish-enterprise.com/trainingforwork

Focus for Work in Northern Ireland

The Department for Employment and Learning in Northern Ireland offers a range of measures aimed at assisting unemployed people to boost their prospects of gaining employment, through the provision of occupational training and work experience opportunities under the title of Focus for Work.

The programmes offering training opportunities within Focus for Work are described below.

Training for Work

Training for Work aims to assist clients with an identified training need to improve their chances of getting a job. A key objective of the programme is to help the client develop and maintain positive work attitudes, in a programme lasting up to 26 weeks. Enterprise Ulster (a Non-Departmental Public Body) is piloting the programme on behalf of the Department during the pilot period, which runs until April 2005. Applicants do not have to be Jobseeker's Allowance claimants. Once on the programme, clients receive a training allowance, help with expenses, ongoing jobsearch training and retraining for a change of career if needed.

Bridge to Employment

This programme aims to provide customised training courses to equip unemployed people aged 18+, and in particular those who are long-term unemployed, with skills to compete for new job opportunities. The programme further assists inward investors and local expanding companies find suitably trained staff. Clients apply for specific Bridge to Employment vacancies, which are advertised by employers, through the Jobcentre/Jobs and Benefits office. Trainees continue to receive their benefits, plus help with travel, lodging expenses in some cases and, for lone parents, childcare. 80% of those who successfully complete the programme find employment.

Contact local Jobs and Benefits offices/Jobcentres.

> **Department for Employment and Learning** – Adelaide House, 39-49 Adelaide Street, Belfast, Co.Antrim BT2 8FD.
> Tel: 029 9025 7777 or information point: 028 9025 7793.
> Email del@nics.gov.uk
> www.delni.gov.uk

New Deal

New Deal is part of the Government's Welfare to Work strategy, giving special help to unemployed people or those in certain disadvantaged groups. It is a national programme that offers help in getting a job through advice, support, education, training and work experience. Each participant has their own personal adviser throughout the programme.

At first, participants will have up to four months of concentrated, personal advice and help – known as the Gateway. This will help them identify a route for entry into employment and prepare for work, while improving their job-seeking skills. If the participant is still unemployed after this period, they go on to the Options/Intensive Activity Period (IAP) stage, which can include work experience with a commercial or voluntary organisation, a subsidised job, self-employment support, courses to develop work skills and training for a specific job. The client's personal adviser can continue to help them during a follow-up stage.

All the New Deal options include possibilities of education and training, mostly either short courses or training in the workplace. Preparation for self-employment is available. Opportunities for full-time education and training are generally for those in the 18-24 age group. Each applicant's needs for training or education are assessed individually.

New Deal for those aged 18-24: full-time education or training is one of the options available if an unsubsidised job cannot be found during the initial Gateway stage of New Deal. The full-time education and training option is for those who do not have qualifications at or above NVQ 2 or equivalent, or if they do, need to gain further vocational qualifications to enable them to get a job. The full-time education and training option is also available for those needing help with basic skills. The training includes workplace training, or training in a realistic work environment. Help can be given towards the cost of books or materials. The programme is mandatory for clients aged between 18 and 24 who have been claiming JSA for six months or more.

New Deal for people aged 25 plus: education and training may be selected as the most appropriate programme of help during the Options/IAP stage of New Deal 25 plus. It provides the chance to develop relevant job skills up to and including NVQ level 3, whilst the participant remains on Jobseeker's Allowance. While most courses are short, it may be possible to study or train for up to a year. The education and training undertaken must be vocational, and must help the participant to find work. It could involve a short course to boost existing skills, or training for new skills. This programme is mandatory for people aged 25+ who have been claiming JSA for 18 months.

Part-time, short course or workplace training and education – as well as preparation for self-employment and advice about training – are also available as options in the other, voluntary, New Deal schemes – for **people aged 50 plus, people with disabilities, lone**

parents and **unemployed partners of people claiming certain benefits.** New Deal 50+ also includes a possible £1,500 training grant for approved training which is relevant to the client's job.

For further information, consult New Deal booklets available from the Jobcentre Plus/ Jobcentre offices.

New Deal telephone information line: 0845 606 2626 or textphone 0845 606 0680.

New Deal website (which includes a 'discovery tool' for clients to find out if they are eligible for the programme): www.newdeal.gov.uk

The New Deal in Northern Ireland is administered by the Department for Employment and Learning (see above).

A new, more flexible, provision for unemployed adults is likely to be trialled from autumn 2005. See information on *Building on the New Deal* on www.dwp.gov.uk

N.B. The Workstep programme for people with disabilities in England, Scotland and Wales can include access to learning and development. Disability Employment Advisers will have details.

Apprenticeships

Apprenticeships in England have been developed by employers and training organisations. They are generally aimed at young people wishing to gain the skills and qualifications needed to become the technicians and managers of the future.

To do an Apprenticeship, a young person needs to be aged 16-24 and not taking part in full-time education. If they start an Apprenticeship before their 25th birthday, they can continue until they have completed it. Apprenticeships offer structured training leading to NVQ level 2 or 3 (depending on the Apprenticeship) and a Technical Certificate, and include key skills. Trainees are normally employed, and earn a wage set by their employer. Apprenticeships are available in a wide range of occupational areas.

Information on Apprenticeships is available in England through information, advice and guidance services, local LSCs, and see www.apprenticeships.org.uk

- **In Scotland**, Modern Apprenticeships, which form part of the Skillseekers Programme, offer similar training, but with no upper age limit, although 16-17 year-olds have priority.

- **In Wales,** Modern Apprenticeships are also available, leading to training at NVQ level 3 and above. Clients should check availability with the careers service.

- **In Northern Ireland**, young people may be eligible for the Jobskills training programme, which includes Modern Apprenticeships.

Apprenticeships for adults

New apprenticeships for adults are being trialled from early 2005, aimed at people aged 25 and over. These Apprenticeships are being developed by Sector Skills Councils (the bodies with responsibility for skills development and training in particular occupational areas) and local Learning and Skills Councils. The trials are being run across England, and will be in the fields of engineering, health and construction. Participants will include those who are employed who have skills but are without qualifications, as well as those who are unemployed, or facing unemployment and wanting to change the type of work they do. Those interested need to check with their local Learning and Skills Council (LSC), which administers the programme, for advice and information.

And finally ...

There are changes in the pipeline. The Government Skills Strategy White Paper proposes that all adults who lack a level 2 qualification (equivalent to five GCSEs at A*-C) should be entitled to free learning to achieve this. There will also be opportunities to target those lacking level 3 (equivalent to A levels).

Further information

Welfare to Work Handbook –published by the Centre for Economic and Social Inclusion. 2004 edition £22.95 plus postage. Can be ordered online on www.cesi.org.uk

2:19

Learning in the workplace

Topics covered:

- Learning providers
- Organisations concerned with workplace learning
- Initiatives to encourage workplace skills development

With the UK's future economic prosperity dependent on having a highly skilled and qualified workforce, there is much focus on ensuring that those already in the workplace are provided with opportunities to develop their skills and qualifications. The rapid pace of change in relation to ICT developments alone illustrates the need for on-going training and skills updating.

It has always been recognised that an employer has responsibility for training staff in the skills of the job they are employed to do. Training may take the form of:

- 'on-the-job' training with a supervisor, on an individual basis

- organised in-company training, so that several employees can update their skills at the same time

- participation in short or part-time courses at a local learning centre, such as a further education college

- undertaking a distance learning package

- online learning – perhaps through an open learning centre within the company.

Some employees are given encouragement or assistance by their employer to study for work-related qualifications in paid work time. Others are expected to study in their own time. Employers may support employees financially – through paying for, or towards, course fees or other costs.

Line managers should be able to advise on which qualifications are 'essential' and which ones are 'desirable'. Personnel or human resources and development managers in larger companies can also be a useful source of advice to their employees.

Those wanting to acquire new knowledge may have to stop work for a while to study full-time on a college or university course. Alternatively, part-time, open or distance-learning courses may be available – these modes of study are well suited to career development because studies can be fitted around time in work.

Employee development schemes

Some companies run formal employee development schemes. There are many variations but all aim to develop the workforce. Some, such as Ford's Employee Development and Assistance Programme (EDAP) urge participants to undertake learning that is not related to their job, encouraging staff to appreciate the wider benefits of learning. Other company programmes have a close bearing on their area of work. Many companies find that actively supporting learning leads to increased staff motivation and loyalty, which in turn, can result in increased productivity.

➢ **LSCs** and **LECs** (details in the gazetteer) may be able to provide information about local enterprises that operate employee development schemes.

Learning additional skills and knowledge at work

If training in job-specific skills is considered largely the responsibility of the employer, such things as enabling employees to acquire competence or understanding in additional areas may not be. Depending on the particular job, the employing organisation and the proposed mode of learning, employees may be able to present a business case to their employer for supporting them, at least partially.

For example, for employees in the sales section of a company with European customers, it may be useful to speak another language. The employer might contribute to course fees for modern language evening classes. However, if customers speak good English, an employer may see no obvious advantage to the company in offering this assistance.

Learning providers

Learning providers include:

- colleges of further education

- higher education institutions

- open/distance learning providers – including the Open University

- independent/commercial learning providers

- professional bodies.

More information about further and higher education, and open and distance learning can be found elsewhere in *Second Chances: 2:8 – Further and adult education; 2:14 – Higher education – first degrees; 2:15 – Higher education – higher degrees; 2:16 – The Open University (OU); 2:17 – Open/distance and other independent learning.*

Of particular relevance to the workplace are courses offered by learndirect, including the Learning through Work initiative, described below.

learndirect

While learndirect online courses are delivered through public learndirect centres, or can be accessed online by people learning at home (see *2:17 – Open/distance and other independent learning*), learndirect courses may also be accessed within the workplace. Many employers, large and small, use learndirect packages with their employees. Some companies have created learndirect centres within their workplaces. Packages available cover the areas of information and communications technology, business skills and basic numeracy and literacy, and courses related to specific sectors, such as engineering, visual communications and the automotive industry.

➤ **learndirect business** has been set up to help businesses of all sizes benefit from learndirect services. For more information, view: www.learndirect-business.co.uk

Learning through Work (LtW)

LtW is an initiative delivered through learndirect in partnership with higher education institutions. LtW allows employees to achieve a higher education qualification. With guidance and specialist advice from a higher education tutor, a learning plan is devised that builds on the individual's previous work experience and particular learning needs. The plan specifies what the employee needs to do in order to achieve the qualification they wish to gain. LtW can be used to gain a new qualification, or to top up an existing qualification – such as an HNC to degree level. The employee learns at a time and pace to suit themselves. Support is available from learndirect lifelong learning advisers initially, and from higher education tutors throughout the programme.

There are no set entry requirements. Each higher education institution will consider applicants on their individual merits.

Each higher education institution sets their own fees. Financial support towards some of the tuition fee costs is paid by the Government direct to the institution. Employers may choose to provide financial support, or support in other ways e.g. allow dedicated time to undertake learning activities, access to resources, supervision and mentoring. LfW is also open to self-employed people.

Participating institutions are: Anglia Polytechnic University, University of Central Lancashire, University College Chester, City University (London), University of Derby, University College Northampton, Northumbria University, Thames Valley University and the University of the West of England (Bristol). Obviously, as LtW is an online initiative, participants may be based anywhere geographically.

Available qualifications, all at higher education level, range from Certificates and Diplomas in Higher Education through to postgraduate qualifications. A range of subject areas is available – including business, IT and engineering. Students can also take short programmes and gain credits.

➤ For further information on LtW, view: www.learndirect-ltw.co.uk

Organisations concerned with workplace learning

Trade unions

Trade unions have long been champions of developing greater and improved opportunities for employees' training and educational development.

TUC Learning Services

TUC Learning Services was set up in 1998 to help unions and their members to contribute to realising the vision of creating a learning society. It provides the strategic framework to support trade unions in learning and skills, and training and support to union learning representatives.

The role of a union learning rep is to help their members access learning opportunities in the workplace. Such opportunities could be anything from improving communication and language skills to an introduction to computers. In particular, learning reps aim to reach and encourage non-traditional learners, especially those with literacy and numeracy needs. Advice, guidance and support to help learners make sound decisions about learning opportunities is an important aspect of the role of a union learning rep, as well as ongoing support once learning has begun.

Union learning reps also work with employers to create and extend workplace learning opportunities, and encourage the development of initiatives like employee development schemes, or basic skills assessment for employees.

There are currently over 7000 union learning reps. The Government has introduced legislation giving them the same rights as other union representatives, including reasonable paid time off for activities related to their role.

> **TUC Learning Services** – tel: 0151 236 7678.
> Email: learningservices@tuc.org.uk
> www.learningservices.org.uk

Union Learning Fund (ULF)

The ULF was set up by the Government in 1998 to support the role of unions in learning. So far, funding has been given to over 350 projects, involving over 70 unions, in around 3000 workplaces. Projects range from basic and key skills, to continuing professional development. ULF projects aim to support the development of people and systems, e.g. to improve access to learning (including the training of union learning reps), to open workplace learning centres (66 have been created), to involve non-traditional and new learners, and to involve people from minority groups. For more information, contact TUC Learning Services (see contact details above).

Trade union representatives

Trade union representatives, including health and safety and learning reps, have a legal right to paid time off from work for education and training connected with their duties. TUC regional officers organise accredited courses for members to train for such roles. Training is delivered through day release, at colleges of further and higher education. The TUC National Education Centre also provides a range of courses for union reps, and online courses are also available.

Full-time officers or union branch secretaries should be able to provide information about training for representative roles, as can TUC regional education officers.

TUC Regional Education Offices

> **Midlands** – 24 Livery Street, Birmingham B3 2PA. Tel: 0121 236 4464

> **Northern, Yorkshire and Humberside** – Friends Provident House, 13-14 South Parade, Leeds LS1 5QS. Tel: 0113 242 9296

> **North West** – Suite 506-510, The Cotton Exchange, Old Hall Street, Liverpool L3 9UD. Tel: 0151 236 7678

> **Southern and Eastern** – Congress House, Great Russell Street, London WC1B 3LS. Tel: 020 7467 1238

> **Wales** – Transport House, 1 Cathedral Road, Cardiff CF11 9SD. Tel: 029 2034 7010

> **South West** – Church House, Church Road, Filton, Bristol BS34 7BD. Tel: 0117 947 0521

> **Scotland** – 4th Floor, 145-165 West Regent Street, Glasgow G2 4RZ. Tel: 0141 221 8545

> **Northern Ireland** – Northern Ireland Committee, Irish Congress of Trade Unions (ICTU), 3 Crescent Gardens, Belfast BT7 1NS. Tel: 028 9024 7940

For more information, see the TUC website: www.tuc.org.uk or www.ictuni.org for the Northern Ireland Committee.

Individual unions

All unions are concerned with training their officials (whether full- or part-time).

Many have their own education service. For example, UNISON (the public service union) offers a wide range of courses through UNISON Open College, ranging from basic education through to professional-level qualifications. Amicus-AEEU runs its own vocational and technical programmes.

In general, courses are only for members of the union concerned. Trade union newspapers or journals provide information about opportunities.

Larger unions may have scholarships or offer financial help so that members can study – especially those attending adult residential colleges. These awards are usually additional to other grants.

General Federation of Trade Unions (GFTU) Educational Trust

The GFTU is the federation for specialist unions; currently there are 35 affiliated unions. Through their Educational Trust, the GFTU offers a wide range of trade union courses for union members, reps and officers. Courses are accredited through the Open College Network.

The GFTU Educational Trust also makes small grants for full-time and Open University students. However, there are limiting criteria. People must be studying subjects within economic theory and history, industrial law, history and principles of industrial relations. Individual trade unions may have other schemes.

> **The General Federation of Trades Unions Educational Trust** – Central House, Upper Woburn Place, London WC1H 0HY.
> Tel: 020 7387 2578.
> Email: gftuhq@gftu.org.uk
> www.gftu.org.uk

Sector Skills Councils (SSCs)

SSCs are independent, UK-wide organisations developed by groups of influential employers in industry or business sectors of economic or strategic significance. SSCs are employer-led and actively involve trade unions, professional bodies and other stakeholders in the sector. SSCs are licensed by the Secretary of State for Education and Skills, in consultation with Ministers in Scotland, Wales and Northern Ireland, to tackle the skills and productivity needs of their sector throughout the UK.

SSCs give responsibility to employers to provide leadership for strategic action to meet their sector's skills and business needs. In return they receive substantial public investment and dialogue with government departments across the UK. This enables employers to have a far greater impact on policies affecting skills and productivity in their sector, and increases their influence with education and training partners.

Each SSC will agree sector priorities and targets with its employers and partners to address four key goals:

- reducing skills gaps and shortages

- improving productivity, business and public service performance

- increasing opportunities to boost the skills and productivity of everyone in the sector's workforce, including action on equal opportunities

- improving learning supply, including apprenticeships, higher education and national occupational standards.

➤ **Sector Skills Development Agency** – 3 Callflex Business Park, Golden Smithies Lane, Wath-Upon-Dearne, South Yorkshire S63 7ER.
Tel: 01709 765 444.
Email: info@ssda.gov.uk
www.skillsforbusiness.org.uk

Capita Learning and Development

Formerly known as Industrial Society Learning and Development, Capita Learning and Development runs public open courses and customised in-company learning and development programmes. Each year, they manage the design, administration and delivery of over 5000 learning events. They also offer publications through Spiro Press.

➤ **Capita Learning and Development** – 17-19 Rochester Row, London SW1P 1LA.
Tel: 0870 400 1000.
Email: info@capita-ld.co.uk
www.capita-ld.co.uk

Association of Learning Providers (ALP)

ALP is the major national association for learning providers, and represents the interests of its members at local, regional and national levels. The Association works closely with policy makers, and runs seminars and conferences on matters related to training. There are a number of sectors and regional groups within ALP.

➤ **Association of Learning Providers** – Colenso House, 46 Bath Hill, Keynsham, Bristol BS31 1HG.
Tel: 0117 986 5389.
Email: enquiries@learningproviders.org
www.learningproviders.org.uk

Initiatives to encourage workplace skills development

LSC Employer Training Pilots

Employer training pilot schemes (now operating until August 2005) are being run in 20 Learning and Skills Council areas, to assist thousands of low-skilled employees to improve their skills.

In each area, the LSC identifies volunteer employers, from the private, public or voluntary sectors. Participating employers release low-skilled employees during work time to achieve basic skills such as literacy or numeracy, or to work towards a vocational qualification at level 2. The aim is to involve employers who have not previously been involved in training towards qualifications. The LSC usually offers the employer compensation for some of the wage costs, in respect of the employees' time away from the workplace. The LSC also pays the training costs, and provides advice and guidance.

The participating LSC areas are: Birmingham and Solihull, Derbyshire, Essex, Greater Manchester, Tyne and Wear, Wiltshire and Swindon, South Yorkshire, Kent, Leicestershire, London East, Berkshire, Shropshire, Northumberland, County Durham and Tees Valley, Lancashire, West Yorkshire, Black Country, Cambridgeshire and Devon and Cornwall.

Different names have been given to the Employer Training Pilot schemes operating in the different pilot areas. For instance, in Wiltshire and Swindon and in Berkshire, the scheme is currently known as Free2Learn, whereas in Birmingham and Solihull, it is called Train2Gain.

➤ For more information, see local LSC websites or: www.lsc.gov.uk

Investors in People (IiP)

This award is given to organisations which can demonstrate that they meet certain quality standards, including the training and development of their staff. If a company is interested in working towards the Investors in People Standard, evidence of actively supporting staff in learning is essential. Once a company has achieved the award, it will have to prove, at intervals of no more than three years, that it maintains the quality standards.

➤ **Investors in People UK** – 7-10 Chandos Street, London W1G 9DQ.
   Tel: 020 7467 1900.
   Email: information@iipuk.co.uk
   www.investorsinpeople.co.uk

Career Development Loans (CDLs)

CDLs help people to pay for vocational education or training by offering a deferred repayment bank loan. They can be used for any course whether full-time, part-time, open or distance learning, as long as the course is vocational and lasts no longer than two years (plus, if relevant, up to one year's practical work experience, if part of the course). CDLs can also support 24 months of a longer course. CDLs may not be used to pay for anything that is being funded by another source. For example, applicants are not entitled to a CDL if they are employed and the employer receives a grant for their training. Subject to the above, CDLs provide a useful source of financial support for those wishing to develop their employment skills and qualifications.

More information, including eligibility criteria, is given in *2:7 – Money*.

> **Career Development Loans Information Line** – Freephone 0800 585 505 (for help, advice and a free information pack and application form); from 8am to 10pm Monday to Sunday.
> www.lifelonglearning.co.uk/cdl

Further information

Adult Learning Yearbook 2004/5 – published annually by NIACE, £21.95. Comprehensive information on adult education organisations and providers. Includes a section on trade union education with a list of many trade union contacts.

Education Year Book 2004/5 – a Financial Times/Prentice Hall publication, published by Pearson Education, £100. Contains lists of education officers for most of the major unions.

British Vocational Qualifications – published by Kogan Page, £37.50. Includes details of more than 3500 vocational qualifications.

2:20

Training for self-employment

Topics covered:

- Considerations for those thinking of self-employment
- Sources of support and advice
- Organisations offering training
- Possible sources of financial assistance
- Course providers
- Useful publications

Many people find the idea of working independently very appealing, and it is a popular occupational choice. About 12% of all workers are self-employed – around 3.2 million.

Recent trends in self-employment have moved towards franchised contracts, freelance consultancy, teleworking and working from home, in addition to individuals delivering a service to others – the more traditional mode of self-employment.

Checklist for those thinking about self-employment:

- a business idea – which has the potential to succeed

- trade or job skills in the area planned for trading

- business skills – from market research and publicity, to book-keeping and tax records

- personal skills – enthusiastic approach to problem-solving, determination etc.

Support and advice

There are plenty of sources of business advice and guidance to help those who intend to start their own business. It is essential to do thorough research and preparation, seeking as much help as possible before becoming self-employed.

Effective planning before business start-up is the key factor in the survival of new business ventures – considering the possibilities of peaks and troughs in demand and variations in cash flow, and planning accordingly.

Some of the main sources of help are listed below; other useful information resources are the business sections of public libraries, and local authority environmental services or economic development units where up-to-date local business and labour market information is gathered. Some local unitary authorities may provide help with marketing, premises, training and fund raising.

Business Link

Business Link is part of the Small Business Service, a Government agency established by the Department of Trade and Industry (DTI), which aims to deliver independent and impartial business advice, information and a range of services to help small firms and those trying to set up a new business. A network of 45 Business Link operators around the UK are on hand to give practical advice on day-to-day issues. The aim is to offer a single point of contact for every kind of business need.

Regardless of the nature of their business inquiry, individuals can expect to receive assistance, either through the help of information officers or business advisers based within local Business Links, or by referral to partner organisations, such as Learning and Skills Councils, Local Enterprise Companies or Chambers of Commerce.

➤ Local **Business Link** operators can be contacted on 0845 600 9 006 or by minicom on 0845 606 2666.

The Business Link initiative also has a website carrying useful information: www.businesslink.org

In Wales, through 31 regional centres, the initiative is entitled **Business Eye**. Those seeking advice should dial the main number – 08457 96 97 98 – their details will be taken and forwarded to an appropriate adviser. Further details and links to sources of funding and advice can be found on the website: www.businesseye.org.uk

Organisations offering training and support

Business Link (see above) can advise individual enquirers about available training, but individuals interested in becoming self-employed may be directed to make contact with some of the following:

Learning and Skills Councils in England, Local Enterprise Companies in Scotland (LECs), Education and Learning Wales (ELWa) and Invest Northern Ireland.

These organisations provide a wide range of training and enterprise measures, including programmes designed to help unemployed people train for self-employment. The programmes are locally determined – specifically designed to meet the needs of local businesses – so provision varies from area to area. The kinds of training available can include:

● initial support and advice

● enterprise awareness – events which help people interested in working for themselves to understand the implications of setting up and running a business

- business planning – help for managers who want to learn how to develop a business and training plan. There are free planning kits for businesses at various stages of development, backed by professional support at special rates

- business training – available through short and part-time courses to help participants to set up or develop a business. This is supported by open learning facilities, seminars in book-keeping, marketing, management, and other skills for established owner-managers of small firms

- low-cost consultancy – helps firms review their strategy for training and development and is available to help established companies develop their management team, develop new training arrangements and work with other businesses to meet future skill needs

- ongoing mentoring.

Contact addresses of local organisations can be found in the Gazetteer.

learndirect

Help is available through this free national helpline for those seeking up-to-date information on training courses offered by the full range of education training bodies in their area, to include those programmes designed to support businesses and commercial enterprises, and business start-ups. Online advisers have links with comprehensive databases of training opportunities which it may also be possible to access at information, advice and guidance services.

➤ **learndirect** free helpline – 0800 100 900 from 8am to 10pm seven days a week. For Typetalk/minicom users, prefix the number with 18001. The website includes links to pages about learndirect in Wales and in Northern Ireland. www.learndirect-advice.co.uk

For information specifically about learndirect's own courses and learning centres phone 0800 101 901. Lines are open from 8am to 8pm every day. www.learndirect.co.uk

or in Scotland 0808 100 9000 from 7.30am to 11pm Monday to Friday; 9am to 6pm weekends www.learndirectscotland.com

Shell LiveWIRE

This organisation operates throughout the UK. Shell LiveWIRE coordinators can offer advice to young people, aged between 16 and 30, who are considering starting their own business. There is an annual competition for new businesses.

➤ **Shell LiveWIRE** national help-line: 0845 757 3252 for information on how to get started. www.shell-livewire.org

Instant Muscle

Instant Muscle is an organisation with 45 centres across England and Wales providing help to disadvantaged and disabled unemployed people, including a business advisory service for those setting up their own business.

> **Instant Muscle Ltd** – Impact Centre, 115/123 Powis Street, Woolwich, London SE18 6JE.
> Tel: 020 8319 5660.
> Email: ho@instantmuscle.org.uk

Business in Prisons

The Business in Prisons Self-Employment project is a registered charity that aims to reintegrate offenders into the labour market, focusing on self-employment as a viable post-release option. Serving prisoners can register on a programme that offers free advice and support on a one-to-one basis, covering all aspects of self-employment.

> **Business in Prisons** – c/o HMP Sudbury, Ashbourne, Derbyshire DE6 5HW.
> Tel: 01283 584139.
> Email: businessinprison@aol.com
> www.businessinprisons.co.uk

The Telework Association

The Association advises and assists individuals and organisations to implement remote working or telework. Information sent out includes a weekly email listing news and work, a bimonthly magazine and a copy of the Teleworking Handbook.

> **The Telework Association** – Dodd Meadow, Wallingford Road, Kingsbridge TQ7 1NF.
> Tel: 0800 616008.
> Email: info@telework.org.uk
> www.telework.org.uk

Business start-up

Assistance through New Deal

Those who are unemployed may be eligible for financial support and assistance with starting a new business through the **New Deal** initiative, operating through their local Jobcentre Plus/Jobcentre. Assisted by a personal adviser, they will receive help in finding out about self-employment and writing a business plan – necessary if they need to apply for funding. The personal adviser will continue to be available for up to two years after leaving the New Deal.

> Contact the **local Jobcentre Plus/Jobcentre** for full details, telephone the New Deal information line on 0845 606 2626, textphone 0845 606 0680, or view: www.newdeal.gov.uk

High Street banks

Most major banks offer free advice and a package of special services for those considering business start-up. Low interest-rate loans of between £5,000 and £250,000 – to assist with spending on business assets, or to cover the cost of materials, research and development etc – can be awarded to help those with insufficient security to cover a normal bank loan. This financial help is made available through the DTI's Small Business Service's Small Firms Loan Guarantee scheme.

> Information about the scheme can be found on: www.sbs.gov.uk

The Prince's Trust

The Prince's Trust offers practical solutions to help people aged 14 to 30 to make the most of their lives. The Prince's Trust helps people to develop their confidence, skills and job chances through a 12-week personal development programme, start their own business and overcome barriers, and get their lives working with cash development awards and mentor support for those leaving care. The priority is to help people who are educational underachievers, offenders and ex-offenders, long-term unemployed and in or leaving care.

➤ **The Prince's Trust** – Head Office, 18 Park Square East, London NWI 4LH.
Freephone: 0800 842 842.
Email: info@princes-trust.org.uk
www.princes-trust.org.uk

➤ **The Prince's Trust Wales** - Baltic House, Mount Stuart Square, Cardiff CF10 5FH.
Freephone: 0800 842 842.
Email: info@princes-trust.org.uk
www.princes-trust.org.uk

➤ **The Prince's Trust Scotland** – 1st Floor, The Guildhall, 57 Queen Street, Glasgow G1 3EN.
Freephone: 0800 842 842.
Email: info@princes-trust.org.uk
www.princes-trust.org.uk

➤ **The Prince's Scottish Youth Business Trust** – 6th Floor, Mercantile Chambers, 53 Bothwell Street, Glasgow G2 6TS.
Tel: 0141 248 4999.
Email: firststep@psybt.org.uk
www.psybt.org.uk

➤ **The Prince's Trust Northern Ireland** - Block 5, Jennymount Court, North Derby Street, Belfast BT15 3HN.
Tel: 028 9074 5454.
Email: ptnire@princes-trust.org.uk
www.princes-trust.org.uk
www.wiredup.net

Enterprise agencies across the UK

England

National Federation of Enterprise Agencies

The National Federation of Enterprise Agencies represents over 130 members in England. Its principal activities are business counselling and follow-up, business training, financial support and help with managed workspace.

Local enterprise agencies and trusts offer free counselling and advice. Their target market is start-ups and microfirms of up to ten employees.

- **National Federation of Enterprise Agencies** – 12 Stephenson Court, Fraser Road, Priory Business Park, Bedford MK44 3WH.
  Tel: 01234 831623.
  Email: enquiries@nfea.com
  www.nfea.com
  or www.smallbusinessadvice.org.uk
  or www.nesprogramme.org

Wales

Welsh Development Agency

The WDA works in partnership with ELWa (Education and Learning Wales). The Agency can advise on programmes offering support and training for entrepreneurs, and its website has links to other sources of information.

- **Welsh Development Agency** – Plas Glyndur, Kingsway, Cardiff CF10 3AH.
  Tel: 01443 845500.
  Email: enquiries@wda.co.uk
  www.wda.co.uk

For specific advice and help for self-employment and business start-up:

- **Business Eye** – Ynysbridge, Morganstown, Cardiff CF15 9YD.
  Tel: 08457 96 97 98.
  Email: assistance@businesseye.org.uk
  www.businesseye.org.uk

Scotland

In addition to delivering local development and training, Local Enterprise Companies (LECs) are responsible for advising and supporting those people wishing to set up in business and those running existing small businesses. They are accountable to either Scottish Enterprise, or the Highlands and Islands Enterprise, depending on location.

Scottish Enterprise

Scottish Enterprise is located across the southern half of Scotland. It provides a range of services to individuals and firms through its network of 12 LECs. These services include advice, training, financial and property assistance, environmental projects and business development advice. For further information on business start-up and for business development advice in these areas of Scotland:

- **Scottish Enterprise** – 5 Atlantic Quay, 150 Broomielaw, Glasgow G2 8LU.
  Tel: 0141 248 2238.
  Network helpline: 0845 607 8787.
  Email: network.helpline@scotent.co.uk
  www.scottish-enterprise.com

Local **LEC** addresses can be found on the Scottish Enterprise website, or in the Gazetteer section of this publication.

For those interested particularly in starting their own business, the **Business Gateway** is a single access point for information. It offers assistance with business start-up – access to market research, one-to-one sessions with an adviser etc – and business growth.

> **The Business Gateway** on 0845 609 6611 – 9am to 5pm, Mondays to Fridays.
> www.bgateway.com

Highlands and Islands Enterprise

The Highlands and Islands Enterprise Network (HIE) covers half of Scotland, delivering skills to people, businesses and organisations in the Highlands and Islands, and strengthening the economy and the community.

The HIE network manages government training initiatives such as Modern Apprenticeships and supports a wide range of other skills and learning initiatives.

The HIE network also offers all-age career planning and guidance services through Careers Scotland.

The headquarters are in Inverness and most of its services are delivered through a network of ten LECs and ten Careers Scotland localities.

> **Highlands and Islands Enterprise (HIE)** – Cowan House, Inverness Retail and
> Business Park, Inverness IV2 7GF.
> Tel: 01463 234171.
> Email: hie.general@hient.co.uk
> www.hie.co.uk
> www.careers-scotland.org.uk

Northern Ireland

Enterprise Northern Ireland

Enterprise Northern Ireland, the association of Enterprise Agencies in Northern Ireland, supports small business and local enterprise. Through its Start a Business Programme, it provides a package of support to anyone interested in setting up their own business – including an advisory service, training courses and financial planning.

> **Enterprise Northern Ireland** – Aghanloo Industrial Estate, Aghanloo Road, Limavady
> BT49 0HE.
> Tel: 028 7776 3555.
> Email: pa@enterpriseni.com
> www.enterpriseni.com

Enterprise Northern Ireland is in partnership with Invest Northern Ireland – an organisation that aims to accelerate economic development in Northern Ireland.

> **Invest Northern Ireland** – 44-58 May Street, Belfast BT1 4NN.
> Upper Galwally, Belfast BT8 6TB.
> 17 Antrim Road, Lisburn BT28 3AL.
> Tel: (for all) 028 9023 9090.
> Email: info@investni.com
> www.investni.com

Help in areas of deprivation

Under the umbrella organisation of the **Regional Development Agency**, there will be local initiatives supporting all aspects of urban regeneration, including business enterprise. In many areas, multi-agency partnerships have successfully bid for all sorts of regeneration support from the European Union. Projects vary from area to area.

There are 2000 **Enterprise Areas** across the UK, where assistance for new businesses may include stamp duty exemption, help from neighbourhood renewal projects etc.

➤ Contact the local **Regional Development Agency, Learning and Skills Council** or **LEC** (see the Gazetteer) or **Business Link, Business Eye** or **Invest Northern Ireland** (see above).

Co-operative business

Workers' co-operatives are owned and democratically controlled by their employees, who work together as equals. This can be a way of reducing the solitude of self-employment. There are co-operatives active in all business sectors.

Co-operatives UK

Co-operatives UK is the national organisation that promotes co-operative solutions, works to increase awareness and understanding of co-operative values and principles, and supports the development and growth of new and existing co-operatives. As part of their work, they provide information and advice to individuals and groups considering setting up co-operative enterprises.

➤ **Co-operatives UK** – Holyoake House, Hanover Street, Manchester M60 0AS.
  Tel: 0161 246 2953.
  Email: info@cooperatives-uk.coop
  www.cooperatives-uk.coop

Business schools

Business schools throughout the UK run short or part-time courses aimed at people about to set up a small business, or who are already running one. Training can cover all aspects of the support that is needed in starting and launching a business; from formulating a business plan and seeking financial backing to product marketing and employment law. Some charge a fee for training, but this is often nominal as financial support is commonly given by the local Learning and Skills Council or LEC, or by the DTI. There is no training allowance.

The Association of Business Schools (ABS)

The Association has over 100 higher education member institutions of high professional standing. Located throughout the UK, they offer a range of services both to companies and to individuals, which will vary slightly according to regional industrial profiles and with established specialisms.

Full information about the wide range of courses offered by schools of the Association is available in their *ABS Directory of UK Business and Management Courses* which is regularly updated and free online.

> **Association of Business Schools (ABS)** – 334-354 Gray's Inn Road, London WC1X 8BP.
> Tel: 020 7837 1899.
> Email: abs@the-abs.org.uk
> www.the-abs.org.uk

Adult education courses

Many adult education centres, colleges, universities and the Workers' Educational Association (WEA), run short or part-time courses on self-employment and starting a small business. They may also offer courses on topics related to running a business, such as book-keeping, employment law or general management. Some of these courses may involve open learning.

> Contact local colleges, universities, WEA or community education centres.

> learndirect free helpline – 0800 100 900, or in Scotland 0808 100 9000.

Open learning courses

A variety of distance learning colleges, like the National Extension College, the International Correspondence Schools and RRC Business Training, offer both general courses in business management and specific ones in subjects like marketing or accountancy. The Open University Business School also runs professional business-related courses.

See *2:17 Open/distance and other independent learning.*

> learndirect free helpline – 0800 100 900, or in Scotland 0808 100 9000.

ICS

ICS offers the ICS diploma course in Starting Your Own Business. The course takes participants from the initial business idea through to the business plan, and cover all aspects of basic finance and budgeting. The whole course costs £249, to include all materials and tutor support.

There is also an ICS diploma course in Business Management, which covers team leadership and decision-making, as well as fundamental aspects of human resource management, financial management, and marketing. This course costs £479, including all materials and tutor support, and a diploma is awarded upon successful completion. ICS also offers many other courses in business and practical skills.

Courses can be paid for in full or by interest-free instalments. Students can study at their own pace.

> **ICS** – Freepost 882, Glasgow G3 8BR.
> Tel: 0500 888 003.
> Email: icscourseadvisors@ics-uk.co.uk
> www.icslearn.co.uk

National Extension College (NEC)

NEC courses are accredited by the ODL QC, the national body for quality in open and distance learning. Their business courses include:

Business Basics – short courses that provide an insight into a key business topic and deliver practical business benefits. Courses in marketing, book-keeping and personal skills for managers.

Book-keeping – training for a number of nationally-recognised qualifications at a choice of levels – *Essential Book-keeping* (manual or computerised book-keeping) to develop basic book-keeping skills and *Advanced Book-keeping.*

Business Start Up – covers the knowledge and skills needed to start up a business from financial and legal planning to market testing, business planning and securing premises.

Every NEC course comes complete with personal tuition from an experienced tutor.

> ➤ **National Extension College** – Student Advisers, The Michael Young Centre, Purbeck Road, Cambridge CB2 2HN.
> Tel: 0800 389 2839.
> Email: info@nec.ac.uk
> www.nec.ac.uk/courses

Distributed Learning

The Distributed Learning group works in collaboration with leading academic partners – such as Edinburgh Business School at Heriot-Watt University and the University of Portsmouth – to develop and deliver off-campus academic qualifications to students around the world through supported self-study. The academic programmes combine text-based study materials and online learning support. Students may begin courses at any time and take examinations in centres around the world

Programmes available include:

Master of Business Administration (MBA)

Doctor of Business Administration (DBA)

MSc Internet Systems Development

Diploma in Marketing

Certificate in Project Management.

> ➤ **Distributed Learning** – Student Services Team, Edinburgh Gate, Harlow, Essex CM20 2JE.
> Tel: 01279 623112.
> Email: student.services@pearson.com
> www.ebsmba.com or www.portsmouthonlinecourses.com

The Open University Business School

The OU offers a range of business courses, including an MBA and a Professional Certificate in Management, which comprises freestanding modules that each take three months to complete and cost around £620.

> ➤ **The Open University Business School** – School of Management, The Open University, Walton Hall, Milton Keynes MK7 6AA.
> Tel: 08700 100311.
> www.open.ac.uk/oubs

RRC Business Training

RRC Business Training provides complete training packages to meet the needs of those seeking to gain professional qualifications or to develop their business and office skills. RRC has over 70 years' experience in developing comprehensive, up-to-date and effective open and distance learning courses. RRC also provides a full range of training and consultancy services for companies of all sizes. Areas of expertise include health and safety, environmental management, book-keeping, payroll, credit management, marketing, sales management, quality assurance, administration and management.

RRC is accredited by the Open and Distance Learning Quality Council (ODLQC) for its overall distance learning operation, and by awarding bodies for its distance and open learning courses.

➤ **RRC Business Training** – Customer Service Team, 27-37 St George's Road, London SW19 4DS.
Tel: 020 8944 3100.
Email: info@rrc.co.uk
www.rrc.co.uk

Further information

There are numerous guides to self-employment available.

The No-nonsense Guide to Government Rules and Regulations for Setting Up your Business – free from Business Link.

The Teleworking Handbook – published by the Telework Association, £16 inc. p&p.

Kogan Page titles include:

How to Set Up and Run Your Own Business – £12.99

Guide to Buying Your First Franchise – £7.99

A Guide to Working for Yourself – £12.99

Running a Home-based Business – £12.99

How to Prepare a Business Plan – £10.40

Starting a Successful Business – £14.99.

How To Books titles include:

The Ultimate Business Plan – £4.99 (£4.24 if bought online)

Book-keeping and Accounting for the Small Business – £9.99 (£8.49 if bought online)

Going for Self-Employment – £9.99 (£8.49 if bought online)

Starting Your Own Business – £9.99 (£8.49 if bought online).

These books, and other relevant titles, may be held in public libraries or may be accessed at information, advice and guidance agencies.

Leaflets on tax and National Insurance for self-employed people are available through public offices such as the Tax Office and the Jobcentre Plus/Jobcentre.

2:21

Volunteering

Topics covered:

- Considerations before undertaking voluntary work
- The breadth of opportunities for volunteers
- National and regional voluntary organisations

The range of voluntary work and the variety of groups who need volunteer helpers is enormous. The tasks undertaken should always:

- be of value to the organisations or to the individuals that volunteers work with
- benefit the individual volunteer.

Positive aspects:

- opportunities for training
- learning new skills
- acquisition of qualifications
- acquisition of language skills
- a job trial.

Prospects:

- further training
- paid employment
- other voluntary work
- improved employability.

Benefits for the volunteer:

- sense of achievement
- meeting other people

– regular activity

– positive use of skills and energy

– work experience

– acquiring adaptability, leadership, initiative skills.

Benefits for the recipient:

– things get done which, perhaps, would not otherwise have happened

– quality of life is improved.

- The experience of a new area of work is useful to those considering a change of career. Some professions – for example, social work and youth work – ask for voluntary experience before accepting training entrants.

- The breadth of opportunity means that potential volunteers can always find an activity to match their skills and interests. For the unemployed or retired, voluntary work can help to maintain skills and develop new interests. Often, maturity is an asset.

- Although the majority of volunteers do not receive financial reward, many express satisfaction at being able to assist a particular cause. However, some volunteers do receive payment to cover reasonable expenses, while a small number go on to get a paid job with the organisation.

- Some voluntary bodies – for example The Samaritans – require volunteers to undergo a thorough training programme. Many organisations assist their voluntary workers to gain qualifications on-the-job.

- Voluntary work keeps people active and in contact with others, often leading to a widening of friendships.

- Volunteers who are unemployed will not stop receiving benefits if they are still available for full-time work and are actively seeking work. Details can be checked with the local Jobcentre Plus/Jobcentre.

- Through the Government's Millennium Volunteers scheme, 16-24 year-olds can do voluntary work within their local communities and gain formal recognition of their achievements. They will have MV on their CV, and receive a certificate after 100 hours of volunteer work, and an MV Award of Excellence after 200 hours.

- The National Trust, BTCV, RSPB, The Wildlife Trusts, and the YHA are all participating in the Employee Volunteering Programme, funded by the Home Office's Active Community Unit. This programme encourages employing organisations to enable their employees to spend time on voluntary projects – as a one-off teamwork exercise, part of a personal development programme or on an individual long-term secondment.

Voluntary opportunities

Before opting for one particular area, potential volunteers should consider the following points.

- A volunteer should choose an organisation which interests them and which they care about – perhaps selecting an activity that they enjoy doing or want to learn to do.

- As a first step, potential volunteers need to get information and advice on all aspects of volunteering from their local volunteer bureau, which will be listed in the telephone directory. Alternatively, they should contact one of the national agencies.

Counselling

Organisations like Relate or The Samaritans provide a long and thorough training for volunteers. Other counselling organisations may be listed in *Yellow Pages*.

Education

Volunteers can assist with basic skills training – in adult literacy programmes or numeracy tutoring – or help in special schools or sheltered work places, working with people who have learning difficulties. Training is usually given.

➤ Contact the local education authority, library, community centre, school or adult education department.

For those interested in being a volunteer tutor in Northern Ireland:

➤ **Educational Guidance Service for Adults (EGSA)** – 4th Floor, 40 Linenhall Street, Belfast BT2 8BA.
Tel: 028 9024 4274.
Email: info@egsa.org.uk
www.egsa.org.uk

Advice and information

Volunteers work in Citizens Advice Bureaux, independent advice centres, legal aid centres and law surgeries, and for welfare rights projects. Most of these organisations provide training. Look in the phone book, or in *Yellow Pages,* under counselling and advice, or see other local directories.

Environmental work

Volunteers help to conserve the countryside – conserving energy, animal and plant life and natural resources, to preserve urban wildlife, conserve buildings and landscapes. Many organisations for the environment offer training in environmental skills, which can lead to a new career or can offer valuable work experience for career development. Some offer short, residential working breaks.

Some of the organisations offering voluntary opportunities are described below.

Friends of the Earth (FoE)

Their activities are divided into local and national levels. At national level, campaign areas include GM food, corporates, global trade, transport, safer chemicals, climate change, waste and biodiversity. At local level, groups are involved in practical projects – these activities may vary from area to area as each group acts independently. The head office has the addresses of active local groups.

➤ **Friends of the Earth** – 26-28 Underwood Street, London NI 7JQ.
Tel: 020 7490 1555.
Email: info@foe.co.uk
www.foe.co.uk

Council for the Protection of Rural England (CPRE)

The CPRE works towards maintaining a living and beautiful countryside through action on conservation issues and planning casework. There is a branch in every county and committees in many district boroughs. It is a registered charity. The national office has details of local branches and their training programmes.

➤ **CPRE** – 128 Southwark Street, London SE1 0SW.
Tel: 020 7981 2800.
Email: info@cpre.org.uk
www.cpre.org.uk

BTCV

BTCV is the UK's leading practical conservation charity. Every year it supports the activities of over 130,000 volunteers from all sections of the community in activities to promote and improve their environment.

The work involved is diverse – from a few hours a week to full-time, from planting a local community garden to an international conservation holiday. Areas of expertise include tree planting, fencing, drystone walling, path work, coppicing and nature garden design.

Training is provided and there are opportunities to manage projects. Training can lead to nationally-recognised qualifications. Many of the volunteers go on to successful careers in environmental and related fields.

Conservation Volunteering – How and Why can be downloaded from their website.

➤ **BTCV** – Conservation Centre, 163 Balby Road, Doncaster DN4 0RH.
Tel: 01302 572 244.
Email: information@btcv.org.uk
www.btcv.org.uk

➤ **Conservation Volunteers Northern Ireland (CVNI)** – Beech House, 159 Ravenhill Road, Belfast BT6 0BP.
Tel: 028 9064 5169.
Email: cvni@btcv.org.uk
www.cvni.org

➤ **BTCV Cymru** – Wales Conservation Centre, Forest Farm Road, Whitchurch, Cardiff CF14 7JJ.
Tel: 029 2052 0990.
Email: help-wales@btcv.org.uk
www.btcvcymru.org

> **BTCV Scotland** – Balallan House, 24 Allan Park, Stirling FK8 2QG.
> Tel: 01786 479 697.
> Email: scotland@btcv.org.uk

The Tree Council (UK)

The Tree Council promotes the improvement of the environment by the planting and conservation of trees and woods in town and country throughout the UK. Its annual programme includes Seed Gathering Sunday, National Tree Week, Trees Love Care and Walk in the Woods month, supporting the groups organising local events. It also coordinates the national volunteer Tree Warden scheme and operates a fund giving tree-planting grants to schools and communities.

> **The Tree Council** – 71 Newcomen Street, London SE1 1YT.
> Tel: 020 7407 9992.
> Email: info@treecouncil.org.uk
> www.treecouncil.org.uk

Greenpeace

Greenpeace is an independent and non-political, international organisation, dedicated to the protection of the environment by peaceful means.

> **Greenpeace** – Canonbury Villas, London N1 2PN.
> Tel: 020 7865 8100.
> Email: info@uk.greenpeace.org
> www.greenpeace.org.uk

National Trust

There are opportunities for voluntary work at National Trust properties or offices throughout the country.

> **The National Trust** – Volunteering & Community Involvement Office, Rowan, Kembrey Park, Swindon SN2 8YL
> Tel: 0870 609 5383.
> Email: volunteers@nationaltrust.org.uk
> www.nationaltrust.org.uk/volunteering

The National Trust also offers working holidays in England, Wales and Northern Ireland on outdoor conservation schemes on the Trust's many properties, often in remote places. You can find details on the website.

> **National Trust Working Holidays** – Sapphire House, Roundtree Way, Norwich NR7 8SQ.
> Tel: 0870 429 2428 (for a brochure).
> Email: working.holidays@nationaltrust.org.uk

Marine Conservation Society

The Society sometimes offers voluntary work at the offices in Ross-on-Wye. It can also help with setting up local voluntary groups.

> **Marine Conservation Society** – Unit 3, Wolf Business Park, Alton Road, Ross-on-Wye, Herefordshire HR9 5NB.
> Tel: 01989 566017.
> Email: info@mcsuk.org
> www.mcsuk.org

Volunteering and the New Deal

The **New Deal** programme for jobseekers may, as part of an individually-designed programme, includes voluntary work as a means of providing you with skills and experience that will make you more useful to an employer.

> See chapter *2:18 – Work Based Learning for Adults and other government-funded training* for more information about the New Deal.

> Contact **New Deal personal advisers**, based at the Jobcentre Plus/Jobcentre.

Work with children and young people

Youth work, organised by local education or leisure departments and other organisations – nurseries, crèches and toddler activity clubs, play groups, social clubs, Guides, Scouts, Woodcraft Folk, St John Ambulance, British Red Cross – requires volunteer helpers. Most groups provide training for their volunteers. Many paid youth workers started out as voluntary helpers. Volunteers working with young people have to agree to undergo criminal record checks.

Contact the organisations listed above, either at local level or through their national headquarters, or contact:

> **National Council for Voluntary Youth Services (NCVYS)** – 2nd Floor, Solecast House, 13-27 Brunswick Place, London N1 6DX.
> Tel: 020 7253 1010.
> Email: mail@ncvys.org.uk
> www.ncvys.org.uk

Social and health services

Thousands of volunteers help in hospitals and with social services departments or the probation service.

Contact the Voluntary Service Organiser (VSO) based in hospitals, social services departments or within the probation service.

In the community

Many volunteers have ideas for new projects in their area, but may need advice and support to enable them to make a start. Projects may include building an adventure playground, clearing up wasteland, running a campaign for safer roads, assisting with crime prevention, starting up a local Link scheme or a lunch club for elderly people.

> Contact the local **Council for Voluntary Service (England), Wales Council for Voluntary Action, CVS Scotland, Northern Ireland Council for Voluntary Action (NICVA)** or **Rural Community Council**. These bodies can inform potential volunteers about on-going local initiatives and can advise on how to go about a project, the legal position, how to raise money and so on. They may also run training courses for members of local projects.

National and regional voluntary organisations

- Council for Voluntary Service/Action (if there is no volunteer bureau)

- Rural Community Council (if there is no volunteer bureau).

Addresses are in the phone book.

At the national level:

The organisations listed below can provide information and advice on most aspects of volunteering. They produce publications and provide training courses, or can steer enquirers to other organisations that help individuals to find suitable voluntary work.

England

Volunteering England

This is an integrated, national volunteer development agency for England and can provide useful free factsheets to those sending an A4 stamped addressed envelope. The envelope should be marked clearly with the names of the leaflets requested.

TimeGuide – a guide for people who want to volunteer (needs a 33p stamp); also, *Finding out about volunteering in your area; Residential volunteering in the UK; National Minimum Wage; Volunteering overseas: a list of information sources; Accreditation of voluntary work; Volunteer drivers; Volunteering and State Benefits; Careers in the Voluntary Sector; Who can Volunteer?*

➤ **Volunteering England** – Information Sheets, Regent's Wharf, 8 All Saints Street, London N1 9RL.
Tel: 0845 305 6979.
Email: information@volunteeringengland.org
www.volunteering.org.uk

Millennium Volunteers (MV)

16- to 24-year-olds can do voluntary work within their local communities and gain recognition of their achievements. The Department for Education & Skills (DfES) funds a large number of voluntary projects, in areas as wide-ranging as language development for ethnic communities, football training, crime prevention, mentoring and study support. MV can signpost local organisations which have successfully bid for funds to run volunteer projects.

➤ Telephone helpline: 0800 917 8185.
Email: millennium.volunteers@dfes.gsi.gov.uk
www.mvonline.gov.uk (with links to Wales, Scotland and Northern Ireland equivalents)

Northern Ireland

Volunteer Development Agency

Organises annual Volunteers' Week in June, and offers information about volunteering opportunities and relevant training. Their useful publications may be ordered or downloaded from the website.

> ➤ **Volunteer Development Agency** – 4th Floor, 58 Howard Street, Belfast BT1 6PG.
> Tel: 028 9023 6100.
> Email: info@volunteering-ni.org
> www.volunteering-ni.org

Voluntary Service Bureau

Arranges voluntary work opportunities for its own projects and those of 600 other user agencies. VSB also supports NI Cares Initiative, a programme designed to promote employer-supported volunteering by encouraging teams to take up a challenge for a community group.

> ➤ **Voluntary Service Bureau** – 34 Shaftesbury Square, Belfast BT2 7DB.
> Tel: 028 9020 0850 or freephone: 0800 052 2212.
> Email: info@vsb.org.uk
> www.vsb.org.uk
> www.nicares.co.uk

Scotland

> ➤ **Volunteer Development Scotland** – Stirling Enterprise Park, Stirling FK7 7RP.
> Tel: 01786 479593.
> Email: information@vds.org.uk
> www.vds.org.uk

Learning Link Scotland (LLS)

LLS can be contacted for information, networking, support and exchange opportunities for the voluntary adult education sector.

> ➤ **Learning Link Scotland (LLS)** – Suite 6, 2 Commercial Street, Edinburgh EH6 6JA.
> Tel: 0131 553 7992.
> Email: info@learninglinkscotland.org.uk
> www.learninglinkscotland.org.uk

Wales

> ➤ **Wales Council for Voluntary Action (WCVA)** – Volunteering Team, Baltic House,
> Mount Stuart Square, Cardiff CF10 5FH.
> Helpdesk for all enquiries: 0870 607 1666.
> Email: help@wcva.org
> www.wcva.org.uk

Voluntary work away from home

CSV

CSV specialises in placing people in full-time voluntary work away from home, helping people in need, for periods of between four and twelve months. Has a special section for over-50s. Volunteers receive full board and accommodation, travel costs and pocket money. Regional offices are listed in local phone directories.

> **CSV** – 237 Pentonville Road, London NI 9NJ.
> Tel: 020 7278 6601.
> Email: information@csv.org.uk
> www.csv.org.uk

> **CSV Scotland** – Wellgate House, 200 Cowgate, Edinburgh EH1 1NQ.
> Tel: 0131 622 7766.
> Email: scotinfo@csv.org.uk

> **CSV Wales** – 4th floor, Arlbee House, Greyfriars Road, Cardiff CF1 3AE.
> Tel: 029 2066 6737.
> Email: csvcymru@dialpipex.com

Voluntary work overseas

This usually requires a commitment of one or more years. The main overseas voluntary organisations usually ask for professionally trained people to go to a particular country for at least a year. However, it is possible to go for shorter periods.

VSO

Offers a range of overseas volunteering opportunities for people with experience and relevant skills, up to the age of 75.

> **VSO** – 317 Putney Bridge Road, London SW15 2PN.
> Tel: 020 8780 7500.
> Email: enquiry@vso.org.uk
> www.vso.org.uk

Worldwide Volunteering

A charity which holds a computer database of volunteer opportunities – mainly for young people but many of which are also suitable for adults – which can be matched to an individual's availability and experience. The website tells you where you can access the database locally.

> **Worldwide Volunteering** – 7 North Street Workshops, Stoke sub Hamdon, Somerset TA14 6QR.
> Tel: 01935 825588.
> Email: worldvol@worldvol.co.uk
> www.worldwidevolunteering.org.uk

Skillshare International

Recruits development workers and health trainers, with qualifications and experience, for projects in Africa and India.

➤ **Skillshare International** – 126 New Walk, Leicester LE1 7JA.
Tel: 0116 254 1862.
Email: info@skillshare.org
www.skillshare.org

Returned Volunteer Action (RVA)

RVA publishes a number of booklets on volunteering and development work overseas. An introductory pack for volunteers is available for £3.50 plus a 56p stamped, addressed envelope.

➤ **RVA** – 1 Amwell Street, London ECIR 1TH.
Tel: 020 7278 0804.

Further information

learndirect – the free information helpline: 0800 100 900, can provide information on regional and local volunteering opportunities.

Leaflet JSAL7 – *Financial help if you are working or doing voluntary work* – can be obtained from the Jobcentre Plus/Jobcentre.

➤ Websites which list volunteering opportunities include: www.timebank.org.uk www.do-it.org.uk

The following are examples of books published by Vacation Work Publications – some may be available in local reference libraries:

Green Volunteers – £10.99

World Volunteers – £10.99

Archaeo-Volunteers – £10.99 (world-wide archaeological and heritage volunteering)

Gap Year for Grown Ups – £11.95

Kibbutz Volunteer – £10.99

Working with the Environment – £11.95 (includes volunteering opportunities)

Working with Animals – The UK, Europe & Worldwide – £11.95 (includes volunteering opportunities).

A Year Off... A Year On? – published by Lifetime Careers Publishing, £10.99.

2:22

Learning opportunities abroad

Topics covered:

- Reasons for studying outside the UK
- Different modes of studying abroad
- Issues, such as finance and the validity of qualifications
- Specific initiatives to assist study abroad

Why study outside the UK?

Many people are interested in spending a period of time studying or working abroad. Besides the usual primary objective of developing modern language skills, many are intrigued by the possibility of absorbing a different culture and approaching their studies from an alternative social and economic perspective. Others, wanting to work abroad in the future, look forward to gaining awareness of a different business culture and of being able to contrast another country's industrial and commercial focus with that of Britain. Before following up ways into studying abroad, there are positive and negative considerations to assess.

Advantages

The benefits of studying abroad include:

- learning a new language or improving existing language skills

- studying subjects not offered in the UK

- getting useful experience which could help with finding employment abroad (or in the UK)

- advances in personal maturity, adaptability, open-mindedness

- the opportunity, perhaps, to study in a 'centre for excellence' in a particular field, for example, to study history of art in Italy

- the course of study abroad might be less expensive.

Disadvantages

The drawbacks of studying abroad include:

- qualifications obtained may not be acceptable to employers or research departments in UK universities

- the cost can be high – some European countries consider EU students as home students and do not charge for tuition, but registration and examination fees may have to be paid

- there may be an exacting language test prior to course entry

- there may prove to be difficulties with the change in culture

- teaching methods differ; there may be problems keeping pace with studies.

Different ways to study abroad

- Clients could undertake a full degree course alongside the country's indigenous students.

- They could study for dual (sometimes, triple) qualifications. Some UK universities offer degree courses where study time is split between countries, leading to the award of a foreign degree or diploma, in addition to the British qualification.

- A UK qualification – for example, on a European studies or modern foreign language course – can involve periods of up to a year spent studying abroad.

- Clients could undertake a short-term study programme as part of a UK course of higher education. Erasmus – the European-funded student mobility scheme – is part of the Socrates European community education programme which operates for mature students as well as younger participants. Studies undertaken abroad in another participating European country are recognised as part of higher education courses run by participating UK HE institutions and may be in any subject area. Applications to the programme must be made through the students' HE institution. The UK Socrates-Erasmus Council can provide further information on the programme and funding.

➤ **UK Socrates-Erasmus Council** – Research and Development Building, The University of Kent, Canterbury CT2 7PD.
Tel: 01227 762712.
Email: info@erasmus.ac.uk.
www.erasmus.ac.uk

Issues to consider

Language

Knowledge of the particular country's language is essential for learners to gain benefit from a period spent studying abroad.

Immigration

Each country has different rules. People considering studying overseas should contact the relevant embassy or high commission.

Money for studies

Unless an intended course of study abroad forms part of a UK higher education course which is linked to the Socrates-Erasmus scheme, people who intend to follow a course of study abroad must be self-funding or seek sponsorship, grants from charitable trusts or apply to other possible sources of finance. Some employers may finance the cost of taking a course of study abroad.

It may be possible to receive assistance through the Student Loans Company or to take out a Career Development Loan of between £300 and £8000. Career Development Loans are only available for vocational courses of two years or less and for people who are going to come back to work in the UK. If the course is longer, the CDL can be used to finance part of the course, for example, the last two years. Learning providers must be registered with the DfES. Clients should contact their **local education authority's finance department** for information about financing their studies.

> **Career Development Loans** – freephone: 0800 585 505 (8am to 10pm, Monday to Sunday).
> www.lifelonglearning.co.uk/cdl

> **Student Loans Company** – freephone: 0800 40 50 10 (9am to 5.30am Monday to Friday).
> www.slc.co.uk

There are some schemes which may pay for a period overseas. For example, the Winston Churchill Memorial Trust offers Fellowships for eligible people to conduct a worthwhile project oversees. See www.wcmt.org.uk for more information.

Also, there are a small number of scholarships available, such as those from NATO, The Fulbright Commission and the Association of Commonwealth Universities. There is strong competition for scholarships and most schemes have an upper age limit.

Health and state benefits

Healthcare overseas is expensive. However, many countries have reciprocal arrangements with the UK, allowing free or reduced-rate health care. The situation with respect to National Insurance Contributions and benefits must be explored, as going abroad may affect eligibility for benefits. The organisations listed below can provide information.

> **Inland Revenue, National Insurance Contributions Office** – International Services, Longbenton, Newcastle-upon-Tyne, NE98 1ZZ.
> Tel: 0845 915 4811.
> www.inlandrevenue.gov.uk/nic

> **Pensions and Overseas Benefits Directorate** – Customer Service Unit, Tyneview Park, Benton, Newcastle-upon-Tyne NE98 IBA.
> Tel: 0191 218 7878.
> www.dwp.gov.uk

> **Department for Social Development (Northern Ireland)** – Overseas Benefits Agency, Castle Building, Stormont Estate, Belfast BT4 3UD.
> Tel: 028 9052 0520.
> www.dsdni.gov.uk

Income tax

For those who have dependants, own property or who are likely to work in the country they are proposing to study in, the tax position is likely to be complicated. Their liability will largely depend on whether or not they are regarded as a UK resident.

The **local tax office** can provide leaflets and advice. It may be necessary to consult with an accountant or to seek assistance through a **Citizens Advice Bureau.**

Qualifications

The validity of foreign qualifications in the UK needs to be carefully checked. Some degrees and professional qualifications are not of comparable standing. UK NARIC – the National Recognition Information Centre for the UK – can provide guidelines and comparability statements to individuals enquiring about formal recognition of particular qualifications. Individuals considering courses of study abroad leading to overseas qualifications might want to establish their relevance for future employment in the UK. The majority of higher educational institutions in the UK subscribe to the UK NARIC service as provided over the internet.

> **UK NARIC** – Oriel House, Oriel Road, Cheltenham, Gloucestershire GL50 1XP.
> Tel: 0870 990 4088.
> Email: info@naric.org.uk
> www.naric.org.uk

There is also a service for individuals enquiring about formal recognition of vocational qualifications. UK NARIC runs UK NRP – the National Reference Point for Vocational Qualifications. UK NRP provides information on vocational qualifications at skilled worker, trade and technician levels.

> **UK NRP** – Oriel House, Oriel Road, Cheltenham, Gloucestershire GL50 1XP.
> Tel: 0870 990 4088.
> Email: info@uknrp.org.uk
> www.uknrp.org.uk

Refer to *2:6 – Qualifications* and *3:27 – Overseas students, refugees and asylum seekers* for further information.

The European Union

The EU is made up of 25 member states and several other countries are seeking to gain entry. Nationals of the following countries are EU citizens:

Spain, Austria, Sweden, Finland, Denmark, Belgium, Germany, the Netherlands, France, Luxembourg, Italy, Greece, Portugal, Ireland, United Kingdom, Poland, Hungary, the Czech republic, Slovakia, Slovenia, Estonia, Latvia, Lithuania, Malta and Cyprus.

Citizens of these countries, as well as those from Iceland, Norway, Liechtenstein, Central and Eastern Europe, have 'freedom of movement'. This means that they have the opportunity to live, study and be employed in any of the member states of the EU or European Economic Area (EEA) on the same basis as those countries' nationals.

European initiatives

The Europe Commission funds several specific initiatives to improve education and training in EU and EEA member states. Organisations such as training bodies, colleges, universities and schools design a project and bid competitively for funds to finance it. Individuals do not receive funds directly but may benefit by participating in a fund-winning project. The initiatives include the European Social Fund, Socrates and Leonardo. Information on current projects can be obtained from local education and colleges etc. Further details on the schemes themselves may be obtained from the British Council (see later).

Socrates

Part of the Socrates programme aims to strengthen the European dimension in adult education and lifelong learning. A range of projects and initiatives is available for adult learners, teachers and trainers. www2.britishcouncil.org/socrates

Leonardo

The Leonardo da Vinci initiative includes vocational work placements in other European countries for trainees of all ages. The placements are for a minimum of three weeks. www.leonardo.org.uk

More information on Europe

Careers Europe

Local careers professionals have access to the Careers Europe information centre in Bradford which provides a range of products such as the *Eurofacts* and *Globalfacts* factsheets and the *EXODUS* database. These are information resources covering aspects of studying, living and working in Europe, the USA, Australia, New Zealand and many other countries. Careers Europe can provide help and advice to professional guidance workers. Individuals cannot approach the organisation themselves, although the factsheets and *EXODUS* may be available for callers to adult information, advice and guidance agencies.

> **Careers Europe** – Onward House, Baptist Place, Bradford, BD1 2PS.
> Tel: 01274 829600.
> Email: europe@careersb.co.uk
> www.careerseurope.co.uk

Local education authorities

Often these public bodies have a European liaison officer/ European awareness adviser or similar. Many further education colleges and universities have a European officer who may be able to help, although their main task is usually coordinating EU-funded programmes.

Eurodesk

This is an information service mainly for young people (classed as under 30) who want to know about European opportunities and funding. Eurodesk provides information on working, studying, volunteering and travelling abroad and is funded by the European Commission.

> **Eurodesk (UK contact point)** – Rosebery House, 9 Haymarket Terrace, Edinburgh EH12 5EZ.
> Tel: 0131 313 2488.
> Email: eurodesk@youthlink.co.uk
> www.eurodesk.org

Beyond Europe

Commonwealth universities

There are opportunities to study at both undergraduate and postgraduate level in the Commonwealth, though there are relatively few scholarships/awards available for undergraduate study outside an individual's own country. Enquirers should contact the immigration section of the respective high commission in London, for details of visa requirements for individual countries.

General enquiries may be made to the Association of Commonwealth Universities' (ACU) library (located in London) which has a substantial collection of prospectuses, reference books and scholarship information. Prospective students are advised to refer to the detailed information sheets on study in Australia, Canada, New Zealand and the Commonwealth in general. These, and related information sources, are available on the ACU website (click on 'library' and then 'student information summaries'). In addition, detailed information on the Commonwealth Scholarships and other awards administered by the ACU is available on the CFSP website: www.cfsp-online.org

> **Association of Commonwealth Universities (ACU)** – John Foster House, 36 Gordon Square, London WC1H 0PF.
> Tel: 020 7380 6700 (Monday to Friday 9.30am to 1pm and 2pm to 5.30pm).
> Email: info@acu.ac.uk
> www.acu.ac.uk
> Library opening hours: Monday to Friday 10am to 1pm and 2pm to 5pm.

American universities

All US universities are fee-paying and the private universities usually charge higher fees. State universities are usually less expensive but costs may vary widely. State universities charge more for out-of-state students (which includes foreign students).

Unlike in Britain, there is generally no uniformity of approach or entrance requirements to US universities. Applicants should anticipate completing applications which may vary greatly from one university to another. There is a separate application fee for each university of between \$40 to \$100. In addition, students are commonly required to take standardised admission tests and submit these scores as an application requirement.

Funding is a very important consideration when researching US universities and applicants are encouraged to contact the universities' admissions offices as well as the department in which they wish to study. Generally, private universities have more scholarship funding to distribute but also have a higher cost of attendance. Bursaries are generally offered only for higher degrees, although some institutions have scholarships for first-degree foreign students. It is worth checking with a particular institution's Dean of Admissions.

US universities have a much more flexible course structure than those in the UK.

Permission to work off campus is rarely given to overseas students in the US and proof must be presented to the immigration authorities that intending students can support themselves and pay their fees without recourse to employment. Furthermore there is no guarantee that students will be permitted to stay in the US beyond their course of study.

The Fulbright Commission's US Educational Advisory Service (EAS) is the first point of contact for people considering studying in the USA. The EAS can provide free information on all aspects of studying in the USA and has a public reference library for the use of prospective students.

> **The Fulbright Commission** – US Educational Advisory Service, Fulbright House, 62 Doughty Street, London WC1N 2JZ.
Tel: 020 7404 6994.
Email: education@fulbright.co.uk
www.fulbright.co.uk/eas

British Council Education and Training Group

The British Council is the UK's international organisation for education and cultural relations. The Education and Training Group promotes quality education and training in the UK and worldwide by:

- delivering a range of international education and training programmes

- strengthening cooperation between the UK and other countries in education and training

- increasing international recognition of learning opportunities provided by the UK

- supporting education and training reform

- sharing best practice between the UK and other countries.

The British Council holds information on a wide range of international services in the field of education and training.

> **The British Council Education and Training Group** – 10 Spring Gardens, London SW1A 2BN.
Tel: 020 7389 4004.
Email: education.enquiries@britishcouncil.org
www.britishcouncil.org/education

Further information

The European Choice – A Guide to Opportunities for Higher Education in Europe – a free booklet published by the Department for Education & Skills. Contains information about financial support and details on the EU and EEA countries' higher education systems. Also available on the DfES website: www.dfes.gov.uk/echoice

Study Abroad – published by UNESCO. 2004-05 edition, £17.50. Available from the Stationery Office, tel: 0870 600 5522. Includes information about scholarships.

Published by Careers Europe:

- *Eurofacts* leaflets – factsheets providing information on over 240 topics, including working, studying and training within the EU – updated annually

- *Globalfacts* leaflets – similar to the above but on international careers topics

- *EXODUS* – database on living, working and studying opportunities in Europe, the USA, Australia and Canada.

Experience Erasmus 2005: The UK Guide – published annually by the UK Socrates-Erasmus Council, £14.95. A UK guide to institutions offering degree and diploma courses which can be combined with Erasmus.

Degree Course Offers 2005 – published by Trotman, £26.99. Includes a list of courses which involve a period of work experience abroad.

Commonwealth Universities Yearbook 2005 – published by the ACU, this new edition available January 2005, £200. A two-volume comprehensive guide to university institutions.

Getting into American Universities – published by Trotman, £11.99.

The following directories are published by Palgrave Macmillan and are edited by the International Association of Universities:

World List of Universities and Other Institutions of Higher Education – £130. A concise directory providing critical information on over 16,000 higher education institutions and national academic bodies in over 180 countries. A new edition is due in 2004.

International Handbook of Universities – £225. A guide to the administrative structure of over 7300 university-level institutions in 175 countries.

World Higher Education Database 2004/5 – £225. A comprehensive CD-ROM which combines information from the above two directories.

3:23

People with children and other dependants

Topics covered:

- National Childcare Strategy

- Carers of children – finances; how and when to study

- Childcare provision

- Organisations that can help

- Help for carers of other dependants

National Childcare Strategy

The Government's National Childcare Strategy was launched in 1998, and is delivered through 150 local authorities in England, with similar arrangements in other parts of the UK. The strategy (now part of the wider Sure Start initiative) aims to:

- ensure that accessible, affordable and quality childcare for children up to the age of 14, and 16 for those with special needs, is available in every area.

To meet these aims, the Government is spending millions of pounds (much of it through local authorities) on:

- creating new childcare places and provision

- targetting support in the most disadvantaged areas, including actively encouraging more integrated early years and family services through Sure Start local programmes and Neighbourhood Nurseries

- developing and increasing the size of the childcare workforce

- enhancing and sustaining quality, for example through National Standards for Under Eights Daycare, Ofsted inspection and registration of provision, and the Investors in Children initiative

- providing substantial help with childcare costs through the childcare element of Working Tax Credit.

The strategy has been very successful in achieving:

- a major expansion in childcare with substantially increased numbers of places, particularly in the private and voluntary sectors in a variety of settings such as day nurseries, playgroups, out of school clubs and childminding

- over 920,000 new childcare places benefitting more than 1.6 million children since 1997.

There are further targets to continue this expansion by creating another 250,000 new places by 2006 and 100,000 more by 2008.

The Government's Childcare Review and the Future

This took place in 2001-2 and reviewed levels of provision and used research evidence showing the benefits of integrating early education and childcare to inform a vision of childcare for the 21st Century. The government is now further transforming services for children and families by developing:

- a network of children's centres in the most disadvantaged areas to deliver services which combine quality childcare with early education, training and employment advice, and family and health services

- Sure Start, Early Excellence Centres and Neighbourhood Nurseries.

Carers of children

Fulfilling the role of parent or carer while taking a course of education or training is very demanding. Childcare should be organised around a suitable course, while time to study needs to fit in with the family routine. Forward planning, involving all those who are likely to be affected, is essential. Levels of childcare vary and there is generally a cost. For those caring for pre-school children, the government are committed to ensuring that all three and fours year olds have access to a free, part-time early years education place.

Financial assistance

Child Benefit

Child Benefit is a tax-free social security benefit paid to people who are bringing up children. It does not depend upon income or savings. It is paid for those with children under 16, or for 16- to18-year-olds studying for GCE Advanced level or equivalent, or for 16- or 17-year-olds registered with the Connexions or careers service (Training and Employment Agency in Northern Ireland) as looking for work or training. A higher amount is payable for the eldest child, and for lone parents in certain circumstances.

➤ Tel: 028 9054 9000 (Monday to Friday 9am-5pm)
www.dwp.gov.uk/childbenefit

Child Tax Credit and Working Tax Credit

Child Tax Credit

Child Tax Credit is available to all families, whether or not they are working, up to a maximum joint income of £58,000 (up to £66,000 if any child is under one year old). Support is available for those with children up to the age of 16, or 18 if they are studying full-time, or registered as looking for work or training. The amount payable varies according to income and the number of children in the family.

Working Tax Credit

Working Tax Credit is a payment to supplement the earnings of working people in low incomes, with or without children. Additional financial support is also available towards the costs of registered or approved childcare. This childcare element is only available to those working at least 16 hours a week. The payment is worth up to 70p in tax credit for every £1 a week that is spent on approved child care, up to a limit of £135 a week for one child and up to £200 a week for two or more children. This corresponds to a maximum tax credit of £94.50 for one child, and £140 a week for two or more children.

➤ Helpline: 0845 300 3900
   Textphone: 0845 300 3909 (local rates)
   www.inlandrevenue.gov.uk/taxcredits

Child Support Agency

Divorced or separated parents can contact the Child Support Agency about getting maintenance from their ex-partner. The Agency automatically gets involved in cases where the parent is claiming means tested benefits. Those not in receipt of benefits can request the help of the Agency. The amount payable for new cases is 15% of the income of the parent not living with the child for those with one child, 20% for two children, and 25% for three or more.

➤ Child Support National Agency enquiry line: 08457 133 133 (for information about the Child Maintenance Premium)
   www.csa.gov.uk

➤ Information on all childcare benefits can also be found on: www.dwp.gov.uk

New Deal

New Deal for Lone Parents is a voluntary programme available to all lone parents who are not working, or who are working less than 16 hours per week, and whose youngest child is under 16 years old. The programme helps lone parents find a job or training to fit around their family commitments. A designated personal advisor will offer help and support with finding work or training and provide assistance on a range of matters from government financial help to finding suitable childcare. Help with expenses to attend meetings, job interviews, or training, including fares and registered childcare costs may also be given.

Existing benefits may continue for the duration of the programme and top-ups may also be paid. Contact the Jobcentre Plus/Jobcentre for details.

➤ New Deal for Lone Parents Information Line: 0800 868 868
   Textphone: 0845 606 0680
   www.newdeal.gov.uk

➤ Information line for Northern Ireland: 0800 35 35 30

More details about financial assistance for childcare under New Deal can be found in *2:18 – Work Based Learning for Adults and other government-funded training.*

How and when to study

Those with children who are under school age can:

- find someone to look after them such as a childminder

- study at home

- find a college or training centre where they have childcare or crèche facilities. There may be a charge for this, although special rates are usually offered to those in receipt of benefits.

Those with children of school age can:

- find a course which fits in with the school day

- organise after-school care

- study at home.

Often there isn't a single solution to the problem of childcare, and in practice parents will opt for a combination.

- Studying at home via open or flexible learning enables parents to combine family commitments and study.

- Many colleges offer courses during school hours from 9.30am-3pm.

- Course tutors will discuss childcare concerns with the student – courses may often be organised in a flexible way. It is sometimes possible to extend the length of the course and lighten the workload in each year if this is appropriate.

- It may not be necessary for mature students to complete all modules of the course. Previous experience may qualify the student for accreditation of prior learning (APL) or accreditation of prior experiential learning (APEL). APL and APEL give credit for experience and related qualifications. Students will be required to prove their previous qualifications and experience with certificates and references, and be ready to demonstrate their skills to a tutor. Tutors will know exactly what is required to gain exemption from individual modules.

For general information about education and training opportunities, see *2:5 – A brief guide to education and training.*

> The **learndirect** helpline: 0800 100 900 (can advise on childcare for those returning to education or training. Available from 8am to 10pm seven days a week)
> www.learndirect.co.uk

> In Scotland, tel: 0808 100 9000 from 7.30am to 11pm Monday to Friday; 9am to 6pm weekends
> www.learndirectscotland.com

Open/distance learning

Open learning is a possibility for those who want to study in a more flexible way. This usually involves the individual in study at home supported by course notes, videos, tapes, radio and television broadcasts as well as email and the internet. There are often opportunities for tutorials as well. The Open University has a range of diploma and degree courses and there are no formal entry requirements for undergraduate courses. The main entry criterion is the will to study. There is a residential element to some OU courses which lasts from two days to one week. Children are not normally allowed at these summer schools, so care arrangements will have to be made. See *2:16 – The Open University* and *2:17 – Open/distance and other independent learning.*

Childcare provision

There are various kinds of childcare provision. Ofsted (the Office for Standards in Education) is responsible for the inspection and regulation of providers of childcare for children under the age of eight, including day nurseries, playgroups, pre-schools, children's centres and some family centres, crèches, out of school clubs, holiday playschemes and childminders in England. Information about the standards Ofsted maintains, and how to contact regional Ofsted Early Years centres is available on: www.ofsted.gov.uk/childcare

Parents should be aware that even friends and relatives who offer childcare regularly, for more than a couple of hours at a time, for reward – which does not necessarily mean money – may need to register with Ofsted as childminders.

ChildcareLink

ChildcareLink is a government-funded service providing a freephone helpline, which can give information about local Children's Information Services. The CIS can put parents in touch with childcare providers in their area – as well as giving information about choosing appropriate childcare. The service covers England, Scotland and Wales. Information is available on touch-screen kiosks in some locations.

➤ Tel: 08000 96 02 96 (from 8am-8pm Monday to Friday and 9am-12 noon on Saturdays).
 Email: childcarelink@opp-links.org.uk
 www.childcarelink.gov.uk

Nurseries

Some colleges have a college crèche or nursery and may offer places to students for free or at subsidised rates.

There are privately-run and workplace nurseries which may accommodate children for part of, or the whole, day, generally opening between 8am and 6pm daily. Local authority or other community-based nurseries generally have more restricted opening times – usually for the normal school day.

Pre-schools or playgroups

Pre-school playgroups offer government-funded places for all three and four year old children. Places are usually offered for two to three hours a day for up to five mornings a week. There is a charge for two year olds, although five year olds also receive a free place before starting school if their parents wish.

➤ **Pre-school Learning Alliance** – Unit 213-216, 30 Great Guildford Street, London SE1 0HS.
 Tel: 020 7620 0550.
 Email: pla@pre-school.org.uk
 www.pre-school.org.uk

➤ **Wales Pre-school Playgroups Association** – Ladywell House, Newtown, Powys SY16 1JB.
Tel: 01686 624573.
Email: info@walesppa.org
www.walesppa.org

➤ **Scottish Pre-school Play Association** – 45 Finnieston Street, Glasgow G3 8JU.
Tel: 0141 221 4148.
Email: info@sppa.org.uk
www.sppa.org.uk

➤ **NIPPA – The Early Years Organisation** – 6c Wildflower Way, Apollo Road, Belfast BT12 6TA.
Tel: 028 9066 2825.
Email: mail@nippa.org
www.nippa.org

N.B. The availability of government-funded places for children may vary in Northern Ireland – the local Education Boards can provide more information.

Playgroup Network

A national educational charity supporting playgroups and parent and toddler groups with training, advice and information to allow them to provide for the needs of children and families through community groups.

➤ **Playgroup Network** – PO Box 401, Middlesborough, Cleveland TS5 4WZ.
Tel: 0191 230 5520.
Email: playgroupnetwork@playgroup.fsnet.co.uk
www.playgroup-network.org.uk

The National Childminding Association (NCMA)

Childminders are people other than relatives who look after other people's children at their home, for reward. The Association provides information for parents and those thinking of becoming a childminder. Registered childminders are inspected and registered by Ofsted.

➤ **NCMA** – 8 Mason's Hill, Bromley BR2 9EY.
Tel: 020 8464 6164..
Information line: 0800 169 4486 (freephone; Monday to Friday 10am-noon and 2pm-4pm)
Email: info@ncma.org.uk
www.ncma.org.uk

➤ **Scottish Childminding Association** – Suite 3, 7 Melville Terrace, Stirling FK8 2ND.
Tel: 01786 445377.
Advice line: 01786 449063 (Tues and Thurs 1.00pm-4.30pm)
Email: information@childminding.org
www.childminding.org

➤ **Northern Ireland Childminding Association** – 16-18 Mill Street, Newtownards, County Down BT23 4LU.
Tel: 028 9181 1015.
Email: info@nicma.org
www.nicma.org

Nannies

Most nannies are trained and have a recognised childcare qualification, such as the Diploma in Childcare and Education. Others may have few or no qualifications, but some experience of childcare. It is up to the employer to check their suitability, as Ofsted inspection and registration does not apply to people caring for children in the family's home. However, it is hoped that this will change in the future. Nannies can be employed on a daily or live-in basis. This option is generally expensive, so increasingly people consider sharing a nanny to keep the costs down.

Out of school schemes and clubs

There is an increasing number of after-school clubs and facilities for primary-age children which also operate in the school holidays.

Schools, libraries or LEAs have information about local schemes, or 4Children can supply contact details for local clubs.

> **4Children** – Bellerive House, 3 Muirfield Crescent, London E14 9SZ.
> Tel: 020 7512 2112.
> Information line: 020 7512 2100 (Monday to Friday 9.00am to 5.30pm)
> Email: info@4children.org.uk
> www.4children.org.uk

Other useful organisations

Working Families

This organisation provides information on childcare options, employment rights, negotiating flexible working with employers, in-work benefits (e.g. Working Tax Credit) and combining paid employment with caring for a disabled child. Working Families produces a range of free factsheets, plus priced publications, and campaigns for family-friendly employment policies.

> **Working Families** – 1-3 Berry Street, London EC1V OAA.
> Tel: 020 7253 7243.
> Free legal helpline for low-income families: 0800 013 0313.
> Email: office@workingfamilies.org.uk
> www.workingfamilies.org.uk

Contact a Family

This organisation offers support and advice to families with disabled children.

> **Contact a Family** – 290-211 City Road, London, EC1V 1JN.
> Helpline: 0808 808 3556 (a freephone for parents and families; open 10am-4pm Monday to Friday).
> Textphone: 0808 808 3556.
> Email: info@cafamily.org.uk
> www.cafamily.org.uk

Daycare Trust

Daycare Trust is the national childcare charity, campaigning for quality, affordable childcare for all and raising the voices of children, parents and carers. They advise parents and carers, providers, employers, trade unions and policymakers on childcare issues. Callers to the helpline can get a free copy of Daycare Trust's, *Choosing Childcare: Your Sure Start Guide to Childcare and Early Education.*

➤ **Daycare Trust** – 21 St George's Road, London SE1 6ES.
Helpline: 020 7840 3350 (10am to 5pm Monday to Friday – includes access to Language Line interpreters for non-English speakers).
Email: info@daycaretrust.org.uk
www.daycaretrust.org.uk

One Parent Families

This is an independent charity offering information, advice and support to lone parents in England and Wales. It publishes a range of free information on issues such as childcare, benefits, returning to work and study, and holidays.

➤ **One Parent Families** – 255 Kentish Town Road, London NW5 2LX.
Tel: 020 7428 5400.
Lone Parent Helpline: 0800 018 5026 (open from 9am-5pm Monday to Friday)
Email: info@oneparentfamilies.org.uk
www.oneparentfamilies.org.uk

One Parent Families Scotland

This organisation provides a range of services for lone parents throughout Scotland, including information, guidance and support for lone parents who wish to access education or training or enter employment. Free information leaflets are available to lone parents, plus some other publications, e.g. *Lone Parents' Rights Guide*, £5.

➤ **One Parent Families – Scotland** – 13 Gayfield Square, Edinburgh EHI 3NX.
Tel: 0131 556 3899 or freephone: 0800 018 5026.
Email: info@opfs.org.uk
www.opfs.org.uk

Gingerbread

Gingerbread is a registered charity run by lone parents to support and advise lone parents in England and Wales. It publishes a series of factsheets available from the London office, which can provide contact details for local groups. All this information is also on the website.

➤ **Gingerbread** – 7 Sovereign Close, Sovereign Court, London E1W 3HW.
Tel: 020 7488 9300.
Advice line: 0800 018 4318 (freephone; from 9am-5pm Monday to Friday).
Email: office@gingerbread.org.uk
www.gingerbread.org.uk

There are separate Gingerbread organisations for Scotland and Northern Ireland.

➤ **Gingerbread Scotland** – 1014 Argyle Street, Glasgow G3 8LX.
Tel: 0141 576 5085.

➤ **Gingerbread Northern Ireland** – 169 University Street, Belfast BT7 1HR.
Tel: 028 9023 1417.
www.gingerbreadni.org

Carers of other dependants

There is much less on offer for this group. Much of the help is in the form of support rather than actual care. There are some useful organisations.

Carers UK

This organisation offers support, information and advice to carers and campaigns and carries out research on their behalf. They can put people in touch with local support groups offering practical advice, and also run a project – Action for Carers and Employment.

> **Carers UK** – 20-25 Glasshouse Yard, London EC1A 4JT.
> Tel: 020 7490 8818.

> **Carers Wales** – River House, Ynysbridge Court, Gwaelod y Garth, Cardiff CF15 9SS.
> Tel: 029 2081 1370.
> Email: mailto:info@careerswales.org.uk

> **Carers Scotland** – 91 Mitchell Street, Glasgow G1 3LN.
> Tel: 0141 221 9141.
> Email: info@carerscotland.org

> **Carers Northern Ireland** – 58 Howard Street, Belfast BT1 6PJ.
> Tel: 028 9043 9843.
> Email: info@carersni.demon.co.uk

> **Carersline**: 0808 808 7777 (freephone; 10am-12noon and 2pm-4pm Wednesday and Thursday only).
> Email: info@ukcarers.org
> www.carersonline.org.uk

Crossroads Caring for Carers

Crossroads has over 200 local schemes in England and Wales alone. Among the support offered to carers would be giving them the chance to attend a course for a few hours per week.

> **Crossroads** – Association Office, 10 Regent Place, Rugby CV21 2PN.
> Tel: 0845 450 0350.
> Email: communications@crossroads.org.uk
> www.crossroads.org.uk

> **Crossroads (Scotland) Caring for Carers** – 24 George Square, Glasgow G2 1EG.
> Tel: 0141 226 3793.
> Email: mailto:enquiries@crossroads-scot.k-web.co.uk

> **Crossroads Caring for Carers (NI) Ltd** – 7 Regent Street, Newtownards, County Down BT23 4AB.
> Tel: 02891 814455.
> Email: mail@crossroadscare.co.uk
> www.crossroadscare.co.uk

The Princess Royal Trust for Carers

The Trust provides information, support and practical help for carers through over 100 Carers' Centres across the UK.

➤ **Princess Royal Trust for Carers** – 142 Minories, London EC3N 1LB.
Tel: 020 7480 7788.
Email: help@carers.org
www.carers.org

Mencap

Mencap is the leading charity in the UK working with children and adults with a learning disability and their families and carers. There are local societies in England, Wales and Northern Ireland.

➤ **Mencap** – 123 Golden Lane, London ECIY 0RT.
Tel: 020 7454 0454.
Helpline: 0808 808 1111
Email: help@mencap.org.uk

➤ **Mencap** – 31 Lambourne Crescent, Cardiff Business Park, Llanishen, Cardiff CF14 5GF.
Tel: 02920 747588.
Helpline: 0808 8000 300 (8am-8pm)
Email: information.wales@mencap.org.uk

➤ **Mencap** – Segal House, 4 Annadale Avenue, Belfast BT7 3JH.
Tel: 02890 691351.
Helpline: 0845 7636227 (9am-5pm Monday-Friday)
Email: mencapni@mencap.org.uk

➤ Or for a list of local groups and details of campaigns see: www.mencap.org.uk

ENABLE

ENABLE is a charity in Scotland providing help for adults and children with learning disabilities.

➤ **ENABLE** – 6th Floor, 7 Buchanan Street, Glasgow G1 3HL.
Tel: 0141 226 4541.
Email: enable@enable.org.uk
www.enable.org.uk

Further information

Choosing Childcare – free guide from the Daycare Trust.

The NCMA Guide to Choosing the Right Childminder – covers issues like finding a childminder, questions to ask, settling children and dealing with problems. Free from the National Childminding Association.

3:24

Women

Topics covered:

- Campaign groups
- General networks
- Organisations providing training and personal development opportunities
- Professional and vocational organisations

Whilst women can use all the usual sources of help and information, there are also many special groups focusing on the particular needs of women in society. Only relevant national groups and networks are featured here; local reference libraries are a good source of information about independent local women's groups or local branches of national organisations.

Campaign groups

Women's National Commission

This is the official independent advisory body, giving the views of women to government. Membership is drawn from many organisations representing political parties, trade unions, religious groups, professional associations and voluntary bodies. As well as giving advice to Government on the views of women's organisations, it produces a directory of women's organisations in the UK (which can be viewed on the website), various working group and conference reports, and a guide for women wishing to gain public appointments.

> **Women's National Commission** – Department of Trade and Industry, 35 Great Smith Street, London SW1P 3BQ.
> Tel: 020 7276 2555.
> Email: wnc@dti.gsi.gov.uk
> www.thewnc.org.uk

Fawcett Society

The Fawcett Society campaigns for change that will lead to equality between women and men at home, at work, and in public life. Fawcett offers a volunteer and work placement programme for students interested in gaining an insight and work experience in a campaign organisation. For further details please see the website below.

> **The Fawcett Society** – 1-3 Berry Street, London EC1V OAA.
  Tel: 020 7253 2598.
  Email: info@fawcettsociety.org.uk
  www.fawcettsociety.org.uk

Equal Opportunities Commission

The Equal Opportunities Commission (EOC) was set up under the Sex Discrimination Act 1975 (SDA) to work towards the elimination of sex discrimination and to promote equality of opportunity towards men and women. The SDA makes it unlawful to discriminate against a person because of their sex in the contexts of education and employment, and in the provision of housing, goods, facilities and services to the public. The Equal Opportunities Commission advises on the Sex Discrimination Act and the Equal Pay Act.

In 2006 the Equal Opportunities Commission will merge with the Commission for Racial Equality and the Disability Rights Commission to form a single organisation, the Commission for Equality and Human Rights.

> **Equal Opportunities Commission** – Arndale House, Arndale Centre, Manchester M4 3EQ.
  Tel: 0845 601 5901.
  Email: info@eoc.org.uk

> **Equal Opportunities Commission** – St Stephens House, 279 Bath Street, Glasgow G2 4JL.
  Tel: 0845 601 5901.
  Email: scotland@eoc.org.uk

> **Equal Opportunities Commission** – Windsor House, Windsor Lane, Cardiff CF10 3GE.
  Tel: 029 2034 3552.
  Email: wales@eoc.org.uk
  www.eoc.org.uk

All phone lines above operate as a telephone helpline between 9am-5pm, Monday-Friday.

General networks

Women Returners' Network

Women Returners' Network (WRN) is the only organisation comprehensively dealing with issues concerning women returning to work or learning. Its aim is to provide innovative and practical support with a genuine 'hands on' approach to meeting the needs of clients.

WRN provides a helpline for women who need advice, guidance and signposting to help them reach their goal of training, returning to education or employment. WRN also works with Government, in particular the Department for Trade and Industry (DTI). WRN works with all the devolved regions of the UK, so helping to ensure that all issues relating to women returners are firmly on the national agenda.

> **WRN** – Chelmsford College, Moulsham Street, Chelmsford, Essex CM2 0JQ.
  Tel: 01245 263796.
  Email: contact@women-returners.co.uk
  www.women-returners.co.uk

British Federation of Women Graduates

The Federation promotes women's opportunities in education and public life; works as part of an international organisation to improve the lives of women and girls; fosters local, national and international friendship; awards scholarships for postgraduate research for students moving into their final year of study for a PhD.

> **British Federation of Women Graduates** – 4 Mandeville Courtyard, 142 Battersea Park Road, London SW11 4NB.
> Tel: 020 7498 8037.
> Email: info@bfwg.demon.co.uk
> www.bfwg.org.uk

Oxford Women's Training Scheme

The Oxford Women's Training Scheme (OWTS) has worked with the DfES and the European Social Fund Unit since the early 1980s to promote best practice on gender and equality in the use and administration of ESF programmes. OWTS is a membership organisation of women's projects and organisations that seek to address the gender pay gap through promoting women's access to new, technical and non-traditional occupations.

OWTS member organisations offer a direct link of women who are training and working in non-traditional occupations. OWTS membership includes:

- women only training courses in the fields of building skills, bench joinery and painting and decorating

- networking and support organisations for women training and working in non-traditional occupations

- providers of guidance and counselling tailored to encourage and support women into non-traditional occupations

- projects working with employers and their organisations to enhance the recruitment and employment of women in non-traditional occupations.

> **Oxford Women's Training Scheme** – Northway Centre, Maltfield Road, Oxford OX3 9RG.
> Tel: 01865 741317
> Email: women@owts.org.uk
> www.owts.org.uk

Organisations providing training and personal development opportunities

YWCA

The YWCA offers a wide range of formal and informal learning programmes for women aged 11-30 from YWCA projects throughout the country.

> **Youth and Community Department, YWCA HQ** – Clarendon House, 52 Cornmarket Street, Oxford OXI 3EJ.
> Tel: 01865 304200.
> Email: info@ywca-gb.org.uk
> www.ywca-gb.org.uk

> **YWCA (Scottish National Council)** – 7b Randolph Crescent, Edinburgh EH3 7TH.
> Tel: 0131 225 7592
> Email: info@ywcascotland.org
> www.ywcascotland.org

National Federation of Women's Institutes of England, Wales, the Channel Islands and the Isle of Man

The WI offers adult education in local institutes, through a travelling tutor scheme, on study tours abroad or at the WI's own Denman College, a residential college for members which has over 500 different courses each year, lasting from two to four days. Non-members are also welcome. Subjects available through the various sources range from public speaking to IT, and from literature and opera to archaeology.

> **National Federation of Women's Institutes of England, Wales, the Channel Islands and the Isle of Man** – 104 New Kings Road, London SW6 4LY.
> Tel: 020 7371 9300.
> Email: hq@nfwi.org.uk
> www.womens-institute.org.uk

> **Denman College** – Marcham, Abingdon OX13 6NW.
> Tel: 01865 391991.
> Email: info@denman.org.uk

Scottish Women's Rural Institute

The Scottish equivalent of the WI, the SWRI offers educational opportunities to members only.

> **Scottish Women's Rural Institute** – 42 Heriot Row, Edinburgh EH3 6ES.
> Tel: 0131 225 1724.
> Email: swri@swri.demon.co.uk
> www.swri.org.uk

Federation of Women's Institutes of Northern Ireland

The Federation offers educational opportunities for members.

> **Federation of Women's Institutes of Northern Ireland** – 209-211 Upper Lisburn Road, Belfast BT10 0LL.
> Tel: 028 9030 1506.
> Email: wini@btconnect.com
> www.wini.org.uk

National Women's Register

This is a network of non-hierarchical groups, with the aim of offering women the opportunity to take part in informal discussions so educating themselves, developing self-confidence and latent talents.

> **National Women's Register** – 3a Vulcan House, Vulcan Road North, Norwich NR6 6AQ.
> Tel: 01603 406767.
> Email: office@nwr.org
> www.nwr.org

National Association of Women's Clubs

The NAWC advances education and provides facilities for leisure in order to improve women's lives. Each club is self-governing, with its own activity programme.

➤ **National Association of Women's Clubs** – 5 Vernon Rise, King's Cross Road, London WC1X 9EP.
Tel: 020 7837 1434.
Email: nawc@tinyworld.co.uk
www.nawc.org.uk

Women's Resource and Development Agency (Northern Ireland)

This organises women-only courses in Northern Ireland. Subjects include health, assertiveness and facilitation skills. The project's primary concern is to support women's groups in Northern Ireland. It offers courses in organisation and management skills, tutor training, training materials and back-up support.

➤ **Women's Resource and Development Agency** – 6 Mount Charles, Belfast BT7 1NZ.
Tel: 028 9023 0212.
Email: futuresearch@wrda.net
www.wrda.net/futuresearch

Professional and vocational organisations

Many organisations, such as the Chartered Management Institute (Women in Management) and the Royal College of Surgeons (Women in Surgery - see website www.rcseng.ac.uk) have women's groups for people already in their professions – or training to enter. There are also many other specialist professional and vocational organisations catering for women in all areas of, mostly, professional work.

Women into Science and Engineering (WISE)

WISE encourages girls and women to consider careers – or to return to careers – in science and engineering. Its website offers links to other useful sites.

➤ **Women into Science and Engineering** – 22 Old Queen Street, London SW1H 9HP.
Tel: 020 7227 8421.
Email: wisecampaign@semta.org.uk
www.wisecampaign.org.uk
www.wiseni.org (for Northern Ireland)
www.wiseinwales.org.uk

The Daphne Jackson Trust

This offers fellowships for women and men wishing to return to careers in engineering, science and technology but in need of retraining.

➤ **The Daphne Jackson Trust** – c/o Department of Physics, University of Surrey, Guildford GU2 7XH.
Tel: 01483 879166.
Email: djmft@surrey.ac.uk
www.daphnejackson.org

Women's Engineering Society

WES promotes the education, training and practice of engineering among women.

> **Women's Engineering Society** – 22 Old Queen Street, London SW1H 9HP.
> Tel: 020 7233 1974.
> Email: info@wes.org.uk
> www.wes.org.uk

Women in Journalism

WIJ is a networking, campaigning, training and social organisation for women journalists in newspapers, magazines and the new media. They undertake education and research and campaign for equal pay for women journalists. Their role also includes aiming to increase the numbers of women at senior levels within the industry.

> Email: wijuk@aol.com
> www.womeninjournalism.co.uk

Women in Film and Television

This group is open to women with at least one year's professional experience in the film and television industry.

> **Women in Film and Television** – 6 Langley Street, London WC2H 9JA.
> Tel: 020 7240 4875.
> Email: info@wftv.org.uk
> www.wftv.org.uk

Business and Professional Women UK Ltd

BPW UK offers networking, training and personal development. Its website lists regional and international contacts.

> **BPW UK** – 24 Knifesmithgate, Chesterfield S40 1XW.
> Tel: 01246 211988.
> Email: hq@bpwuk.org.uk
> www.bpwuk.org.uk

British Women Pilots' Association

The Association exists to promote the role of women in aviation. It offers advice on aviation careers and training through its publication *A Career in Aviation* (£5.50) and through its careers and training advisers. It also provides an annual scholarship and bursary.

> **British Women Pilots' Association** – Brooklands Museum, Brooklands Road, Weybridge KT13 0QN.
> Email:enquiries@bwpa.demon.co.uk
> www.bwpa.demon.co.uk

Further information

The Penguin Careers Guide – published by Penguin Books, £12.99. Information on job opportunities. The book covers areas such as management and working for oneself. A unique feature is the section under each job category which assesses the current position of, and opportunities for, women.

Hobsons Guide for Career Women – Essential Advice on Getting the Right Job for You. Careers Guide published annually by Hobsons, £9.99.

Returning to Work: A Guide to Re-Entering the Job Market – published by How to Books, £9.99.

Women at Work: Strategies for Survival and Success – published by Kogan Page, £8.99.

3:25

Third age

The term 'third age' is popularly used to describe the period in our lives after youth and middle age. The proportion of older people in the population is rising all the time. Currently, there are around 19.6 million people aged 50 and over in the population – 33 % of the adult population. This proportion is growing. In the UK, as in Europe as a whole, people are living longer, staying healthier and, quite rightly, expecting a better quality of life.

Broadly speaking, older people hold fewer qualifications than younger people. Many older people have no formal qualifications. However, with the concept of 'lifelong learning' now very much on the agenda, preconceived ideas of what older people should and could do are disappearing. The fact that many older people are returning to, or continuing with, their education is accepted and, indeed, welcomed.

Older people may wish to undertake learning for many reasons, for example:

- to develop new interests, or further existing ones

- to develop new knowledge or skills for a particular area of voluntary work

- to keep pace with new technology and to be able to benefit from it

- for fun and personal enrichment

- for the social contact it can provide

- in order to continue to play a full role in their community

- to keep the brain active and stimulated

- to enhance skills and knowledge in relation to their paid work – if still active in the employment market.

The Older and Bolder initiative

NIACE (the National Institute of Adult Continuing Education) runs this initiative, which is aimed at addressing the absence from education and training of those aged 50+. It does this through advising and informing all those interested in education and training for older people. NIACE is supported in this by other specialist organisations such as Age Concern, the U3A, and the Pre-Retirement Association.

The Older and Bolder initiative:

- encourages positive planning of future provision to meet the unmet needs of older adults, through the promotion of working partnerships and influencing policy

- collects and disseminates information, including data and examples of good practice

- makes Senior Learner of the Year awards

- organises conferences, seminars and exchanges

- publishes papers and briefing sheets

- produces the *Older and Bolder* newsletter, and runs two email discussion groups.

The initiative has also published a policy discussion paper: *Learning to Grow Older and Bolder.*

➤ Older and Bolder Information Officer, **NIACE** – Renaissance House, 20 Princess Road, Leicester LE1 6TP.
Tel: 0116 204 4200.
Email: enquiries@niace.org.uk
www.niace.org.uk

More general information about the role of NIACE is provided in *2:8 – Further and adult education.*

Older workers

Around 69% of the workforce aged between 50 and state retirement age are currently in employment – a much lower proportion than in the past. Older workers are more likely to be self-employed or working part-time.

Many older people feel that they are discriminated against when applying for jobs, and within their workplace, purely on the basis of their age. The Government has been endeavouring to remedy this – its *Age Positive* campaign aims to influence the attitudes and practices of employers and employees. See the website: www.agepositive.gov.uk which is dedicated to the campaign.

There are various initiatives designed to help older people to start or keep a job:

- In 1999, the Government introduced a voluntary **code of practice** for employers on age diversity in employment, which included guidance on recruitment practices. It covers good practice in six main areas: recruitment; selection; promotion; training and development; redundancy; retirement. Since the Code was issued, the number of companies using age in recruitment has reduced from 27% to 13%. The number of companies having a policy against employing older workers has reduced from 14% to 7%. For further information about the Code, look at the *Age Positive* website.

- The European Union Council of Ministers has adopted the Employment Directive on equal treatment. This requires all 25 EU member states to introduce **legislation** against various forms of discrimination at work, including age discrimination. At present the Government is consulting about how discrimination in employment, vocational training and guidance can be made illegal. 2006 is the agreed deadline for this legislation which will encourage employers to adopt non-ageist employment practices in a market where there are skill shortages.

- **New Deal 50 plus** – a voluntary programme for people over 50 who want to work and are in receipt of any of the following benefits: Jobseeker's Allowance; Income Support; Incapacity Benefit; Severe Disablement Allowance, for at least the last six months. There are also other categories of people who may be eligible, such as those in receipt of National Insurance credits, Invalid Care Allowance or Bereavement Allowance. There is no upper age limit. New Deal 50 plus offers practical help from a Personal Adviser, such as help with job search skills, access to training and self-confidence building. Other benefits of the programme include:

- additional benefits under Working Tax Credits for those working more than 16 hours per week – extra amounts are payable for those on New Deal 50+ and this is paid during the first 52 weeks in employment (depending on family circumstances)

- an in-work training grant of up to £1500 to pay for relevant training and courses

- help and advice for those who wish to start their own business.

➤ For more information about New Deal 50 plus, clients should contact the Jobcentre Plus/Jobcentre, or telephone the New Deal helpline: 0845 606 2626 or textphone: 0845 606 0680 (7am-11pm 7 days a week). The Age Positive web-site also has information: www.agepositive.gov.uk
www.newdeal.gov.uk

Third Age Employment Network (TAEN)

TAEN campaigns for better opportunities for mature people to continue to learn and work. It has a membership of 240 organisations and groups nationwide.

➤ **Third Age Employment Network** – 207-221 Pentonville Road, London N1 9UZ. Information line: 020 7843 1590 (9am-5pm Monday-Friday).
Email: taen@helptheaged.org.uk
www.taen.org.uk

Campaign Against Age Discrimination in Employment (CAADE)

Formed in 1988, CAADE campaigns for the rights of older workers and offers training for older people who are unemployed.

> **Campaign Against Age Discrimination in Employment** – 395 Barlow Road, Altrincham, Cheshire WA14 5HW.
> Tel: 0161 941 2902 or 0845 345 8654.
> Email: enquiries@caade.net
> www.caade.net

Employers Forum on Age (EFA)

The Employers Forum on Age is an independent network of leading employers who recognise the business value of attracting and retaining experienced employees – regardless of their age. Through regular reports, studies and research it constantly highlights and increases knowledge and understanding about the issue of age discrimination at work.

The EFA offers members authoritative advice and practical support on managing the skills and age mix of their organisation via workshops and seminars. It also represents the employers' voice to the Government, and actively campaigns on issues ranging from improving flexible retirement policies to influencing the forthcoming age discrimination legislation.

> **Employers Forum on Age – Mezzanine Floor**, Elizabeth House, 39 York Road, London SE1 7NQ.
> Tel: 0845 456 2495.
> Email: efa@efa.org.uk
> www.efa.org.uk (contains information on current issues related to age discrimination)

Locally-based projects

There are some local projects which provide support and advice and, in some cases, training, to 'third-agers' seeking employment who live in their particular area. Such projects are generally funded from a variety of statutory and voluntary sources. The following are a few examples:

Third Age Challenge is a not-for-profit organisation, with the primary aim of supporting older people to maintain a full working life. It provides information, advice and support to the over-50s in the local area, to assist them back to work, to change career direction and to fulfil their potential through lifelong learning.

> **Third Age Challenge Ltd** – 39 Hawkins Street, Rodbourne, Swindon SN2 2AQ.
> Tel: 01793 533370.
> Email: office@thirdagers.net
> www.thirdagers.net

Target Training offers job seeking advice and training opportunities – particularly IT skills. The service is aimed particularly at those aged 40+ based in its area.

> **Target Training** – Merchant House, 11a Piccadilly, York YO1 9WB.
> Tel: 01904 671171.
> Email: enquiries@targettraining.org.uk
> www.targettraining.org.uk

Third Age Foundation provides training for the over-40s in London area, in computer skills, and personal and business development (including advice on CVs etc).

> **Third Age Foundation** – Britannia House, 1-11 Glenthorne Road, London W6 0LH.
> Tel: 020 8748 9898.
> Email: sylvia@thirdage.org.uk
> www.thirdage.org.uk

The Freshstart Trust provides the over-40s in its local area with assistance in finding work, including general support and job seeking advice, and the chance to update skills.

> **The Freshstart Trust Ltd** – Pembroke House, 7 Brunswick Square, Bristol BS2 8PE.
> Tel: 0117 907 7036.
> Email: info@freshstart.org.uk
> www.freshstart.org.uk

Third Age Network Portsmouth is a forum for lobbying on behalf of mature workers. It offers advice and support to mature jobsearchers in its area, and those seeking education, training etc.

> **Third Age Network Portsmouth** – 6 Cumberland Avenue, Emsworth PO10 7UK.
> Tel: 01243 374567.
> Email: stanspooner@spooner.go-plus.net

Over-50s Employment Bureau is a well-established CAB initiative for jobseekers aged 50+ living in and around the city of London.

> **Over-50s Employment Bureau** – 90 Central Street, London EC1V 8AQ.
> Tel: 020 7608 1395.
> Email: over50semploymentbureau@ukgateway.net

The Jobcentre Plus/Jobcentre and adult information, advice and guidance agencies should have details of any projects operating in their locality.

Pre-retirement courses

The age at which people retire varies enormously. Pre-retirement courses can help with planning – they usually cover money, activities and leisure, health and relationships.

The Pre-Retirement Association (PRA)

The PRA is an independent national organisation in the fields of mid-career and pre-retirement planning and education. The Association runs a range of courses, catering for mid-life planning, career change, redundancy, early retirement and retirement.

Training for pre-retirement professionals is a combination of face-to-face and distance learning. Part-time postgraduate certificate, diploma and MSc courses which offer qualification and accreditation to work as a recognised pre-retirement tutor/organiser are available, validated by Surrey University.

PRA publishes books and reports for pre-retirement professionals.

> **Pre-Retirement Association** – 9 Chesham Road, Guildford GU1 3LS.
> Tel: 01483 301170.
> Email: info@pra.uk.com
> www.pra.uk.com

Can provide list of local associations affiliated to the PRA, including Wales.

Scottish Pre-Retirement Council (SPRC)

SPRC promotes education for retirement throughout Scotland. It organises pre-retirement courses on topics such as money, health, social living and leisure. It also carries out mid-life planning courses for people in their 40s.

➤ **The Scottish Pre-Retirement Council** – Alexandra House, 204 Bath Street, Glasgow G2 4HL.
Tel: 0141 332 9427 .

Workers' Educational Association (WEA)

The WEA runs pre-retirement courses nationwide. (See *2:11 – The Workers' Educational Association* for general information about the WEA.)

➤ **WEA** – Corporate Services, Quick House, 65 Clifton Street, London EC2A 4JE.
Tel: 020 7375 3092.
Email: national@wea.org.uk
www.wea.org.uk

Adult and community education

Adult education/community education services may run pre-retirement evening courses.

Others

A number of financial organisations offer pre-retirement courses. Be aware that many see these courses as a commercial marketing opportunity.

Learning once retired

Many people take up new activities once retired and, in so doing, gain new skills and knowledge without thinking of themselves as formally 'learning'. The following are examples of learning providers offering learning opportunities that may be of interest to those who are no longer working. They are, with the exception of the U3A, also open to people in employment as well as those who are no longer working.

The University of the Third Age (U3A)

U3A is a self-help movement for people no longer in full-time gainful employment, offering a wide range of educational, creative and leisure activities. It operates through a network of over 530 local groups, each of which determines its own programme of courses and activities. Locations of local groups can be found on the organisation's website, or by contacting the National Office. Advice and some resources are available to start new U3As.

➤ **The Third Age Trust (National Office, U3A)** – The Old Municipal Buildings, 19 East Street, Bromley, Kent BR1 1QH.
Tel: 020 8466 6139.
Email: enquiries@u3a.org.uk
www.u3a.org.uk

Adult/community and further education

Adult/community education services and FE colleges offer a huge range of adult learning opportunities, open to people of all ages. Some courses may be geared particularly towards those who are retired. See *2:8 – Further and adult education* and *2:10 – Learning for leisure* for further general information.

Higher education providers

Degree courses and other courses at higher education level are open to people of all ages. Many Open University students are retired people studying for pleasure. The OU offers degree and non-degree courses. See *2:14 – Higher education* and *2:16 – The Open University*.

The Open College of the Arts (OCA)

Courses include art and design, drawing, painting, creative writing, music, photography, sculpture, textiles, garden and interior design and understanding art.

> **Open College of the Arts** – Registration Department, Freepost SF10 678, Barnsley S75 1BR.
> Tel: 01226 730495 or freephone: 0800 731 2116.
> Email: open.arts@ukonline.co.uk
> www.oca-uk.com

The National Extension College (NEC)

The NEC is a non-profitmaking body established to provide high quality home study courses for adults, details of which are listed in their free *Guide to Courses* available on request. See *2:17 – Open/distance and other independent learning* for more information on the NEC and other open/distance learning providers, such as the Open College of the Arts.

> **National Extension College** – Michael Young Centre, Purbeck Road, Cambridge CB2 2HN.
> Tel: 01223 400200.
> Email: info@nec.ac.uk
> www.nec.ac.uk

National Adult School Organisation (NASO)

A national voluntary adult education movement, NASO 'friendship through study' groups meet throughout the country. For more information see *2:10 Learning for leisure*.

> **NASO** – Riverton, 370 Humberstone Road, Leicester LE5 0SA.
> Tel: 0116 253 8333.
> Email: gensec@naso.org.uk
> www.naso.org.uk

The Workers' Educational Association (WEA)

The WEA, already mentioned under 'Pre-retirement courses' above, offers a variety of adult education courses through day and evening classes. See *2:11 – The Workers' Educational Association* for more information.

Broadcast media

The BBC, commercial TV channels and radio stations broadcast programmes that provide opportunities for learning. The BBC, in particular, is well known for its educational broadcasting. See *2:17 – Open/distance and other independent learning* for more information.

Course costs

- Fee concessions may be available in some areas for pensioners attending adult education courses, although this may be confined only to those on benefits.

- For full-time higher education, applications for financial assistance are made to the LEA. Those under the age of 50 can receive a student loan; 50–54-year olds are entitled to a loan if they are planning to return to work after the completion of the course.

For more information on student finance, see *2:7 – Money*.

Voluntary activities

There are many opportunities for retired people to serve their community. Broadly, voluntary work falls into four main categories:

- clerical and administrative

- committee work

- fund-raising

- direct work with the public/clients of the organisation.

Many organisations are willing to train volunteer workers either 'on-the-job' or through special programmes or courses.

➤ **Volunteering England** – Regents Wharf, 8 All Saints Street, London N1 9RL.
 Tel: 0845 305 6979.
 Email: info@volunteeringengland.org
 www.volunteering.org.uk.

➤ **Volunteer Development Scotland** – Unit 157-158 Stirling Enterprise Park, Stirling FK7 7RP.
 Tel: 01786 479593.
 Email: info@vds.org.uk
 www.vds.org.uk

➤ **Wales Council for Voluntary Action (WCVA)** – Baltic House, Mount Stewart Square, Cardiff CF10 5FH.
 Helpdesk: 0870 607 1666.
 Email: enquiries@wcva.org
 www.wcva.org

See also www.volunteering-wales.net which lists local bureaux.

> **Volunteer Development Agency** – 4th Floor, 58 Howard Street, Belfast BT1 6PG.
> Tel: 028 9023 6100.
> Email: info@volunteering-ni.org
> www.volunteering-ni.org

Local volunteer bureaux or volunteer centres exist in most towns to match volunteers to local organisations needing help. The above organisations and their websites can provide information about local bureaux.

For further information about voluntary opportunities, see *2:21 – Volunteering*.

Relevant organisations

Age Concern

Age Concern consists of a network of branches supported by many thousands of volunteers providing community based services which include courses and a range of activities for older people. Local branches should be listed in telephone directories. Copies of factsheet number 30 *Leisure and education* and number 31 *Older Workers* are available through the information line and website.

> **Age Concern England** – Astral House, 1268 London Road, London, SW16 4ER.
> Information Line: 0800 009966.
> Tel: 020 8765 7200.
> www.ageconcern.org.uk
>
> Age Concern also publishes a series of relevant books – for further details tel: 0870 4422120

> **Age Concern Cymru** – 4th Floor, 1 Cathedral Road, Cardiff CFl1 9SD.
> Tel: 029 2037 1566.
> Email: enquiries@accymru.org.uk
> www.accymru.org.uk

> **Age Concern Scotland** – 113 Rose Street, Edinburgh EH2 3DT.
> Tel: 0131 220 3345 or freephone: 0800 00 99 66.
> Email: enquiries@acscot.org.uk
> www.ageconcernscotland.org.uk

> **Age Concern Northern Ireland** – 3 Lower Crescent, Belfast BT7 1NR.
> Tel: 028 9024 5729.
> Information line: 0800 731 4931.
> Email: ageconcern.ni@btinternet.com
> www.ageconcern.org.uk

Help the Aged

Help the Aged is a charity which campaigns of behalf of older people, and provides a variety of advisory services to older people.

> **Help the Aged Head Office** – 207-221 Pentonville Road, London N1 9UZ.
> Tel: 020 7278 1114.
> Email: info@helptheaged.org.uk
> www.helptheaged.org.uk

- ➤ **Scotland:** 11 Granton Square, Edinburgh EH5 1HX.
  Tel: 0131 551 6331.
  Email: infoscot@helptheaged.org.uk
  www.helptheaged.org.uk

- ➤ **Wales**: CSV House, 12 Cathedral Road, Cardiff CF11 9LJ.
  Tel: 029 2034 6550.
  Email: infocymru@helptheaged.org.uk

- ➤ **Northern Ireland**: Ascot House, 24-30 Shaftesbury Square, Belfast BT2 7DB.
  Tel: 028 9023 0666.
  Email: infoni@helptheaged.org.uk

Further information

Good Non Retirement Guide 2004 – published by Kogan Page, £14.99.

The 'Which?' Guide to Making the Most of Retirement – published by Which? Consumer Guides 2003, £10.99.

Yours – a monthly magazine written specially for older people. Available at newsagents, or by subscription (£17.50 for 12 issues, or £26.50 to include four extra quarterly issues). Published by Emap Esprit, tel: 01733 264666.

- ➤ **learndirect** helpline – 0800 100 900 (or 0808 100 9000 in Scotland) – for information and advice on all learning opportunities.

- ➤ www.learndirect.co.uk

- ➤ www.learndirectscotland.com

3:26

People with disabilities

Topics covered:

- Education courses
- Learning at home
- Training courses
- Residential specialist training and further education
- Seeking employment
- Sources of help and information

They may be looking for:

- education for personal development
- education which leads to a qualification
- education with employment in mind
- training for new skills or an update on existing skills
- training with employment in mind.

Options available include:

- attending a course (general or vocational) at a higher education institution or local college
- studying at home – such as an Open University or Open College of the Arts, correspondence course
- training through Work Based Learning for Adults/Training for Work
- attending a course specially designed for people with disabilities at a specialist college of FE or at a residential training college.

Education courses

Higher education institutions and colleges of further education

HE institutions and FE colleges are required under the Disability Discrimination Act to publish disability statements, giving information about their facilities for disabled people. These should include overall policy towards disabled students, admission arrangements, educational facilities and support; physical access to educational and other facilities; names of members of staff with special responsibility for disabled students.

The new **Special Educational Needs and Disability Act (SENDA)** for England, Wales and Scotland makes it unlawful to discriminate against disabled students in the provision of education, training and other services. The Act states that reasonable adjustments involving the provision of auxiliary aids and services (e.g. interpreters) must be made; by September 2005, physical adjustments must have been made.

➤ For further information on the **Disabled Students' Allowance** contact the DfES student support helpline: 01325 392822. www.dfes.gov.uk/studentsupport

The Disability Rights Commission is currently running the **Open 4 All** campaign and also provides a wide range of information and advice for disabled people.

➤ **Disability Rights Commission** – Freepost MID 02164, Stratford upon Avon CV37 9BR.
Helpline: 08457 622 633 (8am-8pm Monday-Friday) .
Textphone: 08457 622 644.
www.drc-gb.org

➤ **Equality Commission for Northern Ireland** – Equality House, 7-9 Shaftesbury Square, Belfast BT2 7DP.
Tel: 028 9050 0600.
Email: information@equalityni.org
www.equalityni.org

Financial assistance

Generally, students aged 19 and over applying for **further** education courses have to pay their own tuition fees. They may apply for additional funds direct from the individual college if they are on a low income or in a particular financial difficulty. If they already receive a means-tested benefit, they may not have to pay tuition fees.

Students offered places on **higher** education courses apply for financial assistance with tuition fees (means-tested) and student loans to:

● their LEA in England and Wales

● the Student Awards Agency in Scotland

● their local Education and Library Board in Northern Ireland.

Disabled Students' Allowance

The Disabled Students' Allowance (non-means tested) is available to help pay for additional support and equipment. The DfES produce a free booklet *Bridging the Gap,* which may be obtained by phoning freephone: 0800 731 9133. It is also available on the internet: www.dfes.gov.uk

See *2:7 – Money* for more details about financing courses in further and higher education.

Education guidance services for adults

There are national adult information, advice and guidance services with details of local facilities and opportunities for people with disabilities.

Lead – Linking Education and Disability

Lead is a voluntary organisation providing guidance and support to access educational opportunities for physically and/or sensory impaired adults in Scotland. Local organisers can visit potential students at home.

> **Lead Scotland** – Queen Margaret University College, 36 Clerwood Terrace, Edinburgh EH12 8TS.
> Tel: 0131 317 3439.
> Email: enquiries@lead.org.uk
> www.lead.org.uk

Basic education

Basic education tuition may be possible in a client's home if he/she is unable to attend classes at a centre or college.

National Federation of Access Centres

Access Centres are based at a number of further and higher education institutions in England, Scotland and Wales. Their purpose is to offer individual students with physical and sensory disabilities an assessment of need for help with their course of study. Students are usually referred by the educational institution they attend or wish to attend. Disabled Students' Allowances are normally used to pay for this. For a list of Access Centres contact:

> **Disability Assist Services** – Access Centre, University of Plymouth, Room 8-11, The Babbage Building, Drake Circus, Plymouth PL4 8AA.
> Tel: 01752 232696.
> Minicom: 01752 232285.
> Email: mmkemp@plymouth.ac.uk
> www.nfac.org.uk

The Learning from Experience Trust

The Learning from Experience Trust publishes a pack to help people with disabilities tackle the barriers they face when seeking employment or training. The pack *Recognising Ability: Make Your Experience Count* contains activities and guidance to help people recognise their abilities and achievements and demonstrate these when applying for a job or a course. Copies of the pack are available from the Trust at a charge of £20 (reduced to £12.00 for non-profit institutions) plus £1.50 postage and packing.

> **Marie Edgar, Secretary, Learning from Experience Trust** – Goldsmiths College, Deptford Town Hall, London SE14 6AE.
> Tel: 020 7919 7739.
> Email: m.edgar@gold.ac.uk
> www.learningexperience.org.uk

Learning at home

There are education schemes aimed at mature students learning at home.

- Open learning and correspondence courses.

- Books and other learning approaches – audiocassettes, videos etc

- BBC Education.

Open University (OU)

The OU has specialist advisers for students with disabilities. Where possible, they also provide extra support, sometimes including helpers for summer schools. Last year, nearly 9500 disabled OU students requested special support services. A copy of the OU booklet *Meeting your Needs* can be obtained from the Regional Centres. The OU Student's Association (OUSA) offers considerable support to members with disabilities.

➤ **The Office for Students with Disabilities** – The Open University, Walton Hall, Milton Keynes MK7 6AA.
Tel: 01908 653745.
Minicom: 01908 655978.

➤ **The OU Students' Association (OUSA)** – Open University, PO Box 397, Walton Hall, Milton Keynes MK7 6BE.
Tel: 01908 652026.
www.open.ac.uk/learners-guide/disability

Open College of the Arts

Linked to the OU, the OCA offers courses in a wide range of subjects, supported by tutors who are themselves practising artists. A bursary of £75 is payable to all students studying with the OCA.

➤ **Open College of the Arts** – Unit 1B, Redbrook Business Park, Wilthorpe Road, Barnsley S75 1JN.
Tel: 0800 731 2116.
Minicom: 01226 205 255.
Email: open.arts@ukonline.co.uk
www.oca-uk.com

National Extension College

NEC offers a range of subjects including GCSEs, A levels, accounting, marketing, IT skills, small business courses, creative writing and counselling skills. It offers distance learning with support from tutors. They are also offering a government-funded programme for students with disabilities and carers aged 16+ (England residents only) offering a reduced fee of £50 for a range of courses with additional support from tutors and mentors.

➤ **National Extension College** – The Michael Young Centre, Purbeck Road, Cambridge CB2 2HN.
Tel: 01223 400 200.
Email: info@nec.ac.uk
www.nec.ac.uk

Open learning through television

The BBC is involved in open learning through TV programmes with supporting materials. There are courses on how to use the internet, as well as educational programmes through The Learning Zone and BBC Knowledge. www.bbc.co.uk/education

See *2:16 The Open University* and *2:17 Open/distance and other independent learning* for more detailed information.

Training courses

Work Based Learning for Adults in England and Wales/Training for Work in Scotland/Training for Work in Northern Ireland

The Jobcentre Plus/Jobcentre in England, LECs in Scotland, ELWa in Wales and the Department for Employment and Learning in Northern Ireland contract with approved training providers to offer training to help unemployed people aged 25 and over to update their existing work skills or learn new ones. The aim is to gain skills and qualifications and to take up employment. People with disabilities can access the training without waiting for the six-month unemployment rule.

In most areas an integrated programme is provided for able-bodied and disabled people. Particular needs will be considered, and a plan for training will be developed, taking into consideration:

- experience
- employment aims
- the needs of the local labour market.

Money

A training allowance, equivalent to any state benefits already received (including Incapacity Benefit and Severe Disablement Allowance), plus an appropriate premium, is paid. This will not normally affect any entitlement to benefits. Help may also be available with such extra expenses as travel costs and childcare. Skill or the Jobcentre Plus/Jobcentre will advise about resuming benefits if the period of training does not secure employment.

Part-time training

Part-time training may be available if the disability prevents full-time training. There may be a minimum number of hours necessary – the Disability Employment Adviser (DEA) can advise.

Additional help

Additional help for those with disabilities may include:

- special aids or equipment – providing the tools and equipment needed to overcome the effects of the disability and make full use of the training

- adaptations to premises or equipment – grants for necessary alterations to training locations and/or equipment

- individually-tailored training programmes where existing contractual local provision is not appropriate

- a readership service for the blind – financial help towards a reader for a trainee with visual impairment

- an interpreter service for the deaf – financial help towards an interpreter for a trainee with a hearing impediment.

More detailed information can be found in *2:18 – Work Based Learning for Adults and other government-funded training.*

Residential Training for Disabled Adults

Residential Training for Disabled Adults is a programme to help unemployed adults with disabilities, particularly those at risk of exclusion from the job market, to secure and sustain employment or self-employment. This is achieved through an individually tailored combination of guidance, learning in the workplace, work experience, training and approved qualifications, carried out in a residential setting. The programme is intended to help disabled adults over the age of 18, who are unable to access suitable local training, to gain skills in a supported and specialist environment. Over 50 courses of vocational training are available, many of which lead to National Vocational Qualifications. Training is provided at a specialist residential college (see below) or a recognised training provider.

➤ Consult the web-site for more information: www.disability.gov.uk/policy/ residentialtraining

➤ The DEA at the Jobcentre Plus/Jobcentre can also provide further information and help.

Residential specialist training and further education

Residential Training Colleges (RTCs)

Residential Training Colleges offer vocational training for unemployed people with all types of disability, including physical, medical or mental health issues, as well as special needs such as dyslexia. RTCs offer specialist facilities, medical and counselling support and expert staff to help people with disabilities gain access to learning and to come to terms with lifestyle changes.

Each college differs in the degree of independence it expects. Training is available to men and women aged 18 and over (some courses are open to 16 year olds). Many trainees have been previously employed and have had an illness or accident necessitating a significant change in lifestyle and retraining for employment. Not all RTCs offer all types of training. All colleges accept trainees from England, Wales and Scotland. A variety of recognised vocational qualifications are available, including City & Guilds and NVQs.

There is no charge to the individual for residential training and benefits are unaffected.

Training courses are available in a wide range of subjects and include:

- business and administration

- bench joinery and woodwork

- book-keeping and accountancy

- car maintenance

- computer-aided design (CAD)

- computer maintenance

- engineering

- food preparation and cookery

- fork-lift truck operating

- horticulture

- information technology

- marketing

- stores, distribution and warehousing

- watch and clock repair.

Training in basic work skills, number and word power and keyboard skills can also be provided.

The DEA at the Jobcentre Plus/Jobcentre can provide further information, or contact one of the colleges directly.

➤ **Finchale Training College** – Durham DH1 5RX.
Tel: 0191 386 2634.
Email: enquiries@finchalecollege.co.uk
www.finchalecollege.co.uk

➤ **Portland College** – Nottingham Road, Mansfield NG 18 4TJ.
Tel: 01623 499111.
Email: college@portland.ac.uk
www.portland.org.uk

➤ **Queen Elizabeth's Foundation Training College** – Leatherhead Court, Leatherhead KT22 0BN.
Tel: 01372 841100.
Email: webmaster@gef.org.uk
www.qef.org.uk

➤ **St Loye's Foundation** – Fairfield House, Topsham Road, Exeter EX2 6EP.
Tel: 01392 255428.
www.stloyes.co.uk
www.training-four-employment.info

Besides vocational training, some RTCs also offer special foundation courses including basic education, independence skills, communication skills and prevocational studies.

Other specialist colleges

There are many specialist colleges, catering for specific disabilities. Most are residential and take students from any area. A wide range of courses is available. DEAs at the Jobcentre Plus/Jobcentre have information about funding. Examples are:

Royal National Institute for the Blind (RNIB)

RNIB Vocational College is a National Specialist College welcoming people with disabilities aged 16 to 63 on a residential or day basis. Most, but not all learners have issues of sight loss. People also come with chronic illness, deafness, learning disabilities, physical mobility difficulties and mental health issues.

The college is situated on the same campus as, and works in close partnership with, Loughborough College of Further Education to provide students with a wide range of mainstream courses and vocational training. The college also provides all the support needed to enable individuals to progress in their lives at work, home and in the community.

Flexible programmes are designed to prepare students for further study or employment. Students are funded either by the Learning and Skills Council or via the Residential Training Unit.

Students can choose from a wide range of academic programmes offered at Loughborough College, including A levels and GCSEs, with full support from the college's visual impairment support service. There are also many courses in a broad range of occupational areas, including administration and secretarial, business, customer service, call centre, complementary therapies, engineering, health and social care, information technology, leisure, travel and tourism, and sports massage.

➤ **RNIB Vocational College** – Radmoor Road, Loughborough LE11 3BS.
 Tel: 01509 611077.
 Email: enquiries@rnibcocoll.ac.uk
 www.rnibvocoll.ac.uk

Royal National College for the Blind (RNCB)

The Royal National College for the Blind exists to enable people who are blind or partially sighted to achieve their independence. They offer a comprehensive range of over 46 course programmes alongside specialist support, services and facilities in a residential setting. Students are prepared for the world of work including self-employment, or for progression to higher education.

➤ **RNCB** – College Road, Hereford, HR1 1EB.
 Tel: 01432 265725.
 Minicom: 01432 276532.
 Email: info@rncb.ac.uk
 www.rncb.ac.uk

The Association of National Specialist Colleges (NATSPEC)

NATSPEC has a membership of over 50 specialist colleges for people with learning difficulties and or disabilities. It publishes a directory containing brief details of member colleges.

> **NATSPEC** – Administration Officer, 36 Gresham Road, East Ham, London E6 6DS.
> Tel: 020 8471 3284.
> Email: janicefaldo.natspec@btinternt.com
> www.natspec.org.uk

Lifetime Careers Wiltshire

Lifetime Careers Wiltshire publishes *COPE* (the directory of post-16 residential education and training for young people with special educational needs), £31.95. *COPE* is updated every two years.

The admissions officer at the individual colleges listed in these directories can provide information and a prospectus.

> **Lifetime Careers Publishing** – 7 Ascot Court, White Horse Business Park, Trowbridge, Wiltshire BA14 0XA.
> Tel: 01225 716023.
> Email: sales@lifetime-publishing.co.uk
> www.lifetime-publishing.co.uk

Seeking employment

Disability Discrimination Act

Following an educational or training course, assistance may be required in obtaining employment. The Disability Discrimination Act (DDA) makes it unlawful for an employer to treat a disabled person less favourably than anyone else because of their disability, unless there is good reason. The DDA also requires employers to make reasonable adjustments to working practices and premises to overcome any substantial disadvantage caused by disability.

> Further information may be obtained from the Disability Rights Commission helpline: 08457 622633. www.drc-gb.org

Working Tax Credit

If working, disabled people may be eligible for the disability element of Working Tax Credit. For further information:

> Helpline (England, Scotland and Wales): 0845 300 3900 (8am-8pm 7 days a week).
> Textphone: 0845 300 3909 .
> Helpline (Northern Ireland): 0845 603 2000.
> Textphone: 0845 607 6078.
> www.inlandrevenue.gov.uk/taxcredits

Government help and schemes for people with disabilities

The Disability Employment Adviser

The Disability Employment Adviser (DEA) based at the Jobcentre Plus/Jobcentre can provide information and support to disabled jobseekers, or disabled people already in work. Various leaflets are available in different formats, such as Braille and audiotape. See: www.jobcentreplus.gov.uk or the DEA can provide help with the programmes and schemes described below.

Access to Work (AtW)

AtW provides practical assistance to help disabled people enter or stay in employment on a more equal basis with their non-disabled colleagues by removing work-related obstacles due to disability. It does this through a system of grants towards the extra costs that result from disability. For example, Access to Work can provide help with:

- communicator support at a job interview

- a support worker to give practical help within the workplace and help with getting to and from work

- equipment to help the individual within the workplace

- alterations to premises and equipment to make them more accessible

- help with additional costs of getting to and from work for people unable to use public transport.

More information can be obtained from the Jobcentre Plus/Jobcentre.

Job Introduction Scheme

A grant is paid to an employer, usually for about six weeks, during which time the employer can assess a person's ability to do a particular job. The scheme allows a disabled applicant for a job to be given, in effect, a trial run. The employer is not obliged to keep the disabled employee after that time, but the actual job (if offered) must be expected to last for at least six months after the trial period ends.

Blind Homeworkers' Scheme

The Blind Homeworkers' Scheme is open to blind and partially sighted people, and others with disabilities who wish to run a business, usually from home.

WORKSTEP

Some people, because of the nature or severity of their disability, require support in the workplace. WORKSTEP can offer all kinds of job opportunities:

- supported placements – disabled people can work with non-disabled colleagues on the same terms and conditions, with support from a WORKSTEP provider

- employment with Remploy – a nationwide organisation, Remploy Interwork, manages placements with employers

- supported factories and businesses – may be run by local authorities and voluntary organisations, or factories run by Remploy Ltd. www.remploy.co.uk

New Deal for Disabled People

The New Deal for Disabled People (NDDP) supports people in receipt of a disability or health-related benefit in finding and retaining paid employment. It is a voluntary programme delivered through a network of Job Brokers across England, Scotland and Wales who:

- help participants understand and compete in the labour market

- agree with each participant the most appropriate route into employment for them

- support participants in finding and keeping paid employment

- work closely with providers of training and other provision where a participant needs additional support

- work with local employers to identify their needs and match them with the skills of their customers

- support participants during their first six months in employment.

Job Brokers are made up of organisations from the private, public and voluntary sector. Clients can choose which Job Broker to register with and, as each operates differently, they are advised to contact the ones in their area before deciding.

➤ NDPP Helpline: 0800 137 177 .
Textphone: 0800 435 550 .
www.newdeal.gov.uk/nddp
www.jobbrokersearch.gov.uk

Further information may be obtained from the DEA at the Jobcentre Plus/Jobcentre.

Specialist Recruitment Agencies

➤ **Total Jobs.com** runs a specialist online recruitment site for people with disabilities entitled 'Jobability', which aims to help break down barriers preventing disabled people from finding suitable employment.
Tel: 020 7769 9200.
www.jobability.com

➤ **Ready, Willing and Able** runs a website which provides information for disabled people who are looking for work, and also has job vacancies.
www.readywillingable.net

Sources of help and useful information

Department for Work and Pensions – disability website

This website provides wide-ranging information for people with disabilities including general advice, details of disability legislation, programmes and initiatives, and links to relevant organisations. www.disability.gov.uk

Skill: National Bureau for Students with Disabilities

Skill promotes opportunities to empower young people and adults with any kind of disability to realise their potential in further and higher education, training and employment throughout the United Kingdom. Skill provides an information service, promotes good practice and influences policy in partnership with disabled people, service providers and policy makers. It organises conferences and seminars around the country, and produces a range of publications.

> **Skill** – 4th Floor, Chapter House, 18-20 Crucifix Lane, London SE1 3JW.
> Tel: 020 7450 0620 (voice/text).
> Helpline: 0800 328 5050 (Tuesday 11.30am-1.30pm, Thursday 1.30pm-3.30pm).
> Textphone: 0800 068 2422.
> Email: info@skill.org.uk
> www.skill.org.uk

> **Skill Scotland** – Norton Park, 57 Albion Road, Edinburgh, EH7 5QY.
> Tel: 0131 475 2348.
> Email: admin@skillscotland.org.uk

> **Skill Northern Ireland** – Unit 2, Jennymount Court, North Derby Street, Belfast, BT15 3HN.
> Telephone/minicom: 028 9028 7000.
> Email: admin@skillni.org.uk

Scottish Accessible Information Forum (SAIF)

SAIF supports the rights of disabled people and carers to have access to accurate information to meet their needs. They produce a variety of publications which can be provided in a variety of formats or downloaded from their website. Examples include: *What Disabled People Should be Able to Expect from Disability Information and Advice Services* and *Making Websites Accessible.*

> **SAIF** – Royal Exchange House, 100 Queen Street, Glasgow G1 3DN.
> Tel: 0141 226 5261.
> Textphone: 0141 226 8459.
> Email: info@saifscotland.org.uk
> www.saifscotland.org.uk

Action for Blind People

Action for Blind People works with, and for, people who are visually impaired, to open up new opportunities so that they can enjoy equal rights and better facilities to lead the lifestyle they choose. It also runs its own services, which include accommodation schemes, holidays and specialist hotels, employment projects, a cash grant scheme and a national information and advice service.

➤ **Action for Blind People** – 14-16 Verney Road, London SE16 3DZ.
Tel: 020 7635 4800.
Helpline: 0800 9154666 (9am-5pm Monday-Friday).
Email: info@afbp.org
www.afbp.org

The Royal National Institute for Deaf People (RNID)
The RNID is the largest charity representing deaf and hard of hearing people in the UK. The Institute:

● campaigns to change laws and government policies

● provides information and raises awareness of deafness, hearing loss and tinnitus

● offers training courses and consultancy on deafness and disability

● provides communication services, including sign language interpreters

● trains interpreters, lipspeakers and speech-to-text operators

● offers employment programmes to help deaf people at work

● offers *Typetalk*, the national telephone relay service for deaf and hard of hearing people

● provides residential and community services for deaf people with special needs

● supplies equipment and products for deaf and hard of hearing people

● undertakes social, medical and technical research.

➤ **RNID Information Line** – 19-23 Featherstone Street, London EC1Y 8SL.
Freephone: 0808 808 0123.
Textphone: 0808 808 9000.
Email: informationline@rnid.org.uk
www.rnid.org.uk

Mencap
Mencap has divisional offices covering England, Wales and Northern Ireland which provide support, advice, and information to people with learning difficulties, and also to their families. It provides help and advice to parents and professionals on all aspects of special education and training for people with learning difficulties. Mencap runs colleges for young people, covering social independence and vocational skills training.

➤ **Mencap** – 123 Golden Lane, London EC1Y 0RT.
Tel: 020 7454 0454.
Helpline: 0808 808 1111 (Monday-Friday, 9am-5pm).
Email: information@mencap.org.uk
www.mencap.org.uk

➤ **Mencap in Northern Ireland** – Segal House, 4 Annadale Avenue, Belfast BT7 3JH.
Tel: 028 9069 1351.
Helpline: 0845 7636227.
Email: mencapni@mencap.org.uk

> **Mencap Cymru** – 31 Lambourne Crescent, Cardiff Business Park, Llanishen, Cardiff CF14 5GF.
> Tel: 029 2074 7588.
> Wales learning disability helpline: 0808 8000 300
> Email: information.wales@mencap.org.uk

Pathway Employment Service

Places people with learning disabilities into appropriate employment and provides on-going support.

> **Mencap Pathway Employment Service** – 6 Nightingale Close, Rotherham, South Yorkshire S60 2AB.
> Tel: 01709 830956.
> Email: information@mencap.org.uk
> www.mencap.org.uk

ENABLE

ENABLE campaigns for better rights and services for people with learning disabilities and their families in Scotland. Over 60 local branches provide support, advice and social activities.

It has a national information service, a legal service and local advocacy projects.

In addition, its service company, ENABLE Scotland, can develop and provide any direct service that someone with a disability might need. In different parts of Scotland, it offers jobs, training, respite short breaks, day services, supported living, housing and support for people with profound learning difficulties.

> **ENABLE** – 6th Floor, 7 Buchanan Street, Glasgow G12 3HL.
> Tel: 0141 226 4541 (1.30pm-4.45pm Monday to Thursday; 1.30pm-3.55pm Friday).
> Email: enable@enable.org.uk
> www.enable.org.uk

Royal Association for Disability and Rehabilitation (RADAR)

A national disability organisation which operates in conjunction with an affiliated network of local and national organisations. It campaigns for disabled people's rights and full integration into society. It runs an information and advisory service, and is active in the fields of employment, mobility, housing, holidays, social service provision, social security, education and civil rights.

> **RADAR** – 12 City Forum, 250 City Road, London ECIV 8AF.
> Tel: 020 7250 3222.
> Email: radar@radar.org.uk
> www.radar.org.uk

Scope

Scope is a national disability organisation whose focus is people with cerebral palsy. It provides a range of support, information and campaigning services both locally and nationally, in addition to providing opportunities in education, employment, residential and day services.

➤ **Scope** – Cerebral Palsy helpline, PO Box 833, Milton Keynes MK12 5NY.
  Tel: 0808 800 3333 (9am-9pm weekdays; 2pm-6pm weekends and bank holidays).
  Email: cphelpline@scope.org.uk
  www.scope.org.uk

Disabled Living Foundation

The Disabled Living Foundation is a national charity providing practical, up-to-date information on many aspects of living with a disability. The DLF's professional advisers respond each year to written enquiries from healthcare professionals and the general public relating mainly to special equipment, clothing and footwear. The DLF has a major and permanent exhibition of over 800 items of disability equipment. Visitors are welcome by appointment. The Foundation also has a helpline service, a letter answering service and an email answering service.

➤ **Disabled Living Foundation** – 380-384 Harrow Road, London W9 2HU.
  Tel: 020 7289 6111.
  Helpline: 0845 130 9177 (Monday to Friday 10am-1pm).
  Helpline (text): 0870 603 9176.
  Email: info@dlf.org.uk
  www.dlf.org.uk

Disability Now

Disability Now is a campaigning newspaper which includes articles, features and links to other organisations and their websites, including those dealing with employment and training issues. *Disability Now* is sent free to disabled people in the UK who can provide photocopied evidence that they are receiving means-tested benefits.

➤ **Disability Now** – 6 Market Road, London N7 9PW.
  Tel: 020 7619 7323.
  Minicom 020 7619 7332.
  Email: editor@disabilitynow.org.uk
  www.disabilitynow.org.uk

Further information

Disability Rights Handbook – available from Disability Alliance, Universal House, 88-94 Wentworth Street, London EI 7SA. Tel: 020 7247 8776. Price for 29th edition £14.90; £10 for individuals on benefits (also available on CD-ROM). Provides annually-updated information on benefits and services for people with disabilities, including education and training.

The Educational Grants Directory 2004/05 – published by the Directory of Social Change, 24 Stephenson Way, London NW1 2DP. Tel: 020 7209 4949. Price £29.95. Lists educational charities for students in need, including help for students with disabilities.

A Guide to Grants for Individuals in Need 2004/05 – published by the Directory of Social Change (address above), £29.95. Lists charitable funds for the relief of individual distress, including grant-making charities for particular illnesses or disabilities.

Hobsons Guide for Students with Disabilities 2004 – £9.99.

All things being equal? A practical guide to widening participation for adults with learning difficulties in continuing education – published by NIACE, 21 De Montfort Street, Leicester LE1 7GE. Tel: 0116 204 4200. Price £8.95.

The Disabled Students' Guide to University – published by Trotman, £21.99.

RWA (Ready Willing Able) – the recruitment bulletin for disabled people – is available on six months' free subscription from RWA, PO Box 295, Witney OX29 4XZ. Tel: 01865 731303.

Skill's *Into* series includes:

Into Higher Education 2005 – £15.00.

Into Science and Engineering; Into Art; Into Architecture; Into Law; Into Teaching; Into Volunteering – all £6.50.

3:27

Overseas students, refugees and asylum seekers

Topics covered:

- Overseas students – finance
- Useful organisations
- Information for refugees/asylum seekers

Students

Coming to the UK to study is an option chosen by thousands of overseas students each year. Nearly all the full-time education opportunities outlined in this book are open to overseas students, but there are extra considerations for those from overseas who wish to study in the UK.

The chosen university or college will send a prospectus on request, with any additional information relating to entry for overseas students, including:

- entry qualifications required

- course fees and examination fees

- accommodation provided by the college and accommodation costs

- an idea of the approximate cost of living in the area

- ability in English language and any entry tests which may be required

- any association or societies run by the institution or its students, for students of different nationalities, which will often provide support and help.

In the UK, overseas students pay the full cost of the course, although students from the EU may qualify for support with fees.

There is information for international students applying to UK universities, including the opportunity to apply online, on the UCAS website: www.ucas.com

Students from EU countries

The only financial assistance available from the UK Government to students from EU countries is help with tuition fees. Prospective students should approach their own home education authorities to check whether any additional support is available from them.

In order to qualify for financial assistance with higher education tuition fees, on a similar means-tested basis to UK students, the following requirements must be met. Students must:

- be a national of an EU country

- have been ordinarily resident in the EEA (European Economic Area) or Switzerland for three years immediately before the start of the first academic year of the course

- attend a designated course (e.g. full-time first degree, foundation degree, HND or DipHE course or full- or part-time postgraduate initial teacher training course). Some help towards fees is also available for those who are on a part-time course that is 50% or more of an equivalent full-time course.

If the student has studied previously in the UK and received help with fees they may not be eligible for further help.

Applicants with migrant worker status are treated as home students, and apply for support through their home LEA.

For study in England and Wales, applicants must complete a form so that their eligibility and entitlement to financial help towards tuition fees can be assessed by the DfES EU Team. Forms may be downloaded from the DfES website listed below. Those applying through UCAS will automatically be sent a copy of the appropriate form (EU4N).

> **DfES European Team** – 2F-Area B, Mowden Hall, Staindrop Road, Darlington, Co Durham DL3 9BG.
> Tel: 01325 391199.
> Email: EUTeam@dfes.gsi.gov.uk
> www.dfes.gov.uk/studentsupport/eustudents

EU students, who meet similar eligibility rules as for England and Wales but who intend to graduate from an HE institution in Scotland, may be entitled to support for their tuition fees for any designated HE course.

> **Student Awards Agency for Scotland (SAAS)** – Gyleview House, 3 Redheughs Rigg, South Gyle, Edinburgh EH12 9HH.
> Tel: 0845 111 1711.
> Email: saas.geu@scotland.gsi.gov.uk
> www.student-support-saas.gov.uk

EU students planning to study in Northern Ireland should apply to the Education and Libraries Board in the area where their university or college is based.

Equivalence of qualifications

UK NARIC (The National Recognition Information Centre for the UK) can provide information about the equivalence of overseas academic qualifications to UK qualifications. Enquirers requiring a written assessment of equivalence can apply for a letter of comparability for a fee of £30 (+VAT for those living in Britain or the EU). See details on the UK NARIC website.

There is also a similar service for individuals enquiring about formal recognition of vocational qualifications. UK NARIC runs UK NRP – the National Reference Point for Vocational Qualifications. UK NRP provides information on vocational qualifications at skilled worker, trade and technician levels.

> **UK NARIC** – Oriel House, Oriel Road, Cheltenham GL50 1XP.
> Tel: 0870 990 4088.
> Email: info@naric.org.uk
> www.naric.org.uk

> **For UK NRP** – contact address and telephone number as above.
> Email: info@uknrp.org.uk
> www.uknrp.org.uk

The private sector

There are many private colleges in the UK. Independent colleges cover a wide range of subjects such as advertising, photography, GCSEs/Standard grades, A levels/Highers, business studies, computing and secretarial courses to name a few. Some of these have formed into Associations in order to guarantee quality standards of teaching and facilities.

British Accreditation Council for Independent Further and Higher Education

BAC was set up in 1984 as the national accrediting body for independent further and higher education. It currently lists over 130 accredited colleges in the UK (as well as some overseas colleges).

> **The British Accreditation Council** – 42 Manchester Street, London W1U 7LW.
> Tel: 020 7224 5474.
> Email: info@the-bac.org
> www.the-bac.org

The Association for Recognised English Language Services

ARELS is the representative body for private accredited English language schools in the UK. ARELS member schools run courses all year and through the summer to suit all ages. They produce a booklet *Learn English in Britain,* free of charge.

> **ARELS** – 56 Buckingham Gate, London SW1E 6AG.
> Tel: 020 7802 9200.
> Email: enquiries@arels.org.uk
> www.arels.org.uk

Independent higher education

The University of Buckingham

The University of Buckingham opened in 1976 as the only independent UK university. Courses start in September, January or July each year and generally last two years for degree level study, as they have four terms per year and fewer holidays.

> **University of Buckingham** – Hunter Street, Buckingham, MK18 1EG.
> Tel: 01280 814080.
> Email: info@buckingham.ac.uk
> www.buck.ac.uk

Correspondence /distance learning

It is possible to study through a distance learning/correspondence course and not come to the UK at all. When choosing a course it is important to check the qualification being offered: the British Council can advise, or see *2:17 – Open/distance and other independent learning*.

Useful organisations

UKCOSA

UKCOSA – The Council for International Education – is an independent body and registered charity. It produces information for prospective students from overseas on various aspects of studying in the UK, and general advice for students once they are in the UK. Information can be accessed through their website. There is also an advice line for would-be students.

> **UKCOSA** – Council for International Education, 9-17 St Alban's Place, London N1 0NX.
> Students' advice line (available Monday to Friday, 1pm-4pm UK time).
> Tel: 020 7107 9922.
> www.ukcosa.org.uk

The British Association of State English Language Teaching

BASELT is an association of UK university and colleges offering English language courses – for leisure, work and as a preparation for further learning. Member institutions are inspected and accredited by the British Council as part of the English in Britain accreditation scheme. BASELT's brochure listing the institutions and courses available can be accessed through their website.

> **BASELT** – c/o University of Gloucestershire, Cornerways, The Park Campus, The Park,
> Cheltenham GL50 2QF.
> Tel: 01242 227099.
> Email: baselt@chelt.ac.uk
> www.baselt.org.uk

The British Council

The purpose of the British Council is to win recognition abroad for the UK's values, ideas and achievements, and to build lasting, mutually beneficial relationships with other countries. It is the UK's international organisation for educational opportunities and cultural relations and is represented in 110 countries worldwide.

The British Council Information Centre (which has taken over the work of the Education Information Service) provides information on the British Council, the UK and UK education, by telephone, fax, email and letter. Students can enquire about any aspect of the UK education system, including funding.

> **British Council Information Centre** – Bridgewater House, 58 Whitworth Street, Manchester M1 6BB.
> Tel: 0161 957 7755.
> Email: general.enquiries@britishcouncil.org
> www.britishcouncil.org
> www.educationuk.org is a British Council website full of information for overseas enquirers.

Careers Europe

Information about international study, training and career opportunities may be available in services which subscribe to Careers Europe, the UK National Resource Centre for International Careers Information.

Refugees/asylum seekers

A **refugee** is defined as someone who has a well-founded fear of persecution on grounds of race, religion, politics etc, and who is therefore unwilling or unable to return home. While their application to stay in this country is being considered, they are known as **asylum seekers**. Asylum seekers are not permitted to work or undertake vocational training until they are given a positive decision on their asylum case, however long that process takes. Individuals, or their advisers, should take advice on what constitutes vocational training.

In higher education, once refugee status is granted, the student is treated as a home student; until then overseas student fees may be charged.

Education and training entitlement

Refugees are free to study any course, at any level, full- or part-time, providing they satisfy the entry requirements of the course, and have the financial means available to pay the course fees, and support themselves. Rules and regulations regarding the rights and entitlements of refugees to **financial support** for education are very complex, and subject to constant change. Much depends on the refugee's particular status. Enquirers are best advised to seek up-to-date information from organisations such as the Refugee Education and Training Advisory Service and other organisations listed below, or consult RETAS's website. Fees are often waived for ESOL courses.

Refugees who have been granted permission to stay and can claim Jobseeker's Allowance are entitled to early entry onto New Deal 25+. Such refugees are also eligible for early entry to Work Based Learning for Adults in England (see *2: 18 – Work Based Learning for Adults and other government-funded training*). The local Jobcentre Plus/Jobcentre can advise further on eligibility for New Deal and Work Based Learning for Adults.

Useful organisations

The Refugee Education and Training Advisory Service

RETAS is a registered charitable organisation offering information, advice and guidance on education, training and employment for refugees. The service is free, confidential and available to adult (16+) asylum seekers, refugees and those with indefinite and exceptional leave to remain granted as a result of an application for asylum. RETAS prioritises marginalised refugees, including refugee women, refugees with disabilities and young refugees. Their aim is to provide independent, impartial information, advice and guidance to help refugees overcome difficulties in accessing education, training and employment, including professional re-qualification. All clients are treated with respect and sympathy.

Services include:

- an office drop-in advice service

- a telephone advice line

- an outreach advice service

- training for service providers

- job search and orientation courses

- a mentoring scheme

- business start-up courses and support

- grants to individuals.

➤ **Refugee Education and Training Advisory Service (RETAS)** – Education Action
  International, 14 Dufferin Street, London EC1Y 8PD.
  Tel: 020 7426 5800.
  Email: retas@education-action.org
  www.education-action.org

Educational Grants Advisory Service

EGAS is part of the Family Welfare Association. EGAS is primarily concerned with helping disadvantaged students, including refugees and asylum seekers. Advice is provided on sources of financial assistance for learning.

➤ **EGAS** – 501-505 Kingsland Road, London E8 4AU.
  Tel: 020 7254 6251 (helpline operates between 10am-12 noon and 2-4pm on Mondays,
  Wednesdays and Fridays).
  Email: egas.enquiry@fwa.org.uk
  www.egas-online.org.uk

The Refugee Council

The Refugee Council helps provide advice and assistance to asylum seekers and refugees. Their Training and Employment Section runs work-related training courses for asylum seekers and refugees, and offers free, confidential and impartial careers advice and guidance, including information and guidance about learning opportunities. The Council's website lists regional offices, and carries information in a dozen different languages.

➤ **Refugee Council** – 3 Bondway, London SW8 1SJ.
  Tel: 020 7820 3000.
  Information line (general enquiries): 020 7820 3085 (operates from 10am to 1pm,
  Mondays, Wednesdays and Fridays)
  Email: info@refugeecouncil.org.uk
  www.refugeecouncil.org.uk

The Immigration Advisory Service

The IAS is a charity with over thirty years' experience and offices throughout the UK. All their advisers are professionals specialising in nationality, immigration and asylum law. The IAS also produces publications and organises events, such as conferences and training.

> **The Immigration Advisory Service** – 3rd Floor, County House, 190 Great Dover Street, London SE1 4YB.
> Tel: 020 7967 1200.
> www.iasuk.org

> Another useful website containing information for refugees and asylum seekers is: www.asylumaid.org.uk

Further information

Information for overseas **postgraduate students** wishing to study in the UK can be viewed on: www.prospects.ac.uk

Eurofacts leaflets – published by Careers Europe, include information on studying and working in the UK for residents of other EU countries.

The Newcomers Handbook: the guide to rights in and out of employment for all working age migrants – published by the Centre for Economic and Social Inclusion, £17.95

Quest for Quality Educational Guidance for Refugees in Europe project report can be downloaded from:

www.ecre.org/publications

British Qualifications – published by Kogan Page, £45.00. A guide to educational, technical, professional and academic qualifications in Britain.

British Vocational Qualifications – published by Kogan Page, £37.50.

University and College Entrance: The Official Guide – published annually by UCAS, 2005 entry edition, £32.50.

International Dictionary of Adult and Continuing Education – published by RoutledgeFalmer, £22.50.

The Educational Grants Directory – published by the Directory of Social Change (tel: 020 7209 5151), £22.95 for 2004-05 edition (due November 2004). A guide to the sources of funding available to students in need, listing trusts and foundations. Covers courses up to and including degree level.

University Scholarships and Awards – published by Trotman. 2004 edition (to be published September 2004), £19.99. Lists university and other awards available to students, including information on awards available to overseas students.

The Hotcourses UK universities, colleges and schools handbook – should be available for reference in British Council offices and other agencies.

Studying in the UK - Sources of funding for international students – free booklet published by the British Council in conjunction with UKCOSA and the FCO.

Studying and Living in the United Kingdom – published by the British Council. The 2004-05 edition can be accessed through their website: www.britishcouncil.org/publications

The following books and student information papers are available direct from The Association of Commonwealth Universities – John Foster House, 36 Gordon Square, London WC1H 0PF. Tel: 020 7380 6700:

International Awards 2001+, £40.

ACU Student Information Papers:

Graduate Study at Universities in the UK

Taking a First Degree at a University in the UK

Single copies are free on receipt of an SAE from the ACU address above. The information papers, and sample chapters of *International Awards 2001+*, can be viewed on: www.acu.ac.uk

A website that provides information on a range of issues, including education and training, relevant to asylum seekers, in a number of languages: www.mulitkulti.org.uk

The Employability Forum is an organisation which works with government departments to improve training and employment prospects for refugees.

See www.employabilityforum.co.uk

3:28

Race/other cultures

Topics covered:

- Race
- Travellers' organisations

All the opportunities outlined in *Second Chances* are open to everyone. There are specialist agencies that can help to promote those opportunities.

Race

Racial equality councils (RECs)

There are over 100 RECs, or similar organisations, many of them funded by the Commission for Racial Equality (see below). RECs help with any problems caused by a person's race, colour, or ethnic origin etc. They can provide information on local initiatives and projects.

Contact **local RECs** through telephone directories or through the **Commission for Racial Equality**. A list of RECs, divided into regions, is available on the CRE's website: www.cre.gov.uk/about/recs.html

Commission for Racial Equality (CRE)

The Commission for Racial Equality was set up by the 1976 Race Relations Act to work towards eliminating discrimination, promote equality of opportunity and good relations between people of different racial groups and keep the workings of the Race Relations Act under review. In December 2003, new regulations came into place outlawing discrimination on the grounds of religion or belief.

The CRE publishes numerous leaflets on equal opportunities and a person's rights under the Race Relations Act.

(N.B. There are plans to create a new equalities commission which will monitor discrimination on the grounds of race, gender, sexual orientation, age, religion and disability.)

➤ **Commission for Racial Equality** – St Dunstan's House, 201-211 Borough High Street, London SE1 1GZ.
Tel: 020 7939 0000.
Email: info@cre.gov.uk
www.cre.gov.uk

- The Commission for Racial Equality also has regional offices around the country:

- 3rd Floor, Lancaster House, 67 Newall Street, **Birmingham** B3 1NA.
  Tel: 0121 710 3000.

- Yorkshire Bank Chambers, 1st Floor, Infirmary Street, **Leeds** LS1 2JP.
  Tel: 0113 389 3600.

- Maybrook House, 5th Floor, 40 Blackfriars Street, **Manchester** M3 2EG.
  Tel: 0161 831 7782.

- The Tun, 12 Jackson's Entry, off Holyrood Road, **Edinburgh** EH8 8PJ.
  Tel: 0131 524 2000.

- Capital Tower, 3rd Floor, Greyfriars Street, **Cardiff** CF10 3AG.
  Tel: 029 2038 8977.

The Windsor Fellowship

The **Windsor Fellowship Undergraduate Programme** is for talented undergraduates from ethnic minorities and aims to equip them with the skills and knowledge necessary for them to compete for senior management and leadership positions within the public and private sectors. The Windsor Fellowship has also developed **Customised Programmes** tailored to the needs of specific employers or particular industries. In addition, the Fellowship runs **Career Focus seminars** aimed at unemployed graduates and final year undergraduates from ethnic minorities. See the website below for details on eligibility, when to apply and how to apply for the various programmes.

- **The Windsor Fellowship** – 138 Kingsland Road, Shoreditch Stables, London E2 8DY.
  Tel: 020 7613 0373.
  Fax: 020 7613 0377.
  Email: office@windsor-fellowship.org
  www.windsor-fellowship.org

Travellers

People who don't live in one place continuously can be disadvantaged when it comes to education.

Local education authority provision

Provision from local education authorities does vary – some provide special facilities at school whilst others will provide a teacher where travellers are living, but education for adults is rarely available. LEAs or Citizens Advice Bureaux have information about what is available in the local area.

Useful organisations

The Gypsy Council for Education, Culture, Welfare and Civil Rights
The Council has contacts nationwide. It liaises with local authorities on behalf of members about site provision etc which may affect adult education.

> **The Gypsy Council for Education, Culture, Welfare and Civil Rights** – 8 Hall Road, Aveley, Essex RM15 4HD.
> Tel. and fax: 01708 868986.
> Email: enquiries@thegypsycouncil.org
> www.thegypsycouncil.org

Romanestan Publications

This publisher produces relevant reports and books.

> **Romanestan Publications** – 22 North End, Warley, Brentwood CM14 5LA.
> Tel: 01277 219491

Friends, Families and Travellers

An advice and information unit for gypsies and travellers which deals mostly with legal issues such as eviction and planning, but can liaise with other organisations on education matters.

> **Friends, Families and Travellers** – Community Base, 113 Queens Road, Brighton BN1 3XG.
> Tel: 01273 234777.
> Emergency 24-hour mobile: 07971 550328.
> Email: fft@gypsy-traveller.org
> www.gypsy-traveller.org

National Association of Teachers of Travellers (NATT)

The Association publishes a directory of traveller education services in the UK, including some that offer adult education.

> **National Association of Teachers of Travellers** – c/o Advisory Service for the Teachers of Travellers, The Harlow Centre, Raymund Road, Oxford OX3 0PT.
> Tel: 01865 256620 (Lucy Beckett).

Further information

Portraits of Black Achievement – published by Lifetime Careers Publishing, £15.95.

Rights for Travellers – £2.00 from the London Irish Women's Centre, 59 Church Street, Stoke Newington, London N16 0AR. Tel: 020 7249 7318.

3:29

Offenders and ex-offenders

Topics covered:

- Legislation relating to offenders and ex-offenders
- Criminal record checks
- Applications for courses and schemes
- Organisations which can help offenders and ex-offenders
- Further sources of advice and information

Legislation and criminal record checks

There are restrictions on the employment of some ex-offenders in certain occupational areas. However, those working with offenders and ex-offenders need to be aware that, in many cases, the restriction is generated by the attitude of individual employers, not by the regulations themselves.

The Rehabilitation of Offenders Act

The Rehabilitation of Offenders Act 1974 (or the Rehabilitation of Offenders (Northern Ireland) Order 1978) is the main piece of UK legal protection for ex-offenders against discrimination based on a criminal record. Under the Act:

- certain criminal convictions can be 'spent' after a rehabilitation period

- it is deemed unlawful for an employer to discriminate against a person on the grounds of a spent conviction

- some kinds of employment are exempt from the Act, including work of national security, work with people from vulnerable groups (such as children and young people, the elderly and people with disabilities), the financial services industry, work connected to law enforcement and certain professions with legal protection.

The publication *I Can't Do That Can I?* (see under further information) provides details of occupational areas where convictions may be relevant, as well as many where there are no specific restrictions on employment.

Some job application forms ask for details of convictions, but do not mention the Act. In these cases, it is advisable for clients to check whether the post applied for is exempt or not.

The legislation relating to offenders is complex so, if in any doubt, clients should seek expert advice. NACRO (see later in this section) and other organisations, e.g. the Apex Charitable Trust (see later) and the Probation Services, produce leaflets on the Rehabilitation of Offenders Act. Further information may also be obtained from the Home Office.

➤ **Home Office** – 50 Queen Anne's Gate, London SW1H 9AT.
   Tel: 0870 000 1585.
   Textphone: 020 7273 3476.
   Email: public.enquiries@homeoffice.gsi.gov.uk
   www.homeoffice.gov.uk

Other Acts relating to work with vulnerable people

In recent years a range of legislation has been introduced intended to prevent unsuitable people from working with children, young people and vulnerable adults. As a result of all these Acts, some people are barred from work with these groups of people. The Criminal Records Bureau (see below) has powers to disclose relevant information to registered employers and voluntary organisations.

The Care Standards Act established a regulatory body for social care and private and voluntary healthcare services in England, known as the National Care Standards Commission. Similar regulatory bodies are setting standards, registering workers and regulating workers in Wales, Northern Ireland and Scotland.

Criminal Records Bureau (CRB)

The CRB is an Executive Agency of the Home Office, set up to improve access to criminal record checks for employment-related and volunteering purposes. In the past, information was only available to a few employers and voluntary organisations.

Through a service called Disclosure, the CRB aims to ensure that public, private and voluntary sector organisations in England and Wales are able to identify candidates who may be unsuitable for certain work. By making more information available from police and other records, the CRB will help to prevent unsuitable people working in jobs that may provide opportunities to harm children and vulnerable adults.

Organisations will be able to ask successful applicants to apply for one of three types of 'Disclosure'. The appropriate one depends on the position applied for and on the type of work involved. The depth of information will depend upon the level of Disclosure. Once a check is complete, one of three Disclosures will be issued. A fee is charged, except for Standard and Enhanced Disclosures for voluntary workers. The organisation requesting the Disclosure must comply with a strict code of practice on its use.

- All employers can ask potential employees to obtain a **Basic Disclosure** which will show convictions held at national level that are not yet spent. The applicant has the right whether or not to show the Disclosure to the employer.

- **Standard Disclosures** are mainly for jobs which involve working with children or regular contact with vulnerable adults (and for certain professions exempt from the

1974 Act). They detail all convictions on record, including spent convictions, plus information about reprimands or warnings. They also give information from lists held by the Department for Employment and Skills and the Department of Health of people unsuitable to work with children.

- For posts involving greater contact with children or particularly vulnerable adults (e.g. in the case of a social worker or doctor), an **Enhanced Disclosure** is issued. Enhanced Disclosures are also issued for those seeking certain statutory licensing purposes or judicial appointments. Local police force records are checked in addition to the checks made for the Standard Disclosure.

➤ **Disclosure Service CRB** – PO Box 110, Liverpool L69 3EF.
Information line: 0870 90 90 811.
www.disclosure.gov.uk
www.crb.gov.uk

Scottish Criminal Record Office (SCRO)

The SCRO Disclosure Scotland Bureau operates in a very similar way to the English and Welsh CRB described above. Basic, Standard and Enhanced Disclosures apply.

➤ **Disclosure Scotland** – PO Box 250, Glasgow G51 1YU.
Helpline: 0870 609 6006.
Email: info@disclosurescotland.co.uk
www.disclosurescotland.co.uk

Applications for courses and programmes

It is important that clients with relevant convictions are prevented from studying courses and then finding they are unacceptable for work placements and subsequent employment.

University degree applications

Clients who apply to universities and other higher education institutions through the UCAS system will find that UCAS application includes a question about criminal convictions. For certain courses, including those leading to teaching, social work and the health professions, applicants must declare any criminal convictions, including spent sentences, reprimands and warnings. Applicants should contact their chosen universities if they need to check whether this applies to the courses they have applied for.

For many university courses that do not include work with children or vulnerable adults etc, it is only necessary for an applicant to declare relevant criminal convictions.

If an applicant indicates that they have a conviction in their UCAS application, the chosen university or universities may ask them to send them more details.

More information about declaring criminal convictions can be found in the Help text for Apply and EAS as well as in UCAS' *How to Apply* booklet.

➤ **UCAS** – Rosehill, New Barn Lane, Cheltenham GL52 3LZ.
Tel: 0870 1122211 for application materials and enquiries, or apply online.
www.ucas.com

Applications to other courses

Applicants to courses outside the UCAS system may also have to declare their convictions. Those applying for postgraduate teacher training courses are expected to indicate any convictions, whether spent or unspent, no matter how minor, when applying for a PGCE through GTTR.

When on work placements, students on further education courses (such as those leading to CACHE qualifications) are never left unsupervised with children or vulnerable adults. Consequently, colleges do not necessarily ask applicants to such courses to declare their convictions. However, it is clearly ill advised for an ex-offender with a relevant conviction to start such a course and then find that they are unable to enter employment in the area. Ask advice from the college, or from agencies such as NACRO.

New Deal programmes

Under the New Deal programme, unemployed ex-offenders who have recently been in custody or on remand may be eligible for early entry onto the programme, rather than waiting for a qualifying period.

For more information on New Deal, see *2.18 – Work Based Learning for Adults and other government-funded training*

➤ **New Deal** helpline: 0845 606 2626.
Textphone: 0845 606 0680.
www.newdeal.gov.uk

Organisations offering information and advice

The following are specialist voluntary organisations which offer advice and information to offenders and ex-offenders, including on issues relating to education and training.

NACRO

NACRO, the crime reduction charity, has a number of centres in England and Wales which offer training in a wide range of vocational areas and in basic skills such as literacy and numeracy. They can also offer careers and employment advice.

NACRO's services are available to offenders and ex-offenders, whether or not they have been in prison, and to young disadvantaged people.

The education and training fund scheme offers financial assistance to ex-offenders for education or training. The scheme is not open to serving prisoners.

➤ **NACRO** – 169 Clapham Road, London SW9 0PU.
Tel: 020 7582 6500.
Resettlement Plus helpline: 020 7840 6464.
Email: helpline@nacro.org.uk and publications@nacro.org.uk
www.nacro.org.uk

➤ **NACRO Cymru** – 35 Heathfield, Swansea SA1 6EJ.
Tel: 01792 468400.
Email: helpline@nacrocymru.org.uk
www.nacro.org.uk/cymru

SACRO

Safeguarding Communities and Reducing Offending in Scotland, or SACRO, aims to promote community safety. SACRO does this by providing services to reduce conflict and offending and by influencing, through consultation, government polices and legislation.

The services SACRO provides across Scotland range from community mediation, consultancy and training through to mediation and reparation, intensive group work, supported accommodation and transitional care.

> **SACRO National Office** – 1 Broughton Market, Edinburgh EH3 6NU.
> Tel: 0131 624 7270.
> Email: info@national.sacro.org.uk
> www.sacro.org.uk

> The website has links to the 20 regional branches of SACRO.

NIACRO

NIACRO, the Northern Ireland Association for the Care and Resettlement of Offenders, is a charity providing services to prisoners, ex-offenders and their families. NIACRO also provides a range of training and employment opportunities under government-funded programmes, such as the New Deal, and European Union programmes targeting social inclusion. It works in partnership with Extern and the Probation Board for Northern Ireland to ensure service provision suited to the individual needs of the offender. A National Lottery project, Lift Off, targets young adults who, for whatever reason, do not participate in mainstream education and training programmes.

In all its work, NIACRO makes direct contact with employers to ensure that there is equality of opportunity in recruitment and selection.

NIACRO's training and employment programmes are provided across Northern Ireland, and details and locations may be obtained by contacting HQ below.

> **NIACRO** – 169 Ormeau Road, Belfast BT7 1SQ.
> Tel: 028 9032 0157.
> Email: niacro@niacro.org
> www.niacro.org

Apex Charitable Trust

The Apex Charitable Trust assists people with criminal records to obtain jobs or self-employment by providing them with the skills they need in the labour market; it also works to break down the barriers to their employment and increase employment opportunities in communities with high levels of crime and unemployment. The JobCheck helpline (see below) is available for advice and guidance to offenders, ex-offenders, their families and employers.

> **Apex Charitable Trust Ltd** – St Alphage House, Wingate Annexe, 2 Fore Street, London EC2Y 5DA.
> Tel: 020 7638 5931.
> JobCheck helpline: 0870 608 4567 (open Monday to Friday, 10am to 5pm).
> Email: jobcheck@apextrust.com
> www.apextrust.com

> **Apex Scotland** – 9 Great Stuart Street, Edinburgh EH3 7TP.
> Tel: 0131 220 0130.
> Email: admin@apexscotland.org.uk
> www.apexscotland.org.uk

Business in Prisons

The Business in Prisons Self-Employment project is a registered charity which aims to reintegrate offenders into the labour market, focusing on self-employment as a viable post-release option. Serving prisoners can register on a programme which offers free advice and support on a one-to-one basis, covering all aspects of self-employment.

> **Business in Prisons** - c/o HMP Sudbury, Ashbourne, Derbyshire DE6 5HW.
> Tel: 01283 584139.
> Email: businessinprison@aol.com
> www.businessinprisons.co.uk

BEAT

Business, Enterprise, Advice and Training (or BEAT) is a charity which gives prisoners, offenders, ex-offenders and other disadvantaged people training in the skills needed to run their own businesses. This includes helping individuals on a one-to-one basis to produce a business plan, to market their business and to raise the finance. If the training takes place in prison, after the prisoner has been released representatives from BEAT support them in establishing their own business. On-going support is provided for two years.

> **BEAT** – Southbank House, Black Prince Road, London SE1 7SJ.
> Tel: 020 7793 4294..
> Email: beatenterprises@aol.com

Further information

Wiping the Slate Clean – produced by the Home Office. A free leaflet explaining the Rehabilitation of Offenders Act 1974. Available from Citizens Advice Bureaux, libraries, Jobcentre Plus/Jobcentre offices or from the Home Office (see address above).

Criminal Records and Employment (Leaflet ER 22) – for information about Northern Ireland's legislation. Available from the Department for Employment & Learning, Adelaide House, 39/49 Adelaide Street, Belfast BT2 8FD.

I Can't Do That Can I? – published by Lifetime Careers Publishing, price £39.95. A directory of occupations and the relevance of criminal convictions.

Straight for Work – practical advice on disclosure, published by the Apex Trust, price £3.50.

The following leaflets, and others, are available from NACRO (address above). Single copies are usually free:

Sorting yourself out guide: Applying for Work – advice on how to complete application forms and write a CV.

Finding a Job – includes advice on job hunting, training and employment on release from prison.

4

The Gazetteer

The Gazetteer provides a listing of contact points for organisations providing information, advice and guidance, and for learning providers. The Gazetteer is organised by geographical area on a regional basis. In England, regions are subdivided into areas based on Learning and Skills Councils' boundaries.

Within each area, full contact details are provided for the following:

- organisations providing information, advice and guidance on learning opportunities i.e. next**step*** providers and Connexions services in England; Careers Wales and Careers Scotland in Wales and Scotland respectively; EGSAs in Northern Ireland

- the local Learning and Skills Council in England; ELWa (Education and Learning Wales) regional office in Wales; LECs in Scotland; Department for Employment and Learning Jobcentres/Jobs and Benefits offices in Northern Ireland

- LEAs (adult/community education services where applicable)

- further education colleges (where colleges have several campuses, one main contact address is normally provided)

- higher education institutions

- specialist colleges (listed under 'Other colleges', such as land-based colleges, drama and art colleges etc which may offer courses at further and/or higher education level)

- the contact agency providing advice on business-start up: Business Link (England); Business Eye (Wales); Small Business Gateway (Scotland); Enterprise Northern Ireland.

Apart from the further and higher education institutions listed in the Gazetteer, there are likely to be other learning providers and training organisations operating in the area, including private providers or those from further afield providing opportunities through distance or open learning. Further information on these may be available from local agencies providing information, advice and guidance, or from public libraries. Please note that most further education colleges also offer courses at higher education level.

*At the time of updating, the transition to nationally branded next**step** services was underway, but not completed. Therefore, some contact details are likely to change. Visit www.nextstep.org.uk for further information. Contact addresses given for next**step** providers are the main contractors for each LSC area.

Gazetteer contents

South West Region

Bournemouth, Dorset and Poole

nextstep provider

nextstep – Gaunts Business Centre, Petersham Lane, Gaunts, Wimbourne BH21 4JT. Freephone: 0800 138 5550. Email: dorsetiag@tribalhubs.com www.nextstep-bdp.org

Connexions service

Connexions Bournemouth, Dorset and Poole – Partnership Office, Ansbury House, 2 Pendruffle Lane, Poundbury, Dorchester, Dorset DT1 3WJ. Tel: 01305 260600. Fax: 01305 264545. www.connexions-bdp.co.uk

LSC

Learning and Skills Council – Provincial House, 25 Oxford Road, Bournemouth BH8 8EY. Tel: 0845 019 4148. Fax: 01202 652666. Email: bdpinfo@lsc.gov.uk www.lsc.gov.uk

LEAs

Bournemouth Borough Council – Adult Education Service, Punshon Centre, Exeter Road, Bournemouth BH2 5AJ. Tel: 01202 456223. Fax: 01202 456191. Email: punshon.centre@bournemouth.gov.uk www.bournemouth.gov.uk

Dorset County Council – Education Directorate, County Hall, Colliton Park, Dorchester DT1 1XJ. Tel: 01305 251000. Fax: 01305 224499. Email: adult.ed@dorsetcc.gov.uk www.dorsetcc.gov.uk

Poole Borough Council – Poole Adult Learning, Oakdale Centre, Wimborne Road, Poole BH15 3DL. Tel: 01202 633633. Fax: 01202 262307. Email: information@poole.gov.uk www.poole.gov.uk

FE colleges

Bournemouth and Poole College – North Road, Poole BH14 0LS. Tel: 01202 205205. Fax: 01202 205719. Email: enquiries@thecollege.co.uk www.thecollege.co.uk

Kingston Maurward College – Dorchester DT2 8PY. Tel: 01305 215000. Fax: 01305 215001. Email: administration@kmc.ac.uk www.kmc.ac.uk

Weymouth College – Cranford Avenue, Dorset DT4 7LQ. Tel: 01305 761100. Fax: 01305 208892. Email: igs@weymouth.ac.uk www.weymouth.ac.uk

HE institutions

Bournemouth University – Fern Barrow, Poole, Dorset BH12 5BB. Tel: 01202 524111. Fax: 01202 702736. Email: enquiries@bournemouth.ac.uk www.bournemouth.ac.uk

Other colleges

Arts Institute at Bournemouth – Wallisdown, Poole BH12 5HH. Tel: 01202 533011. Email: general@aib.ac.uk www.aib.ac.uk

Business Link

Business Link Wessex Ltd – Merck House, Seldown Lane, Poole BH15 1TD. Tel: 08454 588558. Fax: 08454 588554. Email: info@businesslinkwessex.co.uk www.businesslinkwessex.co.uk

Devon and Cornwall

(Areas covered: Devon, Cornwall, Plymouth, Torbay and the Isles of Scilly)

nextstep provider

nextstep – Tamar Business Park, Pennygillam Industrial Estate, Launceston PL15 7ED. Tel: 0845 850 5070. Fax: 01566 777713. www.nextstep-cds.org.uk

Connexions service

Connexions Cornwall and Devon – Tamar Business Park, Pennygillam Industrial Estate, Launceston, Cornwall PL15 7ED. Tel: 01566 777713.
Email: partnership@connexions-cd.org.uk
www.connexions-cd.org.uk

LSC

Learning and Skills Council – Foliot House, Budshead Road, Crownhill, Plymouth PL6 5XR. Tel: 0845 019 4155. Fax: 01752 754040.
Email: devonandcornwallinfo@lsc.gov.uk
www.lscdevonandcornwall.org

LEAs

Cornwall County Council – Education Services, County Hall, Truro, Cornwall TR1 3AY. Tel: 01872 322000. Fax: 01872 270340.
Email: aecentral@cornwall.gov.uk
www.cornwall.gov.uk

Council of the Isles of Scilly – Education Department, Town Hall, St Mary's, Isles of Scilly TR21 0LW. Tel: 01720 422537. Fax: 01720 422202. Email: adultlearning@scilly.gov.uk
www.scilly.gov.uk

Devon County Council – Education Department, County Hall, Topsham Road, Exeter EX2 4QD. Tel: 01392 383444. Fax: 01392 382203. Email: acl@devon.gov.uk
www.devon.gov.uk

Plymouth City Council – Department of Lifelong Learning, Windsor House, Derriford, Plymouth PL6 5UF. Tel: 01752 307400. Fax: 01752 307403.
Email: lifelong.learning@plymouth.gov.uk
www.plymouth.gov.uk

Torbay Council – Education Directorate, Oldway Mansion, Torquay Road, Paignton TQ3 2TE. Tel: 01803 208208. Fax: 01803 208225.
Email: education@torbay.gov.uk
www.torbay.gov.uk

FE colleges

Camborne Pool Redruth College – Trevenson Road, Pool, Redruth TR15 3RD. Tel: 01209 611611. Fax: 01209 611612.
Email: enquiries@cornwall.ac.uk
www.camborne.ac.uk

Cornwall College St Austell – Trevarthian Road, St Austell PL25 4BU. Tel: 01726 226626. Fax: 01726 226627. Email: info@st-austall.ac.uk
www.st-austell.ac.uk

Cornwall College Saltash – Church Road, Saltash PL12 4AE. Tel: 01752 848147. Fax: 01752 842028. Email: information@saltash.ac.uk
www.saltash.ac.uk

Duchy College – Stoke Climsland, Callington PL17 8PB. Tel: 01579 372222. Fax: 01579 372200. Email: stoke.enquiries@duchy.cornwall.ac.uk
www.duchy.ac.uk

East Devon College – Bolham Road, Tiverton EX16 6SH. Tel: 01884 235264.
Email: admissions@admin.eastdevon.ac.uk
www.edc.ac.uk

Exeter College – Victoria House, 33-36 Queens Street, Exeter EX4 3SR. Tel: 01392 205222. Email: reception@exe-coll.ac.uk
www.exe-coll.ac.uk

North Devon College – Old Sticklepath Hill, Barnstaple EX31 2BQ. Tel: 01271 345291. Fax: 01271 338121.
Email: postbox@ndevon.ac.uk
www.ndevon.ac.uk

Penwith College – St Clare Street, Penzance TR18 2SA. Tel: 01736 335000. Fax: 01736 335100.
Email: enquiries@penwith.ac.uk
www.penwith.ac.uk

Plymouth College of Further Education – Kings Road Centre, Devonport, Plymouth PL1 5QG. Tel: 01752 305300. Fax: 01752 305343.
Email: reception@pcfe.ac.uk www.pcfe.ac.uk

South Devon College – Newton Road, Torquay TQ2 5BY. Tel: 01803 400700. Fax: 01803 400701. Email: courses@southdevon.ac.uk
www.southdevon.ac.uk

Truro College – College Road, Truro TR1 3XX. Tel: 01872 267000. Fax: 01872 267100. www.trurocollege.ac.uk

HE institutions

College of St Mark and St John – Derriford Road, Plymouth PL6 8BH. Tel: 01752 636700. Email: admissions@marjon.ac.uk www.marjon.ac.uk

Dartington College of Arts – Totnes, Devon TQ9 6EJ. Tel: 01803 862224. Fax: 01803 861666. Email: registry@dartington.ac.uk www.dartington.ac.uk

Falmouth College of Arts – Woodlane, Falmouth TR11 4RH. Tel: 01326 211077. Fax: 01326 213880. Email: admissions@falmouth.ac.uk www.falmouth.ac.uk

University of Exeter – Northcote House, The Queen's Drive, Exeter EX4 4QJ. Tel: 01392 661000. Fax: 01392 263108. Email: admissions@exeter.ac.uk www.exeter.ac.uk

University of Plymouth – Drake Circus, Plymouth PL4 8AA. Tel: 01752 600600. Fax: 01752 232141. Email: admissions@plymouth.ac.uk www.plymouth.ac.uk

Other colleges

Bicton College of Agriculture – East Budleigh, Budleigh Salterton EX9 7BY. Tel: 01395 562400. Fax: 01395 567502. Email: enquiries@bicton.ac.uk www.bicton.ac.uk

Plymouth College of Art and Design (University of Plymouth) – Tavistock Place, Plymouth PL4 8AT. Tel: 01752 203434. Fax: 01752 203444. Email: enquiries@pcad.ac.uk www.plymouth.ac.uk

Business Link

Business Link Devon and Cornwall – Tamar Science Park, Derriford, Plymouth, Devon PL6 8BT. Tel: 0845 600 9966. Fax: 01752 770184. Email: enquiries@bldc.co.uk www.blinkdandc.com

Gloucestershire

nextstep provider

nextstep – c/o Connexions, Southgate House, Southgate Street, Gloucester GL1 1UB. Tel: 01452 833656. Fax: 01452 833601. Email: iaginfo@connexionsglos.org.uk www.go-iag.org.uk

Connexions service

Connexions Gloucestershire Ltd – Southgate House, Southgate Street, Gloucester GL1 1UB. Tel: 01452 833600. Fax: 01452 833601. Email: info@connexionsglos.org.uk www.connexionsglos.co.uk

LSC

Learning and Skills Council – Conway House, 33-35 Worcester Street, Gloucester GL1 3AJ. Tel: 01452 450001. Fax: 01452 450002. Email: gloucesterinfo@lsc.gov.uk www.lsc.gov.uk

LEA

Gloucestershire County Council – Education Office, Shire Hall, Westgate Street, Gloucester GL1 2TG. Tel: 01452 425000. Fax: 01452 425496. Email: speakout@gloucestershire.gov.uk www.gloscc.gov.uk

FE colleges

Cirencester College – Fosse Way Campus, Stroud Road, Cirencester GL7 1XA. Tel: 01285 640994. Fax: 01285 644171. Email: student.services@cirencester.ac.uk www.cirencester.ac.uk

Gloucestershire College of Arts and Technology – Gloucester Campus, Brunswick Road, Gloucester GL1 1HU. Tel: 01452 532000. Email: info@gloscat.ac.uk www.gloscat.ac.uk

The Royal Forest of Dean College – Five Acres, Coleford, Gloucester GL16 7JT. Tel: 01594 833416. Fax: 01594 545396. Email: enquiries@rfdc.ac.uk www.rfdc.ac.uk

Stroud College of Further Education – Stratford Road, Stroud GL5 4AH. Tel: 01453 763424. Fax: 01453 753543. Email: enquire@stroudcol.ac.uk www.stroud.ac.uk

HE institutions

University of Gloucestershire – PO Box 220, The Park, Cheltenham GL50 2QF. Tel: 01242 532700. Fax: 01242 532810. Email: admissions@glos.ac.uk www.glos.ac.uk

Other colleges

Hartpury College – Hartpury House, Gloucestershire GL19 3BE. Tel: 01452 700283. Fax: 01452 700629. Email: enquire@hartpury.ac.uk www.hartpury.ac.uk

Royal Agricultural College – Stroud Road, Cirencester GL7 6JS. Tel: 01285 652531. Fax: 01285 650219. Email: admissions@royagcol.ac.uk www.royagcol.ac.uk

Business Link

Business Link Gloucestershire – Chargrove House, Main Road, Shurdington, Cheltenham GL51 4GA. Tel: 01242 863863. Fax: 01242 864101. Email: info@glos.businesslink.co.uk www.glos.businesslink.co.uk

Somerset

nextstep provider

nextstep – Tamar Business Park, Pennygillam Industrial Estate, Launceston PL15 7ED. Tel: 0845 850 5070. Fax: 01566 777713. www.nextstep-cds.org.uk

Connexions service

Connexions Somerset – 1 Mendip House, High Street, Taunton TA1 3SX. Tel: 01823 423450. Fax: 01823 423479. Email: info@connexions-somerset.org.uk www.connexions-somerset.org.uk

LSC

Learning and Skills Council – East Reach House, East Reach, Taunton TA1 3EN. Tel: 0845 019 4161. Fax: 01823 256174. Email: somersetinfo@lsc.gov.uk www.lsc.gov.uk

LEAs

Somerset Lifelong Learning Directorate – County Hall, Taunton TA1 4DY. Tel: 01823 355455. Fax: 01823 355332. Email: education@somerset.gov.uk www.somerset.gov.uk/learning

FE colleges

Bridgwater College – Bath Road, Bridgwater TA6 4PZ. Tel: 01278 441234. Fax: 01278 444363. Email: guidance@bridgwater.ac.uk www.bridgwater.ac.uk

Richard Huish College – South Road, Taunton TA1 3DZ. Tel: 01823 320800. Fax: 01823 320801. Email: rhc@richuish.ac.uk www.richuish.ac.uk

Somerset College of Arts and Technology – Wellington Road, Taunton TA1 5AX. Tel: 01823 366331. Fax: 01823 366418. Email: enquiries@somerset.ac.uk www.somerset.ac.uk

Strode College – Church Road, Street BA16 0AB. Tel: 01458 844400. Fax: 01458 844411. Email: courseinfo@strode-college.ac.uk www.strode-college.ac.uk

Yeovil College – Mudford Road, Yeovil BA21 4DR. Tel: 01935 423921. Fax: 01935 429962. Email: info@yeovil-college.ac.uk www.yeovil-college.ac.uk

Other colleges

Cannington College – Cannington, Bridgwater TA5 2LS. Tel: 01278 655000. Fax: 01278 655055.
Email: enquiries@cannington.ac.uk
www.cannington.ac.uk

Business Link

Business Link Somerset – Creech Castle, Taunton TA1 2DX. Tel: 08457 211112. Fax: 01825 274862. Email: enquiry@blsl.co.uk
www.somerset.businesslink.co.uk

West of England

(Areas covered: Bristol, Bath and North East Somerset, South Gloucestershire and North Somerset)

nextstep provider

nextstep – 4 Colston Avenue, Bristol BS1 4ST. Tel: 0800 923 0323.
Email: enquiries@connexionswest.org.uk
www.mychoices.info

Connexions service

Connexions West of England – Floor 2, 4 Colston Avenue, Bristol BS1 4ST. Tel: 0800 923 0323. Fax: 0117 987 3701.
Email: enquiries@connexionswest.org.uk
www.connexionswest.org.uk

LSC

Learning and Skills Council – 7th Floor, St Lawrence House, 29-31 Broad Street, Bristol BS99 7HR. Tel: 0845 019 4168. Fax: 0117 922 6664. Email: westofenglandinfo@lsc.gov.uk
www.lsc.gov.uk

LEAs

Bath and North East Somerset Council – Adult and Community Education, 16A Broad Street, Bath BA1 5LJ. Tel: 01225 396453. Fax: 01225 396457. www.bathnes.gov.uk

Bristol City Council – Education and Lifelong Learning, The Council House, College Green, Bristol BS1 5TR. Tel: 0117 903 6958. Fax: 0117 903 7963.
www.bristol-lea.org.uk

North Somerset Council – Education Department, Town Hall, Walliscote Grove Road, Weston-Super-Mare BS23 1UJ. Tel: 01934 888888. Fax: 01934 418194.
www.n-somerset.gov.uk

South Gloucestershire Council – Education Service, Bowling Hill, Chipping Sodbury, Bristol BS37 6JX. Tel: 01454 868686. Fax: 01454 863309. Email: acls@southglos.gov.uk
www.southglos.gov.uk

FE colleges

City of Bath College – Avon Street, Bath BA1 1UP. Tel: 01225 312191. Fax: 01225 444213. Email: enquiries@citybathcoll.ac.uk
www.citybathcoll.ac.uk

City of Bristol College – Brunel Centre, Ashley Down Road, Bristol BS7 9BU. Tel: 0117 904 5000. Fax: 0117 904 5050.
Email: enquiries@cityofbristol.ac.uk
www.cityofbristol.ac.uk

Filton College – Filton Avenue, Filton, Bristol BS34 7AT. Tel: 0117 931 2121. Fax: 0117 931 2233. Email: info@filton.ac.uk
www.filton.ac.uk

Norton-Radstock College – South Hill Park, Radstock, Bath BA3 3RW. Tel: 01761 433161. Fax: 01761 436173. Email: courses@nortcoll.ac.uk www.nortcoll.ac.uk

Weston College – Knightstone Road, Weston-Super-Mare BS23 2AL. Tel: 01934 411411. Fax: 01934 411410.
Email: mktg@weston.ac.uk
www.weston.ac.uk

HE institutions

Bath Spa University College – Newton Park, Newton St Loe, Bath BA2 9BN. Tel: 01225 875875. Fax: 01225 875444. Email: enquiries@bathspa.ac.uk
www.bathspa.ac.uk

University of Bath – Bath BA2 7AY. Tel: 01225 388388. Fax: 01225 826366. Email: admissions@bath.ac.uk www.bath.ac.uk

University of Bristol – Senate House, Tyndall Avenue, Bristol BS8 1TH. Tel: 0117 928 9000. Fax: 0117 925 1424. Email: admissions@bristol.ac.uk www.bristol.ac.uk

University of the West of England (Bristol) – Frenchay Campus, Coldharbour Lane, Bristol BS16 1QY. Tel: 0117 965 6261. Fax: 0117 344 2810. Email: admissions@uwe.ac.uk www.uwe.ac.uk

Other colleges

Bristol Old Vic: Theatre School – 2 Downside Road, Bristol BS8 2XF. Tel: 0117 973 3535. Fax: 0117 923 9371. Email: enquiries@oldvic.ac.uk www.oldvic.ac.uk

Trinity College (Bristol) – Stoke Hill, Stoke Bishop, Bristol BS9 1JP. Tel: 0117 968 2803. Fax: 0117 968 7470. Email: admissions@trinity-bris.ac.uk www.trinity-bris.ac.uk

Business Link

Business Link West Ltd – 16 Clifton Park, Bristol BS8 3BY. Tel: 0117 973 7373. Fax: 0117 923 8024. Email: info@businesswest.co.uk www.businesswest.co.uk

Wiltshire and Swindon

nextstep provider

nextstep – c/o VT Southern Careers Ltd, Office Suite 3, Crusader House, Roman Way, Crusader Park, Warminster BA12 8SJ. Tel: 01985 217567. Fax: 01985 216124. Email: peter.blackburn@vtplc.com www.steps-to-learning.org.uk

Connexions service

Lifetime Careers Wiltshire Ltd – 7 Ascot Court, White Horse Business Park, Trowbridge BA14 0XA. Tel: 01225 716000. Fax: 01225 716019. www.lcw.uk.com

LSC

Learning and Skills Council – The Bora Building, Westlea Campus, Westlea Down, Swindon SN5 7EZ. Tel: 0845 019 4176. Fax: 01793 608003. www.lsc.gov.uk

LEAs

Swindon Borough Council – Education Department, Sanford House, Sanford Street, Swindon SN1 1QH. Tel: 01793 463902. Fax: 01793 488597. Email: info@swindon.gov.uk www.swindon.gov.uk

Wiltshire County Council – Education Department, County Hall, Bythesea Road, Trowbridge BA14 8JB. Tel: 01225 713000. Fax: 01225 713982. Email: customercare@wiltshire.gov.uk www.wiltshire.gov.uk

FE colleges

New College Swindon – New College Drive, Swindon SN3 1AH. Tel: 0808 172 1721. Fax: 01793 436437. Email: admissions@newcollege.ac.uk www.newcollege.co.uk

Salisbury College – Southampton Road, Salisbury SP1 2LW. Tel: 01722 344344. Fax: 01722 344345. Email: enquiries@salisbury.ac.uk www.salisbury.ac.uk

Swindon College – Regent Circus, Swindon SN1 1SX. Tel: 01793 491591. Fax: 01793 641794. Email: admissions@swindon-college.ac.uk www.swindon-college.ac.uk

Wiltshire College Chippenham – Cocklebury Road, Chippenham SN15 3QD. Tel: 01249 464644. Fax: 01249 465326. Email: info@wiltscoll.ac.uk www.wiltscoll.ac.uk

Wiltshire College Lackham – Lacock, Chippenham SN15 2NY. Tel: 01249 466800. Fax: 01249 444474. Email: info@wiltscoll.ac.uk www.wiltscoll.ac.uk

Wiltshire College Trowbridge – College
Road, Trowbridge BA14 0ES. Tel: 01225 766241.
Fax: 01225 777148. Email: info@wiltscoll.ac.uk
www.wiltscoll.ac.uk

Business Link

Business Link Berkshire and Wiltshire Ltd –
Emlyn Square, Swindon SN1 5BP. Tel: 0845 600
4141. Fax: 01793 485186. Email: info@blbw.co.uk
www.businesslinkberksandwilts.co.uk

South East Region

Berkshire

(Areas covered: West Berkshire, Bracknell Forest, Reading, Slough, Windsor and Maidenhead and Wokingham)

nextstep provider

next**step** – 1st floor, 69 High Street, Maidenhead SL 6 1JX. Tel: 0845 601 8595. Email: info@berkshire-iag.org.uk

Connexions service

Connexions Berkshire – Pacific House, Imperial Way, Reading, Berkshire RG2 0TF. Tel: 0118 987 0040. Fax: 0118 975 5048. Email: info@connexions-berkshire.org.uk www.connexions-berkshire.org.uk

LSC

Learning and Skills Council – Pacific House, Imperial Way, Reading RG2 0TF. Tel: 0845 019 4147. Fax: 0118 908 2109. Email: berkshire@lsc.gov.uk www.lsc.gov.uk

LEAs

West Berkshire Council – Education Department, Avonbank House, West Street, Newbury RG14 1BZ. Tel: 01635 519060. Fax: 01635 519811. Email: aclteam@westberks.gov.uk www.westberks.gov.uk

Bracknell Forest Borough Council – Education Department, Seymour House, 38 Broadway, Bracknell RG12 1AU. Tel: 01344 354000. Fax: 01344 354001. Email: education@bracknell-forest.gov.uk www.bracknell-forest.gov.uk

Reading Borough Council – Education and Community Services, PO Box 2623, Reading RG1 7WA. Tel: 0118 939 0568. Fax: 0118 939 0675. www.reading.gov.uk

Slough Borough Council – Education Department, Town Hall, Bath Road, Slough SL1 3UQ. Tel: 01753 875700. Fax: 01753 875716. www.slough.gov.uk

Royal Borough of Windsor and Maidenhead – Education Department, Town Hall, St. Ives Road, Maidenhead SL6 1RF. Tel: 01628 798888. Fax: 01628 796907. adult.education@rbwm.gov.uk www.rbwm.gov.uk

Wokingham District Council – Education and Cultural Services, Lifelong Learning, PO Box 156, Wokingham, Berkshire RG40 1WN. Tel: 0118 974 6164. Fax: 0118 974 6135. www.wokingham.gov.uk

FE colleges

Bracknell and Wokingham College – Church Road, Bracknell RG12 1DJ. Tel: 0845 330 3343. Email: study@bracknell.ac.uk www.bracknell.ac.uk

East Berkshire College – (Maidenhead, Windsor, Langley), Boyn Hill Avenue, Maidenhead SL6 4EZ. Tel: 0800 923 0423. Fax: 01753 793316. Email: info@eastberks.ac.uk www.eastberks.ac.uk

Newbury College – Main Campus, Monks Lane, Newbury RG14 7TD. Tel: 01635 845000. Fax: 01635 845312. Email: info@newbury-college.ac.uk www.newbury-college.ac.uk

Reading College and School of Arts & Design – Crescent Road, Reading RG1 5RQ. Tel: 0118 967 5000. Fax: 0118 967 5301. Email: enquiries@reading-college.ac.uk www.reading-college.ac.uk

HE institutions

Thames Valley University – Slough Campus, Wellington Street, Slough SL1 1YG. Tel: 0800 036 8888. Fax: 01753 574264. www.tvu.ac.uk

University of Reading – Whiteknights, PO Box 217, Reading RG6 6AH. Tel: 0118 987 5123. Fax: 0118 931 4404. www.reading.ac.uk

Other colleges

Berkshire College of Agriculture – Hall Place, Burchetts Green, Maidenhead SL6 6QR. Tel: 01628 824444. Fax: 01628 824695. Email: enquiries@bca.ac.uk www.bca.ac.uk

College of Estate Management – Whiteknights, Reading RG6 6AW. Tel: 0118 986 1101. Fax: 0118 975 5344. Email: info@cem.ac.uk www.cem.ac.uk

Reading Adult Community College – Wilson Centre, Wilson Road, Reading RG3 2RW. Tel: 0118 901 5262. Fax: 0118 901 5692. www.adultlearningatreading.org.uk

Business Link

Business Link Berkshire and Wiltshire Ltd – Emlyn Square, Swindon SN1 5BP. Tel: 0845 600 4141. Fax: 01793 485186. Email: info@blbw.co.uk www.businesslinkberksandwilts.co.uk

Hampshire and the Isle of Wight

(Areas covered: Hampshire, Isle of Wight, Portsmouth and Southampton)

nextstep provider

nextstep – Link2Learn Hampshire and the Isle of Wight, 1st Floor, 24 West Street, Fareham PO16 0LF. Tel: 01329 236740. Fax: 01329 236824. Email: info@link2learn.co.uk www.link2learn.co.uk

Connexions service

Connexions South Central – South Central Partnership, Eagle Point, West Wing, Little Park Farm Road, Segensworth, Fareham PO15 5TD. Tel: 01489 566990. Fax: 01489 578340. www.connexions-southcentral.org

LSC

Learning and Skills Council – 1st Floor, 1000 Parkway, Whiteley, PO15 7AA. Tel: 0845 019 4182. Fax: 01489 558600. Email: info@lsc.gov.uk www.lsc.gov.uk

LEAs

Hampshire County Council – Education Department, County Office, The Castle, Winchester, SO23 8UG. Tel: 01962 846452. Fax: 01962 842355. www.hants.gov.uk

Isle of Wight Council – County Hall, Newport, Isle of Wight PO30 1UD. Tel: 01983 821000. Fax: 01983 823333. www.iwight.gov.uk

Portsmouth City Council – Lifelong Learning, Education Department, Civic Offices, Guildhall Square, Portsmouth PO1 2EA. Tel: 023 9284 1712. Fax: 023 9284 1725. learnportsmouth@portsmouthcc.gov.uk www.portsmouth.gov.uk

Southampton City Council – Education Services, 5th Floor, Frosbier House, Nelson Gate, Southampton SO15 1BZ. Tel: 023 8083 3466. Fax: 023 8083 3324. Email: info@southampton.gov.uk www.southampton.gov.uk

FE colleges

Alton College – Old Odiham Road, Alton GU34 2LX. Tel: 01420 592200. Fax: 01420 592253. Email: enquiries@altoncollege.ac.uk www.altoncollege.ac.uk

Barton Peveril College – Chestnut Avenue, Eastleigh SO50 5ZA. Tel: 023 8036 7200. Fax: 023 8036 7228. Email: enquiries@imail.barton.ac.uk www.barton-peveril.ac.uk

Basingstoke College of Technology – Worting Road, Basingstoke RG21 8TN. Tel: 01256 354141. Fax: 01256 306444. Email: information@bcot.ac.uk www.bcot.ac.uk

Brockenhurst College – Lyndhurst Road, Brockenhurst SO42 7ZE. Tel: 01590 625555. Fax: 01590 625526. Email: enquiries@brock.ac.uk www.brock.ac.uk

Cricklade College – Charlton Road, Andover SP10 1EJ. Tel: 01264 360036. Fax: 01264 360010. Email: info@cricklade.ac.uk www.cricklade.ac.uk

Eastleigh College – Chestnut Avenue, Eastleigh S050 5FS. Tel: 023 8091 1000. Fax: 023 8032 2133. Email: goplaces@eastleigh.ac.uk www.eastleigh.ac.uk

Fareham College – Bishopsfield Road, Fareham P014 1NH. Tel: 01329 815200. Fax: 01329 822483. Email: info@fareham.ac.uk www.fareham.ac.uk

Farnborough College of Technology – Boundary Road, Farnborough GU14 6SB. Tel: 01252 407040. Fax: 01252 407041. Email: infor@farn-ct.ac.uk www.farn-ct.ac.uk

Havant College – New Road, Havant PO9 1QL. Tel: 023 9248 3856. Fax: 023 9247 0621. Email: enquiries@havant.ac.uk www.havant.ac.uk

Highbury College of Technology – Dovercourt Road, Highbury, Portsmouth P06 2SA. Tel: 023 9238 3131. Fax: 023 9232 5551. Email: info@highbury.ac.uk www.highbury.ac.uk

Isle of Wight College – Medina Way, Newport, Isle of Wight PO30 5TA. Tel: 01983 526631. Fax: 01983 521707. Email: info@iwcollege.ac.uk www.iwcollege.ac.uk

Peter Symonds College – Owens Road, Winchester SO22 6RX. Tel: 01962 852764. Fax: 01962 849372. Email: psc@psc.ac.uk www.psc.ac.uk

Portsmouth College – Tangier Road, Portsmouth PO3 6PZ. Tel: 023 9266 7521. Fax: 023 9234 4363. Email: registry@portsmouth-college.ac.uk www.portsmouth-college.ac.uk

Queen Mary's College – Cliddesden Road, Basingstoke RG21 3HF. Tel: 01256 417500. Fax: 01256 471501. Email: postmaster@qmc.ac.uk www.qmc.ac.uk

South Downs College – College Road, Waterlooville PO7 8AA. Tel: 023 9279 7979. Fax: 023 9279 7940. Email: college@southdowns.ac.uk www.southdowns.ac.uk

Southampton City College – St Mary Street, Southampton S014 1AR. Tel: 023 8048 4848. Fax: 023 8057 7473. Email: enquiries@southampton-city.ac.uk www.southampton-city.ac.uk

St Vincent College – Mill Lane, Gosport PO12 4QA. Tel: 023 9258 8311. Fax: 023 9251 1186. Email: cio@stvincent.ac.uk www.stvincent.ac.uk

Taunton's College – Hill Lane, Southampton SO15 5RL. Tel: 023 8051 1811. Fax: 023 8051 1991. Email: email@tauntons.ac.uk www.tauntons.ac.uk

Totton College – Calmore Road, Totton S040 3ZX. Tel: 023 8087 4874. Fax: 023 8087 4879. Email: info@totton.ac.uk www.totton.ac.uk

HE institutions

Southampton Institute – East Park Terrace, Southampton S014 OYN. Tel: 023 8031 9000. Fax: 023 8022 2259. Email: postmaster@solent.ac.uk www.solent.ac.uk

University College Winchester – Sparkford Road, Winchester S022 4NR. Tel: 01962 841515. Fax: 01962 842280. www.kingalfreds.ac.uk

University of Portsmouth – University House, Winston Churchill Avenue, Portsmouth PO1 2UP. Tel: 023 9284 8484. Fax: 023 9284 3082. Email: info.centre@port.ac.uk www.port.ac.uk

University of Southampton – Highfield, Southampton S017 1BJ. Tel: 023 8059 5000. Fax: 023 8059 3939. www.soton.ac.uk

Other colleges

Sparsholt College Hampshire – Sparsholt, Winchester S021 2NF. Tel: 01962 776441. Fax: 01962 776587. Email: enquiry@sparsholt.ac.uk www.sparsholt.ac.uk

Winchester School of Art – Park Avenue, Winchester S023 8DL. Tel: 023 8059 6900. Email: askwsa@soton.ac.uk www.wsa.soton.ac.uk

Business Link

Business Link Wessex Ltd – Wates House, Wallington Hill, Fareham PO16 7BJ. Tel: 08454 588 558. Fax: 01329 223 223. Email: info@businesslinkwessex.co.uk www.businesslinkwessex.co.uk

Kent and Medway

nextstep provider

nextstep – 2nd Floor, 22 High Street, Ashford, Kent TN24 8TD. Tel: 01233 640214. Fax: 01233 640215. www.learntowork.org.uk

Connexions service

Connexions Kent and Medway – Woodstock House, 15 Ashford Road, Maidstone, Kent ME14 5DA. Tel: 01622 683155. Fax: 01622 683129. Email: enquiries@connexionskentandmedway.co.uk www.connexionskentandmedway.co.uk

LSC

Learning and Skills Council – 26 Kings Hill Avenue, Kings Hill, West Malling ME19 4AE. Tel: 0845 019 4152. Fax: 01732 876917. Email: kentandmedwayinfo@lsc.gov.uk www.lsc.gov.uk

LEAs

Kent County Council – Kent Adult Education Services, College Road, Sittingbourne, Kent ME10 1LF. Tel: 01795 415900. Fax: 01795 435493 www.kent.gov.uk/adulted

Medway Council – Education Department, Civic Centre, High Street, Strood ME2 4AU. Tel: 01634 306000. Fax: 01634 332576. www.medway.gov.uk

FE colleges

Canterbury College – New Dover Road, Canterbury CT1 3AJ. Tel: 01227 811111. Fax: 01227 811101. Email: courseenquiries@cant-col.ac.uk www.cant-col.ac.uk

Mid-Kent College of Higher and Further Education – Horsted Centre, Maidstone Road, Chatham ME5 9UQ. Tel: 01634 830633. Fax: 01634 830224. Email: courseinformation@midkent.ac.uk www.midkent.ac.uk

North West Kent College – Oakfield Lane, Dartford DA1 2JT. Tel: 0800 074 1447. Fax: 01322 629400. Email: course.enquiries@nwkcollege.ac.uk www.nwkcollege.ac.uk

Orpington College of Further Education – The Walnuts, High Street, Orpington BR6 OTE. Tel: 01689 899700. Email: guidance@orpington.ac.uk www.orpington.ac.uk

South Kent College – The Grange, Shorncliffe Road, Folkestone CT20 2TZ. Tel: 01303 858220 Email: courseinformation@southkent.ac.uk www.southkent.ac.uk

Thanet College – Ramsgate Road, Broadstairs CTIO 1PN. Tel: 01843 605040. Email: student_services@thanet.ac.uk www.thanet.ac.uk

West Kent College – Brook Street, Tonbridge TN9 2PW. Tel: 01732 358101. Fax: 01732 771415. Email: marketing@wkc.ac.uk www.wkc.ac.uk

HE institutions

Canterbury Christ Church University College – North Holmes Road, Canterbury CT1 1QU. Tel: 01227 767700. Fax: 01227 470442. Email: admissions@cant.ac.uk www.cant.ac.uk

Department of Agricultural Sciences, Imperial College of Science, Technology and Medicine – Wye, Ashford TN25 5AH. Tel: 020 7589 5111. Fax: 020 7594 2669. Email: admissions.wye@imperial.ac.uk www.wye.ic.ac.uk

University of Kent at Canterbury – Canterbury CT2 7NZ. Tel: 01227 764000. Email: recruitment@kent.ac.uk www.kent.ac.uk

See also Mid-Kent College of Further and Higher Education listed previously

Other colleges

European School of Osteopathy – Boxley House, The Street, Boxley, Nr Maidstone ME14 3DZ. Tel: 01622 671558. www.eso.ac.uk

Hadlow College of Agriculture and Horticulture – Hadlow, Tonbridge TN11 0AL. Tel: 01732 850551. Email: enquiries@hadlow.ac.uk www.hadlow.ac.uk

Kent Institute of Art and Design – Oakwood Park, Maidstone ME16 8AG. Tel: 01622 757286. Fax: 01622 621100. Email: info@kiad.ac.uk www.kiad.ac.uk

Business Link

Business Link Kent Ltd – 26 Kings Hill Avenue, West Malling ME19 4AE. Tel: 08457 226655. Fax: 01732 841109. Email: info@businesslinkkent.com www.businesslinkkent.com

Milton Keynes, Oxfordshire and Buckinghamshire

nextstep provider

nextstep – c/o Careers Management (Bucks and Milton Keynes), 662 North Row, Central Milton Keynes MK9 3AP. Tel: 0800 1954 700. Fax: 01908 208901. Email: admin@the-advice-network.com www.the-advice-network.com

Connexions service

Connexions Milton Keynes, Oxfordshire and Buckinghamshire – 1st Floor, 9b Alton House Office Park, Gatehouse Way, Aylesbury HP19 8YB. Tel: 01296 392424. Fax: 01296 392246. Email: info@connexions-mob.org.uk www.connexionsmkob.org

LSC

Learning and Skills Council – Lackham House, Langford Business Park, Langford Locke, Kidlington, OX5 1GG. Tel: 0845 019 4154. Fax: 01865 291701. Email: mkobinfo@lsc.gov.uk www.lsc.gov.uk

LEAs

Buckingham County Council – Education Department, County Hall, Aylesbury HP20 1UZ. Tel: 01296 395000. Fax: 01296 382474. Email: adultlearning@bcc.ac.uk www.adultedbucks.org.uk

Milton Keynes Council – Adult Education, Westcroft Training Centre, 6 Wimbourne Crescent, Westcroft, Milton Keynes MK4 4DU. Tel: 01908 523100. Fax: 01908 523101. Email: adult.education@milton-keynes.gov.uk www.mkweb.co.uk/adulteducation

Oxfordshire County Council – Education Department, Macclesfield House, New Road, Oxford OX1 1NA. Tel: 01865 810525. Fax: 01865 810656. Email: adult.learning@oxfordshire.gov.uk www.oxfordshire.gov.uk

FE colleges

Abingdon and Witney College – Woolton Road, Abingdon OX14 1GG. Tel: 01235 555585. Fax: 01235 553168. Email: inquiry@abingdon-witney.ac.uk www.abingdon-witney.ac.uk

Amersham and Wycombe College – (now part of Buckinghamshire Chilterns University College) High Wycombe Campus, Spring Lane, Flackwell Heath, High Wycombe HP10 9HE. Tel: 0800 614016. Fax: 01494 735577. www.amersham.ac.uk

Aylesbury College – Oxford Road, Aylesbury HP21 8PD. Tel: 01296 588588. Fax: 01296 588589. Email: customerservices@aylesbury.ac.uk www.aylesbury.ac.uk

Henley College – Deanfield Avenue, Henley-on-Thames, RG9 1UH. Tel: 01491 579988. Fax: 01491 410099. Email: info@henleycol.ac.uk www.henleycol.ac.uk

Milton Keynes College – Chaffron Way Campus, Woughton Campus West, Leadenhall, Milton Keynes MK6 5LP. Tel: 01908 684444. Fax: 01908 684399. Email: info@mkcollege.ac.uk www.mkcollege.ac.uk

Oxford and Cherwell College – Banbury Campus, Broughton Road, Banbury OX16 9QA. Tel: 01865 551755. Fax: 01295 250381. Email: enquiries@banbury.occ.ac.uk www.occ.ac.uk

Oxford and Cherwell College – Oxford Campus, Oxpens Road, Oxford OX1 1SA. Tel: 01865 550550. Fax: 01865 248871. Email: enquiries@oxford.occ.ac.uk www.occ.ac.uk

Oxford and Cherwell College – Blackbird Leys Campus, Cuddeson Way, Oxford OX4 6HN. Tel: 01865 550550. Fax: 01865 269299. Email: enquiries@oxford.occ.ac.uk www.occ.ac.uk

Oxford and Cherwell College – Bicester Campus, Telford House, Telford Road, Bicester OX26 4LA. Tel: 01865 551155. Fax: 01865 551199. Email: enquiries@occ.ac.uk www.occ.ac.uk

HE institutions

Buckinghamshire Chilterns University College – Queen Alexandra Road, High Wycombe HP11 2JZ. Tel: 01494 522141. Fax: 01494 524392. Email: marketing@bcuc.ac.uk www.bcuc.ac.uk

Oxford Brookes University – Headington Campus, Gipsy Lane Oxford OX3 0BP. Tel: 01865 741111. Fax: 01865 483983. Email: postmaster@brookes.ac.uk www.brookes.ac.uk

University of Buckingham – Buckingham MK18 1EG. Tel: 01280 814080. Fax: 01280 822245. Email: info@buckingham.ac.uk www.buckingham.ac.uk

University of Oxford – University Offices, Wellington Square, Oxford OX1 2JD. Tel: 01865 270000. Fax: 01865 270708. Email: undergraduate.admissions@admin.ox.ac.uk www.ox.ac.uk

See also Oxford and Cherwell College listed above which offers higher education courses.

Other colleges

National Film & TV School – Beaconsfield Studios, Station Road, Beaconsfield, Bucks HP9 1LG. Tel: 01494 671234. Fax: 01494 674042. Email: admin@nftsfilm-tv.ac.uk www.nftsfilm-tv.ac.uk

The Oxford School of Drama – Sansomes Farm Studios, Woodstock OX20 1ER. Tel: 01993 812883. Fax: 01993 811220. Email: info@oxforddrama.ac.uk www.oxford.drama.ac.uk

Business Link

Business Link Solutions – Eastern Bypass, Thame OX9 3FF. Tel: 01844 210400. Fax: 01844 358068. Email: info@businesslinksolutions.co.uk www.businesslinksolutions.co.uk

Surrey

nextstep provider

nextstep – 2nd Floor, Sutton House, Weyside Park, Catteshall Lane, Godalming GU7 1XJ. Tel: 0800 085 6872. Email: enquiries@intouchsurrey.co.uk www.intouchsurrey.org.uk

Connexions service

Connexions Surrey – 2nd Floor, Connexions House, 83 East Street, Epsom, Surrey KT17 1DN. Tel: 01372 746500. Fax: 01372 720400. Email: info@connexionssurrey.co.uk www.connexionssurrey.co.uk

LSC

Learning and Skills Council – Technology House, 48-54 Goldsworth Road, Woking GU21 6LE. Tel: 0845 019 4145. Fax: 01483 803330. Email: surreyinfo@lsc.gov.uk www.surreylsc.gov.uk

LEA

Surrey County Council – Education Department, County Hall, Kingston upon Thames KT1 2DJ. Tel: 020 8541 8800. Fax: 020 8541 9004. www.surreycc.gov.uk

FE colleges

Brooklands College – Heath Road, Weybridge KT13 8TT. Tel: 01932 797700. Fax: 01932 797800. Email: info@brooklands.ac.uk www.brooklands.ac.uk

East Surrey College – Claremont Road, Gatton Point, Redhill RH1 2JX. Tel: 01737 772611. Fax: 01737 768641. Email: studentservices@esc.ac.uk www.esc.ac.uk

Esher College – Weston Green Road, Thames Ditton KT7 0JB. Tel: 020 8398 0291. Fax: 020 8339 0207. Email: eshercollege@esher.ac.uk www.esher.ac.uk

Farnham College – Morley Road, Farnham GU9 8LU. Tel: 01252 716988. Fax: 01252 723969. Email: enquiries@farnham.ac.uk www.farnham.ac.uk

Guildford College – Stoke Park, Guildford GU1 1EZ. Tel: 01483 448585. Fax: 01483 448600. Email: info@guildford.ac.uk www.guildford.ac.uk

NESCOT – Epsom's College of Further and Higher Education – Reigate Road, Ewell, Epsom KT17 3DS. Tel: 020 8394 3038. Fax: 020 8394 3030. Email: info@nescot.ac.uk www.nescot.ac.uk

Strode's College – High Street, Egham TW20 9DR. Tel: 01784 437506. Fax: 01784 471794. Email: info@strodes.ac.uk www.strodes.ac.uk

See also The Surrey Institue of Art & Design University College, listed below, which offers some FE courses.

HE institutions

Royal Holloway, University of London – Egham Hill, Egham, Surrey TW20 0EX. Tel: 01784 434455. Fax: 01784 437520. Email: admissions@rhbnc.ac.uk www.rhbnc.ac.uk

The Surrey Institute of Art and Design University College – Farnham Campus, Falkner Road, Farnham GU9 7DS. Tel: 01252 722441. Fax: 01252 892616. Email: registry@surrart.ac.uk www.surrart.ac.uk

University of Surrey – Guildford, Surrey GU2 7XH. Tel: 01483 300800. Fax: 01483 300803. Email: information@surrey.ac.uk www.surrey.ac.uk

See also NESCOT listed above

Other colleges

Conservatoire for Acting and Musical Theatre – Millmead Terrace, Guildford GU2 4YT. Tel: 01483 560701. Fax: 01483 535431. Email: enquiries@conservatoire.org www.conservatoire.org

Guildford College – Merrist Wood Campus, Worplesdon, Guildford GU3 3PE. Tel: 01483 884040. Fax: 01483 448600. Email: info@merristwood.ac.uk www.guildford.ac.uk

Business Link

Business Link Surrey – 5th Floor, Hollywood House, Church Street East, Woking GU21 6HJ. Tel: 01483 713300. Fax: 01483 771507. Email: success@businesslinksurrey.co.uk www.businesslinksurrey.co.uk

Sussex

(Areas covered: East Sussex, West Sussex, Brighton and Hove)

nextstep provider

nextstep – Reed House, 47 Church Road, Hove, East Sussex BN3 2BE. Tel: 0800 028 4490. Email: nextstep@sussexcareers.com www.worklearn.co.uk

Connexions service

Connexions Sussex – 53 Queens Road, Brighton BN1 3XB. Tel: 01273 783648. Fax: 01273 730055.
Email: info@connexions-sussex.org.uk www.connexions-sussex.org.uk

LSC

Learning and Skills Council – Prince's House, 53 Queen's Road, Brighton BN1 3XB. Tel: 01273 783555. Fax: 01273 783507. Email: sussexinfo@lsc.gov.uk www.lsc.gov.uk

LEAs

Brighton & Hove Council – Adult Education, Room 400, King's House, Grand Avenue, Hove BN3 2SU. Tel: 01273 293609. Fax: 01273 294924. Email: info@brighton-hove.gov.uk www.brighton-hove.gov.uk

East Sussex County Council – Educational Department, PO Box 4, County Hall, St Anne's Crescent, Lewes BN7 1SG. Tel: 01273 481497. Fax: 01273 487210.
Email: adulted@eastsussexcc.gov.uk www.eastsussexcc.gov.uk

West Sussex County Council – Education Department, County Hall, Chichester PO19 1RF. Tel: 01243 777770. Fax: 01243 777211. www.westsussex.gov.uk

FE colleges

Brighton College of Technology – Pelham Street, Brighton BN1 4FA. Tel: 01273 667788. Fax: 01273 667703. Email: info@ccb.ac.uk www.bricoltech.ac.uk

Chichester College – Brinsbury Campus, North Heath, Pulborough RH20 1DL. Tel: 01243 786321. Email: info@chichester.ac.uk www.chichester.ac.uk

Chichester College – Chichester Campus, Westgate Fields, Chichester PO19 1SB. Tel: 01243 786321. Fax: 01243 539481. Email: info@chichester.ac.uk www.chichester.ac.uk

Crawley College – College Road, Crawley RH10 1NR. Tel: 01293 442200. Fax: 01293 442399. Email: information@crawley-college.ac.uk www.crawley-college.ac.uk

Hastings College of Arts and Technology – Archery Road, St Leonards-on-Sea TN38 0HX. Tel: 01424 442222. Fax: 01424 721763. Email: studentadvisers@hastings.ac.uk www.hastings.ac.uk

Northbrook College – West Durrington, Littlehampton Road, Worthing BN12 6NU. Tel: 01903 606060. Fax: 01903 606073. www.northbrook.ac.uk

Sussex Downs College – Cross Levels Way, Eastbourne BN21 2UF. Tel: 01323 637637. Fax: 01323 637472. Email:eastbourne@sussexdowns.ac.uk www.sussexdowns.ac.uk

Sussex Downs College – 1 Mountfield Road, Lewes BN7 2XH. Tel: 01273 483188. Fax: 01273 478561. Email: lewes@sussexdowns.ac.uk www.sussexdowns.ac.uk

Varndean College – Surrenden Road, Brighton BN1 6WQ. Tel: 01273 508011. Fax: 01273 542950.
Email: admissions@varndean.ac.uk
www.varndean.ac.uk

HE institutions

University of Brighton – Mithras House, Lewes Road, Brighton BN2 4AT. Tel: 01273 600900. Fax: 01273 642010. www.bton.ac.uk

University College Chichester – College Lane, Chichester PO19 6PE. Tel: 01243 816000. Fax: 01243 816080. www.ucc.ac.uk

University of Sussex – Falmer, Brighton BN1 9RH. Tel: 01273 606755. Fax: 01273 678335.
Email: information@sussex.ac.uk
www.sussex.ac.uk

Other colleges

Brighton and Sussex Medical School – BSMS Admissions, Mithras House, Lewes Road, Brighton BN2 4AT. Tel: 01273 600900. Fax: 01273 642825.
Email: medadmissions@bsms.ac.uk
www.bsms.ac.uk

Plumpton College – Ditchling Road, Plumpton, Lewes BN7 3AE. Tel: 01273 890454. Fax: 01273 890071.
Email: info@plumpton.ac.uk
www.plumpton.ac.uk

Business Link

Sussex Enterprise – Greenacre Court, Station Road, Burgess Hill RH15 9DS.
Tel: 01444 259259. Fax: 01444 259255.
www.sussexenterprise.co.uk

London Region

London Central

(Areas covered: Camden, City of Westminster, Islington, Kensington and Chelsea, Lambeth, Southwark and Wandsworth)

nextstep provider

nextstep – c/o Lifetime Careers, Congress House, Lyon Road, Harrow, Middlesex HA1 2EN. Tel: 0800 0845 4632. Fax: 020 8901 3723. Email: enquries@lclondon.co.uk

Connexions service

Central London Connexions – Partnership Office, 3rd Floor, 125 Freston Road, London W10 6TH. Tel: 020 7938 8080. Fax: 020 7938 8020. Email: info@centrallondonconnexions.org.uk www.centrallondonconnexions.org.uk

LSC

Learning and Skills Council – Centre Point, 103 New Oxford Street, London WC1A 1DR. Tel: 0845 019 4144. Fax: 020 7896 8686. Email: londoncentralinfo@lsc.gov.uk www.lsc.gov.uk

LEAs

London Borough of Camden – Education Department, Crowndale Centre, 218-220 Eversholt Street, London NW1 1BD. Tel: 020 7974 1525. Fax: 020 7974 1536. Email: education@camden.gov.uk www.camden.gov.uk

London Borough of Islington – Education Department, Laycock Street, London N1 1TH. Tel: 020 7527 5666. Fax: 020 7527 5668. Email: education@islington.gov.uk www.islington.gov.uk

London Borough of Lambeth – Education Department, International House, Canterbury Crescent, Brixton, London SW9 7QE. Tel: 020 7926 1000. Fax: 020 7926 9778. Email: infoservice@lambeth.gov.uk www.lambeth.gov.uk

London Borough of Southwark – Regeneration and Education Department, Laycock Street, Islington N1 1TH. Tel: 020 7527 5898. Fax: 020 7527 5668.

London Borough of Wandsworth – Lifelong Learning, The Professional Centre, Franciscan Road, London SW17 8HE. Tel: 020 8871 8618. www.wandsworth.gov.uk

Royal Borough of Kensington and Chelsea – Education Enquiries Service, Town Hall, Horton Street, London W8 7XN. Tel: 020 7361 3334. Fax: 020 7361 2078. Email: eduadmin@rbkc.gov.uk www.rbkc.gov.uk

Westminster City Council – Westminster Adult Education Service, Amberley Road, London W9 2JJ. Tel: 020 7297 7297. Fax: 020 7641 8140. Email: info@waes.ac.uk www.westminster.gov.uk

FE colleges

City and Islington College – The Marlborough Building, 383 Holloway Road, London N7 0RN. Tel: 020 7700 9200. Fax: 020 7700 9222. Email: enquiries@candi.ac.uk www.candi.ac.uk

City of Westminster College – 25 Paddington Green, London W2 1NB. Tel: 020 7723 8826. Fax: 020 7258 2700. Email: customerservices@cwc.ac.uk www.cwc.ac.uk

Kensington & Chelsea College – Hortensia Road, London SW10 0QS. Tel: 020 7573 3600. Fax: 020 7351 0956. www.kcc.ac.uk

Lambeth College – Clapham Centre, 45 Clapham Common South Side, London SW4 9BL. Tel: 020 7501 5005. Fax: 020 7501 5041. Email: courses@lambethcollege.ac.uk www.lambethcollege.ac.uk

South Thames College – Wandsworth High Street, Wandsworth SW18 2PP. Tel: 020 8918 7000. Fax: 020 8918 7140. Email: studentservices@south-thames.ac.uk www.south-thames.ac.uk

Southwark College – Bermondsey Centre, Keetons Road, London SE16 4EE. Tel: 020 7815 1500. Fax: 020 7261 1301. Email: info@southwark.ac.uk www.southwark.ac.uk

Westminster Kingsway College – Gray's Inn Centre, Sidmouth Street, London WC1H 8JB. Tel: 020 7556 8000. Fax: 020 7556 8003. Email: courseinfo@westking.ac.uk www.westking.ac.uk

HE institutions

Birkbeck College, University of London – Malet Street, London WC1E 7HX. Tel: 020 7631 6000. Fax: 020 7631 6270. www.bbk.ac.uk

City University London – Northampton Square, London EC1V 0HB. Tel: 020 7040 5060. Fax: 020 7477 8562. www.city.ac.uk

Courtauld Institute of Art – Somerset House, Strand, London WC2R 0RN. Tel: 020 7848 2777. Fax: 020 7848 2410. www.courtauld.ac.uk

Heythrop College – University of London, Kensington Square, London W8 5HQ. Tel: 020 7795 6600. Fax: 020 7795 4200. Email: enquiries@heythrop.ac.uk www.heythrop.ac.uk

Imperial College of Science, Technology & Medicine – London SW7 2AZ. Tel: 020 7589 5111. Email: admissions@imperial.ac.uk www.ic.ac.uk

Institute of Education, University of London – 20 Bedford Way, London WC1H 0AL. Tel: 020 7612 6000. Fax: 020 7612 6126. Email: info@ioe.ac.uk www.ioe.ac.uk

King's College London – The Strand, London WC2R 2LS. Tel: 020 7836 5454. Email: ceu@kcl.ac.uk www.kcl.ac.uk

London Business School – Regent's Park, London NW1 4SA. Tel: 020 7262 5050. Fax: 020 7724 7875. www.london.edu

London Metropolitan University – London North Campus, 166-220 Holloway Road, London N7 8DB. Tel: 020 7423 0000. Fax: 020 7133 2255. www.londonmet.ac.uk

London School of Economics and Political Science – Houghton Street, London WC2A 2AE. Tel: 020 7405 7686. Fax: 020 7242 0392. www.lse.ac.uk

London South Bank University – 103 Borough Road, London SE1 0AA. Tel: 020 7928 8989. Fax: 020 7815 8273. www.sbu.ac.uk

Roehampton University of Surrey – Erasmus House, Roehampton Lane, London SW15 3PU. Tel: 020 8392 3000. Email: enquiries@roehampton.ac.uk www.roehampton.ac.uk

Royal Free and University College Medical School – Rowland Hill Street, London NW3 2PF. Tel: 020 7679 2000. www.rfc.ucl.ac.uk

Royal Veterinary College, University of London – Royal College Street, London NW1 0TU. Tel: 020 7468 5000. Email: registry@rvc.ac.uk www.rvc.ac.uk

School of Oriental and African Studies, University of London – Thornhaugh Street, Russell Square, London WC1H 0XG. Tel: 020 7637 2388. Fax: 020 7436 3844. Email: study@soas.ac.uk www.soas.ac.uk

School of Pharmacy, University of London – 29-39 Brunswick Square, Bloomsbury, London WC1N 1AX. Tel: 020 7753 5800. www.ulsop.ac.uk

School of Slavonic and East European Studies, University of London – Senate House, Malet Street, London WC1E 7HU. Tel: 020 7636 8000. Fax: 020 7862 8640. www.ssees.ac.uk

St George's Hospital Medical School, University of London – Cranmer Terrace, London SW17 0RE. Tel: 020 8672 9944. www.sghms.ac.uk

University College London – Gower Street, London WC1E 6BT. Tel: 020 7679 2000. Fax: 020 7679 2000. Email: postmaster@ucl.ac.uk www.ucl.ac.uk

University of Westminster – 309 Regent Street, London W1B 2UW. Tel: 020 7911 5000. Fax: 020 7911 5103.
Email: cav-admissions@wmin.ac.uk
www.wmin.ac.uk

Other colleges

Academy of Live and Recorded Arts Limited (ALRA) – Studio 1, The Royal Patriotic Building, Fitzhugh Grove, Trinity Road, London SW18 3SX. Tel: 020 8870 6475. Fax: 020 8875 0789.
Email: enquiries@alra.co.uk
www.alra.demon.co.uk

Architectural Association, School of Architecture – 36 Bedford Square, London WC1B 3ES. Tel: 020 7887 4000. Fax: 020 7414 0782. Email: admissions@aaschool.ac.uk
www.aaschool.ac.uk

The British School of Osteopathy – 275 Borough High Street, London SE1 1JE. Tel: 020 7407 0222. Fax: 020 7089 5300. Email: admissions@bso.ac.uk www.bso.ac.uk

Central School of Speech and Drama – Embassy Theatre, Eton Avenue, London NW3 3HY. Tel: 020 7722 8183. Fax: 020 7722 4132. Email: enquiries@cssd.ac.uk
www.cssd.ac.uk

The City and Guilds of London Art School – 124 Kennington Park Road, London SE11 4DJ. Tel: 020 7735 2306. Fax: 020 7582 5361. Email: info@cityandguildsartschool.ac.uk
www.cityandguildsartschool.ac.uk

City Lit Centre for Deaf People – Keeley House, Keeley Street, London WC2B 4BA. Tel: 020 7383 7624. Fax: 020 7380 1076. Email: cfdp@citylit.ac.uk www.citylit.ac.uk/cfdp

City Literary Institute – 16 Stukeley Street, Covent Garden, London WC2B 5LJ. Tel: 020 7242 9872. Fax: 020 7405 3347. Email: infoline@citylit.ac.uk www.citylit.ac.uk

European Business School London – Regent's College, Inner Circle, Regent's Park, London NW1 4NS. Tel: 020 7487 7505. Fax: 020 7487 7425. Email: ebsl@regents.ac.uk
www.ebslondon.ac.uk

The London Academy of Music and Dramatic Art – 155 Talgarth Road, London W14 9DA. Tel: 020 8834 0500. Fax: 020 8834 0501. Email: enquiries@lamda.org.uk
www.lamda.org.uk

London Contemporary Dance School – The Place, 17 Duke's Road, London WC1H 9PY. Tel: 020 7387 0161. Fax: 020 7383 4851. Email: info@theplace.org.uk
www.theplace.org.uk

The Marine Society, College of the Seas – 202 Lambeth Road, London SE1 7JW. Tel: 020 7261 9535. Fax: 020 7401 2537. Email: enq@marine-society.org
www.marine-society.org

Morley College – 61 Westminster Bridge Road, London SE1 7HT. Tel: 020 7928 8501. Fax: 020 7928 4074. Email: enquiries@morleycollege.ac.uk
www.morleycollege.ac.uk

Prince of Wales's Institute of Architecture – 14-15 Gloucester Gate, Regent's Park, London NW1 4HG. Tel: 020 7916 7380.

Regents Business School London – Regent's College, Inner Circle, Regent's Park, London NW1 4NS. Tel: 020 7487 7654. Fax: 020 7487 7425. Email: rbsl@regents.ac.uk
www.regents.ac.uk

Royal Academy of Dance – 36 Battersea Square, London SW11 3RA. Tel: 020 7326 8000. Fax: 020 7924 3129. Email: info@rad.org.uk
www.rad.org.uk

Royal Academy of Dramatic Art – 62-64 Gower Street, London WC1E 6ED. Tel: 020 7636 7076. Fax: 020 7323 3865. Email: enquiries@rada.org www.rada.org

Royal Academy of Music – Marylebone Road, London NW1 5HT. Tel: 020 7873 7373. Fax: 020 7873 7374. www.ram.ac.uk

Royal College of Art – Kensington Gore, London SW7 2EU. Tel: 020 7590 4444. Fax: 020 7590 4500. Email: info@rca.ac.uk
www.rca.ac.uk

Royal College of Music – Prince Consort Road, London SW7 2BS. Tel: 020 7589 3643. Fax: 020 7589 7740. Email: info@rcm.ac.uk www.rcm.ac.uk

Trinity College of Music – King Charles Court, Old Naval College, Greenwich, London SE10 9JF. Tel: 020 8305 4444. Fax: 020 8305 9444. Email: info@tcm.ac.uk www.tcm.ac.uk

University of the Arts London, Camberwell College of Arts – Peckham Road, London SE5 8UF. Tel: 020 7514 6302. Fax: 020 7514 6310. Email: enquiries@camberwell.arts.ac.uk www.camberwell.arts.ac.uk

University of the Arts London, Central St Martins College of Art & Design – Southampton Row, London WC1B 4AP. Tel: 020 7514 7000. Fax: 020 7514 7024. Email: enquiries@csm.arts.ac.uk www.csm.linst.ac.uk

University of the Arts London, Chelsea College of Art and Design – Manresa Road, London SW3 6LS. Tel: 020 7514 7751. Fax: 020 7514 7777. Email: enquiries@chelsea.arts.ac.uk www.chelsea.arts.ac.uk

University of the Arts London, Drama Centre London – Saffron House, 10 Back Hill, London EC1R 5LQ. Tel: 020 7514 8778. Fax: 020 7514 8777. Email: drama@arts.ac.uk www.csm.arts.ac.uk/drama

University of the Arts London, London College of Communication – Elephant and Castle, London SE1 6SB. Tel: 020 7514 6500. Fax: 020 7154 6535. Email: info@lcc.arts.ac.uk www.lcc.arts.ac.uk

University of the Arts London, London College of Fashion – 20 John Prince's Street, London W1M 0BJ. Tel: 020 7514 7344. Fax: 020 7514 7484. Email: enquiries@fashion.arts.ac.uk www.fashion.arts.ac.uk

Westminster College of Computing – Warrick House, 64-65 Cowcross Street, London EC1M 6BP. Tel: 0207 608 7011. Fax: 0207 253 7406. Email: training@wcc.co.uk www.wwc.ac.uk

Working Men's College – 44 Crowndale Road, London NW1 1TR. Tel: 020 7255 4700. Fax: 020 7383 5561. Email: info@wmcollege.ac.uk www.wmcollege.ac.uk

Business Link

Business Link for London – Link House, 292-308 Southbury Road, Enfield EN1 1TS. Tel: 0845 6000 787. Fax: 020 8443 7270. Email: info@bl4london.com www.businesslink4london.com

London East

(Areas covered: Barking & Dagenham, Bexley, City of London, Greenwich, Hackney, Havering, Lewisham, Newham, Redbridge and Tower Hamlets)

next**step** provider

next**step** – 7th Floor, Swan House, 52 Poland Street, London W1F 7LR. Tel: 020 8297 3324. Email: info@iaglondon.net www.iaglondon.net

Connexions service

Connexions East London – Unit 6, Stratford Office Village, 4 Romford Road, Stratford, London E15 4BZ. Tel: 020 8536 3630. Fax: 020 8534 2830. Email: info@londoneastconnexions.co.uk www.londoneastconnexions.co.uk

LSC

Learning and Skills Council – Boardman House, 64 Broadway, Stratford, London E15 1NT. Tel: 0845 019 4151. Fax: 020 8929 3802. Email: londoneastinfo@lsc.gov.uk www.lsc.gov.uk

LEAs

Corporation of London – Education Department, PO Box 270, Guildhall, London EC2P 2EJ. Tel: 020 7332 1750. Fax: 020 7332 1621. Email: education@corpoflondon.gov.uk www.corpoflondon.gov.uk

London Borough of Barking & Dagenham – Lifelong Learning, Westbury Centre, Ripple Road, Barking IG11 7PT. Tel: 020 8270 4814. Fax: 020 8270 4877. www.barking-dagenham.gov.uk

London Borough of Bexley – Directorate of Education and Leisure Services, Hill View, Hill View Drive, Welling DA16 3RY. Tel: 020 8303 7777. Fax: 020 8319 4302. www.bexley.gov.uk

London Borough of Greenwich – Lifelong Learning, Riverside House, Woolwich High Street, Woolwich, London SE18 6DF. Tel: 020 8854 8888. Fax: 020 8921 8228. www.greenwich.gov.uk

London Borough of Hackney – Adult and Community Learning Team, The Learning Trust, Technology and Learning Centre, 1 Reading Lane, London E8 1GQ. Tel: 020 8356 2335. Fax: 020 8820 7426. Email: info@hackney.gov.uk www.hackney.gov.uk

London Borough of Havering – Directorate of Children and Lifelong Learning, Broxhill Centre, Broxhill Road, Romford RM4 1XN. Tel: 01708 434343. Fax: 01708 379569. www.havering.gov.uk

London Borough of Lewisham – Community Education, Mornington Centre, Stanley Street, Deptford, London SE8 4BL. Tel: 020 8691 5959. Fax: 020 8694 8446. Email: community.education@lewisham.gov.uk www.lewisham.gov.uk

London Borough of Newham – Education Offices, Broadway House, 322 High Street, Newham, London E15 1AJ. Tel: 020 8430 2000. Fax: 020 8503 0014. www.newham.gov.uk

London Borough of Redbridge – Education Department, Floor 2, Lynton House, 255-259 High Road, Ilford IG1 1NY. Tel: 020 8554 5000. Fax: 020 8553 0895. www.redbridge.gov.uk

London Borough of Tower Hamlets – Lifelong Learning, Town Hall, Mulberry Place, 5 Clove Crescent, London E14 2BG. Tel: 020 7364 5000. Fax: 020 7364 4836. www.towerhamlets-pdc.org.uk

FE colleges

Barking College – Dagenham Road, Romford RM7 OXU. Tel: 01708 770000. Fax: 01708 770007. Email: admissions@barking-coll.ac.uk www.barkingcollege.ac.uk

Bexley College – Tower Road, Belvedere DA17 6JA. Tel: 01332 442331. Fax: 01332 448403. Email: enquiries@bexley.ac.uk www.bexley.ac.uk

Greenwich Community College – 95 Plumstead Road, Plumstead, London SE18 7DQ. Tel: 020 8488 4800. Fax: 020 8488 4899. Email: info@gcc.ac.uk www.gcc.ac.uk

Hackney Community College – Shoreditch Campus, Falkirk Street, London N1 6HQ. Tel: 020 7613 9000. Fax: 020 7613 9003. Email: enquiries@comm-coll-hackney.ac.uk www.comm-coll-hackney.ac.uk

Havering College of Further and Higher Education – Ardleigh Green Campus, Ardleigh Green Road, Hornchurch RM11 2LL. Tel: 01708 455011. Fax: 01708 462788. www.havering-college.ac.uk

Lewisham College – Lewisham Way, London SE4 1UT. Tel: 020 8692 0353. Fax: 020 8694 9163. Email: info@lewisham.ac.uk www.lewisham.ac.uk

Newham College of Further Education – East Ham Campus, High Street South, London E6 6ER. Tel: 020 8257 4000. Fax: 020 8257 4300. Email: on-line.enquiries@newham.ac.uk www.newham.ac.uk

Redbridge College – Little Heath, Romford RM6 4XT. Tel: 020 8548 7400. Fax: 020 8599 8224.
Email: info@redbridge-college.ac.uk
www.redbridge-college.ac.uk

Tower Hamlets College – Poplar Site, Poplar High Street, London E14 0AF. Tel: 020 7510 7510. Fax: 020 7538 9153. Email: towercol@mistral.co.uk www.tower.ac.uk

HE institutions

Goldsmiths College, University of London – New Cross, London SE14 6NW. Tel: 020 7919 7171. Fax: 020 7717 2240.
Email: admissions@gold.ac.uk
www.goldsmiths.ac.uk

London Metropolitan University – City Campus, 31 Jewry Street, London EC3N 2EY. Tel: 020 7320 1000. Fax: 020 7320 1163
Email: admissions@londonmet.ac.uk
www.londonmet.ac.uk

Queen Mary, University of London – Mile End Road, London E1 4NS. Tel: 020 7882 5555. Fax: 020 7882 5556. Email: admissions@qmul.ac.uk www.qmul.ac.uk

University of East London – Barking Campus, Longbridge Road, Dagenham RM8 2AS. Tel: 020 8223 3000. Fax: 020 8590 7799. Email: admiss@uel.ac.uk
www.uel.ac.uk

University of Greenwich – Maritime Greenwich Campus, Old Royal Naval College, Park Row, Greenwich SE10 9LS. Tel: 0800 005 006. Fax: 020 331 8590.
Email: courseinfo@greenwich.ac.uk
www.gre.ac.uk

Other colleges

CECOS London College of IT & Management – 2-10 Osborn Street, London E1 6TP. Tel: 020 7426 0167. Fax: 020 7377 5132. Email: London@cecos.co.uk www.cecos.co.uk

Guildhall School of Drama and Music – Silk Street, Barbican, London EC2Y 8DT. Tel: 020 7628 2571. Fax: 020 7256 9438.
Email: registry@gsmd.ac.uk www.gsmd.ac.uk

Greenwich School of Management – Meridian House, Royal Hill, Greenwich, London SE10 8RD. Tel: 020 8516 7800. Fax: 020 8516 7801.
Email: info@greenwich-college.ac.uk
www.greenwich-college.ac.uk

Laban Centre for Movement and Dance – Creekside, London SE8 3DZ. Tel: 020 8691 8600. Fax: 020 8691 8400.
Email: info@laban.org www.laban.org

Rose Bruford College – Lamorbey Park Campus, Burnt Oak Lane, Sidcup DA15 9DF. Tel: 020 8308 2600. Fax: 020 8308 0542.
Email: enquiries@bruford.ac.uk
www.bruford.ac.uk

Business Link

Business Link for London – Link House, 292-308 Southbury Road, Enfield, London EN1 1TS. Tel: 0845 6000 787. Fax: 020 8443 7270.
Email: info@bl4london.com
www.businesslink4london.com

London North

(Areas covered: Barnet, Enfield, Haringey, Waltham Forest)

nextstep provider

nextstep – c/o Prospects, 137-143 Baker Street, Enfield EN1 3JL. Tel: 020 8370 3530.
Email: iagpartnership@prospects.co.uk
www.learningandwork.org

Connexions service

Connexions North London – New Gallery, Haringey Park, Crouch End, London N8 9HY. Tel: 020 8347 2380. Fax: 020 8347 2390.
www.connexions-northlondon.co.uk

LSC

Learning and Skills Council – Dumayne House, 1 Fox Lane, Palmers Green, London N13 4AB. Tel: 0845 019 4158. Fax: 020 8882 5931.
Email: londonnorthinfo@lsc.gov.uk
www.lsc.gov.uk

LEAs

London Borough of Barnet – Educational Services, Town Hall, Friern Barnet Lane, London N11 3DL. Tel: 020 8359 3029. Fax: 020 8359 3057. www.barnet.gov.uk

London Borough of Enfield – Education Services, Civic Centre, Silver Street, Enfield EN1 3XY. Tel: 020 8366 6565. Fax: 020 8379 3243. Email: enfield.council@enfield.gov.uk www.enfield.gov.uk

London Borough of Haringey – Education Offices, 48 Station Road, Wood Green, London N22 7TY. Tel: 020 8489 2500. Fax: 020 8489 3864. Email: hals@haringey.gov.uk www.haringey.gov.uk

London Borough of Waltham Forest – Lifelong Learning Service, Leyton Neighbourhood Learning Centre, 3 The Square, High Road, Leyton, London E10 5NH. Tel: 020 8558 6805. Fax: 020 8527 8313. Email: wfdirect@lbwf.gov.uk www.lbwf.gov.uk

FE colleges

Barnet College – Wood Street Centre, Barnet, London EN5 4AZ. Tel: 020 8440 6321. Fax: 020 8441 5236. Email: info@barnet.ac.uk www.barnet.ac.uk

College of North East London – Tottenham Centre, High Road, London N15 4RU. Tel: 020 8802 3111. Fax: 020 8442 3091. Email: admissions@staff.conel.ac.uk www.conel.ac.uk

Enfield College – 73 Hertford Road, Enfield EN3 5HA. Tel: 020 8443 3434. Fax: 020 8804 7028. Email: courseinformation@enfield.ac.uk www.enfield.ac.uk

Southgate College – High Street, London N14 6BS. Tel: 020 8982 5050. Fax: 020 8982 5051. Email: admiss@southgate.ac.uk www.southgate.ac.uk

Waltham Forest College – Forest Road, London E17 4JB. Tel: 020 8501 8000. Fax: 020 8501 8001. Email: guidance@waltham.ac.uk www.waltham.ac.uk

HE institutions

Middlesex University – North London Business Park, Oakleigh Road South, London N11 1QS. Tel: 020 8411 5000. Fax: 020 8411 5649. Email: admissions@mdx.ac.uk www.mdx.ac.uk

London Metropolitan University – North Campus, 166-220 Holloway Road, London N7 8DB. Tel: 020 9423 0000. Fax: 020 7753 3271. Email: admissions@londonmet.ac.uk www.londonmet.ac.uk

Other colleges

British College of Osteopathic Medicine – Lief House, 120-122 Finchley Road, London NW3 5HR. Tel: 020 7435 6464. Fax: 020 7431 3630. Email: info@bcom.ac.uk www.bcom.ac.uk

Capel Manor College – Bullsmoor Lane, Enfield EN1 4RQ. Tel: 020 8366 4442. Fax: 01992 717544. Email: enquiries@capel.ac.uk www.capel.ac.uk

Oak Hill College – Chase Side, Southgate, London N14 4PS. Tel: 020 8449 0467. Fax: 020 8441 5996. www.oakhill.ac.uk

Business Link

Business Link for London – Link House, 292-308 Southbury Road, Enfield, London EN1 1TS. Tel: 0845 6000 787. Fax: 020 8443 7270. Email: info@bl4london.com www.businesslink4london.com

London South

(Areas covered: Bromley, Croydon, Kingston-upon-Thames, Merton, Richmond-upon-Thames and Sutton)

next**step** provider

next**step** – IAG at Prospects, 8th Floor, Grosvenor House, 125 High Street, Croydon CR0 1QG. Tel: 020 8649 6400. Fax: 020 8649 6444. Email: mark.baxter@prospects.co.uk

Connexions service

Connexions South London Partnership – Canius House, 1 Scarbrook Road, Croydon CR10 1SQ. Tel: 020 8929 4802. Email: info@connexions-southlondon.org.uk www.connexions-southlondon.org.uk

LSC

Learning and Skills Council – Canius House, 1 Scarbrook Road, Croydon CR10 1SQ. Tel: 0845 019 4172. Fax: 020 8929 4706. Email: londonsouthinfo@lsc.gov.uk www.lsc.gov.uk

LEAs

London Borough of Bromley – Lifelong Learning, Civic Centre, Stockwell Close, Bromley BR7 3UH. Tel: 020 8461 7608. Fax: 020 8313 4708. www.bromley.gov.uk

London Borough of Croydon – Lifelong Learning, Taberner House, Park Lane, Croydon CR9 1TP. Tel: 0870 556 1630. Fax: 020 8760 0871. Email: cets@croydon.gov.uk www.croydon.gov.uk

London Borough of Merton – Education Offices, Civic Centre, London Road, Morden, Surrey SM4 5DX. Tel: 020 8545 3268. Fax: 020 8545 3443. Email: education@merton.gov.uk www.merton.gov.uk

London Borough of Richmond-upon-Thames – Education, Arts and Leisure Department, Regal House, London Road, Twickenham TW1 3QB. Tel: 020 8891 7500. Fax: 020 8891 7714. Email: education@richmond.gov.uk www.richmond.gov.uk

London Borough of Sutton – Learning for Life, The Grove, Carshalton, Surrey SM5 3AL. Tel: 020 8770 5000. Fax: 020 8770 6545. www.sutton.gov.uk

London Borough of Kingston upon Thames – Kingston Adult Education, North Kingston Centre, Richmond Road, Kingston upon Thames, Surrey KT2 5PE. Tel: 020 8547 6758. Fax: 020 8547 6747. Email: adult.education@rbk.kingston.gov.uk www.kingston.gov.uk

FE colleges

Bromley College of Further and Higher Education – Rookery Lane, Bromley BR2 8HE. Tel: 020 8295 7000. Fax: 020 8295 7099. Email: info@bromley.ac.uk www.bromley.ac.uk

Carshalton College – Nightingale Road, Carshalton SM5 2EJ. Tel: 020 8770 6800. Fax: 020 8770 6899. Email: helpline@carshalton.ac.uk www.carshalton.ac.uk

Croydon College – Fairfield Campus, College Road, Croydon, Surrey CR9 1DX. Tel: 020 8686 5700. Fax: 020 8760 5880. Email: info@croydon.ac.uk www.croydon.ac.uk

Kingston College – Kingston Hall Road, Kingston upon Thames KT1 2AQ. Tel: 020 8546 2151. Fax: 020 8268 2900. Email: info@kingston-college.ac.uk www.kingston-college.ac.uk

Merton College – Morden Park, London Road, Morden, Surrey SM4 5QX. Tel: 020 8408 6500. Fax: 020 8408 6666. Email: info@merton.ac.uk www.merton.ac.uk

Orpington College of Further Education – The Walnuts, Orpington, Kent BR6 0TE. Tel: 01689 899700. Fax: 01689 877949. Email: guidance@orpington.ac.uk www.orpington.ac.uk

Richmond upon Thames College – Egerton Road, Twickenham TW2 7SJ. Tel: 020 8607 8000. Fax: 020 8744 9738. Email: courses@rutc.ac.uk www.richmond-utcoll.ac.uk

HE institutions

Kingston University – River House, 53/57 High Street, Kingston upon Thames KT1 1LQ. Tel: 020 8547 2000. Fax: 020 8547 7080. Email: admissions@kingston.ac.uk www.kingston.ac.uk

St Mary's College – Waldergrave Road, Twickenham, Middlesex TW1 4SX. Tel: 020 8240 4000. Fax: 020 8240 4255. www.smuc.ac.uk

Other colleges

The British School of Osteopathy – 275 Borough High Street, London SE1 1JE. Tel: 020 7407 0222. Fax: 020 7089 5300. Email: admissions@bso.ac.uk www.bso.ac.uk

Merton Adult College – Whatley Avenue, London SW20 9NS. Tel: 020 8543 9292. Fax: 020 8544 1421.
Email: info@merton-adult-college.ac.uk www.merton-adult-college.ac.uk

Ravensbourne College of Design and Communication – Walden Road, Elmstead Woods, Chislehurst BR7 5SN. Tel: 020 8289 4900. Fax: 020 8325 8320.
Email: info@rave.ac.uk www.rave.ac.uk

Richmond Adult Community College – Clifden Road, Twickenham TW1 4LT. Tel: 020 8843 7921. Fax: 020 8892 6354.
Email: info@racc.ac.uk www.racc.org.uk

Sutton College of Learning for Adults – St Nicholas Way, Sutton SM1 1EA. Tel: 020 8770 6901. Fax: 020 8770 6933. Email: suttoncentre@scola.ac.uk www.scola.ac.uk

Wimbledon School of Art – Merton Hall Road, London SW19 3QA. Tel: 020 8408 5000. Fax: 020 8408 5050. Email: info@wimbledon.ac.uk www.wimbledon.ac.uk

Business Link

Business Link for London – Link House, 292-308 Southbury Road, Enfield, London EN1 1TS. Tel: 0845 6000 787. Fax: 020 8443 7270. Email: info@bl4london.com www.businesslink4london.com

London West

(Areas covered: Hillingdon, Harrow, Brent, Ealing, Hounslow, Hammersmith and Fulham)

nextstep provider

nextstep – c/o CfBT Advice and Guidance, 6 Lampton Road, Hounslow, Middlesex TW3 1JL. Tel: 0800 085 4632. Fax: 020 8569 5165. Email: enquiries@lclondon.co.uk www.londonwestadvice.com

Connexions service

Connexions London West – Suite 4, 2nd Floor, Alperton House, Bridgewater Road, Wembley, Middlesex HA0 1EH. Tel: 020 8453 5000. Fax: 020 8453 5001. www.connexions-londonwest.com

LSC

Learning and Skills Council – Canius House, 1 Scarbrook Road, Croydon, Surrey. Tel: 0845 019 4172. Fax: 020 8929 4706. Email: londonsouthinfo@lsc.gov.uk www.lsc.gov.uk

LEAs

London Borough of Brent –Education, Arts and Libraries, Chesterfield House, 9 Park Lane, Wembley HA9 7RW. Tel: 020 8937 3000. Fax: 020 8937 3040. Email: education@brent.gov.uk www.brent.gov.uk

London Borough of Ealing – Education Department, Perceval House, 14-16 Uxbridge Road, London W5 2HL. Tel: 020 8579 2424. Fax: 020 8280 1291. www.ealing.gov.uk

London Borough of Hammersmith and Fulham – Town Hall, King Street, London W6 9JU. Tel: 020 8748 3020. Email: information@ibhf.gov.uk www.ibhf.gov.uk

London Borough of Harrow – Education Department, PO Box 22, Civic Centre, Station Road, Harrow HA1 2UW. Tel: 020 8863 5611. Fax: 020 8427 1810.
Email: info@harrow.gov.uk
www.harrow.gov.uk

London Borough of Hillingdon – Adult Education, 86 Long Lane, Ickenham, Middlesex UB10 8SX. Tel: 01895 676690.
Fax: 01895 673089.
Email: adulted@ibhill.gov.uk
www.hillingdon.gov.uk

London Borough of Hounslow – Education Department, Civic Centre, Lampton Road, Hounslow TW3 4DN. Tel: 020 8583 2755. Fax: 020 8583 2751. www.hounslow.gov.uk

FE colleges

Barnet College – Grahame Park Centre, Grahame Park Way, Colindale, London NW9 5RA. Tel: 020 8200 8300. Fax: 020 8502 7177.
www.barnet.ac.uk

College of North West London – Dudden Hill Lane, London NW10 2XD. Tel: 020 8208 5050. Fax: 020 8208 5151. Email: courenq@cnwl.ac.uk www.cnwl.ac.uk

Ealing, Hammersmith and West London College – Giddon Road, Barons Court, London W14 9BL. Tel: 0800 980 2185. Fax: 020 8563 8247. Email: personnel@hwlc.ac.uk
www.hwlc.ac.uk

Harrow College – Lifelong Learning Centre, Harrow-on-the-Hill Campus, Lowlands Road, Harrow HA1 3AQ. Tel: 020 8909 6000. Fax: 020 8909 6050.
Email: enquiries@harrow.ac.uk
www.harrow.ac.uk

Holborn College – Woolwich Road, Charltong, London SE7 8LN. Tel: 020 8317 6000. Fax: 020 8317 6001.
Email: admissions@holborncollege.ac.uk
www.holborncollege.ac.uk

Lansdowne College – 40-44 Bark Place, London W2 4AT. Tel: 020 7616 4400. Fax: 020 7616 4401.
Email: educaton@lansdownecollege.com
www.lansdownecollege.com

Stanmore College – Elm Park, Stanmore HA7 4BQ. Tel: 020 8420 7700. Fax: 020 8420 6502. Email: enquiry@stanmore.ac.uk
www.stanmore.ac.uk

Uxbridge College – Park Road, Uxbridge UB8 1NQ. Tel: 01895 853333. Fax: 01895 853377.
Email: enquiries@uxbridgecollege.ac.uk
www.uxbridge.ac.uk

West Thames College – London Road, Isleworth TW7 4HS. Tel: 020 8326 2020. Fax: 020 8326 2001. Email: info@west-thames.ac.uk
www.west-thames.ac.uk

HE institutions

Brunel University – Kingston Lane, Uxbridge UB8 3PH. Tel: 01895 274000. Fax: 01895 811737.
www.brunel.ac.uk

Thames Valley University – Ealing Campus, St Mary's Road, Ealing, London W5 5RF.
Tel: 0800 036 8888. Fax: 020 8566 1353.
Email: learning.advice@tvu.ac.uk
www.tvu.ac.uk

Other colleges

London College of Music, Media and ICT – Thames Valley University, St Mary's Road, London W5 5RF. Tel: 020 8231 2304. Fax: 020 8231 2546. Email: enquiries.lcm2@tvu.ac.uk
www.elgar.tvu.ac.uk

London School of Theology – Green Lane, Northwood HA6 2UW. Tel: 01923 456000.
Fax: 01923 456001. Email: enquiries@lst.ac.uk
www.lst.ac.uk

Business Link

Business Link for London – Link House, 292-308 Southbury Road, Enfield, London EN1 1TS. Tel: 0845 6000 787. Fax: 020 8443 7270.
Email: info@bl4london.com
www.businesslink4london.com

East of England

Bedfordshire and Luton

nextstep provider

nextstep at Learning for Life – 3 Abbey Court, Fraser Road, Priory Business Park, Bedford MK44 3WH. Tel: 0800 107 4177. Email: iag@learning-for-life-bedfordshire.co.uk www.learning-for-life-bedfordshire.co.uk

Connexions service

Connexions Partnership Bedfordshire & Luton – Partnership House, 6 Cardiff Road, Luton Bedfordshire LU1 1PP. Tel: 01582 727184. Fax: 01582 727318. Email: info@connx.org.uk www.connx.org.uk

LSC

Learning and Skills Council – Woburn Court, 2 Railton Road, Woburn Road Industrial Estate, Kempston MK42 9PN. Tel: 0845 019 4160. Fax: 01234 843211. Email: bedsandlutoninfo@lsc.gov.uk www.lsc.gov.uk

LEAs

Bedfordshire County Council – County Hall, Cauldwell Street, Bedford MK42 9AP. Tel: 01234 228347. Fax: 01234 228993. www.bedfordshire.gov.uk

Luton Borough Council – Lifelong Learning Department, Unity House, 111 Stuart Street, Luton LU1 5NP. Tel: 01582 548021. Fax: 01582 548444. www.luton.gov.uk

FE Colleges

Barnfield College – Enterprise Way, Bramingham, Luton LU3 4BU. Tel: 01582 569500. Fax: 01582 492928. www.barnfield.ac.uk

Bedford College – Cauldwell Street, Bedford MK42 9AH. Tel: 01234 291000. Fax: 01234 342674. Email: enquiries@bedford.ac.uk www.bedford.ac.uk

Dunstable College – Kingsway, Dunstable LU5 4HG. Tel: 01582 477776. Fax: 01582 478801. Email: enquiries@dunstable.ac.uk www.dunstable.ac.uk

Shuttleworth College – Old Warden Park, Nr Biggleswade SG18 9EA. Tel: 01767 626222. Fax: 01767 626235. Email: college@shuttleworth.org www.shuttleworth.ac.uk

HE institutions

Cranfield University – Cranfield MK43 0AL. Tel: 01234 750111. Fax: 01234 750875. Email: info@cranfield.ac.uk www.cranfield.ac.uk

De Montfort University Bedford – Lansdowne Road, Bedford MK40 2BZ. Tel: 01234 351966. www.dmu.ac.uk

University of Luton – Park Square, Luton LU1 3JU. Tel: 01582 734111. Fax: 01582 743400. Email: enquiries@luton.ac.uk www.luton.ac.uk

Business Link

Bedfordshire and Luton Chamber – The Business Centre, Kimpton Road, Luton LU2 0SX. Tel: 01582 522448. Fax: 01582 522450. Email: info@chamber-business.com www.chamber-business.co.uk

Cambridgeshire

(Areas covered: Cambridgeshire and City of Peterborough)

nextstep provider

nextstep – c/o Cambridgeshire and Peterborough IAG Partnership, 7 The Meadow, Meadow Lane, St Ives, Huntingdon PE27 4LG. Tel: 0845 068 1400. www.cambsiag.org.uk

Connexions service

Connexions Cambridgeshire and Peterborough Ltd – 7 The Meadows, Meadow Lane, St Ives PE27 4LG. Tel: 01480 376000. Fax: 01480 376010. www.connexionscp.co.uk

LSC

Learning and Skills Council – Stuart House, St Johns Street, Peterborough PE1 5DD. Tel: 0845 019 4165. Fax: 01733 895260. www.lsc.gov.uk

LEAs

Cambridgeshire County Council – Education Department, Box ELH 1101, Shire Hall, Cambridge CB3 0AP. Tel: 01223 718474. Fax: 01223 718482. Email: info@cambridgeshire.gov.uk www.camcnty.gov.uk

Peterborough City Council – Education Department, Bayard Place, Broadway, Peterborough PE1 1FB. Tel: 01733 748444. Fax: 01733 748002. www.peterborough.gov.uk

FE colleges

Abbey College – 17 Station Road, Cambridge CB1 2JB. Tel: 01223 570280. Fax: 01223 519425. Email: enquiries@abbeycolleges.co.uk www.abbeycolleges.co.uk

Cambridge Regional College – Kings Hedges Road, Cambridge CB4 2QT. Tel: 01223 418200. Fax: 01223 426425. Email: enquiry@mail.camre.ac.uk www.camre.ac.uk

Huntingdonshire Regional College – California Road, Huntingdon PE29 1BL. Tel: 01480 379100. Fax: 01480 379127. Email: college@huntingdon.ac.uk www.huntingdon.ac.uk

Isle College – Ramnoth Road, Wisbech PE13 2JE. Tel: 01945 582561. Fax: 01945 582706. Email: courses@isle.ac.uk www.isle.ac.uk

Peterborough Regional College – Park Crescent, Peterborough PE1 4DZ. Tel: 01733 767366. Fax: 01733 767986. Email: info@peterborough.ac.uk www.peterborough.ac.uk

HE institutions

Anglia Polytechnic University – East Road, Cambridge CB1 1PT. Tel: 01223 363271. Fax: 01223 352973. Email: answers@apu.ac.uk www.apu.ac.uk

University of Cambridge – Cambridge CB2 1TN. Tel: 01223 337733. Fax: 01223 339669. Email: admissions@cam.ac.uk www.cam.ac.uk

Other colleges

College of West Anglia – Landbeach Road, Milton, Cambridge CB4 6DB. Tel: 01223 860701. Fax: 01223 860262. www.col-westanglia.ac.uk

National Extension College – The Michael Young Centre, Purbeck Road, Cambridge CB2 2HN. Tel: 01223 400200. Fax: 01223 400399. Email: info@nec.ac.uk www.nec.ac.uk

Peterborough College of Adult Education – Brook Street, Peterborough PE1 1TU. Tel: 01733 761361. Fax: 01733 703545. www.pals.ac.uk

Business Link

Business Link Cambridgeshire – Centenary House, St Mary's Street, Huntingdon PE29 3PE. Tel: 0845 609 7979. Fax: 01480 846478. Email: enquiries@cambs.businesslink.co.uk www.cambs.businesslink.co.uk

Essex

(Areas covered: Essex, Thurrock and Southend-on-Sea)

nextstep provider

nextstep – 12 Eastgate Business Centre, Basildon SS14 1EP. Tel: 0800 917 8790. Email: waytogo@careersessex.co.uk www.essexwaytogo.com

Connexions service

Connexions Essex, Southend and Thurrock – Westergaard House, The Matchyns, London Road, Rivenhall CM8 3HA. Tel: 01376 391300. Fax: 01376 391400. Email: enquiries@estconnexions.co.uk www.careersessex.co.uk

LSC

Learning and Skills Council – Redwing House, Hedgerows Business Park, Colchester Road, Chelmsford CM2 5PB. Tel: 0845 019 4179. Fax: 01245 451430. Email: essexinfo@lsc.gov.uk www.lsc.gov.uk

LEAs

Essex County Council – Learning Services Department, PO Box 47, County Hall, Chelmsford CM2 6WN. Tel: 01245 492211. Fax: 01245 436319. Email: lifelong.learning@essexcc.gov.uk www.essexcc.gov.uk

Southend-on-Sea Borough Council – Adult Education and Lifelong Learning, Civic Centre, Victoria Avenue, Southend-on-Sea SS2 6ER. Tel: 01702 215921. Fax: 01702 432273. www.southend.gov.uk

Thurrock Council – Grays AEC, Adult & Continuing Education, Richmond Road, Grays, Essex RM17 6DN. Tel: 01375 372476. Email: tacc@thurrock.gov.uk www.thurrock.gov.uk

FE colleges

Basildon College – Nethermayne, Basildon SS16 5NN. Tel: 0845 601 5746. Fax: 01268 373356. Email: enquiry@tab.ac.uk www.basildon.ac.uk

Braintree College – Church Lane, Braintree CM7 5SN. Tel: 01376 321711. Fax: 01376 340799. Email: enquiry@braintree.ac.uk www.braintree.ac.uk

Chelmsford College – Moulsham Street, Chelmsford CM2 0JQ. Tel: 01245 265611. Fax: 01245 266908. Email: information@chelmsford-college.ac.uk www.chelmsford-college.ac.uk

Colchester Institute – Sheepen Road, Colchester CO3 3LL. Tel: 01206 518000. Fax: 01206 763041. Email: info@colch-inst.ac.uk www.colch-inst.ac.uk

Epping Forest College – Borders Lane, Loughton IG10 3SA. Tel: 0845 120 4809. Fax: 020 8502 0186. Email: informationcentre@epping-forest.ac.uk www.epping-forest.ac.uk

Harlow College – Velizy Avenue, Town Centre, Harlow CM20 3LH. Tel: 01279 868000. Fax: 01279 868260. Email: learninglink@harlow-college.ac.uk www.harlow-college.ac.uk

South East Essex College – Carnarvon Road, Southend-on-Sea SS2 6LS. Tel: 01702 220400. Fax: 01702 432320. Email: admissions@southend.ac.uk www.se-essex-college.ac.uk

Thurrock & Basildon College – Woodview Campus, Grays RM16 2YR. Tel: 0845 601 5746. Fax: 01375 373356. Email: enquire@tab.ac.uk www.thurrock.ac.uk

HE institutions

Anglia Polytechnic University – Bishop Hall Lane, Chelmsford CM1 1SQ. Tel: 01245 493131. Fax: 01245 490835. Email: info@apu.ac.uk www.apu.ac.uk

University of Essex – Wivenhoe Park, Colchester C04 3SQ. Tel: 01206 873333. Fax: 01206 873598. Email: admit@essex.ac.uk www.essex.ac.uk

Other colleges

Southend Adult Community College – Ambleside Drive, Southend-on-Sea SS1 2UP. Tel: 01702 445710. Fax: 01702 445739. Email: info@southend-adult.ac.uk www.southend-adult.ac.uk

Writtle College – Chelmsford CM1 3RR. Tel: 01245 424200. Fax: 01245 420456. Email: info@writtle.ac.uk   www.writtle.ac.uk

Business Link

Business Link Essex – Alexander House, 36a Church Street, Great Baddow, Chelmsford CM2 7HY. Tel: 0845 717 1615. Fax: 01245 241500. Email: info@essex.businesslink.co.uk www.essex.businesslink.co.uk

Hertfordshire

nextstep provider

next**step** – Hertfordshire IAG Partnership, Delta House, Avenue One, Letchworth Garden City SG6 2HU. Tel: 01462 704911. Email: nextstep@herts-careers.co.uk www.plumworks.co.uk

Connexions service

Connexions Hertfordshire – 28 Castle Street, Hertford SG14 1HH. Tel: 01992 556320. Fax: 01992 558933. www.connexions-hertfordshire.co.uk

LSC

Learning and Skills Council – 45 Grosvenor Road, St Albans AL1 3AW. Tel: 0845 019 4167. Fax: 01727 733503. Email: hertsinfo@lsc.gov.uk www.lsc.gov.uk

LEAs

Hertfordshire County Council – Education Department, County Hall, Peggs Lane, Hertford SG13 8DE. Tel: 01992 555555. Fax: 01992 555719. Email: hertsdirect@hertscc.gov.uk www.hertsdirect.org

FE colleges

Hertford Regional College – Ware Centre, Scotts Road, Ware SG12 9JF. Tel: 01992 411411. Fax: 01992 411885. Email: info@hertreg.ac.uk www.hertreg.ac.uk

North Hertfordshire College – Monkswood Way, Stevenage SG1 1LA. Tel: 01462 424239. Fax: 01462 443054. Email: enquiries@nhc.ac.uk www.nhc.ac.uk

Oaklands College – St Albans City Campus, St Peter's Road, St Albans AL4 3RX. Tel: 01727 737000. Email: help.line@oaklands.ac.uk www.oaklands.ac.uk

West Herts College – Watford Campus, Hempstead Road, Watford WD17 3EZ. Tel: 01923 812000. Fax: 01923 812556. Email: admissions@westherts.ac.uk www.westherts.ac.uk

HE institutions

University of Hertfordshire – College Lane, Hatfield AL10 9AB. Tel: 01707 284000. Fax: 01707 284115. Email: admissions@herts.ac.uk www.herts.ac.uk

Other colleges

Institute of Sales & Marketing Management – Romeland House, Romelands Hill, St Albans AL3 4ET. Tel: 01727 812500. Fax: 01727 812525. Email: sales@ismm.co.uk www.ismm.co.uk

Business Link

Business Link Hertfordshire – 45 Grosvenor Road, St Albans AL3 1AW. Tel: 01727 813400. Fax: 01727 813404. Email: info@mybusinesslink.co.uk www.mybusinesslink.co.uk

Norfolk

nextstep provider

nextstep – Norfolk Information and Advice Service, 83-87 Pottergate, Norwich NR2 1DZ. Tel: 01603 215300. Email: info@iagnorfolk.co.uk www.iagnorfolk.co.uk

Connexions service

Connexions Norfolk – 2nd Floor, Wensum House, Prince of Wales Road, Norwich NR2 2RR. Tel: 01603 764370. Fax: 01603 227070. Email: enquiries@connexions-norfolk.co.uk www.connexions-norfolk.co.uk

LSC

Learning and Skills Council – St Andrews House, St Andrews Street, Norwich NR2 4TP. Tel: 0845 019 4173. Fax: 01603 218802. Email: norfolkinfo@lsc.gov.uk www.lsc.gov.uk

LEAs

Norfolk County Council – Education Department, County Hall, Matineau Lane, Norwich NR1 2DL. Tel: 01603 222146. Fax: 01603 232119. Email: esinet@norfolk.gov.uk www.norfolk.gov.uk

FE colleges

City College Norwich – Ipswich Road, Norwich NR2 2LJ. Tel: 01603 773311. Fax: 01603 773301. Email: information@ccn.ac.uk www.ccn.ac.uk

The College of West Anglia – Tennyson Avenue, King's Lynn, Norfolk PE30 2QW. Tel: 01553 761144. Fax: 01553 764902. Email: enquiries@col-westanglia.ac.uk www.col-westanglia.ac.uk

Easton College – Easton, Norwich NR9 5DX. Tel: 01603 731200. Fax: 01603 741438. Email: info@easton-college.ac.uk www.easton-college.ac.uk

Great Yarmouth College – Southtown, Great Yarmouth NR31 0ED. Tel: 01493 655261. Fax: 01493 653423. Email: info@gyc.ac.uk www.gyc.ac.uk

HE institutions

University of East Anglia – Norwich NR4 7TJ. Tel: 01603 456161.Fax: 01603 458553. Email: admissions@uea.ac.uk www.uea.ac.uk

Other colleges

Norwich School of Art and Design – St George Street, Norwich NR3 1BB. Tel: 01603 610561. Fax: 01603 615728. Email: info@nsad.ac.uk www.nsad.ac.uk

Business Link

Business Link Norfolk – 39 Turbine Way (PO Box 36), Swaffham, Norfolk PE37 7WZ. Tel: 0845 721 8218. Fax: 01760 726727. Email: success@businesslinknorfolk.co.uk www.businesslinknorfolk.co.uk

Suffolk

nextstep provider

nextstep – Mitre House, 4 Bond Street, Ipswich IP4 1JE. Tel: 0845 603 1059. Email: info@iag.suffolkcc.gov.uk www.suffolkiag.org.uk

Careers/Connexions service

Connexions Suffolk – Orchard House, 35-37 St Helens Street, Ipswich IP4 2JL. Tel: 01473 261900. Fax: 01473 581429. Email: enquiries@connexionssuffolk.org.uk www.connexionssuffolk.org.uk

LSC

Learning and Skills Council – Felaw Maltings, 42 Felaw Street, Ipswich IP2 8SJ. Tel: 0845 019 4180. Fax: 01473 883090. Email: suffolkinfo@lsc.gov.uk www.lsc.gov.uk

LEAs

Suffolk County Council – Community Education, County Hall, Ipswich IP4 2JS. Tel: 01473 583000. Fax: 01473 584610. www.suffolkcc.gov.uk/education

FE colleges

Lowestoft College – St Peters Street, Lowestoft NR32 2NB. Tel: 01502 583521. Fax: 01502 500031. Email: info@lowestoft.ac.uk www.lowestoft.ac.uk

Otley College – Otley, Ipswich IP6 9EY. Tel: 01473 785543. Fax: 01473 785353. Email: info@otleycollege.ac.uk www.otleycollege.ac.uk

Suffolk College – Rope Walk, Ipswich IP4 1LT. Tel: 01473 255885. Fax: 01473 230054. Email: info@suffolk.ac.uk www.suffolk.ac.uk

West Suffolk College – Out Risbygate Street, Bury St Edmunds IP33 3RL. Tel: 01284 701301. Fax: 01284 750561. Email: info@westsuffolk.ac.uk www.westsuffolk.ac.uk

Business Link

Business Link Suffolk – Felaw Maltings, 42 Felaw Street, Ipswich IP2 8PN. Tel: 08457 254 254. Fax: 01473 417070. Email: info@bls.org.uk www.bls.org.uk

West Midlands Region

Birmingham and Solihull

nextstep provider

nextstep – c/o Birmingham & Solihull Connexions, Charter House, 100 Broad Street, Birmingham B15 1AE. Tel: 0800 073 0634. Fax: 0121 248 8002. Email: learning.shop@birmingham.gov.uk or learning.shop@solihull.gov.uk www.iag-bs.org.uk

Connexions service

Connexions Birmingham and Solihull – 100 Broad Street, Birmingham B15 1AE. Tel: 0845 145 0845. Fax: 0121 248 8001. Email: info@cebp.co.uk www.connexions-bs.co.uk

LSC

Learning and Skills Council – Chaplin Court, 80 Hurst Street, Birmingham B5 4TG. Tel: 0845 019 4143. Fax: 0121 345 4503. Email: birminghamsolihullinfo@lsc.gov.uk www.lsc.gov.uk

LEAs

Birmingham City Council – Adult Education, 2nd Floor, Central Library, Chamberlain Square, Birmingham B3 3HQ. Tel: 0121 303 2206. Fax: 0121 303 4187. Email: adult_education@birmingham.gov.uk www.birmingham.gov.uk

Solihull Metropolitan Borough Council – Education Department, PO Box 20, Council House, Solihull B91 3QU. Tel: 0121 704 6656. Fax: 0121 704 6669. Email: education@solihull.gov.uk www.solihull.gov.uk

FE colleges

Bournville College of Further Education – Bristol Road South, Northfield, Birmingham B31 2AJ. Tel: 0121 483 1000. Fax: 0121 411 2231. Email: info@bournville.ac.uk www.bournville.ac.uk

Cadbury Sixth Form College – Downlands Close, Birmingham B38 8QT. Tel: 0121 458 3898. Fax: 0121 433 2619. Email: enquiry@cadcol.ac.uk www.cadcol.ac.uk

City College, Birmingham – Garretts Green Lane, Garretts Green, Birmingham B33 0TS. Tel: 0121 741 1000. Fax: 0121 743 9050. Email: enquiries@citycol.ac.uk www.citycol.ac.uk

Handsworth College – The Council House, Soho Road, Birmingham B21 9DP. Tel: 0121 741 1000. Fax: 0121 523 4447. Email: enquiries@citycol.ac.uk www.citycol.ac.uk

Matthew Boulton College of Further and Higher Education – Sherlock Street, Sparkbrook, Birmingham B5 7DB. Tel: 0121 446 4545. Fax: 0121 446 3105. Email: ask@matthew-boulton.ac.uk www.matthew-boulton.ac.uk

North Birmingham College – Aldridge Road, Great Barr, Birmingham B44 8NE. Tel: 0121 360 3543. Fax: 0121 325 0828. Email: enquire@northbham.ac.uk www.northbham.ac.uk

Solihull College – Blossomfield Road, Solihull B91 1SB. Tel: 0121 678 7001. Fax: 0121 678 7200. Email: enquiries@solihull.ac.uk www.solihull.ac.uk

South Birmingham College – Cole Bank Road, Hall Green, Birmingham B28 8ES. Tel: 0121 694 5000. Fax: 0121 694 6290. Email: info@sbirmc.ac.uk www.sbirmc.ac.uk

Sutton Coldfield College – Sutton Campus, Lichfield Road, Sutton Coldfield, Birmingham B74 2NW. Tel: 0121 355 5671. Fax: 0121 355 0799. Email: info@sutcol.ac.uk www.sutcol.ac.uk

HE institutions

Aston University – Aston Triangle, Birmingham B4 7ET. Tel: 0121 359 3611. Fax: 0121 359 6350. www.aston.ac.uk

Newman College of Higher Education – Genners Lane, Bartley Green, Birmingham B32 3NT. Tel: 0121 476 1181. Fax: 0121 476 1196. Email: registry@newman.ac.uk www.newman.ac.uk

University of Birmingham – Edgbaston, Birmingham B15 2TT. Tel: 0121 414 3344. Fax: 0121 414 3971. Email: postmaster@bham.ac.uk www.bham.ac.uk

University of Central England in Birmingham – Perry Barr, Birmingham B42 2SU. Tel: 0121 331 5595. Fax: 0121 331 6740. Email: info@ucechoices.com www.uce.ac.uk

See also Matthew Boulton College of Further and Higher Education listed previously.

Other colleges

Birmingham College of Food, Tourism and Creative Studies – Summer Row, City Centre, Birmingham B3 1JB. Tel: 0121 604 1000. Fax: 0121 608 7100. Email: marketing@bcftcs.ac.uk www.bcftcs.ac.uk

Birmingham Conservatoire – Paradise Place, Birmingham B3 3HG. Tel: 0121 331 5901. Fax: 0121 331 5906. Email: conservatoire@uce.ac.uk www.conservatoire.uce.ac.uk

Birmingham School of Speech and Drama – The Link Building, Paradise Place, Birmingham B3 3HJ. Tel: 0121 262 6800. Fax: 0121 262 6801. Email: bssd@bssd.ac.uk www.bssd.ac.uk

Business Link

Birmingham CCI – 75 Harborne Road, Edgbaston, Birmingham B15 3DH. Tel: 0121 6070 0809. Fax: 0121 455 8670. Email: info@birmingham.businesslink.co.uk www.birmingham-chamber.com

The Black Country

next**step** provider

next**step** – Prospect Services Ltd, Castlemill, Burnt Tree, Tipton DY4 7UF. Tel: 0800 1950 789. Fax: 0121 557 6290. Email: harsha.patel@prospects.co.uk

Connexions service

Black Country Connexions – 40 Lower High Street, Wednesbury, West Midlands WS10 7AQ. Tel: 0121 502 7400. Fax: 0121 502 7401. Email: info@blackcountryconnexions.co.uk www.connexions-bc.co.uk

LSC

Learning and Skills Council – 1st Floor, Black Country House, Rounds Green Road, Oldbury B69 2DG. Tel: 0121 345 4888. Fax: 0121 345 4777. Email: blackcountryinfo@lsc.gov.uk www.lsc.gov.uk

LEAs

Dudley Metropolitan Borough Council – Education and Lifelong Learning Unit, Westox House, 1 Trinity Road, Dudley DY1 1JQ.
Tel: 01384 814225. Fax: 01384 814216. Email: online@dudley.gov.uk www.dudley.gov.uk

Sandwell Metropolitan Borough Council – Sandwell Education and Lifelong Learning, PO Box 41, Shaftesbury House, 402 High Street, West Bromwich B70 9LT. Tel: 0121 569 2200. Fax: 0121 553 1528. Email: education@sandwell.gov.uk www.lea.sandwell.gov.uk

Walsall Metropolitan Borough Council – Community Education, Civic Centre, Walsall WS1 1TP. Tel: 01922 650000. Fax: 01922 720885. Email: centralreception@walsall.gov.uk www.walsall.gov.uk

Wolverhampton Metropolitan Borough Council – Adult Education Service, Old Hall Street, Wolverhampton WV1 3AU. Tel: 01902 558180. Fax: 01902 558183.
Email: info@old-hallstreet.org.uk
www.wolverhampton.gov.uk

FE colleges

College of Continuing Education in Walsall – Hawbush Road, Walsall WS3 1AG.
Tel: 01922 654510. Fax: 01922 400569.
Email: tbell@walsall.gov.uk

Dudley College of Technology – The Broadway, Dudley DY1 4AS. Tel: 01384 363000.
Fax: 01384 363311.
Email: admissions@dudleycol.ac.uk
www.dudleycol.ac.uk

Halesowen College – Whittingham Road, Halesowen B63 3NA. Tel: 0121 602 7777.
Fax: 0121 585 0369. Email:
info@halesowen.ac.uk www.halesowen.ac.uk

Sandwell College – Wednesbury Campus, Woden Road South, Wednesbury WS10 0PE.
Tel: 0121 556 6000. Fax: 0121 253 6836.
Email: enquiries@sandwell.ac.uk
www.sandwell.ac.uk

Stourbridge College – Hagley Road Centre, Hagley Road, Stourbridge DY8 1QU.
Tel: 01384 344344. Fax: 01384 344345.
Email: info@stourbridge.ac.uk
www.stourbridge.ac.uk

Wolverhampton College – Paget Road Campus, Paget Road, Wolverhampton WV6 0DU. Tel: 01902 317700. Fax: 01902 423070.
Email: mail@wolverhamptoncollege.ac.uk
www.wolverhamptoncollege.ac.uk

Walsall College of Arts & Technology – St Paul's Street, Walsall WS1 1XN. Tel: 01922 657000. Fax: 01922 657083.
Email: info@walcat.ac.uk www.walcat.ac.uk

HE institutions

University of Wolverhampton – City Campus, Wulfruna Street, Wolverhampton WV1 1SB. Tel: 01902 321000. Fax: 01902 322680.
Email: enquiries@wlv.ac.uk www.wlv.ac.uk

Business Link

Black Country Business Link – Dudley Court South, Waterfront East, Brierley Hill, West Midlands DY3 1XN. Tel: 0845 113 1234.
Fax: 01384 360560. Email: info@bccbl.com
www.bccbl.com

Coventry and Warwickshire

nextstep provider

nextstep – Coventry and Warwickshire Partnership, c/o CSWP Ltd, 1st Floor, Tower Court, Foleshill Enterprise Park, Courtaulds Way, Coventry CV6 5QT. Tel: 0800 917 1818.
Email: info@iagcw.org.uk www.iagcw.org.uk

Connexions service

Connexions Coventry and Warwickshire – 1st Floor, Tower Court, Foleshill, Enterprise Park, Courtaulds Way, Coventry CV6 5QT.
Tel: 024 7670 7400. Fax: 024 7670 7401.
Email: info@coventrycareers.co.uk
www.connexions-covandwarks.org.uk

LSC

Learning and Skills Council – Oak Tree Court, Binley Business Park, Harry Weston Road, Coventry CV3 2UN. Tel: 0845 019 4156.
Fax: 024 7645 0242. Email: cwinfo@lsc.gov.uk
www.lsc.gov.uk

LEAs

Coventry City Council – Adult Education, Ground Floor, Civic Centre 1, Earl Street, Coventry CV1 5RR. Tel: 024 7622 3831.
www.coventry.gov.uk

Warwickshire County Council – Community Education Service, 22 Northgate Street, Warwick CV34 4SP. Tel: 01926 738588.
Fax: 01926 412004.
Email: communityed@warwickshire.gov.uk
www.warwickshire.gov.uk

FE colleges

City College Coventry – Butts Centre, Coventry CV1 3GD. Tel: 024 7679 1000. Fax: 024 7652 6789. Email: info@staff.covcollege.ac.uk www.covcollege.ac.uk

Henley College – Henley Road, Bell Green, Coventry CV2 1ED. Tel: 024 7662 6300. Fax: 024 7661 1837. Email: info@henley-cov.ac.uk www.henley-cov.ac.uk

North Warwickshire and Hinckley College – Hinckley Road, Nuneaton CV11 6BH. Tel: 024 7624 3000. Fax: 024 7632 9056. Email: the.college@nwarks-hinckley.ac.uk www.nwhc.ac.uk

Stratford-upon-Avon College – The Willows North, Alcester Road, Stratford-upon-Avon CV37 9QR. Tel: 01789 266245. Fax: 01789 267524. Email: college@stratford.ac.uk www.strat-avon.ac.uk

Warwickshire College – Leamington Centre, Warwick New Road, Leamington Spa CV32 5JE. Tel: 01926 318000. Fax: 01926 318111. Email: enquiries@warkscol.ac.uk www.warkscol.ac.uk

HE institutions

Coventry University – Priory Street, Coventry CV1 5FB. Tel: 0845 055 5850. Fax: 024 7688 7688. Email: genenq.ad@coventry.ac.uk www.coventry.ac.uk

University of Warwick – Coventry CV4 7AL. Tel: 024 7652 3523. Fax: 024 7646 1606. www.warwick.ac.uk

Other colleges

Hereward College – Bramston Crescent, Tile Hill Lane, Coventry CV4 9SW. Tel: 024 7646 1231. Fax: 024 7669 4305. Email: enquiries@hereward.ac.uk www.hereward.ac.uk

Business Link

Coventry & Warwickshire Chamber of Commerce – Oak Tree Court, Binley Business Park, Harry Weston Road, Coventry CV3 2UN. Tel: 024 7665 4321. Fax: 024 7645 0242. www.cw-chamber.co.uk

Hereford and Worcestershire

nextstep provider

nextstep – c/o Connexions, 10/12 Farrier Street, Worcester WR1 3BH. Tel: 0800 915 0032. Fax: 01462 704908. Email: iaginfo@connexions-hw.org.uk www.achievemore.info

Connexions service

Connexions Herefordshire and Worcestershire – County Buildings, St Mary's Street, Worcester WR1 1TW. Tel: 01905 765428. Fax: 01905 765527. Email: hq@connexions-hw.org.uk www.connexions-hw.org.uk

LSC

Learning and Skills Council – Progress House, Central Park, Midland Road, Worcester WR5 1DU. Tel: 0845 019 4188. Fax: 01905 361478. Email: hwinfo@lsc.gov.uk www.lsc.gov.uk

LEA

Hereford Council – Education Department, PO Box 185, Blackfriars Street, Hereford HR4 9ZR. Tel: 01432 260900. Fax: 01432 260957. Email: education@herefordshire.gov.uk www.herefordshire.gov.uk

Worcestershire County Council – Educational Services, PO Box 73, Worcester WR5 2YA. Tel: 01905 766859. Fax: 01905 766860. www.worcestershire.gov.uk

FE colleges

Evesham and Malvern Hills College – Davies Road, Evesham WR11 1LP. Tel: 01386 712600. Fax: 01386 712640.
Email: enquiries@evesham.ac.uk
www.evesham.ac.uk

Herefordshire College of Technology – Folly Lane, Hereford HR1 1LS. Tel: 01432 352235. Fax: 01432 353449.
Email: enquiries@hct.ac.uk
www.hereford-tech.ac.uk

Kidderminster College – Market Street, Kidderminster DY10 1LX. Tel: 01562 820811. Fax: 01562 512006.
Email: admissions@kidderminster.ac.uk
www.kidderminster.ac.uk

North East Worcestershire College – Bromsgrove Campus, Blackwood Road, Bromsgrove B60 1PQ. Tel: 01527 570020. Fax: 01527 572900. Email: info@ne-worcs.ac.uk
www.ne-worcs.ac.uk

Pershore Group of Colleges – Holme Lacy Campus, Hereford HR2 6LL. Tel: 01432 870316. Fax: 01432 870566.
Email: holmelacy@pershore.ac.uk
www.pershore.ac.uk

Worcester College of Technology – Deansway, Worcester WRI 2JF. Tel: 01905 725555. Fax: 01905 28906.
Email: college@wortech.ac.uk
www.wortech.ac.uk

HE institutions

University College Worcester – Henwick Grove, Worcester WR2 6AJ. Tel: 01905 855000. Fax: 01905 855132.
Email: admissions@worc.ac.uk
www.worc.ac.uk

Other colleges

Herefordshire College of Art & Design – Folly Lane, Hereford HR1 1LT. Tel: 01432 273359. Fax: 01432 341099.
Email: hcad@hereford-art-col.ac.uk
www.hereford-art-col.ac.uk

Royal National College for the Blind – College Road, Hereford HR1 1EB. Tel: 01432 265725. Fax: 01432 376628.
Email: info@rncb.ac.uk www.rncb.ac.uk

Business Link

Herefordshire and Worcestershire Chamber of Commerce – Enterprise House, Castle Street, Worcester WR1 3EN. Tel: 0800 104010. Fax: 08454 506101.
Email: enquiries@hwchamber.co.uk
www.hwchamber.co.uk

Shropshire

nextstep provider

nextstep – c/o Connexions STW, Coppice House, Halesfield 7, Telford TF7 4NA. Tel: 01952 580015. www.stiag.org.uk

Connexions service

Connexions Shropshire, Telford and Wrekin – Victoria House, Victoria Quay, Welsh Bridge, Shrewsbury SY1 1HH. Tel: 01743 231464. Fax: 01743 368610.
www.connexionsstw.org.uk

LSC

Learning and Skills Council – The Learning Point, 3 Hawksworth Road, Central Park, Telford TF2 9TU. Tel: 0845 019 4190. Fax: 01952 235556. Email: shropshireinfo@lsc.gov.uk
www.lsc.gov.uk

LEAs

Shropshire County Council – Adult and Community Education, Shirehall, Abbey Foregate, Shrewsbury SY2 6ND. Tel: 01743 254307. Fax: 01743 254415.
Email:
education-dept@shropshire-cc.gov.uk
www.shropshire-cc.gov.uk

Telford and Wrekin Council – Lifelong Learning, PO Box 440, Civic Offices Telford TF3 4WF. Tel: 01952 202100. Fax: 01952 290317. Email: education@telford.gov.uk www.telford.gov.uk

FE colleges

Shrewsbury College of Arts and Technology – London Road, Shrewsbury SY2 6PR. Tel: 01743 342342. Fax: 01743 342343. Email: prospects@shrewsbury.ac.uk www.shrewsbury.ac.uk

Telford College of Arts and Technology – Haybridge Road, Wellington, Telford TF1 2NP. Tel: 01952 642200. Fax: 01952 642263. Email: studserv@tcat.ac.uk www.tcat.ac.uk

Walford and North Shropshire College – Shrewsbury Road, Oswestry SY11 4QB. Tel: 01691 688000. Fax: 01691 688001. Email: enquiries@wnsc.ac.uk www.wnsc.ac.uk

HE institutions

Harper Adams University College – Newport, Shropshire TF10 8NB. Tel: 01952 820280. Fax: 01952 814783. Email: enquiries@harper-adams.ac.uk www.harper-adams.ac.uk

Business Link

Business Link Shropshire – Trevithick House, Stafford Park 4, Telford TF3 3BA. Tel: 01952 208200. Fax: 01952 208208. Email: enquiries@scbl.co.uk www.scbl.co.uk

Staffordshire

(Areas covered: Staffordshire and Stoke-on-Trent)

nextstep provider

nextstep – Foregate House, 70 Foregate Street, Stafford ST16 2PX. Tel: 0800 298 0234. Email enquiries through website: www.staffsiag.com

Connexions service

Connexions Staffordshire – Foregate House, 70 Foregate Street, Stafford ST16 2PX. Tel: 01785 355700. Fax: 01785 355747. Email: info@cxstaffs.co.uk www.cxstaffs.co.uk

LSC

Learning and Skills Council – Festival Way, Festival Park, Stoke-on-Trent ST1 5TQ. Tel: 0845 019 4149. Fax: 01782 463104. Email: staffordshireinfo@lsc.gov.uk www.lsc.gov.uk

LEAs

Staffordshire County Council – Education Department, Tipping Street, Stafford ST16 2DH. Tel: 01785 278653. Fax: 01785 278764. Email: education@staffordshire.gov.uk www.staffordshire.gov.uk

Stoke-on-Trent City Council – Education and Lifelong Learning, Floor 2, Civic Centre, Glebe Street, Stoke ST4 1HH. Tel: 01782 232014. Fax: 01782 236803. www.stoke.gov.uk

FE colleges

Burton College – Lichfield Street, Burton on Trent DE14 3RL. Tel: 01283 494400. Fax: 01283 494800. www.burton-college.ac.uk

Cannock Chase Technical College – The Green, Cannock WS11 1UE. Tel: 01543 462200. Fax: 01543 574223.
Email: enquiries@cannock.ac.uk
www.cannock.ac.uk

Leek College of Further Education & School of Art – Stockwell Street, Leek ST13 6DP. Tel: 01538 398866. Fax: 01538 399506.
Email: admissions@leek.ac.uk
www.leek.ac.uk

Newcastle-under-Lyme College – Liverpool Road, Newcastle under Lyme ST5 2DF. Tel: 01782 715111. Fax: 01782 254241.
Email: enquiries@nulc.ac.uk www.nulc.ac.uk

Stafford College – Earl Street, Stafford ST16 2QR. Tel: 01785 223800. Fax: 01785 259953.
Email: enquiries@staffordcoll.ac.uk
www.staffordcoll.ac.uk

Stoke-on-Trent College – Stoke Road, Shelton, Stoke-on-Trent ST4 2DG. Tel: 01782 208208. Fax: 01782 603504.
Email: info@stokecoll.ac.uk
www.stokecoll.ac.uk

Tamworth and Lichfield College – Croft Street, Upper Gungate, Tamworth B79 8AE. Tel: 01827 310202. Fax: 01827 59437.
Email: enquiries@tamworth.ac.uk
www.tamworth.ac.uk

HE institutions

Keele University – Keele, Staffordshire ST5 5BG. Tel: 01782 621111. Fax: 01782 613847.
Email: undergraduate@keele.ac.uk
www.keele.ac.uk

Staffordshire University – College Road, Stoke-on-Trent ST4 2DE. Tel: 01782 294000. Fax: 01782 744035. Email: study@staffs.ac.uk
www.staffs.ac.uk

Other colleges

Rodbaston College – Rodbaston, Penkridge ST19 5PH. Tel: 01785 712209. Fax: 01785 715701.
Email: rodenquiries@rodbaston.ac.uk
www.rodbaston.ac.uk

Business Link

Business Link Staffordshire – Commerce House, Festival Park, Stoke on Trent ST1 5BE. Tel: 07002 202 122. Fax: 01782 274394.
Email: info@staffs.businesslink.co.uk
www.businesslinkstaffordshire.co.uk

East Midlands Region

Derbyshire

(Areas covered: Derbyshire and City of Derby)

nextstep provider

nextstep – 2 Godkin House, Park Road, Ripley DE5 3EF. Tel: 01773 746174. Email: phil.bradley@diagp.org.uk www.careers4adults.org

Connexions service

Derbyshire Connexions Service – 2 Godkin House, Park Road, Ripley, Derbyshire DE5 3EF. Tel: 01773 746174. Fax: 01773 570865. www.connexions-derbyshire.org

LSC

Learning and Skills Council – St Helen's Court, St Helen's Street, Derby DE1 3GY. Tel: 01332 868301. Fax: 01332 292188. Email: derbyshireinfo@lsc.gov.uk www.lsc.gov.uk

LEA

Derby City Council – Adult Learning, Middleton House, 27 St Marys Gate, Derby DE1 3NN. Tel: 01332 716957. Fax: 01332 716920. Email: dmc@derbyals.org.uk www.adult-learning-derby.org.uk

Derbyshire County Council – Lifelong Learning Division, Chatsworth Hall, Chesterfield Road, Matlock, Derbyshire DE4 3FW. Tel: 01629 580000. Fax: 01629 585776. www.derbyshire.gov.uk

FE colleges

Chesterfield College – Infirmary Road, Chesterfield S41 7NG. Tel: 01246 500500. Fax: 01246 500587. Email: advice@chesterfield.ac.uk www.chesterfield.ac.uk

Derby College – Broomfield Hall Campus, Morley, Ilkeston DE7 6DN. Tel: 01332 757570. Email: enquiries@derby-college.ac.uk www.derby-college.ac.uk

South East Derbyshire College – Field Road, Ilkeston DE7 5RS. Tel: 0115 849 2020. Fax: 0115 849 2121. Email: admissions@sedc.ac.uk www.sedc.ac.uk

HE institutions

University of Derby – Kedleston Road, Derby DE22 1GB. Tel: 01332 590500. Fax: 01332 294861.
Email: admissions@derby.ac.uk www.derby.ac.uk

Other colleges

East Midlands College of Beauty & Massage Therapies – 100 Mansfield Road, Derby DE1 3TT. Tel: 01332 368333. Fax: 01332 205783.

Business Link

Business Link Derbyshire – Commerce Centre, Canal Wharf, Chesterfield S41 7NA. Tel: 0845 601 1038. Fax: 01246 233228 Email: info@derbyshire.org www.derbyshire.org

Leicestershire

(Area covered: Leicestershire and City of Leicestershire)

nextstep provider

nextstep – 82 Charles Street, Leicester LE1 1FB. Tel: 0116 262 9993. Fax: 0116 242 2626. Email: pvickerman@gain-iag.co.uk www.gain-iag.co.uk

Connexions service

Connexions Leicester Shire – 16b Fir Tree Lane, Groby, Leicester LE6 0FH. Tel: 0116 287 7033. Fax: 0116 265 8634. Email: enquiries@connexions-leics.org www.connexions-leics.org

LSC

Learning and Skills Council – 17a Meridian East, Meridian Business Park, Leicester LE19 1UU. Tel: 0845 019 4177. Fax: 0116 228 1801. Email: leicestershireinfo@lsc.gov.uk www.enterprisenet.co.uk

LEA

Leicester City Council – Lifelong Learning, Marlborough House, 38 Welford Road, Leicester LE2 7AA. Tel: 0116 229 4304. Fax: 0116 223 2685. Email: lifelonglearning@leicester.gov.uk www.leicester.gov.uk

Leicestershire County Council – Community Education Department, County Hall, Glenfield, Leicester LE3 8RA. Tel: 0116 265 6631. Fax: 0116 265 6398. Email: education@leics.gov.uk www.leics.gov.uk

FE colleges

Brooksby Melton College – Brooksby Campus, Brooksby, Melton Mowbray LE14 2LJ. Tel: 01664 850850. Fax: 01664 855355. Email: course.enquiries@brooksbymelton.ac.uk www.brooksbymelton.ac.uk

Brooksby Melton College – Melton Campus, Asfordby Road, Melton Mowbray LE13 0HJ. Tel: 01664 850850. Fax: 01664 855455. Email: course.enquiries@brooksbymelton.ac.uk www.brooksbymelton.ac.uk

Leicester College – Freemen's Park Campus, Aylestone Road, Leicester LE2 7LW. Tel: 0116 224 2000. Fax: 0116 224 2190. Email: info@leicestercollege.ac.uk www.leicestercollege.ac.uk

Loughborough College – Radmoor Road, Loughborough LE11 3BT. Tel: 01509 215831. Fax: 01509 618109. Email: loucoll@loucoll.ac.uk www.loucoll.ac.uk

North Warwickshire & Hinckley College – Hinckley Road, Nuneaton CV11 6BH. Tel: 024 3000. Email: the.college@nwhc.ac.uk www.nwhc.ac.uk

Regent College – Regent Road, Leicester LE1 7LW. Tel: 0116 255 4629. Fax: 0116 254 5680. Email: support@regent-college.ac.uk www.regent-college.ac.uk

Stephenson College, Coalville – Bridge Road, Coalville LE67 3PW. Tel: 01530 836136. Fax: 01530 814253. Email: enquiries@stephensoncoll.ac.uk www.stephensoncoll.ac.uk

South Leicestershire College – Station Road, Wigston, Leicester LE18 2DW. Tel: 0116 288 5051. Fax: 0116 228 0823. Email: enquiries@slcollege.ac.uk www.wigston-college.ac.uk

Wyggeston and Queen Elizabeth I College – University Road, Leicester LE1 7RJ. Tel: 0116 223 1900. Fax: 0116 223 1999. Email: admissions@wqeic.ac.uk www.wqeic.ac.uk

HE institutions

De Montfort University – The Gateway, Leicester LE1 9BH. Tel: 0116 255 1551. Fax: 0116 257 7533. Email: enquiry@dmu.ac.uk www.dmu.ac.uk

Loughborough University – Loughborough LE11 3TU. Tel: 01509 263171. Fax: 01509 223905. Email: admissions@lboro.ac.uk www.lboro.ac.uk

University of Leicester – University Road, Leicester LE1 7RH. Tel: 0116 252 2522. Fax: 0116 252 2200. Email: careers@le.ac.uk www.le.ac.uk

Business Link

Business Link Leicestershire – Charnwood Court, 5b New Walk, Leicester LE1 6TE. Tel: 0845 070 0086. Fax: 0116 258 7333. Email: enquiries@blleics.co.uk www.blleics.co.uk

Lincolnshire and Rutland

nextstep provider

nextstep – c/o Prospects, Room 10, Jubilee Place, Lindum Business Park, Station Road, North Hykeham, Lincoln LN6 3QX. Tel: 01522 686515. Email: iaglr@prospects.co.uk www.iaga.co.uk

Connexions service

Connexions Lincolnshire and Rutland – Witham House, Pelham Centre, Canwick Road, Lincoln LN5 8HE. Tel: 01522 875000. Fax: 01522 875411. www.connexions-lincsandrutland.co.uk

LSC

Learning and Skills Council – Lindem Business Park, Station Road, North Hykeham, Lincoln LN6 3FE. Tel: 0845 019 4178. Fax: 01522 508540. Email: lincsrutlandinfo@lsc.gov.uk www.lsc.gov.uk

LEAs

Lincolnshire County Council – Education and Cultural Services, County Offices, Newland, Lincoln LN1 1YL. Tel: 01522 552222. Fax: 01522 552288. Email: education@lincolnshire.gov.uk www.lincolnshire.gov.uk

Rutland County Council – Education Department, Catmose, Oakham, Rutland LE15 6HP. Tel: 01572 722577. Fax: 01572 758479. Email: enquiries@rutland.gov.uk www.rutnet.co.uk

FE colleges

Boston College – Skirbeck Road, Boston PE21 6JF. Tel: 01205 365701. Fax: 01205 313252. Email: enquiry@boston.ac.uk www.boston.ac.uk

Grantham College – Stonebridge Road, Grantham NG31 9AP. Tel: 01476 400200. Fax: 01476 400291. Email: enquiry@grantham.ac.uk www.grantham.ac.uk

Lincoln College – Lincoln Centre, Monks Road, Lincoln LN2 5HQ. Tel: 01522 876000. Fax: 01522 876200. Email: enquiries@lincolncollege.ac.uk www.lincolncollege.ac.uk

Stamford College – Drift Road, Stamford PE9 IXA. Tel: 01780 484300. Fax: 01780 484301. Email: enquiries@stamford.ac.uk www.stamford.ac.uk

HE institutions

Bishop Grosseteste College – Newport, Lincoln LN1 3DY. Tel: 01522 527347. Fax: 01522 530243. Email: registry@bgc.ac.uk www.bgc.ac.uk

University of Lincoln – Brayford Pool, Lincoln LN6 7TS. Tel: 01522 882000. Fax: 01522 882088. Email: admissions@lincoln.ac.uk www.lincoln.ac.uk

Business Link

Business Link Lincolnshire and Rutland – Welton House, Lime Kiln Way, Lincoln LN2 4WH. Tel: 0845 757 4000. Fax: 01522 574005. Email: info@matrixbusinesslink.co.uk www.bllr.co.uk

Northamptonshire

nextstep provider

nextstep – c/o A4e, Ground Floor, Room G10, Moulton Park Business Centre, Redhouse Road, Moulton Park, Northampton NN3 6AQ. Tel: 0800 50 30 80. Email: iagenquiries@a4e.co.uk

Connexion service

Connexions Northamptonshire Ltd – Unit 2, Bouverie Court, The Lakes, Northampton NN4 7YD. Tel: 01604 630033. Fax: 01604 633310. Email: info@connexions-northamptonshire.org.uk www.connexions-northamptonshire.org.uk

LSC

Learning and Skills Council – Royal Pavilion, Summerhouse Road, Moulton Park, Northampton NN3 6BJ. Tel: 0845 019 4175. Fax: 01604 533046. Email: northantsinfo@lsc.gov.uk www.lsc.gov.uk

LEA

Northamptonshire County Council – Lifelong Learning, John Dryden House, 8-10 The Lakes, Northampton NN4 7DD. Tel: 01604 236319. Fax: 01604 237441. www.northamptonshire.gov.uk

FE colleges

Moulton College – West Street, Moulton, Northampton NN3 7RR. Tel: 01604 491131. Fax: 01604 491127. Email: enquiries@moulton.ac.uk www.moulton.ac.uk

Northampton College (including Daventry Tertiary College) – Booth Lane, Northampton NN3 3RF. Tel: 01604 734567. Fax: 01604 734207. Email: enquiries@northamptoncollege.ac.uk www.northamptoncollege.ac.uk

Tresham Institute of Further and Higher Education – St Mary's Road, Kettering, Northamptonshire NN15 7BS. Tel: 0845 658 8990. Fax: 0845 658 8991. Email: info@tresham.ac.uk www.tresham.ac.uk

HE institutions

University College Northampton – Park Campus, Boughton Green Road, Northampton NN2 7AL. Tel: 01604 735500. Fax: 01604 722106. Email: enquiries@northampton.ac.uk www.northampton.ac.uk

See also Tresham Institute of Further and Higher Education listed above

Other colleges

Knuston Hall – Irchester, Wellingborough NN29 7EU. Tel: 01933 312104. Fax: 01933 357596. Email: enquiries@knustonhall.org.uk www.knustonhall.org.uk

Business Link

Business Link Northamptonshire – Royal Pavilion, Summerhouse Road, Moulton Park Industrial Estate, Northampton NN3 6BJ. Tel: 01604 671200. Fax: 01604 670362. Email: info@northants-chamber.co.uk www.businesslinknorthants.org

Nottinghamshire

(Area covered: Nottinghamshire and City of Nottingham)

nextstep provider

nextstep – c/o Working Links, Unit 4/5 Provident Works, Newdigate Street, Nottingham NG7 4FD. Tel: 0115 841 3451. Email: richard.angus@workinglinks.co.uk www.workinglinks.co.uk

Connexions service

Connexions Nottinghamshire – Heathcote Buildings, Heathcote Street, Nottingham NG1 3AA. Tel: 0115 912 6611. Fax: 0115 912 6612. Email: ask@cnxnotts.co.uk www.cnxnotts.co.uk

LSC

Learning and Skills Council – Castle Marina Road, Castle Marina Park, Nottingham NG7 1TN. Tel: 0845 019 4187. Fax: 0115 948 4589. Email: nottsinfo@lsc.gov.uk www.lsc.gov.uk

LEAs

Nottingham City Council – Education Department, Sandfield Centre, Sandfield Road, Lenton, Nottingham NG7 1QH. Tel: 0115 915 0800. Fax: 0115 915 0650. Email: education@lea.nottinghamcity.gov.uk www.nottinghamcity.gov.uk

Nottinghamshire County Council – Lifelong Learning, County Hall, West Bridgford NG2 7QP. Tel: 0115 982 3823. Fax: 0115 981 2824. Email: communications@education.nottscc.gov.uk www.nottinghamshire.gov.uk

FE colleges

Broxtowe College – High Road, Chilwell, Beeston NG9 4AH. Tel: 0115 917 5252. Fax: 0115 917 5200. Email: learn@broxtowe.ac.uk www.broxtowe.ac.uk

New College Nottingham Group – Mansfield Road, Nottingham NG5 1AL. Tel: 0115 910 0100. Email: enquiries@ncn.ac.uk www.ncn.ac.uk

Newark & Sherwood College – Friary Road, Newark-on-Trent, Newark NG24 1PB. Tel: 01636 680682. Fax: 01636 680681. www.newark.ac.uk

North Nottinghamshire College – Carlton Road, Worksop S81 7HP. Tel: 01909 504504. Fax: 01909 504505. Email: contact@nnc.ac.uk www.nnc.ac.uk

People's College Nottingham – Maid Marian Way, Nottingham NG1 6AB. Tel: 0115 912 3500. Fax: 0115 912 8600. Email: admissions@peoples.ac.uk www.peoples.ac.uk

South Nottinghamshire College – Greythorn Drive, West Bridgford, Nottingham NG2 7GA. Tel: 0115 914 6400. Fax: 0115 914 6444. Email: enquiries@south-nottingham.ac.uk www.south-nottingham.ac.uk

West Nottingham College – Derby Road, Mansfield NG18 5BH. Tel: 01623 627191. Fax: 01623 623063. Email: enquiry@westnotts.ac.uk www.westnotts.ac.uk

HE institutions

Nottingham Trent University – Burton Street, Nottingham NG1 4BU. Tel: 0115 941 8418. Fax: 0115 848 4266. Email: cor.web@ntu.ac.uk www.ntu.ac.uk

University of Nottingham – University Park, Nottingham NG7 2RD. Tel: 0115 951 5151. Fax: 0115 951 3666. Email: undergraduate-prospectus@nottingham.ac.uk www.nottingham.ac.uk

Business Link

Business Link Nottinghamshire – 5 Phoenix Place, Phoenix Park, Nottingham NG8 6BA. Tel: 0845 757 3680. Fax: 0115 977 7399. Email: info@blnotts.com www.blnotts.com

Yorkshire and Humberside Region

Humberside

(Areas covered: East Riding, Hull, North Lincolnshire, North East Lincolnshire)

nextstep provider

nextstep – c/o igen Ltd, Centre 88, Saner Street, Analby Road, Hull HU3 2TR. Tel: 0800 138 5995. www.imagine.uk.net

Connexions service

Connexions Humber – 24 Priory Tec Park, Saxon Way, Hessle, East Yorks HU13 9PB. Tel: 01482 350150. Fax: 01482 350151. Email: info@connexionshumber.co.uk www.connexionshumber.co.uk

LSC

Learning and Skills Council Humberside – The Maltings, Silvester Square, Silvester Street, Hull HU1 3HA. Tel: 0845 019 4153. Fax: 01482 383595. Email: humberinfo@lsc.gov.uk www.lsc.gov.uk

LEAs

East Riding of Yorkshire Council – Education Offices, County Hall, Beverley HU17 9BA. Tel: 01482 393939. Fax: 01482 392002. Email: customer.services@eastriding.gov.uk www.eastriding.gov.uk

Hull City Council – Guildhall, Hull HU1 2AA. Tel: 01482 300300. Email: info@hullcc.gov.uk www.hullcc.gov.uk

North East Lincolnshire Council – Directorate of Learning and Child Care, 7 Eleanor Street, Grimsby DN32 9DU. Tel: 01472 323023. Fax: 01472 323020. Email: landCC@nelincs.gov.uk www.nelincs.gov.uk

North Lincolnshire Council – Pittwood House, Ashby Road, Scunthorpe, North Lincolnshire DN16 1AB. Tel: 01724 296296. Email: customerservice@northlincs.gov.uk www.northlincs.gov.uk

FE colleges

Bishop Burton College – Bishop Burton, Beverley HU17 8QG. Tel: 01964 553000. Fax: 01964 553101. Email: enquiries@bishopburton.ac.uk www.bbc.ac.uk

East Riding College – Longcroft Hall, Gallows Lane, Beverley HU17 7DT. Tel: 0845 120 0037. Email: reception@eastridingcollege.ac.uk www.eastridingcollege.ac.uk

Grimsby College – Nuns Corner, Grimsby DN34 5BQ. Tel: 01472 311222. Fax: 01472 879924. Email: infocent@grimsby.ac.uk www.grimsby.ac.uk

Hull College – Queen's Gardens, Hull HU1 3DG. Tel: 01482 329943. Fax: 01482 598733. Email: info@hull-college.ac.uk www.hull-college.ac.uk

North Lindsey College – Kingsway, Scunthorpe DN17 1AJ. Tel: 01724 281111. Fax: 01724 294020. Email: info@northlindsey.ac.uk www.northlindsey.ac.uk

HE institutions

University of Hull – Cottingham Road, Hull HU6 7RX. Tel: 01482 346311. Fax: 01482 465936. Email: admissions@hull.ac.uk www.hull.ac.uk

University of Lincoln – Brayford Pool, Lincoln LN6 7TS. Tel: 01522 882000. Fax: 01522 882088. Email: enquiries@lincoln.ac.uk www.humber.ac.uk

Business Link

Business Link Humber – Owen Avenue, Priory Park West, Hessle HU13 9PD. Tel: 01482 644050. Fax: 01482 641044.
Email: enquiries@blhumber.co.uk
www.blhumber.co.uk

North Yorkshire

(Areas covered: North Yorkshire and York)

nextstep provider

next**step** – c/o Guidance Services, 159-160 High Street, Northallerton DL7 8JZ.
Tel: 01609 773537.
Email: charper@guidance-enterprises.co.uk
www.guidance-services.co.uk

Connexions service

Connexions York and North Yorkshire – 2nd Floor, Marlborough House, Westminster Place, York Business Park, York YO26 6RW. Tel: 01904 799937. Fax: 01904 799931.
Email: info@connexionsyny.org.uk
www.connexionsyorkandnorthyorkshire.org.uk

LSC

Learning and Skills Council North Yorkshire – 7 Pioneer Business Park, Amy Johnson Way, Clifton, Moorgate, York YO30 4TN. Tel: 0845 019 4146. Fax: 01904 385503.
Email: northyorkshireinfo@lsc.gov.uk
www.lsc.gov.uk

LEAs

City of York Council – Lifelong Learning, Mill House, North Street, York YO1 6JD. Tel: 01904 554294. Fax: 01904 554206.
www.york.gov.uk

North Yorkshire County Council – Continuing Education Unit, County Hall, Northallerton DL7 8AD. Tel: 01609 780780. Fax: 01609 778772.
Email: lifelonglearning@northyorks.gov.uk
www.northyorks.gov.uk

FE colleges

Craven College – High Street, Skipton BD23 1JY. Tel: 01756 791411. Fax: 01756 794872.
Email: enquiries@craven-college.ac.uk
www.craven-college.ac.uk

Grantley Hall College – Ripon, North Yorkshire HG4 3ET. Tel: 01765 620259.
Fax: 01765 620443.

Harrogate College – Hornbeam Park, Hookstone Road, Harrogate HG2 8QT. Tel: 01423 878211. Fax: 01423 879829.
www.harrogate.ac.uk

Selby College – Abbot's Road, Selby YO8 8AT. Tel: 01757 211000. Fax: 01757 213137.
Email: info@selby.ac.uk
www.selbycollege.ac.uk

York College – Tadcaster Road, Dringhouses, York YO24 1UA. Tel: 01904 770200. Fax: 01904 770499.
www.yorkcollege.ac.uk

Yorkshire Coast College – Lady Edith's Drive, Scarborough YO12 5RN.
Tel: 01723 372105. Fax: 01723 501918.
Email: admissions@ycoastco.ac.uk
www.yorkshirecoastcollege.ac.uk

HE institutions

University of York – Heslington, York YO10 5DD. Tel: 01904 430000. Fax: 01904 433433.
www.york.ac.uk

York St John College – Lord Mayor's Walk, York YO31 7EX. Tel: 01904 624624. Fax: 01904 612512. Email: admissions@yorksj.ac.uk
www.yorksj.ac.uk

Other colleges

Askham Bryan College – Askham Bryan, York YO23 3FR. Tel: 01904 772211. Fax: 01904 772288. www.askham-bryan.ac.uk

Business Link

Business Link York and North Yorkshire – Arabesque House, Monks Cross Drive, Huntington, York YO32 9WU. Tel: 01904 686000. Fax: 01904 686020. Email: info.centre@blyny.co.uk www.here4business.co.uk

South Yorkshire

(Areas covered: Barnsley, Doncaster, Rotherham and Sheffield)

nextstep provider

nextstep – c/o South Yorkshire Partnership, Watson Chambers, 5-15 Market Place, Castle Square, Sheffied S1 2GH. Tel: 0114 279 9760. www.prospects.co.uk

Connexions service

Connexions South Yorkshire – 1 Arena Link, Broughton Lane, Don Valley, Sheffield S9 2DD. Tel: 0114 261 9393. Fax: 0114 242 6434. Email: info@connexions-sy.org.uk www.connexionssy.org.uk

LSC

Learning and Skills Council South Yorkshire – The Straddle, Victoria Quay, Wharf Street, Sheffield S2 5SY. Tel: 0845 019 4171. Fax: 0114 267 5012. Email: southyorkshireinfo@lsc.gov.uk www.lsc.gov.uk/southyorkshire

LEAs

Barnsley Metropolitan Borough Council – Town Hall, Barnsley, South Yorkshire S70 2TA. Tel: 01226 770770. Fax: 01226 773099. Email: townhall@barnsley.gov.uk www.barnsley.gov.uk

Doncaster Metropolitan Borough Council – Directorate of Education and Culture, PO Box 266, The Council House, College Road, Doncaster DN1 3AD. Tel: 01302 737106. Fax: 01302 737223. Email: acl@doncaster.gov.uk www.doncaster.gov.uk

Rotherham Metropolitan Borough Council – Education, Culture and Leisure Services, Norfolk House, Walker Place, Rotherham S65 1AB. Tel: 01709 822506. Fax: 01709 372056. www.rotherham.gov.uk

Sheffield City Council – Community and Adult Lifelong Learning, Derwert House, 150 Arundel Gate, Sheffield S1 2JY. Tel: 0114 266 7503. Fax: 0114 266 7092. Email: azl@sheffield.gov.uk www.sheffield.gov.uk

FE colleges

Barnsley College – PO Box 266, Church Street, Barnsley S70 2YW. Tel: 01226 216216. Fax: 01226 216553. Email: programme.enquiries@barnsley.ac.uk www.barnsley.ac.uk

Dearne Valley College – Manvers Park, Wath upon Dearne, Rotherham S63 7EW. Tel: 01709 513333. Fax: 01709 513110. Email: learn@dearne-coll.ac.uk www.dearne-coll.ac.uk

Doncaster College – Waterdale, Doncaster DN1 3EX. Tel: 0800 358 7575. Fax: 01302 553559. Email: infocentre@don.ac.uk www.don.ac.uk

Rother Valley College – Doe Quarry Lane, Dinnington, Sheffield S25 2NF. Tel: 01909 559100. Fax: 01909 559003. Email: studentservices@rothervalley.ac.uk www.rothervalley.ac.uk

Rotherham College of Arts and Technology – Eastwood Lane, Rotherham S65 1EG. Tel: 01709 362111. Fax: 01709 373053. Email: info@rotherham.ac.uk www.rotherham.ac.uk

Sheffield College – Granville Road, Sheffield S2 2RL. Tel: 0114 260 2600. Fax: 0114 260 3655. Email: mail@sheffcol.ac.uk www.sheffcol.ac.uk

Thomas Rotherham College – Moorgate Road, Rotherham S60 2BE. Tel: 01709 300600. Fax: 01709 300601. Email: enquiries@thomroth.ac.uk www.thomroth.ac.uk

HE institutions

Sheffield Hallam University – City Campus, Howard Street, Sheffield S1 1WB. Tel: 0114 225 5555. Fax: 0114 225 3398. Email: enquiries@shu.ac.uk www.shu.ac.uk

University of Sheffield – Western Bank, Sheffield S10 2TN. Tel: 0114 222 2000. Fax: 0114 273 9826. www.shef.ac.uk

Business Link

Business Link South Yorkshire – Reresby House, Bow Bridge Close, Rotherham S60 1BY. Tel: 0800 073 7474. Fax: 01709 386330. Email: info@blsy.com www.blsy.com

West Yorkshire

(Areas covered: Bradford, Calderdale, Kirklees, Leeds and Wakefield)

nextstep provider

nextstep – c/o Careers West Yorkshire/ West Yorkshire IAG Partnership, 78 John William Street, Huddersfield HD1 1EH. Tel (central referral point): 0845 0521 040. www.wyiag.org.uk

Connexions service

Connexions West Yorkshire – Park View House, Woodvale Office Park, Woodvale Road, Brighouse, West Yorkshire HD6 4AB. Tel: 01484 727500. Fax: 01484 727548. Email: enquiries@connexionswestyorkshire.co.uk www.connexionswestyorkshire.co.uk

LSC

Learning and Skills Council West Yorkshire – Mercury House, 4 Manchester Road, Bradford BD5 0QL. Tel: 0845 019 4169. Fax: 01274 444009. Email: westyorkshireinfo@lsc.gov.uk www.lsc.gov.uk

LEAs

Calderdale Metropolitan Borough Council – Adult and Community Learning, 4th Floor, Northgate House, Northgate, Halifax HX1 1UN. Tel: 01422 392528. Fax: 01422 392506. www.calderdale.gov.uk

City of Bradford Metropolitan District Council – Lifelong Learning and Community Development, Jacobs Well, Bradford BD1 5RW. Tel: 01274 432612. Fax: 01274 431074. www.bradford.gov.uk

Kirklees Metropolitan Council – Community Education and Regeneration, Oldgate House, 2 Oldgate, Huddersfield HD1 6QW. Tel: 01484 225242. Fax: 01484 225237. www.kirkleesmc.gov.uk

Leeds City Council – Education Leeds, 10th Floor West, 110 Merrion Centre, Leeds LS2 8DR. Tel: 0113 247 5590. Email: education.enquiries@educationleeds.co.uk www.leeds.gov.uk

Wakefield Metropolitan Borough Council – Adult Education Service, Manygates Education Centre, Manygates Lane, Sandal, Wakefield WF2 7DQ. Tel: 01924 303302. Fax: 01924 303317. Email: ACES@wakefield.gov.uk www.wakefield.gov.uk

FE colleges

Bowling Community College – The Centre, Flockton Road, East Bowling, Bradford BD4 7RH. Tel: 01274 773310. Fax: 01274 772298. Email: bowling@legend.co.uk

Bradford College – Great Horton Road, Bradford, BD7 1AY. Tel: 01274 433333. Fax: 01274 741060. Email: admissions@bilk.ac.uk www.bilk.ac.uk

Calderdale College – Francis Street, Halifax HX1 3UZ. Tel: 01422 357357. Fax: 01422 399320. Email: admissions@calderdale.ac.uk www.calderdale.ac.uk

Dewsbury College – Halifax Road, Dewsbury WF13 2AS. Tel: 01924 465916. Fax: 01924 457047. Email: info@dewsbury.ac.uk www.dewsbury.ac.uk

Huddersfield Technical College – New North Road, Huddersfield HD1 5NN. Tel: 01484 536521. Fax: 01484 511885. Email: info@huddcoll.ac.uk www.huddcoll.ac.uk

Joseph Priestley College – Peel Street, Morley, Leeds LS27 8QE. Tel: 0113 307 6111. Fax: 0113 307 6001. Email: helpline@joseph-priestley.ac.uk www.joseph-priestley.ac.uk

Keighley College – Cavendish Street, Keighley BD21 3DF. Tel: 01535 618555. Fax: 01535 618556. Email: info@keighley.ac.uk www.keighley.ac.uk

Leeds College of Technology – Cookridge Street, Leeds LS2 8BL. Tel: 0113 297 6464. Fax: 0113 297 6301. Email: info@lct.ac.uk www.lct.ac.uk

Park Lane College – Park Lane, Leeds LS3 1AA. Tel: 0113 216 2000. Fax: 0113 216 2020. Email: enquiries@parklanecoll.ac.uk www.parklanecoll.ac.uk

Shipley College – Exhibition Road, Shipley BD18 3JW. Tel: 01274 327222. Fax: 01274 327201. Email: enquiries@shipley.ac.uk www.shipley.ac.uk

Thomas Danby College – Roundhay Road, Leeds LS7 3BG. Tel: 0113 249 4912. Fax: 0113 240 1967. Email: info@thomasdanby.ac.uk www.thomasdanby.ac.uk

Wakefield College – Margaret Street, Wakefield WF1 2DH. Tel: 01924 789789. Fax: 01924 789340. Email: courseinfo@wakecoll.ac.uk www.wakcoll.ac.uk

HE institutions

Leeds Metropolitan University – City Campus, Leeds LS1 3HE. Tel: 0113 283 2600. Fax: 0113 283 3142. Email: course-enquiries@lmu.ac.uk www.lmu.ac.uk

Trinity & All Saints University College – Brownberrie Lane, Horsforth, Leeds LS18 5HD. Tel: 0113 283 7100. Fax: 0113 283 7200. Email: admissions@tasc.ac.uk www.tasc.ac.uk

University of Bradford – Bradford BD7 1DP. Tel: 01274 232323. Fax: 01274 235300. Email: course-enquiries@brad.ac.uk www.brad.ac.uk

University of Huddersfield – Queensgate, Huddersfield HD1 3DH. Tel: 01484 422288. Fax: 01484 516151. Email: admissions@hud.ac.uk www.hud.ac.uk

University of Leeds – Leeds LS2 9JT. Tel: 0113 243 1751. Fax: 0113 244 3923. Email: admissions@leeds.ac.uk www.leeds.ac.uk

Other colleges

Leeds College of Art & Design – Jacob Kramer Building, Blenheim Walk, Leeds LS2 9AQ. Tel: 0113 202 8000. Fax: 0113 202 8001. Email: info@leeds-art.ac.uk www.leeds-art.ac.uk

Leeds College of Building – North Street, Leeds LS2 8QT. Tel: 0113 222 6000. Fax: 0113 222 6001. Email: info@lcb.ac.uk www.lcb.ac.uk

Leeds College of Music – 3 Quarry Hill, Leeds LS2 7PD. Tel: 0113 222 3400. Fax: 0113 243 8798. Email: enquiries@lcm.ac.uk www.lcm.ac.uk

Northern School of Contemporary Dance – 98 Chapeltown Road, Leeds LS7 4BH. Tel: 0113 219 3000. Fax: 0113 219 3030. Email: info@nscd.ac.uk www.nscd.ac.uk

Business Link

Business Link West Yorkshire – Unit 4, Meadow Court, Millshaw, Leeds LS11 8LZ. Tel: 0113 383 7733. Fax: 0113 383 7700. Email: info@blwy.co.uk www.blwy.co.uk

North West Region

Cheshire and Warrington

nextstep provider

nextstep – 1st Floor, Clock Tower, Winsford Shopping Centre, Winsford CW7 1AG. Tel: 01606 555715. Fax 01606 591957. Email: info@lwplus.org.uk www.learningandworkplus.org.uk

Connexions service

Connexions Cheshire and Warrington – Brunner Court, 97 Wilton Street, Northwich, Cheshire CW9 5DR. Tel: 0800 980 9877. Fax: 01606 45319. Email: info@connexions-cw.co.uk www.connexions-cw.co.uk

LSC

Learning and Skills Council Cheshire and Warrington – Dalton House, Dalton Way, Middlewich, Cheshire CW10 0HU. Tel: 0845 019 4163. Fax: 01606 320082. Email: cheshireandwarringtoninfo@lsc.gov.uk www.lsc.gov.uk

LEAs

Cheshire County Council – Adult and Community Learning, County Hall, Chester CH1 1SF. Tel: 0845 113 3311. Email: info@cheshire.gov.uk www.cheshire.gov.uk

Warrington Borough Council – Education and Lifelong Learning, New Town House, Buttermarket Street, Warrington WA1 2NJ. Tel: 01925 444400. Fax: 01925 442969. Email: education@warrington.gov.uk www.warrington.gov.uk

FE colleges

Macclesfield College – Park Lane, Macclesfield SK11 8LF. Tel: 01625 410000. Fax: 01625 410001. Email: info@macclesfield.ac.uk www.macclesfield.ac.uk

Mid-Cheshire College – Hartford Campus, Chester Road, Northwich CW8 1LJ. Tel: 01606 74444. Fax: 01606 720700. Email: info@midchesh.ac.uk www.midchesh.ac.uk

Priestley College – Loushers Lane, Warrington WA4 6RD. Tel: 01925 633591. Fax: 01925 413887. www.priestley.ac.uk

Reaseheath College – Reaseheath, Nantwich CW5 6DF. Tel: 01270 625131. Fax: 01270 625665. Email: enquiries@reaseheath.ac.uk www.reaseheath.ac.uk

South Cheshire College – Dane Bank Avenue, Crewe CW2 8AB. Tel: 01270 654654. Fax: 01270 651515. Email: info@s-cheshire.ac.uk www.s-cheshire.ac.uk

Warrington Collegiate Institute – Winwick Road, Warrington WA2 8QA. Tel: 01925 494494. Fax: 01925 816077. Email: learner.services@warr.ac.uk www.warr.ac.uk

West Cheshire College – Eaton Road, Handbridge, Chester CH4 7ER. Tel: 01244 670676. Fax: 01244 670676. Email: info@west-cheshire.ac.uk www.west-cheshire.ac.uk

HE institutions

University College Chester – Parkgate Road, Chester CH1 4BJ. Tel: 01224 375444. Fax: 01224 392820. Email: enquiries@chester.ac.uk www.chester.ac.uk

Business Link

Buisness Link for Cheshire and Warrington – International Business Centre, Delta Crescent, Warrington, Cheshire WA5 7WQ. Tel: 0845 345 4025. Fax: 01925 715005. Email: info@blinkcw.co.uk www.blinkcw.co.uk

Cumbria

nextstep provider

nextstep – Unit 27, Trinity Enterprise Centre, Ironworks Road, Barrow-in-Furness, Cumbria LA14 2PN. Tel: 0800 435 709. www.connexionscumbria.co.uk

Connexions service

Connexions Cumbria – 28 Louther Street, Carlisle, Cumbria CA3 8DH. Tel: 01228 596272. Freephone: 0800 435 709. Fax: 01228 598080. Email: info@connexionscumbria.co.uk www.connexionscumbria.co.uk

LSC

Learning and Skills Council Cumbria – Venture House, Guard Street, Workington, Cumbria CA14 4EW. Tel: 0845 019 4159. Fax: 01900 733302. Email: cumbriainfo@lsc.gov.uk www.lsc.gov.uk

LEAs

Cumbria County Council – Education Department, 5 Portland Square, Carlisle CA1 1PU. Tel: 01228 606877. Fax: 01228 606896. Email: education@cumbriacc.gov.uk www.cumbria.gov.uk

FE colleges

Carlisle College – Victoria Place, Carlisle CA1 1HS. Tel: 01228 822703. Fax: 01228 822710. Email: marketing@carlisle.ac.uk www.carlisle.ac.uk

Furness College – Channel Side, Barrow-in-Furness LA14 2PJ. Tel: 01229 825017. Fax: 01229 870964. Email: course.enq@furness.ac.uk www.furness.ac.uk

Kendal College – Milnthorpe Road, Kendal LA9 5AY. Tel: 01539 814700. Fax: 01539 733714. Email: enquiries@kendal.ac.uk www.kendal.ac.uk

Lakes College – West Cumbria – Hallwood Road, Lillyhall Business Park, Workington, Cumbria CA14 4JN. Tel: 01946 839300. Fax: 01946 839302. Email: info@lcwc.ac.uk www.wcc.ac.uk

HE institutions

University of Central Lancashire –Cumbria Campus, Newton Rigg, Penrith, Cumbria CA11 0AH. Tel: 01768 863791. Fax: 01772 894990. Email: cumbriainfo@uclan.ac.uk www.uclan.ac.uk

Other colleges

Cumbria Institute of the Arts – Brampton Road, Carlisle CA3 9AY. Tel: 01228 400300. Fax: 01228 514491. Email: info@cumbria.ac.uk www.cumbria.ac.uk

Business Link

Business Link Cumbria – Capital Building, Hilltop Heights, London Road, Carlisle, Cumbria CA1 2NS. Tel: 0870 757 1177. Fax: 01228 613258. Email: info@businesslinkcumbria.co.uk www.businesslinkcumbria.co.uk

Greater Manchester

(Areas covered: Bolton, Bury, Manchester, Oldham, Rochdale, Salford, Stockport, Tameside, Trafford and Wigan)

nextstep provider

nextstep – Manchester Enterprises Ltd, Lee House, 90 Great Bridgewater Street, Manchester M1 5JW. Tel: 0161 245 4863. www.citypride-iag.org.uk

Connexions service

Connexions Greater Manchester – 3rd Floor, Turing House, Archway 5, Birley Field, Manchester M15 5RL. Tel: 0161 227 7000. Fax: 0161 342 0095. www.gmconnexions.com

LSC

Learning and Skills Council Greater Manchester – Floor 9, Arndale House, Arndale Centre, Manchester M4 3AQ. Tel: 0845 019 4142. Fax: 0161 261 0370. Email: grmanchesterinfo@lsc.gov.uk www.lsc.gov.uk

LEAs

Bolton Metropolitan Borough Council – Education and Culture Department, PO Box 53, Paderborn House, Civic Centre, Bolton BL1 1JW. Tel: 01204 333333. Fax: 01204 332228. Email: education.reception@bury.gov.uk www.bolton.gov.uk

Bury Metropolitan Borough Council – Education Department, Athenaeum House, Market Street, Bury BL9 0BN. Tel: 0161 253 5652. Fax: 0161 253 5686. Email: education.reception@bury.gov.uk www.bury.gov.uk

Manchester City Council – Manchester Adult Education Service, Hathersage Road, Plymouth Grove, Manchester M13 0BY. Tel: 0161 255 8209. Fax: 0161 255 8212. Email: adult-education@manchester.gov.uk www.manchester.gov.uk

Oldham Metropolitan Borough Council – Education Department, Civic Centre, West Street, Oldham OL1 1XJ. Tel: 0161 911 4260. Fax: 0161 911 4220. Email: enquiries@oldham.gov.uk www.oldham.gov.uk

Rochdale Metropolitan Borough Council – Adult and Community Learning, Hindhill Centre, Hindhill Street, Heywood, Rochdale OL10 1AN. Tel: 01706 867412. Fax: 01706 867389. Email: learnlocal@rochdale.gov.uk www.rochdale.gov.uk

Salford City Council – Adult Education Team, Minerva House, Pendlebury Road, Swinton, Manchester M27 4EQ. Tel: 0161 778 0333. Fax: 0161 835 1561. www.salford.gov.uk

Stockport Metropolitan Borough Council – Adult Education, 3rd Floor, Stopford House, Town Hall, Stockport SK1 3XE. Tel: 0161 474 3875. Fax: 0161 355 6968. Email: adult.education@stockport.gov.uk www.stockport.gov.uk

Tameside Metropolitan Borough Council – Adult Learning, Council Office, Wellington Road, Ashton OL6 6DL. Tel: 0161 342 2838. Email: adult.learning@mail.tameside.gov.uk www.tameside.gov.uk

Trafford Metropolitan Borough Council – Directorate of Lifelong Learning, PO Box 40, Trafford Town Hall, Talbot Road, Stretford, Manchester M32 0EL. Tel: 0161 912 1212. Fax: 0161 912 1220. www.trafford.gov.uk

Wigan Metropolitan Borough Council – Education Department, Progress House, Westwood Park Drive, Wigan WN3 4HH. Tel: 01942 828891. Fax: 01942 828811. Email: education@wiganmbc.gov.uk www.wiganmbc.gov.uk

FE colleges

Bolton Community College – Manchester Road Centre, Manchester Road, Bolton BL2 1ER. Tel: 01204 531411. Fax: 01204 453321. Email: info@bolton-community-college.ac.uk www.bolton-community-college.ac.uk

Bury College – Market Street, Bury BL9 0BG. Tel: 0161 280 8280. Fax: 0161 280 8228. Email: information@burycollege.ac.uk www.burycollege.ac.uk

City College Manchester – Crescent Road, Crumpsall, Manchester M8 5UF. Tel: 0800 013 0123. Fax: 0161 720 6376. Email: admissions@ccm.ac.uk www.ccm.ac.uk

Hopwood Hall College – Middleton Campus, Rochdale Road, Middleton, Manchester M24 6XH. Tel: 0161 643 7560. Fax: 0161 643 2114.
Email: enquiries@hopwood.ac.uk
www.hopwood.ac.uk

Manchester College of Arts and Technology – Ashton Old Road, Openshaw, Manchester M11 2WH. Tel: 0161 953 5995. Fax: 0161 953 3909. Email: enquiries@mancat.ac.uk www.mancat.ac.uk

North Trafford College – Talbot Road, Stretford, Manchester M32 0XH. Tel: 0161 886 7000. Fax: 0161 872 7921. Email: admissions@ntc.ac.uk www.ntc.ac.uk

The Oldham College – Rochdale Road, Oldham OL9 6AA. Tel: 0161 624 5214. Fax: 0161 785 4234. Email: info@oldham.ac.uk
www.oldham.ac.uk

Ridge Danyers College – Marple Campus, Hibbert Lane, Marple, Stockport SK6 7PA. Tel: 0161 484 6600. Fax: 0161 484 6601. Email: info@theridge.ac.uk www.theridge.ac.uk

Salford College – Worsley Campus, Walkden Road, Worsley, Manchester M28 7QD. Tel: 0161 702 8272. Fax: 0161 211 5020.
www.salford-col.ac.uk

South Trafford College – Manchester Road, West Timperley, Altrincham WA14 5PQ. Tel: 0161 952 4600. Fax: 0161 952 4672. Email: enquiries@stcoll.ac.uk
www.stcoll.ac.uk

Stockport College of Further and Higher Education – Wellington Road South, Stockport SK1 3UQ. Tel: 0161 958 3414. Fax: 0161 480 6636. Email: enquiries@stockport.ac.uk
www.stockport.ac.uk

Tameside College – Beaufort Road, Ashton under Lyne OL6 6NX. Tel: 0161 908 6789. Fax: 0161 908 6611.
Email: info@tamesidecollege.ac.uk
www.tamesidecollege.ac.uk

Wigan and Leigh College – PO Box 53, Parson's Walk, Wigan WN1 1RS. Tel: 01942 761600. Fax: 01942 761603.
Email: admissions@wigan-leigh.ac.uk
www.wigan-leigh.ac.uk

HE institutions

Bolton Institute of Higher Education – Deane Road, Bolton BL3 5AB. Tel: 01204 900600. Fax: 01204 399074. Email: enquiries@bolton.ac.uk www.bolton.ac.uk

Manchester Metropolitan University – All Saints Building, All Saints, Manchester M15 6BH. Tel: 0161 247 2000. Fax: 0161 247 6390.
Email: enquiries@mmu.ac.uk
www.mmu.ac.uk

Salford University – Salford, Greater Manchester M5 4WT. Tel: 0161 295 5000.
Fax: 0161 295 5999. Email: course-enquiries@salford.ac.uk www.salford.ac.uk

University of Manchester – Oxford Road, Manchester M13 9PL. Tel: 0161 275 2000.
Email: ug.admissions@man.ac.uk
www.man.ac.uk

UMIST – University of Manchester Institute of Science and Technology – Sackville Street, Manchester M60 1QD. Tel: 0161 236 3311. Fax: 0161 200 4019. Email: ug.admissions@umist.ac.uk www.umist.ac.uk

See also Stockport College of Further and Higher Education listed above.

Other colleges

Royal Northern College of Music – 124 Oxford Road, Manchester M13 9RD. Tel: 0161 907 5200. Fax: 0161 273 7611.
Email: info@rncm.ac.uk www.rncm.ac.uk

Business Link

Business Link for North Manchester – 1-3 The Courtyard, Calvin Street, The Valley, Bolton BL1 8PB. Tel: 0845 608 3388. Fax: 0845 600 9989. Email: info@blnm.co.uk
www.blnm.org.uk

Greater Merseyside

(Areas covered: Halton, Knowsley, Liverpool, St Helens, Sefton and Wirral)

nextstep provider

nextstep – 3rd Floor, Tea Factory, 82 Wood Street, Liverpool L1 4DQ. Tel: 0151 703 7578. Fax: 0151 703 7579. Email: nextstep@connexions-gmerseyside.co.uk

Connexions service

Connexions Greater Merseyside Partnership – Head Office, Tea Factory, 82 Wood Street, Liverpool L1 4DQ. Tel: 0151 703 7400. Fax: 0151 703 7401. Email: hq@connexions-gmerseyside.co.uk www.connexions-gmerseyside.co.uk

LSC

Learning and Skills Council Greater Merseyside – 3rd Floor, Tithebarn House, Tithebarn Street, Liverpool L2 2NZ. Tel: 0845 019 4150. Fax: 0151 672 3405. Email: merseysideinfo@lsc.gov.uk www.lsc.gov.uk

LEAs

Halton Borough Council – Education Department, Grosvenor House, Halton Lea, Runcorn, Cheshire WA7 2WD. Tel: 0151 424 2061. Fax: 0151 471 7321. www.halton-borough.gov.uk

Knowsley Metropolitan Borough Council – Lifelong Learning Department, Huyton Hey Road, Huyton, Knowsley L36 5YH. Tel: 0151 443 3232. Fax: 0151 449 3852. www.knowsley.gov.uk

Liverpool City Council – Education and Lifelong Learning Services, 4th Floor, 4 Renshaw Street, Liverpool L1 4NX. Tel: 0151 233 1600. www.liverpool.gov.uk

Metropolitan Borough of Wirral – Education Department, Hamilton Building, Conway Street, Birkenhead, Wirral CH41 4FD. Tel: 0151 666 2121. Fax: 0151 666 4207. Email: educ@wirral.gov.uk www.wirral.gov.uk

St Helens Metropolitan Borough Council – Family Learning and Community Services, The Rivington Centre, Rivington Road, St Helens, Merseyside WA10 4ND. Tel: 01744 455465. Fax: 01744 455488. www.sthelens.gov.uk

Sefton Metropolitan Borough Council – Education Offices, Town Hall, Oriel Road, Bootle, Merseyside L20 7AE. Tel: 0151 934 3421. Fax: 0151 934 3239. www.sefton.gov.uk

FE colleges

Liverpool Community College – Clarence Street, Liverpool L3 5TN. Tel: 0151 252 1515. Fax: 0151 252 3300. Email: enquiry@liv-coll.ac.uk www.liv-coll.ac.uk

Halton College – Kingsway, Widnes, Cheshire WA8 7QQ. Tel: 0151 257 2800. Fax: 0151 257 2020. Email: studentservices@haltoncollege.ac.uk www.haltoncollege.ac.uk

Hugh Baird College – Balliol Road, Bootle, Liverpool L20 7EW. Tel: 0151 353 4400. Fax: 0151 353 4469. Email: info@hughbaird.ac.uk www.hughbaird.ac.uk

Knowsley Community College – Roby College, Rupert Road, Roby, Huyton L36 9TD. Tel: 0151 447 5777. Fax: 0151 477 5703. Email: info@knowsleycollege.ac.uk www.knowsleycollege.ac.uk

Southport College – Mornington Road, Southport PR9 0TT. Tel: 01704 500606. Fax: 01704 392794. www.southport.ac.uk

St Helens College – Brook Street Campus, St Helens WA10 1PZ. Tel: 01744 733766. Fax: 01744 623400. Email: enquire@sthelens.ac.uk www.sthelens.ac.uk

Wirral Metropolitan College – Conway
Park Campus, Europa Boulevard, Conway
Park, Birkenhead CH41 4NT. Tel: 0151 551 7777.
Fax: 0151 551 7001. Email:
enquiries@wmc.ac.uk www.wmc.ac.uk

HE institutions

Liverpool Hope University – Hope Park,
Liverpool L16 9JD. Tel: 0151 291 3000. Fax: 0151
291 3100. Email: admission@hope.ac.uk
www.hope.ac.uk

Liverpool John Moores University –
Student Recruitment, Roscoe Court, 4
Rodney Street, Liverpool L1 2TZ. Tel: 0151 231
5090. Fax: 0151 231 5632.
Email: recruitment@livjm.ac.uk
www.livjm.ac.uk

University of Liverpool – Liverpool L69 3BX.
Tel: 0151 794 2000. Fax: 0151 708 6502.
Email: ugrecruitment@liv.ac.uk
www.liv.ac.uk

Other colleges

Liverpool Institute of Performing Arts –
Mount Street, Liverpool L1 9HF. Tel: 0151 330
3000. Fax: 0151 330 3131.
Email: admissions@lipa.ac.uk
www.lipa.ac.uk

Business Link

Business Link for Greater Merseyside –
Egerton House, 2 Tower Road, Birkenhead,
Merseyside CH41 1FN. Tel: 0845 330
0151. Fax: 0845 330 0150.
Email: information@gme.org.uk
www.gme.org

Lancashire

*(Areas covered: Burnley, Chorley, Flyde,
Hundburn, Lancashire, Pendle, Preston,
Ribble Valley, Rossendale, South Ribble,
West Lancashire and Wyre)*

nextstep provider

nextstep – 2nd Floor, Guildhall House,
Guildhall Street, Preston PR1 3NU. Tel: 01772
205400. Email:
learndirect@nownetwork.org.uk
www.nowdirect.org.uk

Connexions service

Connexions Lancashire – The Business
Centre, School Lane, Guide, Nr Blackburn
BB1 2QH. Tel: 01254 685120. Fax: 01254 685123.
www.connexions-lancashire.org.uk

LSC

Learning and Skills Council Lancashire –
Caxton Road, Fulwood, Preston PR2 9ZB.
Tel: 0845 019 4157. Fax: 01772 443002.
Email: info@lsc.gov.uk www.lsc.gov.uk

LEAs

Lancashire County Council – Adult and
Continuing Education Service, PO Box 61,
County Hall, Preston PR1 8RJ. Tel: 01772
531939. Fax: 01772 31480.
Email: adult-ed.central@ed.lancscc.gov.uk
www.lancscc.gov.uk

FE colleges

Accrington and Rossendale College –
Sandy Lane, Accrington BB5 2AW. Tel: 01254
389933. Fax: 01254 354001. www.accross.ac.uk

Alston Hall College Residential College –
Alston Lane, Longridge, Preston PR3 3BP.
Tel: 01772 784661. Fax: 01772 785835.
Email: alston.hall@ed.lancscc.gov.uk
www.alstonhall.com

Blackburn College – Feilden Street,
Blackburn BB2 1LH. Tel: 01254 55144. Fax: 01254
682700.
Email: studentservices@blackburn.ac.uk
www.blackburn.ac.uk

Blackpool and the Fylde College –
Bispham Campus, Ashfield Road, Bispham,
Blackpool FY2 0HB. Tel: 01253 352352. Fax:
01253 356127.
Email: admissions@blackpool.ac.uk
www.blackpool.ac.uk

Burnley College – Shorey Bank, Ormerod
Road, Burnley BB11 2RX. Tel: 01282 711200.
Fax: 01282 415063. Email:
student.services@burnley.ac.uk
www.burnley.ac.uk

Lancashire College – Southport Road,
Chorley, Lancashire PR7 1NB. Tel: 01257
276719. Fax: 01257 241370. Email:
insight@ed.lancscc.gov.uk
www.lancashirecollege.com

Lancaster and Morecambe College –
Morecambe Road, Lancaster LA1 2TY.
Tel: 01524 66215. Fax: 01524 843078.
Email: info@lanmore.ac.uk
www.lanmore.ac.uk

Nelson and Colne College – Reedyford
Site, Scotland Road, Nelson BB9 7YT. Tel:
01282 440200. Fax: 01282 440274.
Email: reception@nelson.ac.uk
www.nelson.ac.uk

Preston College – St Vincent's Road,
Fulwood, Preston PR2 8UR. Tel: 01772 225000.
Fax: 01772 225002.
Email: reception@preston.ac.uk
www.preston.ac.uk

Runshaw College – Langdale Road,
Leyland, Preston PR25 3DQ. Tel: 01772 622677.
Fax: 01772 642009. www.runshaw.ac.uk

Skelmersdale College – Westbank
Campus, Yewdale, Skelmersdale WN8 6JA.
Tel: 01695 728744. Fax: 01695 579997.
Email: admissions@skelmersdale.ac.uk
www.skelmersdale.ac.uk

Wigan and Leigh College – PO Box 53,
Parsons Walk, Wigan WN1 1RS. Tel: 01942
761600. Fax: 01942 761533.
Email: admissions@wigan-leigh.ac.uk
www.wigan-leigh.ac.uk

Winstanley College – Winstanley Road,
Billinge, Wigan WN5 7XF. Tel: 01695 633244.
Fax: 01695 633409. www.winstanley.ac.uk

HE institutions

Edge Hill College – St Helen's Road,
Ormskirk, Lancashire L39 4QP. Tel: 01695
575171. Fax: 01695 579997.
Email: enquiries@edgehill.ac.uk
www.edgehill.ac.uk

Lancaster University – Bailrigg, Lancaster
LA1 4YW. Tel: 01524 65201.
Email: ugadmissions@lancaster.ac.uk
www.lancs.ac.uk

St Martin's College – Bowerham Road,
Lancaster LA1 3JD. Tel: 01524 384384.
Fax: 01524 384385. Email:
admission@ucsm.ac.uk www.ucsm.ac.uk

University of Central Lancashire – Preston
PR1 2HE. Tel: 01772 201201. Fax: 01772 894954.
Email: cenquiries@uclan.ac.uk
www.uclan.ac.uk

Other colleges

The Adult College, Lancashire – White
Cross Education Centre, Quarry Road,
Lancaster LA1 3SE. Tel: 01524 60141. Fax: 01524
849458.
Email: adcollege.info@ed.lancscc.gov.uk
www.theadultcollege.org

Myerscough College – Myerscough Hall,
Bilsborrow, Preston PR3 0RY. Tel: 01995
642222. Fax: 01995 642333.
Email: mailbox@myerscough.ac.uk
www.myerscough.ac.uk

Business Link

**Business Link North and Western
Lancashire** – Leyland House, Lancashire
Enterprises Business Park, Leyland,
Lancashire PR26 6TY. Tel: 01772 790200. Fax:
01772 450501.
Email: info@nwl.businesslink.co.uk
www.nwlbusinesslink.co.uk

North East Region

County Durham

nextstep provider

next**step** – Suite 7, Wear Valley Business Centre, 27 Longfield Road, South Church Enterprise Park, Bishop Auckland DL14 6XB. Tel: 01388 776911. www.durham-iag.org.uk

Connexions service

Connexion County Durham - Aykley Heads House, Aykley Heads, Durham DH1 5TS. Tel: 0191 383 1777. Fax: 0191 383 2777. Email: info@connexions-durham.org www.connexions-durham.org

LSC

Learning and Skills Council – Horndale Avenue, Aycliffe Industrial Park, Newton Aycliffe, Co Durham DL5 6XS. Tel: 0845 019 4174. Fax: 01325 372302. Email: countydurhaminfo@lsc.gov.uk www.lsc.gov.uk

LEA

Durham County Council – Adult Education Department, County Hall, Durham DH1 5UJ. Tel: 0191 383 4574. Fax: 0191 383 3288. www.durham.gov.uk

FE colleges

Bishop Auckland College – Woodhouse Lane, Bishop Auckland, Co Durham DL14 6JZ. Tel: 01388 443000. Fax: 01388 609294. Email: enquiries@bacoll.ac.uk www.bacoll.ac.uk

Derwentside College – Front Street, Consett, Co Durham DH8 5EE. Tel: 01207 585900. Fax: 01207 585991. www.derwentside.ac.uk

East Durham and Houghall Community College – Burnhope Way Centre, Burnhope Way, Peterlee, Co Durham SR8 1NU. Tel: 0191 518 2000. Fax: 0191 586 7125. www.edhcc.ac.uk

New College Durham – Framwellgate Moor Centre, Durham DHI 5ES. Tel: 0191 375 4000. Fax: 0191 375 4222. Email: admissions@newdur.ac.uk www.newdur.ac.uk

HE institutions

University of Durham – Old Shire Hall, Durham DH1 3HP. Tel: 0191 374 2000. Fax: 0191 374 7250. www.dur.ac.uk

Business Link

Business Link County Durham – 1st Floor, IMEX Business Centre, Abbey Road, Durham DH1 5JZ. Tel: 0191 374 4000. Fax: 0191 374 4010. Email: ustomerservices@blcd.co.uk www.blcd.co.uk

Northumberland

nextstep provider

next**step** – 27/28 Bamburgh House, Manor Walks, Cramlington, Northumberland NE23 6QE. Tel: 0800 389 0639. www.learningnorthumberland.co.uk

Connexions service

Connexions Northumberland – 7 Sextant House, Freehold Street, Blyth, Northumberland NE24 2BA. Tel: 01670 798180. Fax: 01670 798181. Email: enquiries@connexions-northumberland.org.uk www.connexions-northumberland.org.uk

4 The Gazetteer: England

LSC

Learning and Skills Council Northumberland – 2 Craster Court, Manor Walk, Cramlington NE23 6XX. Tel: 0845 019 4185. Fax: 01670 706212.
Email: northumberlandinfo@lsc.gov.uk
www.lsc.gov.uk

LEA

Northumberland County Council – Community Education for Adults, County Hall, Morpeth, Northumberland NE61 2EF. Tel: 01670 533000. Fax: 01670 533750.
Email: education@northumberland.gov.uk
www.northumberland.gov.uk

FE colleges

Northumberland College – College Road, Ashington NE63 9RG. Tel: 01670 841200.
Fax: 01670 841201.
Email: advice.centre@northland.ac.uk
www.northland.ac.uk

Business Link

Business Link for Northumberland – Wansbeck Business Centre, Wansbeck Business Park, Rotary Parkway, Ashington, Northumberland, NE63 8QZ. Tel: 01670 813322. Fax: 01670 813355. Email: info@n-bs.co.uk
www.n-bs.co.uk

Tees Valley

(Areas covered: Darlington, Hartlepool, Middlesbrough, Redcar and Cleveland, Stockton-on-Tees)

nextstep provider

nextstep – igen Ltd, c/o Middlesbrough Learning Shop, 99-101 Albert Road, Middlesbrough TS1 2PA. Tel: 01642 358099.

Connexions service

Connexions Tees Valley – Calvert's Lane, Stockton-on-Tees TW18 1SW. Tel: 01642 601600. Fax: 01642 633663. Email: enquiries@connexionsteesvalley.co.uk
www.connexionsteesvalley.co.uk

LSC

Learning and Skills Council – 2 Queens Square, Middlesbrough, Cleveland TS2 1AA. Tel: 0845 019 4166. Fax: 01642 232480.
Email: tessvalleyinfo@lsc.gov.uk
www.lsc.gov.uk

LEA

Darlington Borough Council – Education Department, Town Hall, Darlington DL1 5QT. Tel: 01325 380651. Fax: 01325 382032.
Email: enquiries@darlington.gov.uk
www.darlington.gov.uk

Hartlepool Borough Council – Adult Education, Golden Flatts, Seaton Lane, Hartlepool TS25 1HN. Tel: 01429 868616.
Fax: 01429 891673.
Email: adult.education@hartlepool.gov.uk
www.hartlepool.gov.uk

Middlesbrough Borough Council – Acklam Adult Education Centre, Kings Manor School Site, Hall Drive, Acklam, Middlesbrough TS5 7JZ. Tel: 01642 818480.
Fax: 01642 821300.
Email: maes.acklam@adultedboro.com
www.adultedboro.com

Redcar and Cleveland Borough Council – Adult Learning Service, Redcar Education Development Centre, Corporation Road, Redcar TS10 1HA. Tel: 01642 490409. Fax: 01642 492388. Email: adult_education@redcar-cleveland.gov.uk
www.redcar-cleveland.gov.uk

Stockton-on-Tees Borough Council – Adult Education Service, PO Box 228, Municipal Buildings, Church Road, Stockton-on-Tees TS18 1XE. Tel: 01642 393538. Fax: 01642 393501.
Email: member.services@stockton.gov.uk
www.stockton.gov.uk

FE colleges

Hartlepool College of Further Education – Stockton Street, Hartlepool TS24 7NT. Tel: 01429 295000. Fax: 01429 292999. Email: enquiries@hartlepoolfe.ac.uk www.hartlepoolfe.ac.uk

Middlesbrough College – Marton Road, Middlesbrough TS4 3RZ. Tel: 01642 275000. Fax: 01642 313290. Email: courseinfo@mbro.ac.uk www.mbro.ac.uk

Redcar and Cleveland College – Corporation Road, Redcar TS10 1EZ. Tel: 01642 473132. Fax: 01642 490856. www.cleveland.ac.uk

Stockton Riverside College – Harvard Avenue, Stockton-on-Tees TS17 6FB. Tel: 01642 865400. Fax: 01642 865470. www.stockton.ac.uk

HE institutions

University of Durham – Queens Campus, University Boulevard, Thornaby, Stockton TS17 6BH. Tel: 0191 334 2000. Fax: 0191 334 0007. Email: Queens.admissions@durham.ac.uk www.dur.ac.uk/stockton

University of Teesside – Middlesbrough TS1 3BA. Tel: 01642 218121. Fax: 01642 342067. www.tees.ac.uk

Other colleges

Cleveland College of Art and Design – Green Lane, Linthorpe, Middlesbrough TS5 7RJ. Tel: 01642 288000. Fax: 01642 288828. Email: admissions@ccad.ac.uk www.ccad.ac.uk

Business Link

Business Link Tees Valley Ltd – The Tees Valley Business Centre, 2 Queens Square, Middlesbrough, Tees Valley TS2 1AA. Tel: 01642 806666. Fax: 01642 341425. Email: info@tees.businesslink.co.uk www.tees.businesslink.co.uk

Tyne and Wear

(Areas Covered: Gateshead, Newcastle-upon-Tyne, North Tyneside, South Tyneside and Sunderland)

nextstep provider

nextstep – Amber Court, William Armstrong Drive, Newcastle Business Park, Newcastle Upon Tyne NE4 7YA. Tel: 0800 073 0708. Email: info@new-pathways.org.uk www.new-pathways.org.uk

Connexions service

Connexions Tyne and Wear – Interchange Centre, West Street, Gateshead NE8 1BH. Tel: 0191 490 1717. Fax: 0191 477 9971. www.connexions-tw.co.uk

LSC

Learning and Skills Council Tyne and Wear – Moongate House, 5th Avenue Business Park, Team Valley, Gateshead NE11 0HF. Tel: 0845 019 4181. Fax: 0191 491 6159. Email: tyneandwearinfo@lsc.gov.uk www.lsc.gov.uk

LEA

Gateshead Metropolitan Borough Council – Drydon Professional Development Centre, Evistanes Road, Gateshead NE9 5UR. Tel: 0191 433 8646. Email: adultlearning@gateshead.gov.uk www.gateshead.gov.uk

Newcastle-upon-Tyne City Council – Learning City Unit, Room 422, Education and Libraries Directorate, Civic Centre, Barras Bridge, Newcastle-upon-Tyne NE1 8PU. Tel: 0191 211 5332. Fax: 0191 211 4983. Email: learningcityunit@newcastle.gov.uk www.newcastle.gov.uk/education

North Tyneside Council – Adult Education, White Swan Centre, Citadel East, Killingworth NE12 6SS. Tel: 0191 200 8329. Fax: 0191 200 8339. Email: adulteducation@northtyneside.gov.uk www.northtyneside.gov.uk

South Tyneside Metropolitan Borough Council – Adult and Community Learning, Unit 120, Henry Robson Way, Station Road, South Shields, Tyne and Wear NE33 1RF. Tel: 0191 427 4590. Fax: 0191 427 4589. Email: acl@s-tyneside-mbc.gov.uk www.s-tyneside-mbc.gov.uk

Sunderland City Council – Adult and Community Learning, City Library and Arts Centre, 1st Floor, Fawcett Street, Sunderland SR1 1RE. Tel: 0191 553 2500. Fax: 0191 553 2506. Email: acl.info@sunderland.gov.uk www.sunderland.gov.uk

FE colleges

City of Sunderland College – Bede Centre, Durham Road, Sunderland SR3 4AH. Tel: 0191 511 6327. Fax: 0191 511 6380. www.citysun.ac.uk

Gateshead College – Durham Road, Gateshead NE9 5BN. Tel: 0191 490 0300. Fax: 0191 490 2313. Email: start@gateshead.ac.uk www.gateshead.ac.uk

Newcastle College – Rye Hill Campus, Scotswood Road, Newcastle-upon-Tyne NE4 5BR. Tel: 0191 200 4000. Fax: 0191 272 4297. Email: enquiries@ncl-coll.ac.uk www.ncl-coll.ac.uk

North Tyneside College – Embleton Avenue, Wallsend NE28 9NL. Tel: 0191 229 5000. Fax: 0191 229 5301. Email: admissions@ntyneside.ac.uk www.ntyneside.ac.uk

South Tyneside College – St George's Avenue, South Shields NE34 6ET. Tel: 0191 427 3500. Fax: 0191 427 3535. Email: info@stc.ac.uk www.stc.ac.uk

Tynemouth College –Hawkeys Lane, North Shields, Tyne and Wear NE29 9BZ. Tel: 0191 257 8414. Fax: 0191 290 0732. Email: enquiries@tynecoll.ac.uk www.tynecoll.ac.uk

HE institutions

University of Newcastle upon Tyne – Newcastle upon Tyne NE1 7RU. Tel: 0191 222 6000. Fax: 0191 222 6229. www.ncl.ac.uk

University of Northumbria at Newcastle – Ellison Place, Newcastle-upon-Tyne NE1 8ST. Tel: 0191 232 6002. Fax: 0191 227 4017. Email: admissions@northumbria.ac.uk www.northumbria.ac.uk

University of Sunderland – Langham Tower, Ryhope Road, Sunderland SR2 7EE. Tel: 0191 515 2000. Fax: 0191 515 3805. Email: student-helpline@sunderland.ac.uk www.sunderland.ac.uk

Business Link

Business Link Tyne and Wear – Business & Innovation Centre Sunderland Enterprise Park, Wearfield, Sunderland SR5 2TA. Tel: 0191 516 6700. Fax: 0191 516 6777. Email: ask@businesslinktw.co.uk www.businesslinktw.co.uk

Channel Islands and the Isle of Man

Guernsey

Careers service

Guernsey Careers Service – States of Guernsey Education Department, The Grange, St Peter Port, Guernsey GY1 1RQ. Channel Islands. Tel: 01481 733044. Fax: 01481 713015. Email: careers@education.gov.gg www.careers.gg

LEA

States of Guernsey – Education Department, The Grange, St Peter Port, Guernsey GY1 1RQ. Tel: 01481 710821. Fax: 01484 714475. www.gov.gg

College

Guernsey College of Further Education – La Route des Coutanchez, St Peter Port, Guernsey GY1 2TT. Tel: 01481 737500. Fax: 01481 714153. Email: college@cfe.edu.gg www.cfe.edu.gg

Jersey

Careers service

Jersey Careers Service – PO Box 142, St Helier, Jersey JE4 8QJ. Tel: 01534 509351. Fax: 01534 509470. Email: jcs@psilink.co.je www.jcs.co.je

LEA

States of Jersey – Education Department, PO Box 142, St Saviour, Jersey JE4 8QJ. Tel: 01534 509500. Fax: 01534 509400. www.education.gov.je

Colleges

Highlands College – PO Box 1000, St Saviour, Jersey JE4 9QA. Tel: 01534 608608. Fax: 01534 608600. Email: reception@highlands.ac.uk www.highlands.ac.uk

Jersey Business School – PO Box 1000, St Saviour, Jersey JE4 9QA. Tel: 01534 754000. Fax: 01534 754001. Email: jbs@highlands.ac.uk www.jersey-business-school.com

Isle of Man

Careers service

Isle of Man Careers Service – Department of Education, St George's Court, Upper Church Street, Douglas, Isle of Man IM1 1EE. Tel: 01624 685128. Fax: 01624 687016. Email: careers@gov.im www.gov.im

LEA

Isle of Man Government – Department of Education, St George's Court, Upper Church Street, Douglas IM1 2SG. Tel: 01624 685280. Fax: 01624 685834. www.gov.im

Colleges

The Isle of Man College – Homefield Road, Douglas, Isle of Man IM2 6RB. Tel: 01624 648200. Fax: 01624 648201. Email: enquiries@iomcollege.ac.im www.iomcollege.ac.im

IHMES International Hotel School – Windsor House, Port Erin, Isle of Man IM9 6LA. Tel: 01624 832836. Fax: 01624 835365. Email: office@ihmes.com www.ihmes.com

Wales

North West Wales

(Areas covered: Conwy, Denbighshire, Gwynedd And Isle Of Anglesey)

All age careers service

Careers Wales North West – 5 Castle Street, Caernarfon LL55 1SE. Tel: 01286 679199. www.careerswales.com

ELWa

ELWa North Wales – St Asaph Business Park, St Asaph, Denbighshire LL17 0LJ. Tel: 01745 538500. Fax: 01745 538501. www.elwa.org.uk

LEAs

Isle of Anglesey County Council – The Department of Education and Leisure, Park Mount, Glanhwfa Road, Llangefni, Anglesey LL77 7TW. Tel: 01248 752900. Fax: 01248 752999. www.anglesey.gov.uk

Conwy County Borough Council – Education Department, Government Buildings, Dinerth Road, Colwyn Bay, Conwy LL28 4UL. Tel: 01492 575001. Fax: 01492 541311. www.conwy.gov.uk

Denbighshire County Council – Department of Lifelong Learning, Council Offices, Wynnstay Road, Ruthin LL15 1YN. Tel: 01824 706777. Fax: 01824 706780. Email: education@denbighshire.gov.uk www.denbighshire.gov.uk

Gwynedd Council – Education, Culture and Leisure Offices, County Offices, Shirehall Street, Caernarfon, Gwynedd LL55 1SH. Tel: 01286 672255. Fax: 01286 677347. www.gwynedd.gov.uk

FE colleges

Coleg Harlech – Harlech, Gwynedd, LL46 2PU. Tel: 01766 781900. Fax: 01766 780169. Email: infor@fc.harlech.ac.uk www.harlech.ac.uk

Coleg Llandrillo – Llandrillo Road, Rhos-on-Sea, Colwyn Bay, Clwyd LL28 4HZ. Tel: 01492 546666. Fax: 01492 543052. Email: admissions@llandrillo.ac.uk www.llandrillo.ac.uk

Coleg Meirion-Dwyfor – Fford Ty'n Coed, Dolgellau, Gwynedd LL40 2SW. Tel: 01341 422827. Fax: 01341 422393. Email: coleg@meirion-dwyfor.ac.uk www.meirion-dwyfor.ac.uk

Coleg Menai – Ffriddoed Road, Bangor LL57 2TP. Tel: 01248 370125. Fax: 01248 370052. Email: pp@menai.ac.uk www.menai.ac.uk

HE institutions

University of Wales Bangor – Bangor, Gwynedd LL57 2DG. Tel: 01248 351151. Fax: 01248 370451. Email: admissions@bangor.ac.uk www.bangor.ac.uk

Business Eye

Business Eye –3 Ynys Bridge Court, Morganstown, Cardiff CF15 9YD. Tel: 08457 969798. Fax: 029 2081 5399. Email: assistance@businesseye.org.uk www.businesseye.org.uk

North East Wales

(Areas covered: Flintshire, Wrexham and South Denbighshire)

All age careers service

Careers Wales North East – 2nd Floor, St Davids Buildings, Daniel Owen Square, Earl Road, Mold, Flintshire CH7 1DD. Tel: 01352 750456. www.careerswales.com

ELWa

ELWa North Wales – St Asaph Business Park, St Asaph, Denbighshire LL17 0LJ. Tel: 01745 538500. Fax: 01745 538501. www.elwa.org.uk

LEAs

Denbighshire County Council – Department of Lifelong Learning, Council Offices, Wynnstay Road, Ruthin LL15 1YN. Tel: 01824 706777. Fax: 01824 706780. www.denbighshire.gov.uk

Flintshire County Council – Education Department, County Hall, Mold, Flintshire CH7 6ND. Tel: 01352 752121. Fax: 01352 754202. www.flintshire.gov.uk

Wrexham County Borough Council – Education and Leisure Services, Ty Henblas, Queen's Square, Wrexham LL13 8AZ. Tel: 01978 297401. Fax: 01978 297501. Email: education@wrexham.gov.uk www.wrexham.gov.uk

FE colleges

Coleg Llysfasi – Ruthin, Denbighshire LL15 2LB. Tel: 01978 790263. Fax: 01978 790468. Email: admin@llysfasi.ac.uk www.llysfasi.ac.uk

Deeside College of Further Education – Kelsterton Road, Connah's Quay, Deeside CH5 4BR. Tel: 01244 831531. Fax: 01244 814305. Email: enquiries@deeside.ac.uk www.deeside.ac.uk

Yale College – Grove Park Road, Wrexham LL12 7AA. Tel: 01978 311794. Fax: 01978 291569. Email: admissions@yale-wrexham.ac.uk www.yale-wrexham.co.uk

HE institutions

North East Wales Institute of Higher Education – Plas Coch Campus, Mold Road, Wrexham LL11 2AW. Tel: 01978 290666. Fax: 01978 290008. Email: enquiries@newi.ac.uk   www.newi.ac.uk

Other colleges

Welsh College of Horticulture – Northop, Mold CH7 6AA. Tel: 01352 841000. Fax: 01352 841031. Email: info@wcoh.ac.uk www.wcoh.ac.uk

Business Eye

Business Eye –3 Ynys Bridge Court, Morganstown, Cardiff CF15 9YD. Tel: 08457 969798. Fax: 029 2081 5399. Email: assistance@businesseye.org.uk www.businesseye.org.uk

West Wales

(Areas covered: Carmarthenshire, Ceredigion, Neath Port Talbot, Pembrokeshire and Swansea)

All age careers service

Careers Wales West – 69 The Kingsway, Swansea SA1 5JA. Tel: 01792 644444. www.careerswales.com

ELWa

ELWa South West Wales – Ty'r Llyn, Waterside Business Park, Clos Llyn Cwm, Swansea Enterprise Park, Llansamlet, Swansea SA6 8AH. Tel: 01792 765800. Fax: 01792 765801. www.elwa.org.uk

LEAs

Carmarthenshire County Council – Lifelong Learning and Leisure, County Hall, Carmarthen, Carmarthenshire SA13 1JP. Tel: 01267 224501. Fax: 01267 221692. www.carmathenshire.gov.uk

Ceredigion County Council – Education Department, County Offices, Marine Terrace, Aberystwyth, Ceredigion SY23 2DE. Tel: 01970 633600. Fax: 01970 633655. Email: education@ceredigion.gov.uk www.ceredigion.gov.uk

City and County of Swansea – Lifelong Learning, Dan-y-Coet House, Huntingdon Close, Westcroft, Swansea SA3 5AR. Tel: 01792 401548. Fax: 01792 403750. www.swansea.gov.uk

Neath Port Talbot County Borough Council – Education Offices, Civic Centre, Port Talbot SA13 1PJ. Tel: 01639 763298. Fax: 01639 899914. Email: education@neath-porttalbot.gov.uk www.neath-porttalbot.gov.uk

Pembrokeshire County Council – Adult Education, County Hall, Haverfordwest, Pembrokeshire SA16 1TP. Tel: 01437 764551. Fax: 01437 775303. www.pembrokeshire.gov.uk

FE colleges

Coleg Ceredigion – Park Place, Cardigan, Ceredigion SA43 1AB. Tel: 01239 612032. Fax: 01239 612032. www.ceredigion.ac.uk

Coleg Sir Gar – Sandy Road, Llanelli SA15 4DN. Tel: 01554 748000. Fax: 01554 756088. Email: admissions@colegsirgar.ac.uk www.csgcollege.ac.uk

Gorseinon College – Belgrave Road, Gorseinon, Swansea SA4 6RD. Tel: 01792 890700. Fax: 01792 898729. Email: admin@gorseinon.ac.uk www.gorseinon.ac.uk

Neath Port Talbot College – Neath Campus, Dwr-y-felin Road, Neath SA10 7RF. Tel: 01639 648000. Fax: 01639 648009. Email: enquiries@nptc.ac.uk www.nptc.ac.uk

Pembrokeshire College – Haverfordwest, Pembrokeshire SA61 1SZ. Tel: 01437 765247. Fax: 01437 767279. Email: info@pembrokeshire.ac.uk www.pembrokeshire.ac.uk

Swansea College – Tycoch Road, Swansea SA2 9EB. Tel: 01792 284000. Fax: 01792 284074. Email: admissions@swancoll.ac.uk www.swancoll.ac.uk

HE institutions

Swansea Institute of Higher Education – Mount Pleasant, Swansea SA1 6ED. Tel: 01792 481000. Fax: 01792 481085. Email: enquiry@sihe.ac.uk www.sihe.ac.uk

Trinity College – Carmarthen SA31 3EP. Tel: 01267 676767. Fax: 01267 676766. Email: registry@trinity-cm.ac.uk www.trinity-cm.ac.uk

University of Wales – Lampeter, Ceredigion SA48 7ED. Tel: 01570 422351. Fax: 01570 423423. Email: admissions@lamp.ac.uk www.lampeter.ac.uk

University of Wales, Aberystwyth – Old College, King Street, Aberystwyth, Ceredigion SY23 2AX. Tel: 01970 623111. Email: dils@aber.ac.uk www.aber.ac.uk

University of Wales Swansea – Singleton Park, Swansea SA2 8PP. Tel: 01792 205678. Fax: 01792 295157. Email: admissions@swansea.ac.uk www.swansea.ac.uk

Business Eye

Business Eye –3 Ynys Bridge Court, Morganstown, Cardiff CF15 9YD. Tel: 08457 969798. Fax: 029 2081 5399. Email: assistance@businesseye.org.uk www.businesseye.org.uk

Mid Wales

(Area covered: Powys)

All age careers service

Careers Wales Powys – The Lindens, Spa Road, Llandrindod Wells LD1 5EQ. Tel: 01597 825898. Fax: 01597 823988. Email: careers.wales@powys.gov.uk www.careerswales.com

ELWa

ELWa Mid Wales – St Davids House, Newtown, Powys SY16 1RB. Tel: 01686 622494. Fax: 01686 622716. www.elwa.org.uk

LEA

Powys County Council – Education Department, County Hall, Llandrindod Wells LD1 5LG. Tel: 01597 826000. Fax: 01597 826475. www.powys.gov.uk

FE colleges

Coleg Powys – Llanidloes Road, Newtown, Powys SY16 4HU. Tel: 01686 622722. Fax: 01686 622246. Email: enquiries@coleg-powys.ac.uk www.coleg-powys.ac.uk

Business Eye

Business Eye –3 Ynys Bridge Court, Morganstown, Cardiff CF15 9YD. Tel: 08457 969798. Fax: 029 2081 5399. Email: assistance@businesseye.org.uk www.businesseye.org.uk

South East Wales

(Area covered: Cardiff and the Vale of Glamorgan, Gwent and Mid-Glamorgan)

All age careers service

Careers Wales Cardiff and Vale – 53 Charles Street, Cardiff, CF10 2GD. Tel: 029 2090 6700. Fax: 029 2090 6799. www.careerswales.com

Careers Wales Gwent – Tw Glyn, Albion Road, Pontypool NP4 6GE. Tel: 01495 756666. Fax: 01495 768950. Email: info@careerswalesgwent.org.uk www.careerswales.com

Careers Wales Mid-Glamorgan – 10-11 Centre Court, Treforest Industrial Estate, Pontypridd CF37 5YR. Tel: 01443 842207. Fax: 01443 842208. www.careerswales.com

ELWa

ELWa South East Wales – Ty'r Afron, Bedwas Road, Bedwas, Caerphilly CF83 8WT. Tel: 01443 663663. Fax: 01443 663653. www.elwa.org.uk

LEAs

Blaenau Gwent County Borough Council – Education Department, Municipal Offices, Civic Centre, Ebbw Vale NP23 6XE. Tel: 01495 355340. Email: education.department@blaenau-gwent.gov.uk www.blaenau-gwent.gov.uk

Bridgend County Borough Council – Education and Leisure Services, Angel Street, Bridgend CF31 1LX. Tel: 01656 642696. Fax: 01656 668126. Email: education@bridgend.gov.uk www.bridgend.gov.uk

Caerphilly County Borough Council – Community Education, Ystrad Fawr Caerphilly Road, Ystrad Mynach, Hengoed CF82 7SF. Tel: 01443 863238. Fax: 01443 863070. Email: communityeducation@caerphilly.gov.uk www.caerphilly.gov.uk

Cardiff County Council – Education Department, County Hall, Atlantic Wharf, Cardiff CF10 4UW. Tel: 029 2087 2000. Fax: 029 2087 2777. Email: c2c@cardiff.gov.uk www.cardiff.gov.uk

Merthyr Tydfil County Borough Council – Education Directorate, Ty Keir House, Riverside Court, Avenue De Clichy, Merthyr Tydfil CF47 8XD. Tel: 01685 724600. Fax: 01685 721965. Email: education@merthyr.gov.uk www.merthyr.gov.uk

Monmouthshire County Council – Lifelong Learning and Leisure Directorate, County Hall, Cwmbran, Torfaen NP44 2XN. Tel: 01633 644644. Fax: 01633 644666. www.monmouthshire.gov.uk

Newport County Borough Council – Lifelong Learning and Leisure, Civic Centre, Newport NP20 4UR. Tel: 01633 656656. Fax: 01633 233376. www.newport.gov.uk

Rhondda Cynon Taff County Borough Council – Lifelong Learning, The Education Centre, Ty Trevithick, Abercynon, Mountain Ash CF45 4UQ. Tel: 01443 744000. www.rhondda-cynon-taff.gov.uk

Torfaen County Borough Council – Education Department, County Hall, Cwmbran, Torfaen NP44 2WN. Tel: 01495 762200. Fax: 01495 755513. Email: enquiries@torfaen.gov.uk www.torfaen.gov.uk

Vale of Glamorgan Council – Directorate of Learning and Development, Civic Offices, Holton Road, Barry, Vale of Glamorgan CF63 4RU. Tel: 01446 709151. Fax: 01446 709110. Email: educationstaff@valeofglamorgan.gov.uk www.valeofglamorgan.gov.uk

FE colleges

Aberdare College – Cwmdare Road, Aberdare CF44 8ST. Tel: 01685 887500. Fax: 01685 876635. Email: gen.office@aberdare.ac.uk www.aberdare.ac.uk

Barry College – Colcot Road, Barry CF62 8YJ. Tel: 01446 725000. Fax: 01446 732667. Email: enquiries@barry.ac.uk www.barry.ac.uk

Bridgend College of Technology – Cowbridge Road, Bridgend CF31 3DF. Tel: 01656 302302. Fax: 01656 663912. Email: enquiries@bridgend.ac.uk www.bridgend.ac.uk

Coleg Glan Hafren/Cardiff Tertiary College – Trowbridge Road, Rumney, Cardiff CF3 1XZ. Tel: 029 2025 0250. Fax: 029 2025 0339. www.glan-hafren.ac.uk

Coleg Gwent – The Rhadyr, Usk NP5 1XJ. Tel: 01495 333333. Fax: 01495 333526. Email: info@coleggwent.ac.uk www.coleggwent.ac.uk

Coleg Morgannwg – Pontyridd Campus, Ynys Terrace, Rhydyfelin, Pontypridd CF37 5RN. Tel: 01443 662800. Fax: 01443 663028. Email: college@pontypridd.ac.uk www.pontypridd.ac.uk

Merthyr Tydfil College – Ynysfach, Merthyr Tydfil CF48 1AR. Tel: 01685 726000. Fax: 01685 726100. Email: college@merthyr.ac.uk www.merthyr.ac.uk

Ystrad Mynach College – Twyn Road, Ystrad Mynach, Hengoed CF82 7XR. Tel: 01443 816888. Fax: 01443 816973. Email: enquiries@ystrad-mynach.ac.uk www.ystrad-mynach.ac.uk

HE institutions

Cardiff University – PO Box 927, Cardiff CF10 3UA. Tel: 029 2087 4400. Email: prospectus@cardiff.ac.uk www.cardiff.ac.uk

University of Glamorgan – Pontypridd CF37 1DL. Tel: 01443 480480. Fax: 01443 480558. Email: enquiries@glam.ac.uk www.glam.ac.uk

The University of Wales – King Edward VII Avenue, Cardiff CF10 3NS. Tel: 029 2038 2656. Fax: 029 2039 6040. Email: uniwales@wales.ac.uk www.wales.ac.uk

University of Wales, Newport – Caerleon Campus, PO Box 101, Newport NP18 3YH. Tel: 01633 432432. Fax: 01633 432046. Email: uic@newport.ac.uk www.newport.ac.uk

Other colleges

Glamorgan Centre for Art & Design Technology – Glyntaff Road, Glyntaff, Pontypridd CF37 4AT. Tel: 01443 663309. Fax: 01443 663313. Email: college@gcadt.ac.uk www.gcadt.ac.uk

Royal Welsh College of Music and Drama
– Castle Grounds, Cathays Park, Cardiff CF10
3ER. Tel: 029 2034 2854. Fax: 029 2039 1304.
Email: info@rwcmd.ac.uk www.rwcmd.ac.uk

United World College of the Atlantic – St
Donat's Castle, Llantwit Major, Vale of
Glamorgan CF61 1WF. Tel: 01446 799000.
Fax: 01446 799013.
Email: principal@uwcac.uwk.org
www.uwc.org

Business Eye

Business Eye – 3 Ynys Bridge Court,
Morganstown, Cardiff CF15 9YD. Tel: 08457
969798. Fax: 029 2081 5399.
Email: assistance@businesseye.org.uk
www.businesseye.org.uk

Scotland

South West Scotland

(Areas covered: Ayrshire, Dumfriesshire, Kirkcudbrightshire, Lanarkshire and Wigtownshire)

All age careers service

Careers Scotland centres listed by town:

Airdrie – Albert Primary School, 31 North Biggar Road, Airdrie ML6 6EJ. Tel: 01236 762623. Fax: 01236 755451.
www.careers-scotland.org.uk

Ardrossan – 54-56 Princes Street, Ardrossan KA22 8DF. Tel: 01294 468134. Fax: 01294 464018.
www.careers-scotland.org.uk

Ayr – 2b Boswell Park, Ayr KA7 1QF. Tel: 01292 281421. Fax: 01292 618730.
www.careers-scotland.org.uk

Bellshill – Main Street, Bellshill ML4 1AW. Tel: 01698 746985. Fax: 01698 746249.
www.careers-scotland.org.uk

Coatbridge – Community Centre, 2 Corsewall Street, Coatbridge ML5 1QQ. Tel: 01236 424471. Fax: 01236 421104.
www.careers-scotland.org.uk

Cumnock – Glaisnock Business Centre, Townhead Street, Cumnock KA18 1LE. Tel: 01290 423422. Fax: 01290 420530.
www.careers-scotland.org.uk

Dalmellington – 8 High Main Street, Dalmellington KA6 7QN, Tel: 01292 551191.
www.careers-scotland.org.uk

Dumfries – Loreburne Centre, High Street, Dumfries DG1 2BD. Tel: 01387 272500. Fax: 01387 279649. www.careers-scotland.org.uk

East Kilbride – 6 Righead Gate, Town Centre, East Kilbride G74 1NS. Tel: 01355 255478. Fax: 01355 264235.
www.careers-scotland.org.uk

Hamilton – Units1 & 2 Princes Gate, Castle Street, Hamilton ML3 6BU. Tel: 01698 477120. Fax: 01698 477155.
www.careers-scotland.org.uk

Irvine – 36-38 Bank Street, Irvine KA12 0LP. Tel: 01294 272421. Fax: 01294 275863.
www.careers-scotland.org.uk

Kilmarnock – 2 The Cross, Kilmarnock KA1 1LR. Tel: 01563 527165. Fax: 01563 525544.
www.careers-scotland.org.uk

Lanark – South Lanark Council, 3rd Floor, South Vennel, Lanark ML11 9AQ. Tel: 01555 673593. Fax: 01555 673592.
www.careers-scotland.org.uk

Motherwell – 62 Windmillhill Street, Motherwell ML1 1TA. Tel: 01698 266469. Fax: 01698 268195.
www.careers-scotland.org.uk

Newton Stewart – 79 Victoria Street, Newton Stewart DG8 6NL. Tel: 01671 402692.
www.careers-scotland.org.uk

Rutherglen – 380 King Street, Rutherglen G73 1DQ. Tel: 0141 613 5211. Fax: 0141 613 5219.
www.careers-scotland.org.uk

Seafar, Cumbernauld – Muirfield Centre, Brown Road, Seafar, Cumbernauld G67 1AA. Tel: 01236 720889. Fax: 01236 726904.
www.careers-scotland.org.uk

Stranraer – Off Lewis Street, Stranraer DG9 7AL. Tel: 01776 889793.
www.careers-scotland.org.uk

Wishaw – 17 Graham Street, Wishaw ML2 8HR. Tel: 01698 292616. Fax: 01698 292637.
www.careers-scotland.org.uk

LECs

Scottish Enterprise Ayrshire – 17-19 Hill Street, Kilmarnock K3 1HA. Tel: 01563 526623. Fax: 01563 543636.
www.scottish-enterprise.com

Scottish Enterprise Dumfries and Galloway – Solway House, Dumfries Enterprise Park, Tinwald Downs Road, Dumfries DG1 3SJ.
Tel: 01387 245000. Fax: 01387 246224.
www.scottish-enterprise.com

Scottish Enterprise Lanarkshire – New Lanarkshire House, Strathclyde Business Park, Bellshill ML4 3AD. Tel: 01698 745454.
Fax: 01698 842211.
Email: selenquiry@scotent.co.uk
www.scottish-enterprise.com

LEAs

Dumfries and Galloway Council – Educational Department, 30 Edinburgh Road, Dumfries DG1 1NW. Tel: 01387 260427.
Fax: 01387 260453. www.dumgal.gov.uk

East Ayrshire Council – Department of Education and Social Services, Council Headquarters, Kilmarnock KA3 7BU. Tel: 01563 576000. Fax: 01563 576500.
Email: education@east-ayrshire.gov.uk
www.east-ayrshire.gov.uk

North Ayrshire Council – Educational Services, 4th Floor, Cunninghame House, Irvine, Ayrshire KA12 8EE. Tel: 01294 324100.
Fax: 01294 324144.
Email: education@north-ayrshire.gov.uk
www.north-ayrshire.gov.uk

North Lanarkshire Council – Education Department, Municipal Buildings, Kildonan Street, Coatbridge, Lanarkshire ML5 3BT.
Tel: 01236 812239.
Email: education@northlan.gov.uk
www.northlan.gov.uk

South Ayrshire Council – Educational Services, County Buildings, Ayr KA7 1DR.
Tel: 01292 612200. Fax: 01292 612143.
www.south-ayrshire.gov.uk

South Lanarkshire Council – Educational Resources, Council Offices, Almada Street, Hamilton, Lanarkshire ML3 0AE. Tel: 01698 454379. Fax: 01698 454465.
Email: education@southlanarkshire.gov.uk
www.southlanarkshire.gov.uk

FE colleges

Ayr College – Dam Park, Ayr KA8 0EU.
Tel: 01292 265184. Fax: 01292 263889.
Email: admissions@ayrcoll.ac.uk
www.ayrcoll.ac.uk

Barony College – Parkgate, Dumfries DG1 3NE. Tel: 01387 860251. Fax: 01387 860395.
www.barony.ac.uk

Coatbridge College – Kildonan Street, Coatbridge ML5 3LS. Tel: 01236 422316.
Fax: 01236 440266.
Email: admissions@coatbridge.ac.uk
www.coatbridge.ac.uk

Cumbernauld College – Tryst Road, Town Centre, Cumbernauld G67 1HU. Tel: 01236 731811. Fax: 01236 723416. Email: cumbernauld_college@cumbernauld.ac.uk
www.cumbernauld.ac.uk

Dumfries and Galloway College – Heathhall, Dumfries DG1 3QZ. Tel: 01387 261261. Fax: 01387 250006. Email: info@dumgal.ac.uk www.dumgal.ac.uk

Kilmarnock College – Holehouse Road, Kilmarnock KA3 7AT. Tel: 01563 523501. Fax: 01563 538182. www.kilmarnock.ac.uk

Motherwell College – Dalzell Drive, Motherwell ML1 2DD. Tel: 01698 232323.
Fax: 01698 232527.
Email: register@motherwell.ac.uk
www.motherwell.ac.uk

HE institutions

Bell College – Almada Street, Hamilton, Lanarkshire ML3 0JB. Tel: 01698 283100.
Fax: 01698 282131. Email: registry@bell.ac.uk
www.bell.ac.uk

Small Business Gateway

Small Business Gateway – Tel: 0845 609 6611.
www.sbgateway.com

South East Scotland

(Areas covered: Berwickshire, Clackmannanshire, East Lothian, Kinross-shire, Midlothian, Peebles-shire, Roxburghshire, Selkirkshire, Stirlingshire and West Lothian)

All age careers service

Careers Scotland centres listed by town:

Alloa – 39-43 Bank Street, FK10 1HP. Tel: 01259 215214. Fax: 01259 211741.
www.careers-scotland.org.uk

Dalkeith – 20 Croft Street, EH22 3BA. Tel: 0131 663 7287. Fax: 0131 663 2446.
www.careers-scotland.org.uk

Edinburgh – Regional Headquarters, 17 Logie Mill, EH7 4HG. Tel: 0131 556 7384. Fax: 0131 556 0841.
www.careers-scotland.org.uk

Falkirk – 1a Bank Street, FK1 1NB. Tel: 01324 620311. Fax: 01324 624062.
www.careers-scotland.org.uk

Galashiels – Waukrigg Mill, Duke Street, Galashiels TD1 1QD. Tel: 01896 754884. Fax: 01896 758183.
www.careers-scotland.org.uk

Grangemouth – 15 La Porte Precinct, FK3 8AZ. Tel: 01324 472397. Fax: 01324 666729.
www.careers-scotland.org.uk

Hawick – 12 Howegate, TD9 0AB. Tel: 01450 372724. Fax: 01450 372771.
www.careers-scotland.org.uk

Livingston – Cairngorm House, Almondvale Boulevard, Livingston EH54 6NG. Tel: 01506 434249. Fax: 01506 430955.
www.careers-scotland.org.uk

Musselburgh – Adam Ferguson House, Station Road, EH21 7PQ. Tel: 0131 665 3120. Fax: 0131 665 0738.
www.careers-scotland.org.uk

Penicuik – 14a John Street Penicuik, EH26 8AB. Tel: 01968 673760. Fax: 01968 678993.
www.careers-scotland.org.uk

Stirling – 6 Viewfield Place, Stirling FK7 9JQ. Tel: 01786 462036.
www.careers-scotland.org.uk

LECs

Scottish Enterprise Borders – Bridge Street, Galashiels TD1 1SW. Tel: 01896 758991. Fax: 01896 758625.
Email: seb-enquiry@scotent.co.uk
www.scottish-enterprise.com

Scottish Enterprise Edinburgh and Lothian – Apex House, 99 Haymarket Terrace, Edinburgh EH12 5HD. Tel: 0131 313 4000. Fax: 0131 313 4231.
Email: lothian@scotent.co.uk
www.scottish-enterprise.com

Scottish Enterprise Forth Valley – Laurel House, Laurelhill Business Park, Stirling FK7 9JQ. Tel: 01786 451919. Fax: 01786 478123.
Email: forthvalley@scotent.co.uk
www.scottish-enterprise.com

LEAs

City of Edinburgh Council – Education Department, Wellington Court, 10 Waterloo Place, Edinburgh EH1 3EG. Tel: 0131 469 3000. Fax: 0131 469 3141. www.edinburgh.gov.uk

Clackmannanshire Council – Education Department, Lime Tree House, Alloa, Clackmannanshire FK10 1EX. Tel: 01259 452432. Fax: 01259 452440.
Email: edusupport@clacks.gov.uk
www.clacksweb.org.uk

East Lothian Council – Education Offices, John Muir House, Haddington, East Lothian EH41 3HA. Tel: 01620 827631. Fax: 01620 827291. www.eastlothian.gov.uk

Falkirk Council – Community Education – Adult Learning, Park Street, Falkirk FK1 1RE. Tel: 01324 503670. Fax: 01324 503671.
Email: enquiry@falkirk.gov.uk
www.falkirk.gov.uk

Midlothian Council – Adult Education, Fairfield House, 8 Lothian Road, Dalkeith, Midlothian EH22 3ZG. Tel: 0131 271 3708. Fax: 0131 271 3751. Email: education.services@midlothian.gov.uk www.midlothian.gov.uk

Scottish Borders Council – Education Department, Council Headquarters, Newtown St. Boswells, Melrose TD6 0SA. Tel: 01835 824000. Fax: 01835 825091. Email: enquiries@scotborders.gov.uk www.scotborders.gov.uk

Stirling Council – Education Offices, Viewforth, Stirling FK8 2ET. Tel: 01786 443322. Fax: 01786 442782. www.stirling.gov.uk

West Lothian Council – Education Services, Lindsay House, South Bridge Street, Bathgate, West Lothian EH48 1TS. Tel: 01506 776000. Fax: 01506 776378. www.westlothian.gov.uk

FE colleges

Borders College – Head Office, Melrose Road, Galashiels TD1 2AF. Tel: 08700 505152. Fax: 01896 758179. www.borderscollege.ac.uk

Clackmannan College – Branshill Road, Alloa, Clackmannanshire FK10 3BT. Tel: 01259 215121. Fax: 01259 722879. www.clacks.ac.uk

Edinburgh's Telford College – Crewe Toll, Edinburgh EH4 2NZ. Tel: 0131 332 2491. Fax: 0131 343 1218. Email: mail@ed-coll.ac.uk www.ed-coll.ac.uk

Falkirk College of Further and Higher Education – Grangemouth Road, Falkirk FK2 9AD. Tel: 01324 403000. Fax: 01324 403222. Email: info@falkirkcollege.ac.uk www.falkirkcollege.ac.uk

Jewel & Esk Valley College – Milton Road Campus, 24 Milton Road East, Edinburgh EH15 2PP. Tel: 0131 660 1010. Fax: 0131 657 2276. Email: info@jevc.ac.uk www.jevc.ac.uk

Stevenson College – Bankhead Avenue, Edinburgh EH11 4DE. Tel: 0131 535 4700. Fax: 0131 535 4708. Email: info@stevenson.ac.uk www.stevenson.ac.uk

West Lothian College – Almondvale Cresent, Livingston, West Lothian EH54 7EP. Tel: 01506 418181. Fax: 01506 409980. Email: enquiries@west-lothian.ac.uk www.west-lothian.ac.uk

HE institutions

Heriot-Watt University – Edinburgh EH14 4AS. Tel: 0131 449 5111. Fax: 0131 449 5153. Email: enquiries@hw.ac.uk www.hw.ac.uk

Napier University Edinburgh – Information Centre, 10 Colinton Road, Edinburgh ER10 5DT. Tel: 0500 35 35 70. Fax: 0131 445 2588. Email: info@napier.ac.uk www.napier.ac.uk

Queen Margaret University College – Clerwood Terrace, Edinburgh EH12 8TS. Tel: 0131 317 3000. Fax: 0131 317 3256. Email: admissions@qmuc.ac.uk www.qmuc.ac.uk

University of Edinburgh – Old College, South Bridge, Edinburgh EH8 9YL. Tel: 0131 650 1000. Fax: 0131 650 2147. www.ed.ac.uk

University of Stirling – Stirling FK9 4LA. Tel: 01786 473171. Fax: 01786 463000. www.stirling.ac.uk

See also Falkirk College of Further and Higher Education listed above.

Other colleges

Edinburgh College of Art – Lauriston Place, Edinburgh EH3 9DF. Tel: 0131 221 6000. Fax: 0131 221 6001. www.eca.ac.uk

Oatridge Agricultural College – Ecclesmachan, Broxburn, West Lothian EH52 6NH. Tel: 01506 864800. Fax: 01506 853373. Email: info@oatridge.ac.uk www.oatridge.ac.uk

Scottish Agricultural College – King's Building, West Mains Road, Edinburgh EH9 3JG. Tel: 0131 535 4000. Fax: 0131 535 4246. www.sac.ac.uk

The Thomas Chippendale School of Furniture – Myreside Grange, Gifford, Haddington, East Lothian EH41 4JA. Tel: 01620 810680. Fax: 01620 810701. Email: info@chippendale.co.uk www.chippendale.co.uk

Small Business Gateway

Small Business Gateway – Tel: 0845 609 6611. www.sbgateway.com

West Scotland

(Areas covered: Dunbartonshire, Glasgow and Renfrewshire)

All age careers service

Careers Scotland centres listed by town:

Careers Scotland Headquarters, Scottish Enterprise Area – 150 Broomielaw, Atlantic Quay, Glasgow G2 8LU. Tel: 0141 228 2264. Fax: 0141 228 2851.
www.careers-scotland.org.uk

Alexandria – Main Street, Alexandria G83 ONU. Tel: 01389 754987. Fax: 01389 721055. www.careers-scotland.org.uk

Barrhead – 160 Main Street, Barrhead G78 1SL. Tel: 0141 881 2886. Fax: 0141 880 8456. www.careers-scotland.org.uk

Bishopbriggs – Thomas Muir High School, Westercladdens Road, Bishopbriggs G64 1DL. Tel: 0141 722 2318. Fax: 0141 772 5684. www.careers-scotland.org.uk

Clydebank – West Thomson Street, Clydebank G81 3EA. Tel: 0141 952 1454. Fax: 0141 951 4131.
www.careers-scotland.org.uk

Greenock – Laird House, 20 Laird Street, Greenock PA15 1LB. Tel: 01475 721271. Fax: 01475 728826. www.careers-scotland.org.uk

Helensburgh – 46-48 East Clyde Street, Helensburgh G84 7PG. Tel: 01436 678847. www.careers-scotland.org.uk

Johnstone – Floorsburn House, Floors Street, Johnstone PA5 8TW. Tel: 01505 326758. Fax: 01505 331496.
www.careers-scotland.org.uk

Milngavie – 1/11 Douglas Street, Milngavie G62 4BL. Tel: 0141 955 0909. Fax: 0141 955 0907. www.careers-scotland.org.uk

Paisley – 27 Causeyside Street, Paisley PA1 1UL. Tel: 0141 849 0942. Fax: 0141 5614201. www.careers-scotland.org.uk

Port Glasgow – 14 King Street, Port Glasgow PA14 5HZ. Tel: 01475 745566. Fax: 01475 744059. www.careers-scotland.org.uk

LECs

Scottish Enterprise Dunbartonshire – 2nd Floor, Spectrum House, Clydebank Business Park, Clydebank, Glasgow G81 2DR. Tel: 0141 951 2121. Fax: 0141 951 1907. www.scottish-enterprise.com

Scottish Enterprise Glasgow – Atrium Court, 50 Waterloo Street, Glasgow G2 6HQ. Tel: 0141 204 1111. Fax: 0141 248 1600. Email: glasgow@scotent.co.uk www.scottish-enterprise.com

Scottish Enterprise Renfrewshire – 27 Causeyside Street, Paisley PA1 1UL. Tel: 0141 848 0101. Fax: 0141 848 6930. Email: renfrewshire.directory@scotent.co.uk www.scottish-enterprise.com

LEAs

East Dunbartonshire Council – Education Services, Boclair House, 100 Milngavie Road, Bearsden, Glasgow G61 2TQ. Tel: 0141 578 8000. Fax: 0141 578 8653. www.eastdunbarton.gov.uk

East Renfrewshire Council – Education Department, Eastwood Park, Rouken Glen Road, Giffnock, Glasgow G46 6UG. Tel: 0141 577 3404. Fax: 0141 577 3405. www.eastrenfrewshire.gov.uk

Glasgow City Council – Education Services, Wheatley House, 25 Cockrane Street, Merchant City, Glasgow. G1 1HL. Tel: 0141 287 2965. Fax: 0141 287 2936. www.glasgow.gov.uk

Inverclyde Council – Education Services, 105 Dalrymple Street, Greenoak, Inverclyde PA15 1HT. Tel: 01475 712850. Fax: 01475 712875. www.inverclyde.gov.uk

Renfrewshire Council – Education and Children's Services, South Building, Cotton Street, Paisley PA1 1LE. Tel: 0141 842 5663. Fax: 0141 842 5699. www.renfrewshire.gov.uk

West Dunbartonshire Council – Department of Education and Cultural Services, Garshake Road, Dumbarton G82 3PU. Tel: 01389 737301. Fax: 01389 737348. www.west-dunbarton.gov.uk

FE colleges

Anniesland College – Hatfield Drive, Glasgow G12 0YE. Tel: 0141 357 3969. Fax: 0141 357 6557. Email: reception@anniesland.ac.uk www.anniesland.ac.uk

Cardonald College – 690 Mosspark Drive, Glasgow G52 3AY. Tel: 0141 272 3333. Fax: 0141 272 3444. Email: enquiries@cardonald.ac.uk www.cardonald.ac.uk

Clydebank College – Kilbowie Road, Clydebank, Dunbartonshire G81 2AA. Tel: 0141 952 7771. Fax: 0141 951 1574. Email: information@clydebank.ac.uk www.clydebank.ac.uk

James Watt College of Further and Higher Education – Finnart Street, Greenock, Renfrewshire PA16 8HF. Tel: 0800 587 2277. Fax: 01475 888079. Email: enquiries@jameswatt.ac.uk www.jameswatt.ac.uk

John Wheatley College – 1346 Shettleston Road, Glasgow G32 9AT. Tel: 0141 778 2426. Fax: 0141 763 2384. Email: advice@jwheatley.ac.uk www.jwheatley.ac.uk

Langside College – 50 Prospecthill Road, Glasgow G42 9LB. Tel: 0141 649 4991. Fax: 0141 632 5252. www.langside.ac.uk

North Glasgow College – Springburn Campus, 110 Flemington Street, Glasgow G21 4BX. Tel: 0141 558 9001. Fax: 0141 558 9905. Email: admissions@north-gla.ac.uk www.north-gla.ac.uk

Reid Kerr College – Renfrew Road, Paisley PA3 4DR. Tel: 0141 581 2222. Fax: 0141 581 2204. Email: sservices@reidkerr.ac.uk www.reidkerr.ac.uk

South Lanarkshire College – Cambuslang Campus, Hamilton Road, Cambuslang, Glasgow G72 7NY. Tel: 0141 641 6600. www.south-lanarkshire-college.ac.uk

Stow College – 43 Shamrock Street, Glasgow G4 9LD. Tel: 0141 332 1786. Fax: 0141 332 5207. Email: enquiries@stow.ac.uk www.stow.ac.uk

HE institutions

Glasgow Caledonian University – City Campus, 70 Cowcaddens Road, Glasgow G4 0BA. Tel: 0141 331 3000. Fax: 0141 331 3005. www.gcal.ac.uk

University of Glasgow – Glasgow G12 8QQ. Tel: 0141 330 2000. Fax: 0141 339 8855. www.glasgow.ac.uk

University of Paisley – High Street, Paisley PA1 2BE. Tel: 0141 848 3000. Fax: 0141 887 0812. Email: info@paisley.ac.uk www.paisley.ac.uk

University of Strathclyde – 16 Richmond Street, Glasgow G1 1XQ. Tel: 0141 552 4400. Fax: 0141 552 4400. www.strath.ac.uk

See also James Watt College of Further and Higher Education listed above.

Other colleges

Central College of Commerce – 300 Cathedral Street, Glasgow G1 2TA. Tel: 0141 552 3941. Fax: 0141 553 2368. Email: information@central-glasgow.ac.uk www.centralcollege.ac.uk

Glasgow College of Building and Printing – 60 North Hanover Street, Glasgow G1 2BP. Tel: 0141 332 9969. Fax: 0141 332 5170. www.gcbp.ac.uk

Glasgow College of Food Technology – 230 Cathedral Street, Glasgow G1 2TG. Tel: 0141 271 5100. Fax: 0141 553 2370. Email: enquiries@gcft.ac.uk www.gcft.ac.uk

Glasgow College of Nautical Studies – 21 Thistle Street, Glasgow G5 9XB. Tel: 0141 565 2500. Fax: 0141 565 2599.
Email: enquiries@gcns.ac.uk
www.glasgow-nautical.ac.uk

Glasgow School of Art – 167 Renfrew Street, Glasgow G3 6RQ. Tel: 0141 353 4500. Fax: 0141 3534528. www.gsa.ac.uk

Royal Scottish Academy of Music and Drama – 100 Renfrew Street, Glasgow G2 3DB. Tel: 0141 332 4101. Fax: 0141 332 8901.
Email: registry@rsamd.ac.uk
www.rsamd.ac.uk

Small Business Gateway

Small Business Gateway – Tel: 0845 609 6611.
www.sbgateway.com

North East Scotland

(Areas covered: Aberdeenshire, Angus, Banffshire, Fife, Kincardineshire and Perthshire)

All age careers service

Careers Scotland centres listed by town:

Aberdeen – 377 Union Street, Aberdeen AB11 6BT. Tel: 01224 285200. Fax: 01224 285221.
www.careers-scotland.org.uk

Angus – Bellevue House, 5 Springfield Terrace, Arbroath DD11 1EL. Tel: 01241 870441. Fax: 01241 430965.
www.careers-scotland.org.uk

Cowdenbeath – 320 High Street, Cowdenbeath KY4 9NT. Tel: 01383 313141. Fax: 01383 313148.
www.careers-scotland.org.uk

Cupar – 54 Crossgates, Cupar KY15 5HS. Tel: 01334 412240. Fax: 01334 412249.
www.careers-scotland.org.uk

Dundee – Royal Exchange Building, Panmure Street, Dundee DD1 1DU. Tel: 01382 495050. Fax: 01382 495061.
www.careers-scotland.org.uk

Dunfermline – 29 East Port, Dunfermline KY12 7JG. Tel: 01383 312200. Fax: 01383 312199,
www.careers-scotland.org.uk

Glenrothes – Unicorn House, Faulkland Gate, Glenrothes KY7 5NS. Tel: 01592 415188. Fax: 01592 415199.
www.careers-scotland.org.uk

Inverurie – Unit 6, Garioch Centre, Constitution Street, Inverurie AB51 4UY. Tel: 01467 623623. Fax: 01467 623624.
www.careers-scotland.org.uk

Kirkcaldy – 12 Whytescauseway, Kirkcaldy KY1 1XF. Tel: 01592 412555. Fax: 01592 412554.
www.careers-scotland.org.uk

Leven – Greig Institute, Forth Street, Leven KY8 4PF. Tel: 01333 592580. Fax: 01333 592584.
www.careers-scotland.org.uk

Perth – Highland House, St Catherine's Road, Perth PH1 5RY. Tel: 01738 637639. Fax: 01738 445138. www.careers-scotland.org.uk

Peterhead – 9 Marischal Street, Peterhead, AB42 1BS. Tel: 01779 479345. Fax: 01779 470037.
www.careers-scotland.org.uk

LECs

Scottish Enterprise Fife – Kingdom House, Saltire Centre, Glenrothes, Fife KY6 2AQ. Tel: 01592 623000. Fax: 01592 623149.
Email: fife@scotent.co.uk
www.scottish-enterprise.com

Scottish Enterprise Grampian – 27 Albyn Place, Aberdeen AB10 1DB. Tel: 01224 252000. Fax: 01224 213417.
Email: webinfo@scotent.co.uk
www.scottish-enterprise.com

LEAs

Aberdeen City Council – Education Department, Summerhill Education Centre, Stronsay Drive, Aberdeen AB15 6JA. Tel: 01224 346060. Fax: 01224 346061.
Email: furen@education.aberdeen.net.uk
www.aberdeencity.gov.uk

Aberdeenshire Council – Education Office (HQ), Woodhill House, Westburn Road, Aberdeen AB16 5GJ. Tel: 01224 664630. Fax: 01224 664615.
Email: education@aberdeenshire.gov.uk
www.aberdeenshire.gov.uk

Angus Council – Education Department, County Buildings, Market Street, Forfar DD8 3WE. Tel: 01307 461460. Fax: 01307 461848.
Email: education@angus.gov.uk
www.angus.gov.uk

Dundee Council – Education Department, Floor 8, Tayside House, Dundee DD1 3RZ. Tel: 01382 433111. Fax: 01382 433080.
Email: education@dundeecity.gov.uk
www.dundeecity.gov.uk

Fife Council – Education Services, Fife House, North Street, Glenrothes KY7 5LT. Tel: 01592 414141. Fax: 01592 413696.
www.fife.gov.uk

Perth and Kinross Council – Education and Children's Services, 2 High Street, Perth PH1 5PH. Tel: 01738 475000. Fax: 01738 475710.
Email: enquiries@pkc.gov.uk
www.pkc.gov.uk

FE colleges

Aberdeen College – Gallowgate, Aberdeen AB25 1BN. Tel: 01224 612000. Fax: 01224 612001.
Email: enquiry@abcol.ac.uk
www.abcol.ac.uk

Angus College – Keptie Road, Arbroath, Angus DD11 3EA. Tel: 01241 432600. Fax: 01241 876169. Email: marketing@angus.ac.uk
www.angus.ac.uk

Banff and Buchan College of Further Education – Henderson Road, Fraserburgh, Aberdeenshire AB43 9GA. Tel: 01346 586100. Fax: 01346 515370.
Email: admin@banff-buchan.ac.uk
www.banff-buchan.ac.uk

Dundee College – Old Glamis Road, Dundee DD3 8LE. Tel: 01382 834800. Fax: 01382 858117. Email: enquiry@dundeecoll.ac.uk
www.dundeecoll.ac.uk

Elmwood College – Carsiogie Road, Cupar, Fife KY15 4JB. Tel: 01334 658800. Fax: 01334 658888. Email: contact@elmwood.ac.uk
www.elmwood.ac.uk

Fife College of Further and Higher Education – St Brycedale Avenue, Kirkcaldy, Fife KY1 1EX. Tel: 01592 268591. Fax: 01592 640225. Email: enquiries@fife.ac.uk
www.fife.ac.uk

Glenrothes College – Stenton Road, Glenrothes, Fife KY6 2RA. Tel: 01592 772233. Fax: 01592 568182.
Email: college@glenroths.ac.uk
www.glenrothes-college.ac.uk

Lauder College – Halbeath, Dunfermline, Fife KY11 8DY. Tel: 01383 845000. Fax: 01383 845001. Email: customerservices@lauder.ac.uk
www.lauder.ac.uk

Perth College – Crieff Road, Perth PH1 2NX. Tel: 01738 877000. Fax: 01738 631364.
Email: pc.enquiries@perth.uhi.ac.uk
www.perth.ac.uk

HE institutions

Robert Gordon University – Schoolhill, Aberdeen AB10 1FR. Tel: 01224 262000. Fax: 01224 262185. Email: admissions@rgu.ac.uk www.rgu.ac.uk

University Of Aberdeen – Regents Walk, Aberdeen AB24 3FX. Tel: 01224 272000. Fax: 01224 273613. www.abdn.ac.uk

University of Abertay Dundee – Bell Street, Dundee DD1 1HG. Tel: 01382 308000. Fax: 01382 308877.
Email: enquiries@abertay.ac.uk
www.abertay.ac.uk

University of Dundee – Dundee DD1 4HN. Tel: 01382 344000. Fax: 01382 201604. Email: srs@dundee.ac.uk www.dundee.ac.uk

University of St Andrews – College Gate, North Street, St Andrews, Fife KY16 9AJ. Tel: 01334 476161. Fax: 01334 463388.
www.st-andrews.ac.uk

See also Fife College of Further and Higher Education listed above.

Other colleges

SAC: The National College for Food, Land & Environmental Studies – Craibstone Estate, Bucksburn, Aberdeen AB21 9YA. Tel: 01224 711000. Fax: 01224 711290. www.sac.ac.uk

Small Business Gateway

Small Business Gateway – Tel: 0845 609 6611. www.sbgateway.com

The Highlands and Islands

(Areas covered: Argyllshire, Bute-shire, Caithness, Inverness-shire, Morayshire, Nairnshire, Orkney, Ross-shire & Cromartyshire, Shetland and Sutherland)

All age careers service

Careers Scotland centres listed by town:

Campbeltown – 4 Castle Hill, Campbeltown, PA28 6AN. Tel: 01586 552795. Fax: 01586 553877. www.careers-scotland.org.uk

Dingwall – 2b Fodderty Way, Dingwall Business Park, Dingwall IV15 9XB. Tel: 01349 864914. Fax: 01349 865484. www.careers-scotland.org.uk

Dunoon – 24 Argyll Street, PA23 7HJ. Tel: 01369 705816. Fax: 01369 703045. www.careers-scotland.org.uk

Elgin – 7 Commerce Street, Elgin IV30 1BS. Tel: 01343 548884. Fax: 01343 550113. www.careers-scotland.org.uk

Fort William – Lochabar College, An Aird, Fort William PH33 6AN. Tel: 01397 874550. Fax: 01397 706092. www.careers-scotland.org.uk

Inverness – Cowan House, Inverness Retail & Business Park, IV2 7GF. Tel: 01463 244547. Fax: 01463 244338. www.careers-scotland.org.uk

Inverness – 4th Floor, River House, Young Street, IV3 5BQ. Tel: 01463 252100. Fax: 01463 243231. www.careers-scotland.org.uk

Isle of Benbecula – Taigh Cheann A Locha, Lionacleit, HS7 5PJ. Tel: 01870 604927. Fax: 01870 604928. www.careers-scotland.org.uk

Isle of Bute – 9 Victoria Street, Rothesay, PA20 9HA. Tel: 01700 503600. Fax: 01700 503130. www.careers-scotland.org.uk

Isle of Islay – Flora Street, Bowmore, PA43 7JY. Tel: 01496 810133. Fax: 01496 810131. www.careers-scotland.org.uk

Isle of Skye – Elgin Hostel, Dunvegan Road, Portree, IV51 9EE. Tel: 01478 612328. Fax: 01478 613256. www.careers-scotland.org.uk

Kirkwall – 2 Albert Street, KW15 1HP. Tel: 01856 872460. Fax: 01856 875515. www.careers-scotland.org.uk

Lerwick – Toll Clock Shopping Centre, 26 North Road, ZE1 0DE. Tel: 01595 695791. Fax: 01595 694011. www.careers-scotland.org.uk

Lochgilphead – Manse Brae, PA31 8RA. Tel: 01546 602725. Fax: 01546 602750. www.careers-scotland.org.uk

Oban – Albany Street, Oban PA34 4AG. Tel: 01631 564697. Fax: 01631 564699. www.careers-scotland.org.uk

Stornoway – 30 Francis Street, Isle of Lewis HS1 2ND. Tel: 01851 701333. Fax: 01851 701444. www.careers-scotland.org.uk

Thurso – 2 Princes Street, Thurso, Caithness KW14 7BQ. Tel: 01847 895310. Fax: 01847 893740. www.careers-scotland.org.uk

LECs

Highlands and Islands Enterprise – Cowan House, Inverness Retail and Business Park, Inverness IV2 7GF. Tel: 01463 234171. Fax: 01463 244469. Email: hie.general@hient.co.uk www.hie.co.uk

HIE Network Data Centre – Benbecula – Taigh Cheann a' Locha, Lionacleit, Isle of Benbecula HS7 5PJ. Tel: 01870 604900. Fax: 01870 604901. Email: hie.general@hient.co.uk www.hie.co.uk

Argyll and The Islands Enterprise – The Enterprise Centre, Kilmory, Lochgilphead, Argyll PA31 8SH. Tel: 01546 602281. Fax: 01546 603964. Email: aie@hient.co.uk www.hie.co.uk

Caithness and Sutherland Enterprise – Tollemache House, High Street, Thurso, Caithness KW14 8AZ. Tel: 01847 896115. Fax: 01847 893383. Email: case@hient.co.uk www.hie.co.uk

Inverness and Nairn Enterprise – The Green House, Beechwood Business Park North, Inverness IV2 3BL. Tel: 01463 713504. Fax: 01463 712002. Email: ine.general@hient.co.uk www.hie.co.uk

Lochaber Enterprise – St Mary's House, Gordon Square, Fort William PH33 6DY. Tel: 01397 704326. Fax: 01397 705309. Email: lochaber@hient.co.uk www.hie.co.uk

Moray Badenoch and Strathspey Enterprise – The Apex, Forres Enterprise Park, Forres, Moray IV36 2AB. Tel: 01309 696000. Fax: 01309 696001. Email: mbse@hient.co.uk www.hie.co.uk

Orkney Enterprise – 14 Queen Street, Kirkwall, Orkney KW15 1JE. Tel: 01856 874638. Fax: 01856 872915. Email: oe@hient.co.uk www.hie.co.uk

Ross and Cromarty Enterprise – 69-71 High Street, Invergordon, Ross-shire IV18 0AA. Tel: 01349 853666. Fax: 01349 853833. Email: race@hient.co.uk www.hie.co.uk

Shetland Enterprise – Toll Clock Shopping Centre, 26 North Road, Lerwick, Shetland ZE1 0DE. Tel: 01595 693177. Fax: 01595 693208. Email: shetland@hient.co.uk www.hie.co.uk

Skye and Lochalsh Enterprise – King's House, The Green, Portree, Isle of Skye IV51 9BS. Tel: 01478 612841. Fax: 01478 612164. Email: sale@hient.co.uk www.hie.co.uk

Western Isles Enterprise – James Square, 9 James Street, Stornoway, Isle of Lewis HS1 2QN. Tel: 01851 703703. Fax: 01851 704130. Email: wie@hient.co.uk www.hie.co.uk

LEAs

Argyll and Bute Council – Education Department, Argyll House, Alexander Parade, Dunoon PA23 8AJ. Tel: 01369 704000. Fax: 01369 708584. www.argyll-bute.gov.uk

Comhairle Nan Eilean Siar (Western Isles) – Community Education, Sandwick Road, Stornoway, Isle of Lewis HS1 2BW. Tel: 01851 709450. Fax: 01851 709372. Email: comed@cne-siar.gov.uk www.cne-siar.gov.uk

Highland Council – Community Education Office, Town House, Inverness IV1 1JJ. Tel: 01463 724278. Fax: 01463 712836. www.highland.gov.uk

The Moray Council – Educational Services, High Street, Elgin, Morayshire IV30 1BX. Tel: 01343 563267. Fax: 01343 563478. www.moray.gov.uk

Orkney Island Council – Department of Education & Recreational Services, Council Offices, Kirkwall, Orkney KW15 1NY. Tel: 01856 873535. Fax: 01856 870302. www.orkney.gov.uk

Shetland Islands Council – Education Services, Hayfield House, Hayfield Lane, Lerwick, Shetland ZE1 0QD. Tel: 01595 744000. Fax: 01595 692810. Email: education@shetland.gov.uk www.shetland.gov.uk

FE colleges

Inverness College – Longman Campus, 3 Longman Road, Inverness IV1 1SA. Tel: 01463 273000. Fax: 01463 711977. Email: inverness.college@inverness.uhi.ac.uk www.inverness.uhi.ac.uk

Lews Castle College – Stornoway, Isle of Lewis HS2 0XR. Tel: 01851 770000. Fax: 01851 770001. Email: aofficele@lews.uhi.ac.uk www.lews.uhi.ac.uk

Lochaber College – An Aird, Fort William PH33 6AN. Tel: 01397 874000. Fax: 01397 874001. Email: lochaber.college@groupwise.uhi.ac.uk www.lochaber.uhi.ac.uk

Moray College – Moray Street, Elgin, Morayshire IV30 1JJ. Tel: 01343 576000. Fax: 01343 576001. Email: mc.admissions@moray.uhi.ac.uk www.moray.ac.uk

The North Highland College – Ormile Road, Thurso KW14 7EE. Tel: 01847 889000. Fax: 01847 889001. Email: northhighlandcollege@thurso.uhi.ac.uk www.nhcscotland.com

Orkney College – Kirkwall, Orkney KW15 1LX. Tel: 01856 596000. Fax: 01856 596001. Email: orkney.college@uni.ac.uk www.orkney.uhi.ac.uk

Sabhal mor Ostaig – Sleat, Isle of Skye IV44 8RQ. Tel: 01471 888000. Fax: 01471 888001. Email: oifis@groupwise.uhi.ac.uk www.smo.uhi.ac.uk

Shetland College – Gremista, Lerwick ZE1 0PX. Tel: 01595 771000. Fax: 01595 771001. Email: shetland.college@shetland.uhi.ac.uk www.shetland.uhi.ac.uk

HE institutions

UHI Millennium Institute – Caledonia House, 63 Academy Street, Inverness IV1 1LU. Tel: 01463 279000. Fax: 01463 279001. Email: EO@uhi.ac.uk www.uhi.ac.uk

Other colleges

North Atlantic Fisheries College – Port Arthur, Scalloway, Shetland Isles ZE1 0UN. Tel: 01595 772000. Fax: 01595 772001. Email: info@nafc.ac.uk   www.nafc.ac.uk

Stromness Academy Nautical Department – Stromness, Orkney KW16 3JS. Tel: 01856 850660. Fax: 01856 850171. Email: enquiries.stromness@orkneyschools.org.uk www.stromnessacademy.orkney.sch.uk

Business start-up

Contact the relevant LEC (see previous listing).

Northern Ireland

Belfast

EGSAs

EGSA Connecting Adults with Learning – 4th Floor, 40 Linenhall Street, Belfast BT2 8BA. Tel: 028 9024 4274. Fax: 028 9027 1507. Email: info@egsa.org.uk www.egsa.org.uk

Careers/employment service

N.B. Jobcentres are being replaced by Jobs and Benefits offices.

Department for Employment and Learning – Adelaide House, 39-49 Adelaide Street, Belfast BT2 8FD. Tel: 028 9025 7777. Email: del@nics.gov.uk www.delni.gov.uk *(Head Office for Northern Ireland)*

Andersonstown Jobcentre – 1st Floor, Kennedy Centre, 564-566 Falls Road, Andersonstown, Belfast BT11 9AB. Tel: 028 9087 1880. Fax: 028 9087 1888. Email: andersontown.jc@delni.gov.uk www.jobcentreonline.com

East Belfast Jobcentre – 3rd Floor, Gloucester House, 57 Chichester Street, Belfast BT1 4RA. Tel: 028 9025 2222. Fax: 028 9025 2267. Email: eastbelfast.jc@delni.gov.uk www.jobcentreonline.com

North Belfast Jobcentre – 2nd Floor, Gloucester House, 57 Chichester Street, Belfast BT1 4RA. Tel: 028 9025 2222. Fax: 028 9025 2397. Email: northbelfast.jc@delni.gov.uk www.jobcentreonline.com

South Belfast Jobcentre – Conor Building, 107 Great Victoria Street, Belfast BT2 7AG. Tel: 028 9054 5500. Fax: 028 9054 5511. Email: southbelfast.jc@delni.gov.uk www.jobcentreonline.com

Falls Road Jobs and Benefits office – 19 Falls Road, Belfast BT12 4PH. Tel: 028 9025 1346. Fax: 028 9054 2750. Email: fallsroad.jc@delni.gov.uk www.jobcentreonline.com

Holywood Road Jobs and Benefits office — 106-108 Holywood Road, Belfast BT4 1JU. Tel: 028 9052 8900. Fax: 028 9052 8905. Email: eastbelfast.jc@delni.gov.uk www.jobcentreonline.com

Knockbreda Jobs and Benefits office – Upper Knockbreda Road, Belfast BT8 8SY. Tel: 028 9054 5600. Fax: 028 9054 5620. Email: knockbreda.jc@delni.gov.uk www.jobcentreonline.com

Shankill Road Jobs and Benefits office – 178-180 Shankill Road, Belfast BT13 2BH. Tel: 028 9025 1456. Fax: 028 923 9330. Email: shankillroad.jc@delni.gov.uk www.jobcentreonline.com

LEA

Education and Library Board – 40 Academy Street, Belfast BT1 2NQ. Tel: 028 9056 4000. Fax: 028 9033 1714. Email: info@belb.co.uk www.belb.org.uk

FE colleges

Belfast Institute of Further and Higher Education – College Square Building, College Square East, Belfast BT1 6DJ. Tel: 028 9026 5000. Fax: 028 9026 5001. Email: information_services@belfastinstitute.ac.uk www.belfastinstitute.ac.uk

Ulster People's College – 30 Adelaide Park, Belfast BT9 6FY. Tel: 028 9066 5161. Fax: 028 9066 8111.

HE institutions

Open University – 40 University Road, Belfast BT7 1SU. Tel: 028 9032 3722. Fax: 028 9023 0565. Email: ireland@open.ac.uk www.open.ac.uk

The Queen's University, Belfast – University Road, Belfast BT7 1NN. Tel: 028 9024 5133. Fax: 028 9024 7895.
Email: admissions@qub.ac.uk
www.qub.ac.uk

St Mary's University College – 191 Falls Road, Belfast BT12 6FE. Tel: 028 9032 7678. Fax: 028 9033 3719.
Email: admissions@stmarys-belfast.ac.uk
www.stmarys-belfast.ac.uk

Stranmillis University College – Stranmillis Road, Belfast BT9 5DY. Tel: 028 9038 1271. Fax: 028 9066 4423. www.stran-ni.ac.uk

University of Ulster – Belfast Campus, York Street, Belfast BT15 1ED. Tel: 08700 400 700.
Email: online@ulst.ac.uk www.ulst.ac.uk

See also Belfast Institute of Higher and Further Education.

Enterprise Northern Ireland

Enterprise Northern Ireland – Aghanloo Road, Limavady, Belfast BT49 0HE. Tel: 028 7776 3555. www.enterpriseni.com

North Eastern Area

(Area covered: Co Antrim and Co Londonderry)

EGSAs

EGSA Connecting Adults with Learning – Magheraflelt Area, North East Institute of Further and Higher Education, Magherafelt Campus, 22 Moneymore Road, Magherafelt BT46 6AE. Tel: 028 7930 1388. Fax: 028 7930 1388.
Email: info@egsa.org.uk www.egsa.org.uk

EGSA Connecting Adults with Learning – Ballymoney Area, 29-31 Church Street, Ballymoney BT53 6HS. Tel: 028 2766 9500. Fax: 028 2766 9500.
Email: info@egsa.org.uk www.egsa.org.uk

EGSA Connecting Adults with Learning – East Antrim Area, East Antrim Institute of Further and Higher Education, 400 Shore Road, Newtownabbey BT37 9RS.
Tel/fax: 028 9086 3377.
Email: info@egsa.org.uk www.egsa.org.uk

EGSA Connecting Adults with Learning – Londonderry Area, Derry Central Library, Foyle Street, Londonderry BT48 6AL. Tel: 028 7127 1899. Fax: 028 7127 1899.
Email: info@egsa.org.uk www.egsa.org.uk

Careers/employment service

Ballymena Jobcentre – 35-39 Bridge Street, Ballymena BT43 5EL. Tel: 028 2566 0777. Fax: 028 2566 0766. Email:
Ballymena.jc@delni.gov.uk
www.jobcentreonline.com

Ballymoney Jobs and Benefits office – 37-45 Johns Street, Ballymoney BT53 6DT. Tel: 028 276 60100. Fax: 028 276 61038.
Email: ballymoney.jc@delni.gov.uk
www.jobcentreonline.com

Carrickfergus Jobs and Benefits office – 41 Davys Street, Carrickfergus BT38 8DJ. Tel: 028 9335 1811. Fax: 028 9336 6909.
Email: carrickfergus.jc@delni.gov.uk
www.jobcentreonline.com

Coleraine Jobcentre – 41 Church Street, Coleraine BT52 1AW. Tel: 028 7032 2880. Fax: 028 7032 2888.
Email: coleraine.jc@delni.gov.uk
www.jobcentreonline.com

Foyle Jobs and Benefits office – Asylum Road, Londonderry BT47 7EA. Tel: 028 7131 9500. Email: foyle.jc@delni.gov.uk
www.jobcentreonline.com

Larne Jobcentre – 75 Main Street, Larne BT40 1HH. Tel: 028 2827 3371. Fax: 028 2827 0178. Email: larne.jc@delni.gov.uk
www.jobcentreonline.com

Limavady Jobs and Benefits office – 9 Connell Street, Limavady BT49 0T2. Tel: 028 7776 0500. Fax: 028 7772 2245.
Email: limavady.jc@delni.gov.uk
www.jobcentreonline.com

Lisburn Jobcentre – 71 Bow Street, Lisburn BT28 1BJ. Tel: 028 9262 3300. Fax: 028 9262 3401. Email: lisburn.jc@delni.gov.uk www.jobcentreonline.com

Lisnagelvin Jobs and Benefits office – 2 Cresent Road, Lisnagelvin, Londonderry BT47 2NJ. Tel: 028 7131 9315. Fax: 028 7131 9376. Email: lisnagelvin.jc@delni.gov.uk www.jobcentreonline.com

Magherafelt Jobs and Benefits office – 31 Station Road, Magherafelt BT45 5DJ. Tel: 028 7930 2000. Fax: 028 7930 2001. Email: magherafelt.jc@delni.gov.uk www.jobcentreonline.com

Newtownabbey Jobs and Benefits office – 39-41 Church Road, Newtownabbey BT36 7LB. Tel: 028 9025 0888. Fax: 028 9054 8110. Email: newtownabbey.jc@delni.gov.uk www.jobcentreonline.com

Richmond Chambers Jobcentre – The Diamond, Londonderry BT47 1FP. Tel: 028 7126 7741. Email: richmondchambers.jc@delni.gov.uk www.jobcentreonline.com

LEA

North Eastern Education and Library Board – County Hall, 182 Galgorm Road, Ballymena BT42 1HN. Tel: 028 2565 3333. Fax: 028 2564 6071. www.neelb.org.uk

FE colleges

Causeway Institute of Further & Higher Education – Coleraine Campus, Union Street, Coleraine BT52 1QA. Tel: 028 7035 4717. Fax: 028 7035 6377. Email: info@causeway.ac.uk www.causeway.ac.uk

East Antrim Institute of Further & Higher Education – 400 Shore Road, Newtonabbey BT37 9RS. Tel: 028 9085 5000. Fax: 028 9086 2076. Email: info@eaifhe.ac.uk www.eaifhe.ac.uk

North East Institute of Further & Higher Education – Antrim Campus, Fountain Street, Antrim BT41 4AL. Tel: 028 9446 3916. Fax: 028 9446 5132. Email: enquiries@nei.ac.uk www.nei.ac.uk

HE institutions

University of Ulster – Coleraine Campus, Cromore Road, Coleraine BT52 1SA. Tel: 08700 400 700. Email: online@ulst.ac.uk www.ulst.ac.uk

See also Institutes of Further and Higher Education listed above.

Other colleges

The College of Agriculture, Food and Rural Enterprise – Greenmount Campus, 22 Greenmount Road, Antrim, Co Antrim BT41 4PU. Tel: 028 9442 6601. Fax: 028 9442 6606. Email: enquiries@dardni.gov.uk www.greenmount.ac.uk

Northern Ireland Hotel and Catering College – Ballywillan Road, Portrush BT56 8JL. Tel: 028 7082 3768. Fax: 028 7082 4733. Email: contact@nihcc.ac.uk www.nihcc.ac.uk

The Rural College – Derrynoid Road, Draperstown BT45 7DW. Tel: 028 7962 9100.

Enterprise Northern Ireland

Invest Northern Ireland – Aghanloo Road, Limavady, Belfast BT49 0HE. Tel: 028 7776 3555. www.enterpriseni.com

South Eastern Area

(Area covered: Co Down)

EGSAs

EGSA Connecting Adults with Learning – Newry Area, Ballybot House, 28 Corn Market, Newry BT35 8DG. Tel: 028 3025 6255. Fax: 028 3025 6255. Email: info@egsa.org.uk www.egsa.org.uk

Careers/employment service

Ballynahinch Jobcentre – 20 High Street, Ballynahinch BT24 8AB. Tel: 028 9756 2986. Fax: 028 9756 5144.
Email: ballynahinch.jc@delni.gov.uk
www.jobcentreonline.com

Bangor Jobcentre – 65 High Street, Bangor BT20 5BE. Tel: 028 9127 9999. Fax: 028 9146 5747.
Email: bangor.jc@delni.gov.uk
www.jobcentreonline.com

Downpatrick Jobcentre – Rathkeltair House, Market Street, Downpatrick BT30 6LZ. Tel: 028 4461 8023. Fax: 028 4461 8026.
Email: downpatrick.jc@delni.gov.uk
www.jobcentreonline.com

Newcastle Jobcentre – 113 Main Street, Newcastle BT33 0AE. Tel: 028 4372 5001. Fax: 028 4372 6302.
Email: newcastle.jc@delni.gov.uk
www.jobcentreonline.com

Newtownards Jobcentre – 9 Conway Square, Newtownards BT23 4DA. Tel: 028 9181 8653. Fax: 028 9182 4911.
Email: newtownards.jc@delni.gov.uk
www.jobcentreonline.com

LEA

Education and Library Board – 40 Academy Street, Belfast BT1 2NQ. Tel: 028 9056 4000.
Fax: 028 9056 6266. Email: info@belb.co.uk
www.belb.org.uk

FE/HE colleges

Castlereagh College of Further Education – Montgomery Road, Belfast BT6 9JD. Tel: 028 9079 7144. Fax: 028 9040 1820.
Email: enquiry@castlereagh.ac.uk
www.castlereagh.ac.uk

Lisburn Institute of Futher and Higher Education – 39 Castle Street, Lisburn BT27 4SU. Tel: 028 9267 7225. Fax: 028 9267 7291.
Email: admissions@liscol.ac.uk
www.liscol.ac.uk

North Down and Ards Institute of Further & Higher Education – Castle Park Road, Bangor BT20 4TF. Tel: 028 9127 6600. Fax: 028 9127 6601. Email: info@ndai.ac.uk
www.ndai.ac.uk

Enterprise Northern Ireland

Invest Northern Ireland – Aghanloo Road, Limavady, Belfast BT49 0HE. Tel: 028 7776 3555. www.enterpriseni.com

Southern Area

(Area covered: Co Armagh)

EGSAs

EGSA Connecting Adults with Learning – Craigavon Area, Craigavon Training Centre, Upper Bann Institute of Further and Higher Education, Lurgan Road, Portadown BT65 5HY. Tel: 028 3835 1493. Fax: 028 3835 1493. Email: info@egsa.org.uk www.egsa.org.uk

Careers/employment service

Armagh Jobcentre – 56 Scotch Street, Armagh BT61 7PU. Tel: 028 3751 5970. Fax: 028 3752 7994. Email: armagh.jc@delni.gov.uk
www.jobcentreonline.com

Banbridge Jobcentre – 50 Newry Street, Banbridge BT32 3HA. Tel: 028 4066 2149. Fax: 028 4062 6872.
Email: banbridge.jc@delni.gov.uk
www.jobcentreonline.com

Cookstown Jobcentre – 17 Oldtown Street, Cookstown BT80 8EE. Tel: 028 8676 6950. Fax: 028 8676 1231.
Email: cookstown.jc@delni.gov.uk
www.jobcentreonline.com

Dungannon Jobs and Benefits office – Crown Buildings, Thomas Street, Dungannon BT70 1HN. Tel: 028 8775 4870. Fax: 028 8775 4327.
Email: dungannon.jc@delni.gov.uk
www.jobcentreonline.com

Kilkeel Jobs and Benefits office – Newry Street, Kilkeel BT34 4DN. Tel: 028 4176 1400. Fax: 028 4161 1433. Email: kilkeel.jc@delni.gov.uk www.jobcentreonline.com

Lurgan Jobs and Benefits office – Alexander Crescent, Lurgan BT66 6BB. Tel: 028 3831 3213. Fax: 028 3831 3244. Email: lurgan.jc@delni.gov.uk www.jobcentreonline.com

Newry Jobs and Benefits office – 40 Bridge Street, Newry BT35 8AJ. Tel: 028 3026 5522. Fax: 028 3025 4185. Email: newry.jc@delni.gov.uk www.jobcentreonline.com

Portadown Jobs and Benefits office – 140 Jervis Street, Portadown BT62 3DA. Tel: 028 3839 7200. Fax: 028 3839 7244. Email: portadown.jc@delni.gov.uk www.jobcentreonline.com

LEA

Education and Library Board – 3 Charlemont Place, The Mall, Armagh BT61 9AX. Tel: 028 3751 2200. Fax: 028 3751 2490. Email: selb.hq@selb.org www.selb.org

FE colleges

Armagh College – Lonsdale Camous, College Hill, Armagh BT61 7HN. Tel: 028 3752 2205. Fax: 028 3752 2845. Email: enquiries@armaghcollege.ac.uk www.armaghcollege.ac.uk

East Down Institute of Further and Higher Education – Market Street, Downpatrick BT30 6ND. Tel: 028 4461 5815. Fax: 028 4461 5817. Email: admin@edifhe.ac.uk www.edifhe.ac.uk

East Tyrone College of Further Education – Circular Road, Dungannon BT71 6BQ. Tel: 028 8772 2323. Fax: 028 8775 2018. Email: info@etcfhe.ac.uk www.etcfhe.ac.uk

Newry and Kilkeel Institute of Further and Higher Education – Patrick Street, Newry BT35 8DN. Tel: 028 3026 1071. Fax: 028 3025 9662. Email: institute@newry-kilkeel.ac.uk www.nkifhe.ac.uk

Upper Bann Institute of Further & Higher Education – Castlewellan Road, Banbridge BT32 4AY. Tel: 028 3839 7700. Fax: 028 3839 7701. Email: info@ubi.ac.uk www.ubifhe.ac.uk

HE institutions

The Queen's University, Belfast – Armagh Campus, 39 Abbey Street, Armagh BT61 7EB. Tel: 028 3751 0678. Fax: 028 3751 0679. Email: qua@qub.ac.uk www.qub.ac.uk

See also Colleges of Further and Higher Education listed above.

Other colleges

Coalisland Training Services – 51 Dungannon Road, Coalisland, Co Tyrone BT71 4HP. Tel: 028 8774 8512. Email: info@coalislandtraining.com www.coalislandtraining.com

Enterprise Northern Ireland

Invest Northern Ireland – Aghanloo Road, Limavady, Belfast BT49 0HE. Tel: 028 7776 3555. www.enterpriseni.com

Western Area

(Area covered: Co Tyrone and Co Fermanagh)

EGSAs

EGSA Connecting Adults with Learning – Dungannon Area, Branch Library, Market Square, Dungannon BT70 1JD. Tel: 028 8775 0226. Email: info@egsa.org.uk www.egsa.org.uk

EGSA Connecting Adults with Learning – Omagh Area, Omagh Community House, 2 Drumragh Avenue, Omagh BT78 1DP. Tel: 028 8225 2669. Fax: 028 8225 2669. Email: info@egsa.org.uk www.egsa.org.uk

Careers/employment service

Enniskillen Jobs and Benefits office – Crown Buildings, Queen Elizabeth Road, Enniskillen BT74 7JD. Tel: 028 6634 3333. Fax: 028 6632 1979. Email: enniskillen.jc@delni.gov.uk www.jobcentreonline.com

Omagh Jobs and Benefits office – Crown Buildings, 7 Mountjoy Road, Omagh BT79 7BB. Tel: 028 8225 4222. Fax: 028 8225 4333. Email: omagh.jc@delni.gov.uk www.jobcentreonline.com

Strabane Jobcentre – 23 Upper Main Street, Strabane BT82 8AS. Tel: 028 7138 2332. Fax: 028 7138 2172. Email: strabane.jc@delni.gov.uk www.jobcentreonline.com

LEA

Education and Library Board – Headquarters Offices, 1 Hospital Road, Omagh, Co Tyrone BT79 0AW. Tel: 028 8241 1411. Fax: 028 8241 1400. Email: info@welbni.org www.welbni.org

FE/HE colleges

Fermanagh College – Fairview, 1 Dublin Road, Enniskillen BT74 6AE. Tel: 028 6632 2431. Fax: 028 6632 6357. Email: info@fermanaghcoll.ac.uk www.fermanaghcoll.ac.uk

Limavady College of Further & Higher Education – Main Street, Limavady BT49 0EX. Tel: 028 7776 2334. Fax: 028 7772 2229. Email: limcollege@limavady.ac.uk www.limavady.ac.uk

North West Institute of Further & Higher Education – Strand Road, Londonderry BT48 7AL. Tel: 028 7127 6000. Fax: 028 7126 0520. Email: info@nwifhe.ac.uk www.nwifhe.ac.uk/

Omagh College of Further Education – Mount Joy Road, Omagh BT79 7AH. Tel: 028 8224 1440. Fax: 028 8224 1440. Email: info@omagh.ac.uk www.omagh.ac.uk

Other Colleges

Enniskillen College of Agricultural – Levaghy, Enniskillen, Co Fermanagh BT74 4GF. Tel: 028 6634 4853. Fax: 028 6634 4888. Email: enquiries@dardni.gov.uk www.enniskillen.ac.uk

Enterprise Northern Ireland

Invest Northern Ireland – Aghanloo Road, Limavady, Belfast BT49 0HE. Tel: 028 7776 3555. www.enterpriseni.com

Publishers' contact details

Airlift Book Company – 8 The Arena, Mollison Avenue, Enfield EN3 7NL. Tel: 020 8804 0400. Fax: 020 8804 0044. Email: info@airlift.co.ukwww.airlift.co.uk

Association of Commonwealth Universities (ACU) – John Foster House, 36 Gordon Square, London WC1H 0PF. Tel: 020 7380 6700. Fax: 020 7387 2655. Email: info@acu.ac.uk   www.acu.ac.uk

ADSET – Britannia House, 29 Station Road, Kettering NN15 7HJ. Tel: 01536 410500. Fax: 01536 414274. Email: info@adset.org.uk www.adset.org.uk

British Council Education and Training Group – 10 Spring Gardens, London SW1A 2BN. Tel: 020 7389 4004. Fax: 020 7389 4426. Email: info@britishcouncil.org.uk www.britishcouncil.org/cbiet

Careers Europe – 3rd Floor, Midland House, 14 Cheapside, Bradford BD1 4JA. Tel: 01274 829600. Fax: 01274 829610. Email: europe@careersb.co.uk   www.careerseurope.co.uk

Careers Service Unit – Higher Education (CSU) – Prospects House, Booth Street East, Manchester M13 9EP. Tel: 0161 277 5200. Fax: 0161 277 5210. Email: publications@csu.ac.uk www.prospects.ac.uk

Continuing Education Gateway – 199 Nithsdale Road, Glasgow G41 5EX. Tel: 0141 422 2301.

Continuum – The Tower Building, 11 York Road, London SE1 7NX. Tel: 020 7922 0880; 01202 665432 (sales) www.continuumbooks.com

Department for Education and Skills – Connexions Service National Unit – PO Box 99, Sudbury, Suffolk CO10 2SN. Tel: 0845 60 222 60. Fax: 01787 375920. Email: connexions@prolog.uk.com www.connexions.gov.uk/

Department for Education and Skills (DfES) Publications – PO Box 5050, Sherwood Park, Annesley, Nottingham NG15 0DJ. Tel: 0845 60 222 60. Fax: 0845 60 333 60. Email: dfes@prolog.uk.com   www.dfes.gov.uk/publications

Directory of Social Change Publications – 24 Stephenson Way, London NW1 2DP. Tel: 0207 209 5151. Fax: 0207 391 4804. Email: ujonsson@dsc.org.uk

Hobsons Publishing *(for CRAC publications)* – Challenger House, 42 Adler Street, London E1 1EE. Tel: 020 7958 5000; 01752 202301 (sales). Fax: 020 7958 5001. www.hobsons.com

How To Books – 3 Newtec Place, Magdalen Road, Oxford OX4 1RE. Tel: 01865 793806; 01752 202301 (sales). Fax: 01865 248780. Email: info@howtobooks.co.uk www.howtobooks.co.uk

Independent Schools Careers Organisation (ISCO) – 12A Princess Way, Camberley, Surrey GU15 3SP. Tel: 01276 21188. Fax: 01276 691833. Email: info@isco.org.uk www.isco.org.uk

Kogan Page – 120 Pentonville Road, London N1 9JN. Tel: 020 7278 0433; 01903 828800 (sales). Fax: 020 7837 6348. Email: kpsales@kogan-page.co.uk www.kogan-page.co.uk

Learning Partners – Marquis House, 2 North Street, Winchcombe, Gloucestershire GL54 5LH. Tel/fax: 01242 604060. Email: lp.books@argonet.co.uk

Lifetime Careers Publishing – 7 Ascot Court, White Horse Business Park, Trowbridge BA14 0XA. Tel: 01225 716023; 01202 665432 (sales). Fax: 01225 716025. Email: sales@lifetime-publishing.co.uk www.lifetime-publishing.co.uk

Management Books 2000 – Forge House, Limes Road, Cirencester, Gloucestershire GL7 6AD. Tel: 01285 771441. Fax: 01285 771055. Email: m.b.2000@virgin.net www.mb2000.com

National Extension College (NEC) – The Michael Young Centre, Purbeck Road, Cambridge CB2 2HN. Tel: 01223 400350. Fax: 01223 400399. Email: info@nec.ac.uk www.nec.ac.uk

National Institute for Adult Continuing Education (NIACE) – 21 De Montfort Street, Leicester LE1 7GE. Tel: 0116 204 4200. Fax: 0116 285 4514. Email: enquiries@niace.org.uk www.niace.org.uk

Open University (OU) – Open University Worldwide Ltd, Walton Hall, Milton Keynes MK7 6AA. Tel: 01908 858785. Fax: 01908 858787. Email: ouwenq@open.ac.uk www.ouw.co.uk

Palgrave Macmillan – Palgrave Orders, Brunel Road, Houndmills, Basingstoke RG21 6XS. Tel: 01256 302699. Fax: 01256 330688. Email: orders@palgrave.com www.palgrave.com

Pearson Education – Edinburgh Gate, Harlow, Essex CM20 2JE. Tel: 01279 623623. Fax: 01279 413059. Email: customer.enquiries@pearsoned-ema.com www.pearsoned-ema.com

Penguin Books – Distribution Centre, Bath Road, Harmondsworth, West Drayton, Middlesex UB7 0DA. Tel: 020 8757 4000. Fax: 020 8757 4099. Email: penguin@penguin.co.uk www.penguin.co.uk

The Stationery Office – Orders Department, PO Box 29, Norwich NR3 1GN. Tel: 0870 600 5522. Fax: 0870 600 5533. Email: book.orders@tso.co.uk www.tso.co.uk/bookshop

Trotman – 2 The Green, Richmond, Surrey TW9 1PL. Tel: 020 8486 1160. Fax: 020 8486 1161. Email: tracy@trotman.co.uk www.careers-portal.co.uk

Universities and Colleges Admissions Service (UCAS) – Rosehill, New Barn Lane, Cheltenham GL52 3LZ. Tel: 01242 222444. Fax: 01242 544960. Email: enq@ucas.ac.uk www.swotbooks.com

Vacation Work Publications – 9 Park End Street, Oxford OX1 1HJ. Tel: 01865 241978. Fax: 01865 790885. Email: info@vacationwork.co.uk www.vacationwork.co.uk

Which? Books – Castlemead, Gascoyne Way, Hertford SG14 1LH. Tel: 0800 252 100. Fax: 0800 533 053. Email: which@which.net www.which.net/

Index

4 Index

4 Index

4 Index

4 Index